MW00358861

THE

APPEARANCES

OF

MEMORY

THE
APPEARANCES
OF
MEMORY

Mnemonic Practices of Architecture
and Urban Form in Indonesia

Abidin Kusno

Duke University Press
Durham and London
2010

© 2010 Duke University Press

All rights reserved

Printed in the United States of America on acid-free paper ∞

Designed by Heather Hensley

Typeset in Adobe Jenson Pro by Tseng Information Systems, Inc.

Library of Congress Cataloging-in-Publication Data appear
on the last printed page of this book.

The Canada Foundation for Innovation provided a generous
subvention toward the publication of this book.

FOR TONY, ISAAK, AND HONG

CONTENTS

ILLUSTRATIONS

ACKNOWLEDGMENTS

When I started writing the essays in this book in 2000, the effects of the fall of the Suharto regime were just unfolding, especially in the capital city of Jakarta. Since then I have sought to make sense of these effects as they were represented and experienced in the visual environment of the city. This attempt to reflect on the present has pushed me back, often to a quite distant past, only to be pulled back again to the absorbing present where I belong. Both the shape and the contents of this book thus represent my encounter and engagement with the effects, problems, and sense of the movement of time as they have been articulated in the physical environment. They also represent my own movement over the past ten years across different institutions in both Indonesia and North America. I thus owe a good deal to many people for their help in making this book possible.

Anthony D. King read all the chapters sequentially at various times over the past ten years. He was there before the beginning of this book, and his critical intellect and endless generosity have seen it through. I am indebted and immensely grateful to him, and I hope he will be pleased by what he sees. Greig Crysler and Michael Leaf have inspired and humbled me through their continuing intellectual companionship over many years. There are also many friends, colleagues, and teachers to whom I owe a debt of gratitude for their conversations and for reading so generously some chapters of this book. Outside Indonesia, I am particularly thankful to Rifaat and Barbara Abou-El Haj, Karen Bakker, Bulent Batuman, Thomas Bender, Dikmen Bezmez, Manneke Budiman, Charles Burroughs, Peter Carrol, Freek Colombijn, Lisa Drummond, John Friedmann, Michael Gilsenan, Jim Glassman, Benglan Goh, Laura Hein, Tineke Hellwig, Lakhbir Jassal, Kivanc Kilinc, Fouad Makki, Terry McGee, Sherry McKay,

Peter Nas, Ravi Palat, Intan Paramaditha, Peter Post, Rhodri Windsor-Liscombe, and Gwendolyn Wright.

As will be apparent to the reader, this book could not have been written without the existence of path-breaking scholarship on Indonesia, notably on the subjects of nationalism and technological change by Benedict Anderson, Rudolf Mrázek, Takashi Shiraishi, and James Siegel. I am thankful for their inspiring works. Several institutions have also helped me to complete this book. Graham Foundation for Advanced Studies in the Fine Arts supported the beginning of this study. The Netherlands Institute for War Documentation (NIOD) provided a Summer research fellowship to use the resources of the KITLV. Canada Social Sciences and Humanities Research Council offered me research grants to sustain my field trips. The UBC-Peter Wall Institute for Advanced Studies and the Swedish Collegium for Advanced Studies gave me a fellowship to complete this project. I am very grateful to these institutions and the directors with whom I have had the opportunity to work. I want to thank Dianne Newell and Olav Slaymaker of the Peter Wall Institute, Göran Therborn, Babro Klein, and Björn Wittrock of the Swedish Collegium, and Peter Post, Remco Raben, and Els Bogaerts of NIOD. They have not only offered me a truly interdisciplinary intellectual environment but also their relentless support and friendship. The group of scholars, especially Simon Bekker, Swati Chattopadhyay, Koh Keng We, Laura Kolbe, Fernando Perez-Oyarzun, Igor Torbakov, and Karl Schlögel, they put together during my stay has affected my understanding of the potentials and limits of this study.

Having taught at the University of Indonesia and the University of Gadjah Mada and having made many visits to Jakarta to experience its changes and to gather materials (especially at the library of Tarumanagara University), I found myself no less dependent on scholars and friends there for their expertise and insights into the changing appearances of Jakarta and the otherwise ungraspable urban life that structure those changes. Melani Budianta, Iswanto Hartono, Damar Harsanto, Suryono Herlambang, Herlily Stefanus Huwae, Michelle Kooy, Lilawati Kurnia, Marco Kusumawijaya, Budi Lim, Mona Lohanda, Wastu Pragantha, Pratiwo, Danang Priatmodjo, Josef Prijotomo, Adi Purnomo, Fransiska Prihadi, Bambang Purwanto, Jo Santoso, Rudy Surya, Gunawan Tjahjono, Johannes Widodo, Nanda Widyarta, Wardah Hafidz, and friends at the

Urban Poor Consortium provided not only time, insight, and hospitality but also their own works as activists, intellectuals, historians, architects, and planners, without which this book would not have been possible. I would also like to thank two anonymous readers for Duke University Press who offered insightful comments and generously helped me see what this book is about. My thanks also go to Reynolds Smith and Sharon Torian from Duke University Press for their conscientious support, and to Tim Elfenbein and Michael Wakoff who managed and copy edited the manuscript with care.

Finally, to Hong Kal, with whom I have lived both together and apart for the period I have been working on this book, I offer my profound gratitude for her loving companionship, spirited intellect, and good humor and for all she has taught me about her own stimulating work. I also want to thank Isabel Lee and Christine Chung for sharing with me, over numerous years, many moments of fun and, increasingly today, exchanging ideas about art, the environment, and politics. This writing would not have been possible without the unconditional support of my parents, brothers, and sisters in Indonesia. Whether they knew it or not, their own everyday experiences of Jakarta were always in my mind. I am grateful to them, especially to my brother Isaak, who read every draft, visited sites, and brought to my attention things he found important in newspapers and in urban life. I offer him this book with my respect and admiration for his good-naturedness and willingness to give the city yet another chance.

Earlier versions of some chapters have appeared elsewhere. Chapter 1 was published in *Urban Studies* 41, no. 12 (2004); chapter 4 in *Public Culture* 15, no. 1 (2003); chapter 5 in *The Past in the Present*, edited by Peter J. Nas and published by the NAI Press, Rotterdam in association with KITLV Leiden in 2007; chapter 7 was published in *Kota Lama, Kota Baru*, edited by Freek Colombijn et al. and published by Ombak Press, Yogyakarta in 2005; chapter 8 was published in *Journal of Architectural Education* 57, no. 1 (2003); and chapter 9 was published in *Indonesia* 81 (April 2006). I want to thank the editors and publishers of these journals and books for their permission to reuse these materials.

INTRODUCTION

So let's give back to the spatial and the visual the place they deserve in the history of political and social relations. — UMBERTO ECO, *TRAVELS IN HYPERREALITY*

In April 1920 someone named Doelriadi wrote the following for the front page of the Indonesian newspaper *Persatoean Hindia*, an "anticolonial" Indisch nationalist newspaper in Indonesia, then still under Dutch imperial rule:

> The notion of "moving" [*bergerak* in Malay-Indonesian] not only means "striking" [*pemogokan*]. It also refers to what in Javanese is called "change" [*obah*]. Ten years ago, the movement [*pergerakan*] of our nation [*bangsa Hindia*] was marked by the desire [*kemaoean*] among young people to obtain a job in the government. The reason was that a government job presupposed honor [*kehormatan*] even though the salary is small. The desire of people for honor could not be stopped. But what moved them? It was neither an elf [*peri*] nor a human. Instead it was the era [*zaman*] itself that moved their desire. . . . Since then, the movement has gone in a different direction. Now the era asked for a different thing. It is no longer interested in the notion of honor. Instead it honors money. Our young people will go where there is money [*mengejar wang*]. A lot of high school graduates are no longer interested in working for the government as civil servants or teachers. They do not listen to their elders who keep asking them to work in the offices of the government for they do not find satisfaction anymore in the respect of the elderly and students. Instead they prefer to work in the shops and companies that give them no honor, but only more money. . . . Recently however, the move-

ment has gone in yet another direction. Besides the pursuit of money, people are looking for "human rights" [*hak kemanoesiaan*] and freedom [*kemerdikaan*]. In this era, virtually everyone in our nation, young and old, men and women, are chasing freedom and human rights. These two words are their favorite [*buah bibir*]. These two words have been exploding the world of the master and the capitalist. Who is moving us so? It is the era that wants to see this happening. There will be casualties, but the "movement" will not die out and it cannot be stopped. It will only accelerate because it is the will of the era.[1]

We do not know who Doelriadi was, but, living in colonial Java, he articulated a profound sense of anxiety and amazement over the rapid and unprecedented series of changes in his time, and he understood them, almost teleologically, as a product of "the will of the era (zaman)." Doelriadi thus titled his article, "Zaman baharoe (The New Times): What Is Moving Us So?" to represent the spirit of his time, which we know today as the popular radical phrase "age in motion."[2] Although it may seem ironic in the retrospective light of the rapid death of popular radicalism in colonial Indonesia, the "new times" of Doelriadi represented a peak of anxious optimism regarding not only the possibility of liberation from Dutch colonialism and the colonially tainted "feudal tradition" of Java but also of moving forward.

In his declaration, Doelriadi expressed a chronological sequence of cultural habits and, in the final instance, reinscribed the will of "the new times" as something inevitable, and thus something that ought to be remembered, understood, and accepted by Indonesians for, as he expected, the present new time was accelerating to a desired future.[3] In efforts to cope with the profound changes generated by the new times, Doelriadi evoked memories of different actions and aspirations in the development of Indonesian society and reinscribed the authoritative "will of the era" to overcome them in order to register a new phenomenon. He reassembled earlier contradictory cultural habits and remembered them by means of a chronological sequence to construct the idea of change and thus bridge the gap between the different wills of the past, the present, and the future.

I have used this scene and scenario from the early twentieth century as a brief illustrative example of how members of a particular society articulate their sense of new times in responding to a profound but still uncertain feeling of social and political change. In addition, perhaps more importantly, this instance suggests that the theme of movement or moving forward has been a crucial concept and problem of modern Indonesia for much of the last century. This book focuses on the visual environment and the ways in which it helps to articulate a general anxiety over the sense of change in everyday life. I am concerned with those aspects of the visual environment that reveal how the discourses of space, nation, and community have historically managed this anxiety. Such concern also entails an exploration of the way unmanaged anxieties of the past have continued and of their effects on the new configuration of both aesthetic and ethical life in the present. Seeing architecture and urban space as bound up with historical experiences, this book conceives the built environment as encompassing both the practices of reproduction and performance.[4] That is, buildings serve as a reminder of the practices of the past and the starting point for both the performance of unfinished fantasies and the desire to overcome troubling memories and remake oneself within, as well as beyond, one's particular time and place.

I start with the present, known problematically as the "new Indonesia" and analyze its built environment in terms of what Raymond Williams called "the long revolution . . . of a still changing society and my own experience of it."[5] I examine a range of architectural and spatial features that Indonesia has produced since the political revolution that led to the fall of the Suharto regime and study their roles in helping to constitute new social and political identities as well as to reinforce old hierarchies. I then move back in time to retrieve various past attempts to create a sense of new times, the responses to which in one way or another have contributed to the transformation of Indonesian society. My aim is to tease out some layers of the spatial history of Indonesia, including that of the late colonial era, where techniques of power became the bases for modes and processes of identity formation on the one hand and the breaking of that formation on the other. I want to show that there are many responses to urban change at different moments in the nation's history. There are thus various voices in this book of both contemporary and historical figures — radical youths, conservative elites, revolutionary wonderers, religious leaders, literary figures, visionary architects, and social reformists — who speak not only with words but also through the built environment they have helped to shape. I also want to show that their senses of subjectivity are connected not only to material space but also to the imagining of places outside the boundary of the nation.

Placing the struggles of the present, its desires, concerns, and contradictions within the larger spatial and temporal contexts of the long twentieth century (which means encompassing the power effects of colonial and postcolonial conditions), this book examines the roles that architecture and urban space play in the making and unmaking of a history still in formation. How do architecture and the urban environment help to shape social memories and political consciousness in the colonial and postcolonial world? How do they come to terms with experiences of crisis, violence, and the struggles for resolution? How do different members of society, from leaders and architects to radicals and commoners, cope with troubling memories of the past in the present? How do they endure and contest forms of historical experience inscribed in the city? How do they reconfigure time and space?

I explore these questions, and though I have no straightforward answers to them, I show how attempting to answer them helps uncover some of the difficulties, dilemmas, and contradictions experienced by those who lived in and attempted to imagine new spaces, cultures, and histories. I do not write a narrative history of twentieth-century urban Indonesia. Instead, I choose to look at different encounters, themes, sites, personages, and events in that history, in part because I believe that recounted histories appear discursively through multilayered and fragmented, real or imagined, spatial images, even though these histories are often narrated in terms of a coherent and singular flow of time.

The significance of physical space and spatial images in the narrative of this book can be seen as stemming from what I believe to be a gradual erosion of, and challenge to, the historicist narrative of "development."[6] The seamless march of history which once guided nationalists' discourse of progress, moving in multiple paths from one stage of development to the next, has been challenged (internally) by the urban spaces it has helped to produce.[7] The most visible signs of this contradiction have been the increasing gaps and unevenness of development and the concomitant emergence of various claims of "rights to (survive in) the city." The disjuncture between time and space can no longer hide a range of social differences. This unevenness has generated different strategies of urban governance, including a new framing of knowledge in spatial products, such as the provision of public transport, the preservation of urban heritage, and the construction of large-scale superblock complexes as a way to reconquer space, culture, and history. A distinctive relation of the present to the past is invented in order to create, problematically, new commonality and to produce the everyday anew.

This book thus engages with architecture and urban theory, and it is structured by different encounters, sites, personages, and events that take both history and theory into consideration. It is divided into four thematic sections. They are chosen in such a way that their theoretical issues can be scrutinized, reframed, and extended out of the historically specific materials. The objective is to delineate the intermingling of global and historical forces and the regimes of power that operate in the city and to deconstruct the meaning of the post-Suharto era as it appears in the built landscape of contemporary Indonesia. By "post" I mean the new historical conditions that remain an unknowing host for the return of the past.[8] The main examples are drawn from Jakarta and, to a lesser degree, other cities in Java, for the capital city is still significantly and problematically the "exemplary center" of the nation that continues to shape the psychic life of the Indonesian people. How do contemporary architects, city governments, and urban dwellers reconfigure time by remaking space?

GOVERNMENTALITY

Indonesians today remember a decade since the fall of President Suharto (1966–98). However, no one seems sure how different the present era is in comparison with the previous one. A profound sense of anxiety has developed in regard to how things have changed since 1998. Some point to an unprecedented democratic tendency in state-societal relations, even though violence and undemocratic predatory practices continue to mark the social life of Indonesians.[9] Others trace the ways in which Indonesians have revisited their contested past (including the massacre of 1965) and are "beginning to remember" the historical injustices following decades of living in amnesia.[10] Still others indicate the unprecedented reassertion of identities and claims to citizenship by several social groups through identity politics of various kinds. These social groups range in class, local regional identity, religion, and ethnicity, thus challenging the once and still encompassing metanarrative of "Indonesia."[11] Yet others argue that one of the key components of the post-Suharto era is nothing other than the specific reconfigurations of the economy and power relations characteristic of the previous era.[12]

The first section of the book aims to contribute to the study of the post-Suharto era in at least two ways: by focusing on the role of architecture and urban space in defining social changes associated with the new Indonesia and by examining the role such spaces play in the formation of social and political identities. What kind of creative programs have been set in motion to remanage the urban population, displace prior forms of social relations and social memories, and stimulate new desires for individual and collective identity and identification? How did architectural programs of image enhancement and urban spectacle affect the domains of governance and public life in post-Suharto Jakarta? What forms of knowledge were created for, and directed at, the discourse of demolition and preservation of particular urban sites? Who was enabled and disabled by the urban programs of rehabilitation and alteration? According to what rationales were architecture and urban space put into play by various groups under the global influence of neoliberalism, structural changes in economic activity, and specific histories of post-Suharto Indonesia?

The book starts with an examination of spatial and physical forms of representations and the strategies and values that have marked post-Suharto Jakarta and considers them as a submission to, and a form of negotiation with, the relations of power that the new Indonesia has produced. I first analyze the social environment of post-Suharto Jakarta by bringing together ways that people of various backgrounds conceptualize, represent, and experience their urban environment in response to the profound and uncertain social and spatial changes brought about by the transformation in political regime. In chapter 1, "Whither Nationalist Urbanism? Public Life in Governor Sutiyoso's Jakarta," I deal with memory conflicts and the contradictory uses of urban space. I look at the ground of Jakarta as the site of memory retrieval and contestation. This chapter shows how Jakarta has been engaged in an unprecedented politics of memory since the collapse of Suharto's regime (1966–98). I argue that the nationalist discourses of the city dressed in the ideology of "nationalist urbanism" no longer appear to hold the influence that it once did in the face of the changing regime. This situation has given rise to a sense of "looseness" at the center. This in turn has encouraged both the government and citizens (of both the middle- and the underclass) to safeguard their space in the city by way of remembering and forgetting the past as well as the present.

In tandem with the new democratic politics and the deepening power of neoliberalism, one of the key characteristics of the post-Suharto era is an emphasis on economic recovery that guarantees the well-being of the city after its physical and symbolic destruction in May 1998 (see chapter 4). Foreign investment is represented as the key index of improvement in the image of the city, a priority to which other forms of rights are subordinated. Architecture and urban renewal are essential to this spectacle of urban makeup, which allows people to bypass the memories of political violence that took place in the city. Meanwhile, there are attempts on the part of the state to strengthen its authority and control over the population. As members of the society seek to liberate themselves from the encroachment of the once authoritarian state, the mission of the state is to find a new way to reenter the public life of the urban population.

In chapter 2, I turn to the spectacle of a new bus transportation system, known as the busway, which allows special buses to use separate lanes so that they can go faster than other vehicles. I see this as the state's attempt to mediate the imagination of a passage to a new era by managing the urban population. I argue that one of the most significant reconfigurations of urban space to constitute a new time took place in 2004, when the municipality of Jakarta, through Governor Sutiyoso, launched its new busway as part of what was claimed to be a comprehensive and integrated master plan of the city's transportation system. Chapter 2, "The Regime, the Busway, and the Construction of the Urban Subjects in an Indonesian Metropolis," focuses on some of the discourses around the busway in Jakarta as an example of urban violence, spectacle, and governmentality, in which the sights and anxieties of state power (embodied in the figure of the governor) and citizen groups are mapped onto the sites of the city. The point of this chapter is, emphatically, not to argue against much-needed mass transportation for the city. Rather it is to offer a different context in which to understand how political cultures of the state and the experiences of urbanism intersect. The busway can be seen as a postauthoritarian apparatus of power that, through their experience of riding buses across the city, seeks to reintegrate Indonesians into the state through imageries of national progress, political authority, and popular consumption. The target of the state's technique of embodiment in the city's urban space is the population at large (instead of a small section of society), thus not only producing the idea of the "public" for the political culture of the post-Suharto era but also relinking the public back to the body of the authority. In this sense, riding the busway can also be seen as a passage between Suharto and the postauthoritarian spatial order.

I close this section with a different urban makeup that constitutes yet another post-Suharto urban governmentality.[13] If the busway could be read as an attempt by the city government to regulate the psyche of the urban population, the current urban architectural complex known as the "super-block" provides yet another sense of the new times. In chapter 3, "'Back to the City': Urban Architecture in the New Indonesia," I examine two types of urban architecture associated with the (upper) middle-class imagination (a class to which architects belong): the ordinary "private" house and the "public-oriented" superblock (defined as a large multifunctional commercial space consisting of residences, offices, entertainment venues, and places to shop). I conceive of them as representatives of different attempts to both reinvigorate and dematerialize the conflictual realm of the city in the new Indonesia. These discourses arose from attempts to manage the urban population in the new times. They are discursively related to the city government's attempt in the past five years to clean up the central part of Jakarta, to evict squatters, and to reclaim public spaces for the revitalization of the city. They are propelled by developers, urban designers, as well as citizens' groups who are seeking to find practical and beneficial solutions to "urban" problems in a time of crisis, often by means of the language of sustainability, promoting a healthy environment, and preserving the cultural heritage of the historic city.

This aspiration for the new, which has become a central theme to architects and urban designers, indicates to us only that architecture in the post-Suharto Indonesia is as much a feature of political symbolism as of societal (re)organization. It registers the importance of the "urbanism" as opposed to the suburbanism of the middle class (which was central to the politics of space in the Suharto era).[14] The discourse of "back to the city" is symptomatic of the post-Suharto spatial products that help constitute the sense of the new times.

REMEMBERING AND FORGETTING

The acting out of violence on the built environment—especially through the ritualized destruction of the improvised housing of the marginalized population, the property of the urban poor and the ethnic Chinese—has long been a part of nation-building practices in Indonesian history. The sense of Jakarta's vulnerability as the site of state and societal violence has increased since 1998 and encouraged the formation of multiple and autonomous "communities" as a prime source of security. The state, the city government, professionals, religious elites, ethnic groups, nationalists, and neoliberals—each seems to act within a different temporal and spatial framework, a condition that often results in violent expressions in urban space. Perhaps, with memories of violence embedded somewhere in the inner psyche of the urban residents of Jakarta, the city is being conceived as an unfolding space of fear and terror to which the occasional response is the invention of techniques of creating spatial order and physical environments that themselves generate even more violence. With fear and terror posed as a core of identity, the state, the urban middle class, and the poor perform an equally spectacular form of violence through the ways that spaces are formed and transformed. Access to citizenship is thus carried out in and through physical and symbolic violence, both of which, as this book shows, are expressed in the built environment. This section on remembering and forgetting raises further questions: How is violence produced, ignored, or reinscribed through the production of buildings and urban spaces? How does it codify the space of past violence? How does the city refigure its space for the future?

In looking at the making of new times and spaces, this section pays particular attention to the refashioning of the physical environment and how the new space could be seen as managing the continuation of the past into the present. The series of scenes presented in this section exhibits the intermingling of memories and responses to these memories of the various social actors coping with a series of new situations and irresolvable contradictions in the urban centers of Indonesia. It pays attention to particular citizens' groups who are implicated in the mutual unpacking and repacking of social memories for the new times. The challenge however is not so much to discover how memories (of both official and popular kinds) contested each other but also how the official came to be a popular memory and vice versa. How did people with various memories internalize a particular hegemonic version of memory as their particular past? What is the possible role of architecture in memory work in places like Jakarta? Can buildings adequately stand for memories as many architectural theorists seem to believe? Or on the contrary, should we say that architecture, in all of its experiments with the preservation of memory, is actually an "art of forgetting" or a struggle with forgetfulness,[15] the success of which lies in reminding people only of what remains just beyond what architecture seeks to represent?

Chapter 4, "Glodok on Our Minds: Chinese Culture and the Forgetting of the May Riots," takes up the theme of forgetting, memory suppression, and its specific spatial and architectural consequences. It deals with issues around memory, violence, and urban renewal by considering the effects of the state's failure to recognize historical injustice in the wake of the 1998 anti-Chinese riots and gang rapes in Jakarta. It analyzes the architectural reconstruction of Glodok (a key Chinese business district) that was heavily damaged in the riots and demonstrates the failure of new buildings and the subsequent production of "Chinese cultures" (by the state and among the ethnic Chinese) to work through or even acknowledge the trauma. It then takes up an illustrated story, set in the future, and tracks the retrieval of the suppressed memories through private stories and their effects on the urban inhabitants. This chapter shows how collective memories are invested in the built environment and how new buildings contribute to the retrieval and suppression of those memories as well as help to reinvent new ones. But it also shows that buildings cannot adequately stand in for memory. Nor are architects, developers, and the state capable of controlling the meaning and use of buildings even as they are taking part in constructing them.

In my view, memory and architecture mutually constitute each other but in a most problematic way.[16] They need each other even as they are inadequate for each other.[17] It is memory's demand for representation from buildings (among others) coupled with the impossibility of memory being adequately represented that makes the interplay between memory and architecture both beneficial and problematic. A building can trigger memory and political action, but it cannot be relied upon to deliver an intended consciousness. It can never adequately represent memory, yet it can initiate something beyond the memory itself. The visual environment can be seen as a medium through which to interrogate what lies within as well as beyond the representation. It can unpack what it sought to forget and remember what it cannot quite represent. It is in this sense that the visual environment (be it architecture, public space, or an ordinary building that no one intends to become a monument) plays a role in mediating politics and histories and in registering public memories.[18] Everyday built environments embody collective memories that are not only arbitrary but are also implied and blurred rather than clearly stated. As a form of a banal "technology of memories,"[19] the built environment can nevertheless contribute to the recalling as well as the forgetting of the past, the present, and the future.

The interplay between memory and the city is particularly central to countries undergoing profound social and political transformation. In times of economic dislocation and rapid cultural and political change associated with decolonization, for instance, what kinds of memories structure architecture and urbanism? Under such circumstances, postcolonial memories remain unsettled and are played out in the city through the contestation over heritage, identity, and difference.[20] Postcolonial nations seek to construct a new identity even as this identity is often articulated in an ironic and contradictory relation with the colonial past. Chapter 5, "The Afterlife of the Empire Style, *Indische Architectuur*, and Art Deco," shows how certain stylistic conventions of colonial architecture shaped and were shaped by the ways architects and the Indonesian middle class confronted the period of economic dislocation and rapid social change during and after Suharto's New Order. How did architects and their clients symbolically visualize their identity and role under the shadow of the state production of national culture and capitalist development? This chapter demonstrates how architects as "specific intellectuals," in a time of crisis and working under the social environment of the New Order, reinvent colonial architectural styles to work both with and against the grain of state interests.[21] It looks at the ways in which the three prevailing architectural styles of Dutch colonial society—neoclassical, regionalist Indies architecture, and modernist art deco—instead of representing forms of dominance, are refashioned as an imaginary resolution to the question and contradiction of the time within which they are embedded. It raises questions related to the issue of remembering and forgetting both the past and the present through the architectural styles inherited from colonial times.

The idea that "collective memory" is embodied in buildings becomes un-
tenable when postcolonial memory, as geographer Brenda Yeoh points out,
is "a fraught terrain, contestory and multistranded, and woven around the
politics of inclusion and exclusion, of remembering and forgetting."[22] In
this sense, approaches to the study of postcolonial cities cannot be based
on the presumed coherence of a "collective memory" even though such an
approach is desired, especially by the nation-state as well as its critics, the
progressive thinkers of inclusive nationalism. Regardless of the importance
of collective memory, the coherence of this category must be questioned by
showing how it is made collective under particular historical circumstances
and also how it is contested.

In postcolonial Indonesia, the question of the role of the urban environment in registering both power and collective memories and in the process
of social forgetting is of real significance. It is connected to the increasing
awareness among Indonesian intellectuals today that the life history of the
nation cannot be separated from urban changes since the beginning of the
twentieth century. In 2004, I had the opportunity to participate in what
has been called "the first international conference on urban history" in
Surabaya and engaged in an intensive workshop on "urban symbolism" in
Yogyakarta with Indonesian historians from various parts of the country.[23]
This event, concerned with the time period of late colonialism and early
independence, the 1930s to the 1960s, is connected to the broader, perhaps
global, phenomenon of "coming to terms with the past." Issues of historical
injustices, including those left unresolved and frozen in bitter memories
related to Dutch colonialism, Japanese occupation, and the revolutionary
war for independence, have been revisited, partly as a response to changing discourses of nationalism in post-Suharto Indonesia. Dutch scholars,
led by the Netherlands Institute for War Documentation, have also been
working together with Indonesian historians in recent years to address the
complex issues surrounding memories of "decolonization." While Indonesian and Dutch historians have been involved, formally as well as infor-
mally, in the project of rewriting both nations' traumatic history, they are
also, in a way, involved in historical reconciliation.

The current interest in urban history in Indonesia is thus more than
an act of measuring up to forgotten past realities. Rather, the urban has

become a present political site for the rethinking of historiography. This entails a reformulation of colonial urban space as not merely a "form of dominance" (a target of nationalist criticism) but also as the site of identity formation and an arena for the production of new social and political consciousness.[24] In this sense, what does the architecture and urban design of the colonial world look like when considered from the perspective of the colonized, anticolonial nationalists as well as the revolutionaries? Where the earlier sections of this book are centered on contemporary scenes, they also allude to the importance of the colonial past. This section takes up the appearance and suppression of political consciousness in and through urban space during Dutch colonialism. It reveals the connectedness between the present crisis of the center, the fragmentary and contradictory claims of rights to the city, and the past emergence of urban modernity, including the suppressions of popular radicalism and the nationalists' goal to separate themselves from global imperialism. I suggest that the contemporary preoccupation with redefining memory in post-Suharto Indonesia is not in opposition to these efforts of the early twentieth century. Spatializing memories (instead of periodizing them) would allow us to see the otherwise unrelated cultural practices of both the past and the present. This section shows that today's political consciousness carries the mark of the early twentieth century's struggles with the idea and value of constructing a new time—a historical relationship that constitutes the long revolution of Indonesian modernity.

My interest in the relation between political consciousness and the urban form of the recent past is further encouraged by recent works on urbanism in Asia that show that the modern city of the early twentieth century triggers new forms of individual and collective identities.[25] Historians of Indonesia have also indicated that popular urban radicalism brought about by early twentieth-century urban changes had no equivalent in the previous era. In *Engineers of Happy Land*, historian Rudolf Mrázek precisely shows the effects of the utopian and dystopian forces of "colonial modernity" (in the form of various technologies) as they worked through the lives of people in a colony.[26] He shows how changes in the urban centers of the colony in the early twentieth century were characterized by a liberatory disruption of the link to prior forms of representation. At the heart of this cultural and historical dislocation was, however, a demand from intellectuals of the colonial world not for continuity with the irretrievable past but for new modes of representation that would adequately portray the new era. For sure these intellectuals felt intensely the pressure of "zaman baharoe" (the new era as proclaimed by Doelriadi earlier), but they did not see themselves as victims of colonial misery. In what came to be known as "an age in motion," many of them engaged socially and politically in the spirit of "development" as the will of the time (zaman) against the colonial state and attempted to imagine a new time.[27] They nevertheless felt that from this moment on memory could no longer be a merely transparent expression of the past. Instead, it had become a cultural enterprise that needed to be actively produced, represented, and contested. This legacy, as this book will show, has continued to generate the hopes and anxieties that have been at work in the era of decolonization.

This section of the book seeks to contribute to the current effort to rethink urban history in Indonesia. It aims to dispose of the narrative of victimhood often embedded in postcolonial studies. It suggests an alternative account by asking how the politics of architecture and urbanism, instead of simply producing forms of dominance, are bound up with the making of new subjectivities. The title of the book *The Appearances of Memory* thus refers neither to the sense of victimhood nor to the melancholic nostalgia for a return to a lost precolonial, supposedly glorious age. Instead, it refers to the formation of a critical consciousness, to working through both managed and unmanaged memories of hopes and anxieties, the tension of which can be traced in the discourses and values of architecture and urbanism as well as in the reception to them. I aim to show how this self-critical consciousness did not come out of thin air. Instead it is formed in and through the changing realm of the visual and spatial environment. I represent architecture and urban space as concrete social artifacts, both in terms of strategies of regulation and tactics of identity formation that are both disciplining and empowering. I intend to show the ways architecture and urban space participate in the ever-changing sense of a history still in formation and how they provide materials to imagine anew the space of our present.

I begin this section by asking what are the exact connections between the new visual environment and political consciousness? To what extent was the emergence of popular radicalism in early twentieth-century Indonesia a result of the transformation of urban form in Dutch colonial society? Chapter 6, "Colonial Cities in Motion: Urban Symbolism and Popular Radicalism," examines a case of this process of new identity formation in the princely town of Java. It explores how the palatial compound—the authoritative orientation of the city in an earlier era—was gradually displaced by, or became outdated in comparison with, the emerging new visual environment in the early twentieth century. By default, and perhaps not by intention, the provision of urban structures such as the railway and the commercial buildings of the main streets created a new "cognitive map" for the image of the city.[28] This transformation of urban symbolism displaced the realm of the sultanate, which, in the eyes of the city residents, had given way to a new time in motion. This change in the image of the city might well have been an attempt by the colonizer to undermine or negotiate with the power of the traditional court. At the same time, however, the new visual environment led to the formation of a profoundly anticolonial and antifeudal political consciousness among the urban population. Such a moment, when urban form was beginning to be recognized as signifying the rise and fall of the colonial inflected "feudal tradition," might be seen as the emergence of Indonesian modernity, a process that occurred in tandem with the appearance of consumerist urban culture.

If the colonized in the early twentieth century refashioned themselves as radicals aspiring for liberation from colonial power in the wake of the new urban modernity, the colonial state closed the era with the construction of yet another new urban environment and a new form of spatial regulation. Chapter 7, "Urban Pedagogy: The Appearance of Order and Normality in Late Colonial Java, 1926–42," analyzes the appearance of a distinctive visual order in the urban environment associated with the *zaman normal*, the "era of normalcy" (1926–42). It interprets images and drawings produced by urban designers of the time to convey the arrival of yet another new time and space. Haunted by memories of violence, the images of buildings, the scenes of the streets, and the site plan of the town operate as the appearance of a new era that offered the colonial state and its urbanites a weird sense of normalcy. However, beneath the surface, this chapter argues, was the suppression of memories of popular radicalism in order to ensure their permanent death. The surveillance effect of the new environment and the cultivation of a sense of living in a new time and space associated with peace and harmony was thus bound up with the architectures of forgetting.

The late colonial urban design thus resulted from the Dutch East Indies government's intensification of its grip over the colony by means of an extensive surveillance apparatus. Following the violent death of the communist revolt in 1926–27, the colonial space of Indonesia was contained in a "house of glass," where suspected "subversive" movements of individuals were monitored and disciplined. So effective was this control that Indonesians growing up in the 1930s and 1940s remember this period as *zaman normal* (the age of normalcy) — a term that signified the end of the preceding radical era of *zaman pergerakan* (the age in motion) (see chapter 6). To ensure peace and order, zaman normal came together with a tight control over the contents of newspapers, journals, and, as we will see in chapter 7, the functioning of urban spaces.

By the end of the 1920s there were fewer and fewer newspapers openly critical of colonialism, and more and more urban spaces were emptied of demonstrations and social unrest. Where had the anticolonial imagination gone in the calm of zaman normal? Fantasies of liberation did not just disappear in the social environment of "peace and order." They took various cultural forms, one of which was a genre of popular fiction known as the dime novel (*roman picisan*). Between 1938 and 1942, some four hundred titles of roman picisan were published.[29] Roman picisans were extremely popular, especially among boys and men, not only because they were inexpensive (they cost only a dime) and available on a regular basis (many roman picisans were written in a few weeks and some in just a day) but also because they were deeply immersed in adventures and fantasies of liberation that ran counter to the social environment of zaman normal. Written largely in Sino-Malay "street" language, roman picisans often escaped the screening of colonial authority and thus became a covert form of "public space" in which fantasies of liberation were often articulated. The most popular series of roman picisans was *Patjar Merah* (The Scarlet Pimpernel), a detective novel flavored with stories of espionage intrigue, heroic romance, exile, and uncanny happenings. Under the regime of order and normality of the late colonial era, we could imagine various political reasons why *Patjar Merah* was popular, but the crucial thing for us is that Patjar Merah, the superhero of the series, took on the appearance of Tan Malaka (1897–1949), a real-life Indonesian anticolonial nationalist who was wanted by the colonial regime but was never captured or identified. Tan Malaka and the dime novel of *Patjar Merah* moved beneath and above the material constructs of the zaman normal.

If the chapters above and the case of Tan Malaka delineate a condition of Indonesian modernity in which forms of anxiety and critical consciousness emerged and eventually dominated, we might say that the very formation of such a moment is not only urban but also inherently transnational. We can see this when various strands of urban-based politics confronted colonial authority in different parts of Asia. This transnational lineage helped constitute a radical nationalist world of anticolonial modernity, even as this world was conceived through a harnessing of up-to-date "Western" scientific innovations. A number of scholars on Asia (as well as elsewhere) from diverse disciplines have suggested that, in the early twentieth century (and parallel to the West), a new way of perceiving space and time emerged in the cultural imagining of the East and Southeast Asian world.[30] The impact of railways, the public clock, a new form of urban life, popular culture, and mass media circulating in urban spaces provided their inhabitants with new ways of conceiving time and space. The relatively autonomous universes of Asia were opened up such that they conceived themselves to be interrelated with the larger world, instead of being, as predicated by modernization theory, behind the West. The largely colonized subjects of the region began to see themselves (in mutual identification with each other) as agents of change, not only as victims of the colonizers. They did not merely respond with astonishment to the modern urban environment of the time but played a part in its rapid transformation. In this way they attained a sense of being subjects of history (even if these new subjects often came to be identified with the rhetoric of antiurbanism). This consciousness relied on a self-reflexive sense of being both "urban" and "transnational," and it carried a political implication: a sense of anticolonial nationalism.

The making and unmaking of the critical transnational lineage of modernity, enabled in part by the "spectre of comparison" across different urban environments, provoked fantasies of liberation in the colonial and postcolonial world.[31] The responses often took the form of a collective transnational anticolonial imagination even though the site for the political practice remained national. This cultural enterprise, which had already started in the early twentieth century (as in the case of Indonesia), however, remained unfinished. It is in this sense that the early twentieth-century past has become part of the present. And the present is part of the way the past is remembered. They find connection with each other through the ways in which the colonial, in shaping the memory of contemporary practice, is foiled and displaced to resolve the dilemma and questions of the present. This book, however, does not intend to resolve the contradiction or trace the origin of the critical present. Instead, it aims to show the contemporary moment (of Indonesia) as the question, the dilemma, and the contradiction of a broader and longer twentieth century to which the built environment continues to emerge as both an imaginary and real response.

MENTAL NEBULAE

I have explored elsewhere specific episodes in the biography of Tan Malaka, who found himself in Shanghai as it was engulfed in the hostilities between China and Japan in January 1932.[32] The adventure in Shanghai shaped the way Tan Malaka confronted colonialism and the political intrigue in Jakarta in the 1940s. His anticolonial consciousness and views on Indonesia developed from his being in Shanghai in particular, among other colonial cities, and his experience of this city influenced even his recollections of Amsterdam, his views of the Dutch, and his assessments of the course of the Indonesian revolution in the 1940s. The diverse geographies of colonial power and the recovery from them of the meaning invested in those spaces by colonials like Tan Malaka indicate how mnemonic practices and geographical imaginings were profoundly shaped by mobility, travel, and the experience of exile, rather than by any spatially bounded forms of indigenous knowledge. It shows how specific urban responses to colonial Java were articulated in and through the rhizomatic experiences of place and the imaginative geographies of transnational revolution, anti-colonialism, and anti-imperialism.

Tan Malaka's experience of moving from city to city across regions revealed to him less the normalcy of colonialism than the limits of Western imperialism. His memoir brought together several worlds to illuminate the European presence as no more than one of the global powers. In a way, Tan Malaka "provincialized" the West by comparing it with other Asian powers.[33] Perhaps, for him, the history of Western colonialism was simply one layer among other layers of histories that made up the "mental nebulae" of his Indonesia.[34] Yet, written at the moment of decolonization and in the jail of his own country, Tan Malaka's memory work reminded his contemporary public of the importance of thinking nationalism strategically across national boundaries and historically across layers of historical experiences. He showed that there are other imaginaries, other narratives, and other temporalities within as well as beyond the structure of western modernity.

The last section of this book seeks to move beyond the nexus of East and West that has characterized much of colonial and postcolonial studies. The attention given to the East-West connection tends to homogenize cultural production and marginalize other connections. Western colonialism is one particularly powerful historical force that has overdetermined the production of culture after decolonization, but there were also other coexisting powerful phenomena. In "Carrefour Javanais," the late French historian Denys Lombard demonstrated the coexistence of several time frames and several worlds (with the West as only one among them) that have underpinned the Indonesian experience of modernity.[35] He identified the intermingling of several layers of "mental nebulae" over a *longue durée* that continues to shape the complex life of the nation in the present. The "mental nebulae" can be seen as identifiable forms of historical experience that still resurface in various formats and in more or less visible manifestations, shaping the mentality of the present.

Drawing from Lombard's insights, this section demonstrates how particular styles of mosques and gatehouses in Java have been produced and perceived through several layers of social memories and how they were involved in the making of the new times. Through a longue-durée analysis of mosques and gatehouses, we see the appearance of various forms of the past that still produce more or less visible manifestations as they pass through different social formations and power relations. However, unlike in Lombard's approach, this section shows that there were ruptures and crises that required not only the making of new space, time, and identity but also a confrontation with the "mental nebulae" that demands, as well as resists, the call for different representations.

Chapter 8, "'The Reality of One-Which-Is-Two': Java's Reception of Global Islam" considers the way Java responds to the global architectural flows of Islam. It shows how architecture became the site of negotiation between global Islam and the Javanese world in the creation of a new faith. It then explores the dispute over identity and the representation of Islam in Java through various events in the present and the past. It discusses the debate over the design of a university's mosque in Jakarta in the 1980s, the

confrontation between Javanese and Middle Eastern Islam in the building of the first "great mosque" in the fifteenth century, the discourses of
mosque building of the two previous postcolonial presidents of Indonesia,
and the struggle in the intellectual culture of contemporary architecture
over what constitutes "Indonesian architecture."

While chapter 8 takes up the theme of memory and symbolic struggle
over identity and place in the form of the mosque, the last chapter, "Guardian of Memories: The *Gardu* in Urban Java," provides the Indonesian form
of gatehouses (called *gardu*) with a memory that is concomitant with the
emerging, as well as the declining, social and political order of the country.
As the repositories for memories about various eras of Indonesian history,
gardus are also sites for struggles over the ideas and values of remaking
time, space, and identity. This chapter thus examines the political roles
and the changing meaning of the gardu, genealogically, from our own times
back to the past to show how it has continued to be a political medium
through which the public is formed and transformed. Instead of showing
the gardu as merely a symptom of a recent global urban form associated
with the rise of disciplinary society and gated communities worldwide, this
chapter aims to reflect on the gardu as an institution that embodies specific
histories and has over time shaped the collective memories of people who
lived through those histories.

Taken together, the chapters in this book (organized from the everyday
present to the events of the past) constitute a palimpsest "history of the
present," which demonstrates the memory work and the resistance to it of
Indonesian modernity in the twentieth century and how this is played out
in the visual environment.[36] The chapters conceive buildings and physical
space as one of the tools through which people reconfigure their social
and private world in the wake of a profound unsettling change in their
surroundings.

The Appearances of Memory thus refers to moments of producing, encountering, and engaging with the new time, through mnemonic practices
in architecture and urban form in Indonesia. It asks questions about how
building and urban space engage in defining (as well as contesting) the
sense of fragmentation, collective memories, new forms of governmentality, and different hopes for the future. And finally it asks what it means
to construct a new space at a moment marked by colonial legacies, post-

colonial historical injustices, and global influences of neoliberalism. These questions are certainly larger than this book, but they are necessary for a meaningful engagement with Indonesian modernities in formation and for making some sense of the city and the nation in motion and the continuous remaking of the new times.

GOVERNMENTALITY

CHAPTER 1   **WHITHER NATIONALIST URBANISM?**
Public Life in Governor Sutiyoso's Jakarta

Beginning is not only a kind of action; it is also a frame of mind, a
kind of work, an attitude, a consciousness . . . beginning is making or
producing difference. —EDWARD SAID, *BEGINNINGS: INTENTION AND
METHOD*

Since independence, Jakarta has loomed large as a powerful place in the
Indonesian imagination. The significance of this city derives from the
fact that it has been produced and reproduced over time, largely through
state policies, as a space of power in terms of the concentration of capital exchange, political authority, and cultural assets.[1] The most important
sources of the city's power, however, are discourses of national prestige
through which the political elites of the country produce Jakarta as a city
of influence. By insisting that the nation needs all its development, infrastructure, and monuments in one place, they transform the physical spaces
of the city. If a *kampung* (poor urban neighborhood) has to be demolished
and the master plan changed, the further development of the nation provides sufficient justification. This—what I would call "nationalist urbanism"—aims at providing a unifying image of Jakarta as the center that
represents the nation for citizens living in the city (as well as elsewhere
in the country). Out of this ideology, the coexistence of two seemingly
contradictory sets of relationships emerged during the reign of President
Suharto (1966–98). On the one hand, there is a familiar Western economic
liberalization (dictated by the International Monetary Fund) implemented
through the discourses of development. On the other hand, there is the
nationalist discourse of power centered on the authority of Jakarta. The

difference between these two discourses does not add up to an opposition between economics and culture, or the global and the local. Instead, they coexist, and it is this coexistence that has made Jakarta a city of power and influence. As inhabitants of the capital city, the residents of Jakarta thus live city life as much as national life. Living in Jakarta, one thinks of oneself as experiencing a cosmopolitan globalscape, and yet as a citizen of Indonesia, one also consequently lives in deference to the authority of national discourses.

The riots of May 1998, which toppled the rule of President Suharto, have changed the lives of many people in Jakarta. To the amazement of the people, the powerful, relatively stable and repressive regime of Suharto was dismantled in just a few days by what seemed to be forces from below. The majority of the city populace had never seen in their lifetime how large-scale protests, demonstrations, and the physical destruction of the built environment could contribute to the overthrowing of an authoritarian regime. The damage that was done to the city and its inhabitants during the riots, however, was also deep and of lasting consequence. The riots and the spectacle of *reformasi* (a rallying word that accompanied the overthrown of Suharto) have profoundly changed the sensitivity of Jakarta's residents toward the nation and the governance of the city. They have also shown that people have the right to the city and that, as one resident put it, "people rejected spaces that have been created in the city."[2]

The collapse of Suharto's New Order has finally brought down the framework of "nationalist urbanism" with which the state's elites have been playing since independence. The residents of Jakarta, from various classes, found themselves in a more advantageous position to criticize developmental projects in the city that seek to represent the image of the nation. More importantly, unlike in the past, Jakarta's inhabitants now know that their protests over city administration and planning will not easily be put down by using the apparatus of violence. This chapter tells one such story that unfolded in Jakarta during the few years after the collapse of the Suharto regime. It deals with the attempts of the authority of Jakarta to recreate another round of "nationalist urbanism" as the city witnessed the decline of its political and economic power. It considers the spatial effects of the city government's attempts to revive the image of the city by initiating the "nationalist urbanism" of the previous regimes and considers the critical responses of the public.

In this sense, this chapter deals with the politics of memory. It shows how Jakarta has been engaged in an unprecedented politics of memory that, on the one hand, involves the remembering of the city as the beacon of the nation and, on the other, the forgetting of national consciousness as the formation of city power. "Memory" in this chapter is thus not just a term referring to the state of the human mind concretely remembering and forgetting the past. Instead, it also refers, more abstractly, to the ways in which the past, consciously or unconsciously, structures how one lives the present. It concerns how a particular past continues to live on as traces of the normalized present while other memories are forgotten or return only to haunt the sense of that normality constructed in the aftermath of 1998. What is thus important is not what has been forgotten and remembered, but how and why certain memories are institutionalized, transformed, and invested with particular meaning for the reregulation of the public. The public, however, can, in turn, open these same memories for appropriation, contestation, and intervention. To account for both the condition underlying current urban change in Jakarta and its character, I analyze the operations of different networks of urban memories and their spatial consequences that coexist, as well as conflict, with each other. I suggest that while the moment of social, economic, and political crisis and the concomitant refashioning of the city have opened up the possibility for more responsible and democratic urban lives, it has also created spaces for new urban politics that are profoundly egoistic and violent.

The "looseness" at the center, however, was ephemeral. A new powerful phenomenon of "antiterrorism" began to sweep through the city following the October 2002 bombing of Bali.[3] The material for this chapter is largely based on my observation of urban discourses in Jakarta from 1999 to 2002 (prior to the Bali bombing) as represented in urban spaces as well as reported in the newspapers. I focus on the middle-class newspapers to back up my observations of the city for the public claim of the middle class is crucial to understanding the *mentalitet* of the political elites (with whom the middle class has been affiliated), as well as to grasping the unrepresented voices that nevertheless speak, not always through their own representations, but in and through the hegemonic as well as ambiguous articulations of the middle class.

REMEMBERING AND FORGETTING JAKARTA

Toward the middle of the 1990s, at the time when Jakarta was optimistically making up its urban landscape with high-rise buildings, shopping malls, flyovers, and real estate housing for the middle class, Goenawan Mohamad, a noted contemporary Indonesian writer, wrote a reflective essay on the city. The essay, titled "City," is about the commodification of Jakarta and the mentalities of the middle class who live in it.[4] The attraction of Jakarta however lay not only in its economic power. Instead, Goenawan saw Jakarta as the source of national power that attracted people from provinces to the city, recalling Pramoedya's satire more than three decades earlier that "the wind blows through the provinces whispering that one cannot be fully Indonesian until one has seen Jakarta."[5] Going to the capital city meant more than finding a better life, however that may be defined. It included a sense of upward mobility and becoming a full "Indonesian," with the promise of "doing great things and being equal in mind and body to the opportunities one could find."[6] Goenawan nevertheless moves ambiguously against this national myth of equality in Jakarta by showing the gap between the city and the nation. The city is shown as neither controlled by the "Dutch-style fortress," nor by the guiding spirit of the ancient Javanese "Mataram Kingdom," (a regime with which Suharto often associated), but by "something else, something stronger—the economic and political forces around it" that make "us all foreigners here."[7] Perhaps the economic intrigue and political maneuver under Suharto's regime allowed Goenawan to see with unclouded clarity the gap between the imagined fullness of nationalism and the actual lived experiences of the city. Goenawan wrote that the capital city indeed offers many things to people but does not register any connection with them. Yet, people still come and stay in the city because Jakarta is the center for the person who does not "love his place of origin enough to stay there, but yet cannot tie his heart to his new place."[8]

While Jakarta's residents or visitors desire to see themselves as hierarchically higher (and more powerful) than their fellows in their imagined hometowns or villages, we should also not lose sight of their sense of ambivalence toward the city. In reflecting this ambiguity, Goenawan explains that while the city tries to catch and hold people, the latter show themselves to be alienated souls who engage the city in buying and selling everything—"our things, our bodies, our spirits."[9] Yet, the people Goenawan describes did not leave the city (except perhaps during the Islamic New Year—the Idul Fitri), but lived and worked in "the city of their second birth."[10] In Goenawan's prose, there is no "national" glory of being in the city, but there is still a sense that the city is the *center* of human life even as it acknowledges the alienation of that life. It is this ambiguity—this sense of attachment-and-detachment to the city—that has given rise to official discourses of "nationalist urbanism" that aim to control the discursive link between the people and the city to further particular interests of the state and to offer an ideological attachment for urban residents to the nation.

The attempt to align the people in the city with the idea of the nation thus arose from the awareness of the political elites that "Jakarta citizens don't love Jakarta enough, because they have no emotional ties binding them to their city."[11] In a city where it is assumed that everyone has "a place of origin elsewhere," as Indonesian writer Seno Gumira Ajidarma states,[12] it seems almost natural that the "nation" has become a powerful binding trope for everyone to imagine him- or herself as belonging to the city. Yet, as I have detailed elsewhere, the different nationalist urbanisms of Sukarno and Suharto, which aimed at turning the city into the subject of the nation, were essentially based on transforming the city according to the image of the regime in power.[13] As we have seen from Goenawan's depiction of the city, the "national" and "cosmopolitan" inhabitants of Jakarta are simultaneously alienated by the "economic and political forces" around the city.

About a decade after Goenawan wrote "City," Seno Gumira Ajidarma, a prolific young writer, wrote a short essay titled "From Jakarta."[14] This essay grew out of the social environment of post-Suharto Jakarta and revealed a change in the status of the city. On first glance, the essay still seems to be about the centrality of Jakarta, recalling similar stances of Goenawan and Pramoedya. Seno writes, *from Jakarta* means "from a superior place . . . it means excess, wealthier, more knowledgeable, more *modern*, and this has an effect of becoming more powerful."[15] Yet, Seno's story shows a significant change in the perceptions of Jakarta. As in Goenawan's "City," there is no "national" glory of being in the city. However, if Goenawan shows the centrality of living in Jakarta, Seno emphasizes the importance of detaching oneself from the city. In "From Jakarta," there is a displacement of

Jakarta even as the essay acknowledges the power of the city. "If you come to Jakarta, then you will become part of the symbol of superiority that, however, will be read by people (outside Jakarta) as oppression [*penindasan*]."[16] In Seno's work, there is a suspicion of everything from Jakarta, and if one is close to the "hot spot" (the area of riots) outside Jakarta, the advice is: "Don't ruthlessly say you are from Jakarta, for the image of Jakarta has changed. It is now seen as a 'dirty' place where one is playing against another [*pengadu domba*] to maintain power."[17] It seems to me that this unambiguous sense of disappointment with Jakarta appears only after the 1998 May riots, in contradistinction to the time Pramoedya satirically wrote: "The wind blows through the provinces whispering that one cannot be fully Indonesian until one has seen Jakarta."[18] "How is Jakarta today?" asked Seno, "It used to be superior, but now it is inferior."[19] These two imaginings of Jakarta, one from the inside-out (Goenawan) and another, from the outside-in (Seno), can be seen in tandem with discourses critical of state-imposed "nationalist urbanism."

In the following sections, I will explore the falling apart of the ideology of "nationalist urbanism" that for years sustained the transformation of both the physical and the mental space of the city. Perhaps the best way to show this is to demonstrate the change of sensitivity among Jakarta's residents and how the people of Jakarta responded to the policies and practices of the recently retired governor of Jakarta, Lieutenant General Sutiyoso, during the first term of his tenure (1997–2002).

GOVERNOR SUTIYOSO, THE ECONOMIC CRISIS, AND THE UNRULY URBAN MILIEU

Sutiyoso took over the office of the governor in 1997, at a critical juncture in the history of the city, the end of Suharto's regime, and he also inherited the immediate post-1998 social environment of Indonesia.[20] Prior to becoming governor, he was deputy-commander in chief of the Kopassus, the army's Special Action Commandos responsible for warfare and atrocities in East Timor and Aceh. Sutiyoso inherited many techniques of governance associated with Suharto's New Order. Many of these techniques, as I will make clear below, are those of "nationalist urbanism." Throughout his tenure, he drummed up the national conscience of Jakarta's residents through a number of urban projects involving national sentiment. Consistent with the urban paradigm of his predecessors, he also devoted much energy to the basic issues familiar from the previous regime: demolishing kampungs, banning rickshaws, restricting motor-bike taxis, and catching vendors, street musicians (*pengamen*), beggars, scavengers, and sex workers.[21] He also, of course, mismanaged public funds. However, unlike the previous forms of nationalist urbanism officially imposed from above at the height of the state's authority, Sutiyoso's version resulted from the "looseness" of power in the center and thus represents the crisis of that paradigm. Had Suharto stayed in power, I believe Sutiyoso's nationalist urbanism would have confronted only minor resistance, if not full acceptance, by the public.

However, the mood of post-1998 Jakarta is entirely different because the people seem to have found their critical voice. They are suspicious, skeptical, and often angry about urban projects that seek to represent the nation. While they used to be "passive" in resisting the city's programs of "national development" (apart from a few cases),[22] their "passive" resistance has been replaced by explicit protests, rallies, and strikes. This active resistance comes from people's distrust of their national elites and the displacement of the power of the nation-state and the authoritative image of the capital city. The coherent image of "Jakarta as the center of human life" associated with the national ideology is today an obscure imagining. A new consciousness, critical of the nexus between the city and the nation, has emerged from the remnants of the violence associated with nationalist urbanism. But before I discuss the urban discourses of Sutiyoso, it might be useful to get a sense of the changing socioeconomic milieu of post-1998 Indonesia, given the turmoil since the collapse of Suharto's authoritarian rule that has forcefully shaped as well as limited the urban visions of the governor.

The urban discourses of Sutiyoso, initiated to save the authority of the city and the nation, arose, in large measure, from the 1998 economic and political crisis. In contrast to the 1970s and 1980s, Indonesia experienced a deep economic downturn toward the end of the 1990s. According to John Bresnan, "the World Bank estimated that the turnaround in growth in Indonesia, from a positive 7 percent in 1997 to a projected negative 15 percent in 1998 — a net loss of 22 percent — was the worst the world has seen since the Great Depression of the 1930s."[23] As a result, the rates of unemployment, poverty, and urban crime have increased dramatically since 1998.[24] Foreign investment has declined significantly, and investors

Figure 1 Signboards giving direction to the newly established business enterprises at a housing complex of a new town in post-Suharto Jakarta. Photo by A. Kusno.

in Indonesia, complaining about the incapacity of the state to enforce law, have begun to disappear. The number of reports on economic crises and the incapacity of the government to address the issue has increased in the past five years. In 2002, the *Jakarta Post* published the World Investment Report, which showed "Indonesia to be the only country in East Asia to have suffered capital flight since 1998."[25] In Jakarta, a great number of professionals (the so-called managerial class) have been laid off following the closure of many financial and other service industries. A substantial number of these middle- and high-income managers have switched professions or become self-employed. Unable to find jobs in the shrinking formal sector, many have turned their houses and sidewalks into places for making money. They have opened up family businesses, after-school classes, semipermanent shops, small restaurants, and places for gambling. This phenomenon is most visibly expressed in the residential neighborhoods in various parts of Jakarta. These areas have suddenly become filled with different kinds of food stalls, billboards, tents, car parking, and, not least, garbage (see figure 1).

Observing this excess of private enterprises in the residential areas of the city, a newspaper reported: "Especially after the riots of May 1998, many streets are blocked by portals, and behind the blockage, is the phenomenal growth of private enterprises in the housing complex."[26] Meanwhile, in the central business district, where the middle class used to work in high-rise towers, no new office building has been built in the past seven years after the political revolution, though more and more "underclass" vendors concentrate closer and closer to the skyline of Jakarta.

VENDORS, THE STREETS, AND THE MEMORIES OF EVICTIONS

The effects of the economic crisis have been especially severe for the urban poor.[27] Many of them have lost their jobs as manufacturing industries such as electronics, machinery, textiles, shoes, and construction, among others, have closed or scaled down their activities, contributing to the increase of unemployment in the urban world of the underclass. These increasing numbers of unemployed have tremendous effects on the urban environment as most of them (not unlike the middle class) have altered the space of the city to fit their strategies of survival. If members of the middle class have been faking antiques in their garages and setting up café tents and restaurants in the public park, in carports, as well as on the sidewalks of their homes, members of the working class, having lost their jobs in the factories, have been taking up jobs as street vendors, pedicab drivers, donation seekers, beggars, and urban thugs. They operate in every public space and on almost every street in the city: at the traffic lights, on the crossover, under the flyovers, on the toll roads, in the public park, and on the sidewalks of both private and public buildings. Shocked by the phenomenal appearance of vendors in every corner of the city after 1998, a newspaper reported: "The presence of vendors [kaki lima] in the capital city is not surprising. However, today their presences have been extremely ignited [marak]. They do not just display their merchandises on pushcarts or under plastic or canvas tents. Instead they set up their places with permanent stalls, which they also use as their dwellings."[28]

The urban poor are thus competing with the middle class in the public spaces of the city. In the process, self-employment has made Jakarta resemble "a city of vendors," provoking reactions from the municipality to curb their activities not by evicting them, "for the city officers are scared of rioting,"[29] but by changing the physical space of the city: fences are built in public parks, and sidewalks are lined with barbed wire to prevent vendors

Figure 2 Vendors appropriating the fence set up to prevent them from using the sidewalk. Photo by A. Kusno.

from using them. The city administration, the middle class, and the urban poor are thus performing different forms of illegality. They propagate new spatial practices beyond any imagined by urban design paradigms. Most importantly, in the eyes of the government, they have contributed to the declining authority of the city and the nation (see figure 2).

The spatial practices described above are not entirely new. Historically, the street vendors have always been subjected to condemnation, and governors of Jakarta have customarily targeted them as the cause of the city's problems. The raids against vendors have taken various forms, ranging from banning them to minimizing the provision of sidewalks to avoid occupation by vendors.[30] The deeper reason is political since vendors invite the possibility of crowds gathering in the streets, a situation considered as threatening to the orderliness promoted by the state. In this sense, the proliferation of vendors in post-Suharto Jakarta can be seen as a symbol of the struggle for the right to the city concomitant with the change in the political climate. This has altered the relations between citizens and government. In the post-1998 era, one can easily find unprecedented expressions ranging from critical evaluations to a total disregard of the existence of the state: "Why should I care about the state if the state never pays attention to its people? I don't trust them (the people who are running the state)."[31] Similarly, a food seller critically comments: "I used to think that they (legislators) represented us, but observing their performance, now I have changed my mind. They are not the people's representatives anymore."[32] Others have lost patience: "Every time I see them driving their posh cars, I wonder how they are able to earn that much money. I have been working for many years, but I can't afford to even buy a bicycle at the moment.... I swear if they ever pass me by, I will throw stones at the faces of the people's representatives.... Do they recognize the insecurity felt by most vendors?"[33]

In post-1998 Jakarta, the vendors feel insecure even though they have gained an unprecedented degree of control over their own existence. Their revenues have considerably declined, the result of, what they perceive as, the new disorderliness of the city. From their perspective, the main source of disorder lies in the city's administration and planning, which they consider corrupt, unfair, and incompetent. For this reason, this group, at least, feels that they can always neglect or protest against the authority that seeks to displace them, even though their unrest has not prevented their revenues from decreasing. They occupy public spaces at will and are on almost every sidewalk in the city and quite often the streets themselves, causing massive traffic jams. They do not seem to be afraid of the security officers (*tramtib*), "for today's condition is different from that before the reformasi. Today's traders are more daring compared to the past. If they [the security personnel] dismiss us, we will react against them."[34] Indeed, resistance and riots have altered the encounters between police officers and vendors.

The memory of previous clashes continues to worry the middle class. Newspapers (reflecting middle-class fears) often remind readers (or perhaps the authority) of previous incidents, such as: "The resistances of vendors that sparked into riots have taken place in Senen and Glodok as well as Tampuring, South Jakarta."[35] The middle class particularly feels the change in the city. Jakarta is no longer a city of discipline and order as envisioned under nationalist urbanism. Perhaps in accordance with the change in people's behavior, the city authority has also become more tolerant toward vendors. The mayor of the central region of Jakarta states: "We also worry that our officers will be attacked [if we dismiss the vendors], so we just have to be cautious. Hopefully the vendors will leave this place by themselves."[36]

THE "LOOSENESS" AT THE CENTER: THE SOCIOPOLITICAL CRISES AND THE CHANGING MOOD OF THE PEOPLE

Post-1998 Indonesia has witnessed an unprecedented "looseness" at the center. More than before, the press is free to speak, and critical voices of the "people" can be heard; political parties are allowed to organize freely (resulting in various groups forming affiliations, often in order to exclude each other);[37] and public protests are tolerated, generating an impression that "today's Jakarta cannot be separated from protest expressing feeling [*unjuk rasa*] in public."[38] In the post-1998 period, all types of social movements have emerged to complicate the political scene. The political elites, the middle class, and the working class are all visible at the center of politics, transforming relations between politicians and citizens.

In a country with a long tradition of social hierarchy, political suppression, inequality, and authoritarianism, this "looseness" at the center has profound implications for the social environment of the city. It is as if a central support that had stabilized the island of Java for ages has been removed; a sense of restlessness prevails among the inhabitants. There is a sense among the population that the center is no longer there, fixing, watching, and ordering their conduct. The vanishing of the center has created a sense of disorientation and the creation of smaller centers that coexist uneasily with each other. The state is still there, but it has been perceived as merely one center among many others, each looking for opportunities to gain more wealth and power. It is not surprising therefore to see that residents of Jakarta have increasingly felt that they are living in a web of corruption, lawlessness, and violent actions. They feel insecure, vulnerable, and unprotected, even as they acknowledge the ample opportunities to get tougher, richer, and smarter. High officials are jockeying for more power, and officials and mobs are competing for illegal fees. Members of the upper middle class protect themselves and their properties day and night, often with firearms, bulletproof vests, and private security guards. They build many private and community gatehouses to prevent public access and to mark territory as well as identity, with no regard for public use of streets. The less well-off, unable to buy protection and to determine the shape of law enforcement, have also created their own system of security, often by means of mass trials. The "looseness" at the center generates a feeling that "we seem to be a nation that is just beginning to learn about everything."[39]

This sense that the center is falling apart has also created various civilian groups formed either loosely or tightly around identities "below" as well as "above" the nation; familiar groupings include those of class, professional, religious, ethnic, political, as well as moral affiliations. They are all linked to each other by a sense that the nation-state no longer commands any power to protect and rule, or at best, the political elites safeguard only their own interests and completely disregard the rest of the citizens who are left on their own to survive in the worsening realities of urban lives. In the eyes of the urban poor, the city government has never helped them and will perhaps never be able to provide its citizens with solutions. Criticizing the city's neglect of the people's welfare, Marco Kusumawijaya, an urban activist, urges the urban poor to create, if not maintain, their own networks, for "it is time for poor communities to seek solutions favorable to their own interests instead of expecting government policy to help them."[40] In a way, these "social movements," ranging from grassroots activist organizations to professional associations, are both empowered as well as disoriented by the "looseness" at the center. They have been able to form various networks to press the city government to improve its services to urban communities although almost always without success.

The "looseness" at the center encourages citizens of Jakarta to act on their own, creating a condition in which everyone safeguards his or her own space, often without much regard for the public. Some have used violence to show aspirations, others create and advance their own urban agendas. The city government too, having found itself toothless before vendors, has formed affiliations with civilian vigilante groups and urban thugs to save its own authority. Governor Sutiyoso, for instance, cooperated with local militias such as the Front Pembela Islam (FPI), founded after the May riots in 1998, to fight against "immoral" urban life.[41] He participated in the meeting of the leaders of the FPI who have been active in lobbying the city council to shut down the red-light districts of the city.[42] Since 1998, militia groups, some numbering in the tens of thousands, were established to help the governor cope with "trouble situations." The police too supported these militia groups in their beating of what are thought to be "sinful" couples in public, and in the burning of brothels, gambling dens, and restaurants suspected of selling alcohol.

This tradition of harnessing militias to "safeguard" the city is not new. The New Order of Suharto did this under the so-called *Siskamling* system, set up in the middle of the 1980s, in which civil security forces, trained in military camps, were distributed as private security guards to offices, hotels, shopping malls, industrial plants, as well as private residences. However, during the New Order, all these militias were controlled by the state in its effort to form an urban culture dependent on the military. Thus we saw in the 1980s cases of "mysterious corpses" (*matius*) and "mysterious shooters" (*petrus*), the result of state-sponsored killing of some members of the militias and of people identified as "criminals" on the streets of Jakarta.[43] In the post-Suharto era, this tradition of harnessing militias to safeguard the city and control the criminal underworld continues. For example, in 1998, a law was passed to permit police mobilizing masses to solve civilian disputes.[44] However, there are also significant differences. Today, the militias seem to be able to take charge of their own operations without the consent of the police. Indeed, quite often the police have had no better choice than to simply accommodate the wishes of the militias.

In contrast to the New Order state, which used to be the center of authority, constantly controlling and watching the behavior of its subjects, the post-Suharto state is under the gaze of the public. There is indeed a painful truth to Governor Sutiyoso's defense of his failure to manage Jakarta during his accountability speech, five years after being elected governor of Jakarta: "The multidimensional crisis, *the change in people's behavior*, and the fewer job opportunities have all caused difficulties in upholding security and order."[45] It is not easy for the retired army lieutenant general to acknowledge that during his first term as governor between 1997 and 2002, "4,538 demonstrations were staged by Jakartans against me . . . from small-scale rallies to ones that led to anarchy."[46]

REMEMBERING THE NATION: STATUES OF HEROES, THE WATER FOUNTAIN, AND THE FENCING OF THE NATIONAL MONUMENT

To illustrate the city government's attempts to deal with "the change in people's behavior" in post-1998 Jakarta, I now turn to Governor Sutiyoso's urban discourses. Sutiyoso mounted several urban design initiatives to cope with the crisis in the quality of life in the city after he took office.

Figure 3 Vendors' pushcarts parked at the National Monument.
Photo courtesy of F. Prihadi.

These were part of an attempt to revive nationalist urbanism to restore the authority of the city and the nation as one of the bases for power and influence. In particular, the governor made use of the city's monuments to remind citizens of the affinity between the city and the nation. He utilized the symbols of memory linking place with nation. Immediately after he took office, he planned to erect statues of national heroes at every street junction in Jakarta. These statues were to be placed on the streets bearing the names of these national heroes.

The aim of this project, according to Sutiyoso, was to make the public respect the struggle of Indonesian national leaders. Sutiyoso also ordered the fencing of the National Monument (Monas) Park, built by Sukarno in the 1960s (see figure 3). Since the monetary crisis of 1997, the largest park in the capital city has been filled with tents set up by vendors. Monas Park, according to Abdul Kahfi, one of the vice-governors of Jakarta, "has been turned into a storage dump, places where people wash and hang their clothes while many plants have been stepped on."[47]

Furthermore, Monas Park has been a popular site for street rallies against both the governor and the president of Indonesia, whose offices face the park. It was reported that Governor Sutiyoso had been complaining and grumbling about the Monas, "the historical symbol of Indonesia which is now in ruins,"[48] because he felt that the management of Monas Park represented the prestige of his administration. To restore its prestige, Sutiyoso ordered the park paved, vegetation planted, deer kept, and the whole park fenced to "create order and comfort for visitors" as well as to reduce demonstrations and get rid of vendors and the homeless who had been occupying the space in the past few years.[49] Through the office of sanitation, he also ordered that 550 garbage bins be placed in the area and instructed the office to service them twenty-four hours a day.[50] To further restore the area, the governor also planned to erect memorials at the four sides of the National Monument, each symbolizing a chapter in the history of the nation: the glorious time of the ancient kingdoms of Majapahit and Sriwijaya, the turmoil of colonial time, the struggle for independence, and the splendid era of development.[51]

The people of Jakarta, especially those who had set up vending tents and who would be evicted, received the orders with antagonism. Consistent with the mood of post-1998 Jakarta, they fought back. The vendors recognized "the importance of Monas to the pride of the city and that it ought to be clean and orderly," but argued that their right to the city was more important than the pride of the nation.[52] For the vendors of post-1998 Jakarta, Monas Park is merely a place with a vast open space important for enacting their survival in the city. National patriotism is secondary and deserves to be remembered only after the welfare of the residents.

Another urban nationalist initiative of Sutiyoso's was the renovation of the water fountain of the Hotel Indonesia (HI) traffic circle, on a part of which stands the Welcome Statue, built on the instructions of President Sukarno in the 1960s to welcome the Asian Games athletes to the city and "to welcome the future society that is just and prosperous."[53] The HI circle has been a popular spot since it was built. After the collapse of the Suharto regime, it has also become a site for the manifestation of social and political discontent. Partly to curb protests in the area, Sutiyoso initiated a program in 2001 called: "building national pride through lighting."[54] He wanted to see the Welcome Statue renovated and floodlit so that it would unite people and cheer the nation up again.[55] He therefore ordered the installation of new water pumps and hundreds of nozzles for the water fountain, the spray of which would form a red and white configuration (following the red and white national flag). He also hired security guards to patrol the circle on Sundays and public holidays. One observer welcomed this project for, in his eyes, this monument reminded him of the glory of Jakarta as the center of the nation: "There is a need to preserve the Welcome Monument because it is connected to the long history of this great nation."[56]

Although the governor and his supporters considered the renovation important for the image of Jakarta, and thus, the nation, many citizens of Jakarta felt that it was useless and a waste of money. "How could the city administration spend such an amount of money (14 billion rupiahs) for the decorative project?" was the cry in protest.[57] They felt that the project was too luxurious, even if a private cigarette company did fund the renovation of HI circle in exchange for ten strategic places in the city for its company's billboards. The citizens of Jakarta thought that the city of Jakarta should prioritize programs that would solve many of the city's social problems. Sally, a lower middle-class housewife, commented: "The governor seems to concentrate on evicting poor people living on the river banks, and not doing anything useful for Jakartans. The development of the Hotel Indonesia (HI) water fountain is one example of how the administration just wastes people's money."[58] Instead of generating the spirit of nationalism, the HI project provoked more criticism and protests and revealed the declining socioeconomic and political power of the government.

NOSTALGIA FOR ORDERLINESS: BATAVIA AND
THE RESTORATION OF AUTHORITY

To further show how deep the sense of crisis that prevailed in post-1998 Jakarta was, as well as the effort on the part of the city government to restore order and authority, I now take up the discourses surrounding the restoration of the Old Batavia (*Kota Tua*) in North Jakarta. At the outset, the project was meant to attract tourists, but deeper examination reveals an (unconscious) attempt on the part of the city government to restore the nation's image, which was damaged during the May riots. This project is much larger and more utopian than the renovation of HI, the restoration of the Monas, and the erection of statues of national figures on Jakarta's streets. It was also clear that this project would not be realized for a very long time for various reasons including the lack of funds and political will on the part of the citizens, investors, and the government. The project of restoring the Colonial Town could be read as expressing a longing for the orderliness of the old regime and the reassumption of national authority and the city's influence. The colonial past, embedded in the urban structure of the old town, was harnessed to provide a spectral order for the built environment of the postcolonial.

The physical destruction of old buildings during the riots of May 1998,[59] the sense of social disintegration after 1998, and the increased cases of violations of city laws prompted architects, planners, and the city government to reestablish projects of cultural preservation. Unlike in the past when the purpose of preserving the built environment was to attract foreign tourists and to educate the young generation about the nation's history, the city government today feels that the aim of saving old buildings is to restore the authority of the government. In other words, the city government feels that its authority lies in its capacity to save and restore old monuments of Jakarta. In 2000, a journalist reported: "The government has made a firm commitment for the restoration of the remaining buildings in the old part of the city, known as Old Batavia. It has aimed to create in that part of the city a beautiful, comfortable and clean place that will be beneficial to its citizens."[60]

In 2001, Governor Sutiyoso issued a decree (sk Gubernur No. 106 / 2001) to preserve the Old Batavia of Jakarta in order to attract tourists and recreate the image of Jakarta as a city of order. For the governor, the restoration would upgrade the authority of the Indonesian government in the eyes of public as well as the global tourists in contradistinction to the atmosphere of "chaos, hectic, inhumanity, and traffic jams" pervading the area of the Old Batavia "where the authority of the government drops to zero."[61] The preservation of the old town thus aims at "freeing the area from the hullabaloo of vehicles" so that an atmosphere of tranquility could be achieved.[62] The city of the past, neglected for years, is to become the future of Jakarta "to attract tourists, to increase security, to preserve old buildings and their surroundings in order to create an artistic and cheerful atmosphere," the governor declared.[63]

This project of preserving the Colonial Town of Jakarta was to start from the Sunda Kelapa harbor, a fifteenth-century port built by the Padjajaran kingdom, and then subsequently occupied by the Portuguese in 1522 and the Dutch in 1610. From there, the area of preservation will extend to cover 132 locations considered part of the Old Batavia. Receiving "an extraordinary support from the Dutch government," this harbor will be "made up so that it will appear pretty, cute and passionate."[64] As if the old town will provide a sense of orientation and stability to the condition of chaos in the post-1998 city, Martono Yuwono, the head of the development of Sunda Kelapa and a senior conservationist, declared: "Jakarta has entered a new chapter. It is now remembering its glory and pride of the old time through the renovation of the old harbor built by the Netherlands East Indies Company (voc) four hundred years ago. It seeks to restore the honor of the nation by turning the colonial heritage into tourist areas."[65] The objective was not merely to provoke nostalgia for the past, but to educate Indonesians about the importance of history and national struggle. Martono Yuwono further argued that the most important memory in Indonesian history was the awakening of national consciousness (*kebangkitan nasional*) represented by the formation of an organization in Batavia in 1908 by a circle of young Javanese students seeking to remake Javanese culture for the twentieth century. Martono Yuwono strongly felt that this memory, which is now celebrated annually in Indonesia as the Day of National Awakening, ought to be used as a basis for turning Jakarta into the city of national struggle (*Kota Joang*). He proposed the idea of constructing a Jakarta History Corridor (see figure 4), which would extend from the historical harbor of Sunda Kelapa at North Jakarta (where the Old Batavia is located) to the National Monument at the central part of Jakarta. Along this corridor would be found monuments, museums, parks, and various tourist-related facilities to remind the present urban population of the history of the city and the nation.[66]

What is also significant in this "nostalgia for the present" is that the development of Sunda Kelapa is also about restoring the authority of urban design and planning in a time of chaos and disorder that marked post-1998 Jakarta. Martono Yuwono harked back to the modest success in 1972, when the Dutch City Hall was restored along with the breakthrough achievement of "rehabilitating infrastructure of 40 hectares, upgrading roads, paving sidewalks, organizing vendors and garbage, constructing drainage, park, street and traffic lights, and rerouting traffic flow, removing bus terminal, rearranging billboards, planting street plants, providing advices, and restoring and repainting the facade of old buildings in the area."[67]

The memories of the demolition of buildings from the previous era that culminated in the May 1998 riots, the sense that the government has lost

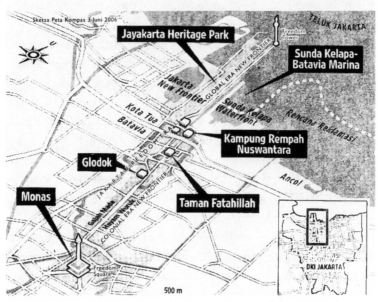

POROS KEHORMATAN BANGSA
"Freedom Square" – "Freedom Trail" – Freedom Tower"

Figure 4 The Jakarta Historical Corridor: Urban renewal and the retrieval of past glory. Reprinted from Martono Yuwono, *Palapa Nusantara 2015: "Kebangkitan semangat wawasan bahari Jakarta"* (Jakarta: Masyarakat Kota Bandar Jakarta, 2008).

its authority to order the city, and the discourses of the restoration of Old Batavia are thus connected. They are part of the nostalgic remembering of the orderliness of the old regimes and the forgetting of the chaotic present. The goal of preserving Old Batavia is thus not merely to educate Indonesians about the importance of both tourism and restoring the memories of the country's colonial past and its struggle for independence. It originates also from a desire on the part of the urban elite to restore an order and authority that are at present deteriorating and to imagine a coherent image of the past in order to regain power and influence.

LOOKING FORWARD: THE HOUSES OF THE WORLD, THE SINGING MALLS, AND THE FORGETTING OF THE PRESENT

For the middle class, this period of unprecedented lawlessness, marked by conflicting civic and state interests, has produced an exceptional sense of instability. In response, there is pressure to build an even stronger bulwark against the poor, the unruly, and the unexpected. Growing up in the cradle of Suharto's regime with its emphasis on "stability," the middle class is most anxious about the change in people's behavior in the city. Their sense of insecurity is expressed in their anxieties over the condition of security in the city and in their demand for more police, which, ironically, they do not trust.[68] Since 1998, the middle-class newspaper, *Kompas*, has devoted much attention to such issues of public safety as bomb threats, murders, kidnaps, rapes, and robberies. Middle-class residents of Jakarta feel extremely unsafe both at home and on the streets. Explosive materials have occasionally been found in the malls, the social space of the middle class; their parked cars have been stolen and broken into; and even their gated housing complexes have been subject to intrusion, robbery, and attack.

To gauge the spatial responses of the middle class to the decline of public safety in Jakarta, it would be appropriate to assess the current position of the New Town and the shopping mall, the two most significant middle-class enclaves inherited from Suharto's regime.[69] The New Town, with its utopian overtones, is a logical starting point to see how the middle class attempt to curb a sense of insecurity and escape from living dangerously in Jakarta. As street crimes dramatically worsened after 1998, significantly higher, sharply pointed fences have been constructed as bulwarks of resistance to the unexpected beyond the gate. Tighter security checkpoints have been established to ensure the control of visitors and passers-by. At some gates, visitors are asked to leave their identification cards with the security guards. Fences, gatehouses, and security guards symbolize not only the prestige of the middle class but also their sense of fear, loss, and the need for a tightened defense.

The architectural design of post-1998 New Town also expresses a yearning to be somewhere else, in a different time and space. In the guarded enclave of Lippo Karawaci, for instance, the developer offers architectural styles of various places from different time periods: Taman Britania (Garden of Britain), Taman Boston (Garden of Boston), Taman Osaka (Garden of Osaka), and Taman Pattaya (Pattaya Garden) are some of the large-scale housing complexes on offer, complemented by smaller-scale, locally themed estates, suggesting an association with the legendary past such as: Taman Legian, Taman Batavia, Taman Diponegoro (Garden of Diponegoro, the Javanese prince who fought against Dutch rule from 1825 to 1830), and Taman Parahyangan (Garden of Parahyangan, the abode of the gods as found in Indic mythology). There is also prairie-style housing named "Taliesin, Woodland and Oak Park," recalling the architectural imagination of Frank Lloyd Wright.[70]

It is more than an accidental metaphor when the most famous real estate company today, the Duta Pertiwi, chose to name the largest of its housing complexes established after 1998, Kota Wisata (Tour Town) and Legenda Wisata (Tour Legend). As if to remove feelings of insecurity, Kota Wisata, the largest real estate housing on the outskirts of southeast Jakarta, offers housing and shopping facilities that would enable people to "go around the world without passport: Visits to beautiful Indonesia, jewels of Paris, German masterpiece, romantic Italy, Japanese heritage, spirit of America, splendor of China."[71] Reminiscent of theme parks and closely connected to the idea of journeying abroad away from the national territory, the architectural styles offered range beyond the boundaries of the nation. They speak of voyaging and a sense of living away from the city and the nation. In the first quarter of 2002, Kota Wisata sold some two hundred upper-class houses (prices in the range of 500 million rupiah). The "most spectacular" market performance has prompted the company to develop six more new housing projects clustered around Euro-American themes: "Kensington, Windsor, Orlando, San Francisco, Beverly Hills, and Florida."[72]

In addition, as a means of escape from the crime-infested city streets, the shopping mall has become a favorite space for the residents to retreat to. As a result, toll roads have become an important avenue of transportation connecting the housing enclaves to the central business district and the shopping malls. Lining the toll roads on the way home "from the West are Mal Ciputra, Mal Taman Anggrek, and Slipi Jaya Plaza. Then up the road are Plaza Senayan and Ratu Plaza. From the main boulevard of MH Thamrin, one could find Plaza Indonesia and Sarinah shopping center. Towards the area of Casablanca, one could find Mal Ambassador. Towards the direction of Menteng, one could find Menteng Plaza and further East is Atrium Plaza at the area of Senen."[73] Customers are attracted to these well-designed malls by their "strategic locations [along the flyovers] and the pleasant interior."[74] Totally shielded from the chaos outside, the interiors of these malls are equipped not only with full air-conditioning but also with entertainment and recreational facilities for the whole family. For example, in Plaza Senayan, "at certain hours, a clock hanging at the lobby will sing, sweetly with melodious voice, to cheer up customers."[75]

Another six malls are reported to be under construction "to fulfill the demand for these places for recreation for everyone."[76] Not unlike the New Town of Kota Wisata, post-1998 shopping malls have also been promoting the tranquility and self-sufficient amenities of their environments. "There is no need to travel to Singapore, Hong Kong, United States, or France to buy brand-name perfume, shoes, and designer clothes" declared an upper middle-class city magazine.[77] If the New Town promises a journey abroad, away from the time and space of the nation, the mall replaces the streets of Jakarta, now filled with vendors, with the fantasy of touring the world in a safely enclosed and guarded interior space for consumption.

People's lifestyles have indeed changed. The *Jakarta Post* reports: "When in the past people would spend their free time at parks or public places, nowadays people flock to the malls scattered around the city."[78] In the 1960s, 1970s, and 1980s, the Welcome Monument at the Hotel Indonesia circle, the Semanggi cloverleaf highway, and the National Monument were the symbols of Jakarta and the residents of Jakarta went there to take pictures. Today, the general sentiment is: "Ngapain ke sana, mending ke mal!" [Why go there? It is better to go to the malls!].[79] Not only is the shopping mall the new symbol of the city, but in post-1998 Jakarta, the centrality of the mall is also closely connected to middle-class anxieties over the worsening street crime in Jakarta.

NEW SUBJECTIVITIES?

In the past, Jakarta was the center of national life, the place where the city's residents identified themselves with the nation and its government. Under the rule of Suharto, Jakarta had built itself up as a city of power by blending authoritative official nationalism with market capitalism to produce a particular type of urbanism that sought to advance along the trajectory of "development." After 1998, even though people in Jakarta still locate the city within the nation, they no longer embrace nationalism as a discourse compatible with the reality of their city lives.

In this chapter, I have outlined how the current power of Jakarta is produced through the engagement of its inhabitants in various urban discourses associated with the memories of the present, the past, and the future. I have shown how Governor Sutiyoso, in drawing on the remnants of the previous Suharto regime, attempted to restore past memories by mobilizing nationalist urbanism to generate the impression that power belongs to Jakarta and not to other cities. With this image, he hoped that Jakarta would reconnect itself to the previous cultural, economic, and political networks. This attempt by the state to link the memory of the past with the reality of the present for the future of the city, however, is overlaid by different sets of public memories involving the city inhabitants and their decentralized networks.

The people of Jakarta today have been witnessing an unprecedented change in their relationships to the nation and its government, a change that I argue results from a critical consciousness of the state—the collapse of the ideology of centralized government, the assaults of the capitalist economic crises, the increase in urban poverty, the spread of unemployment, the deepening culture of corruption, the prevailing sense of lawlessness, the proliferation of violence, and the eruption of ethnic conflicts. These series of crises have put a wedge between the imagined fullness of nationalism and the reality of life in the city, generating a politics of remembering and forgetting that includes a nostalgia for the orderliness associated with the old regime.

This moment of rupture has opened up a possibility for a more responsible, diverse, and democratic urbanism, but it has also created spaces for the formation of a new urban politics that is more egotistic, deliberately unpredictable, and violent. The city has been liberated from the imposed uniformity of the national framework, but other politics of morality have been emerging. Some are more conservative, exclusive, and equally authoritarian, while others are more cosmopolitan, multicultural, and progressive. Out of this struggle to remember and to forget, a set of selected politics of morality will ultimately emerge as norms of public life that will replace, or perhaps return to, the old nationalist urbanism.

CHAPTER 2   **THE REGIME, THE BUSWAY, AND THE CONSTRUCTION OF URBAN SUBJECTS IN AN INDONESIAN METROPOLIS**

> Today's [busway] does not merely convey representational contents, but also contributes to the fabrication of new assemblages of enunciation, individual and collective. —FELIX GUATTARI, "REGIMES, PATHWAYS, SUBJECTS"

> Jakarta's residents are certainly not starved for choice when it comes to transport. The city's streets are clogged with ojek [motorbike taxis], bajaj [three-wheel motor scooter pedicab], minivans, buses, taxis and private cars. Until recently becak [pedicab] still operated in parts of the city. Some hardy individuals ride bicycles. Ojek are popular for their ability to weave in and around traffic, but sometimes a jam is too much even for them. Rising above this traffic mess is the busway. With its dedicated lanes, it is a popular means of transportation for people wanting to skip the traffic. —ALVIN D. SOEDARJO, "BUSWAY MAINTENANCE NEEDED, SAY PASSENGERS," *JAKARTA POST*, 14 AUGUST 2006

"The revolution (thus) has begun on Jakarta's streets," a reporter proclaimed at the end of 2004.[1] That year the city launched its new busway link as the first step in the implementation of what was claimed to be a comprehensive and coherent master plan for the city's transportation system. Under this arrangement, special buses managed by the system have separate lanes in which they can drive faster than other vehicles (see figure 5).

Some forty shelters have been built for commuters under the crossing bridges in the green belt strip along the route. Aspiring to be known as "the father of transportation,"[2] the incumbent governor at the time, Lieutenant General Sutiyoso, claimed that his plan would achieve Jakarta's dream

Figure 5 The exclusive busway lane. Photo by A. Kusno.

of a city free of traffic jams by controlling the operation of private cars
and motorcycles in the city as well as establishing such public transport
as trains, the busway, and the monorail and river systems. Seemingly designed to please everyone, Sutiyoso's urban project represents not only a
radical step to solve the problem of chronic traffic jams and to catch up
with developments in mass transportation but also an attempt to imprint
on the urbanscape the authority, legitimacy, and legacy of his rule in the
city, which, since the fall of the Suharto regime, has been suffering from
"looseness in the center," as detailed in chapter 1.

   This chapter focuses on the cultural politics of the busway in Jakarta
as an example of urban spectacle and governmentality, a politics in which
the desires and anxieties of both the city government and citizen groups
are represented in the sites of the city. This is *not* to argue against the
much-needed mass transportation system for the city. It is rather to offer
an understanding of how the experiences of urbanism interact with political cultures of the state. In this chapter, I show how the busway can be
seen as an "apparatus" of power that, through the experience of riding the
bus across the city, seeks to reintegrate "Indonesians" through imageries
of progress, authority, and discipline. The newly installed busway consti-

tutes a sphere of governmentality that contributes to the production of particular social norms and forms associated with the new environment of governing in the post-Suharto era. First, I will provide some context for the emergence of the busway and the concomitant discourses of discipline, order, and security regarding the streets of Jakarta.

REMINISCENCE: GOVERNOR SUTIYOSO, LOOSENESS IN THE CENTER, AND THE TRAUMATIZED RESIDENTS

Let me start by recalling briefly some aspects of public life in Jakarta during the first five-year term of Governor Sutiyoso (1997–2002), which coincided with the immediate post-Suharto era of "reformasi." In chapter 1, I referred to the beginning of the post-Suharto era in terms of a "looseness in the center," a sense among the population that the center was retreating if not decomposing and was being replaced by many centers that coexisted uneasily. This sense created a profound feeling of disorientation and was one of the effects of the violent end of Suharto's rule, which produced in the urban population of Jakarta a feeling of liberation mixed with fear and uncertainty. The sense of a "looseness in the center" stimulated various social actors (from the state to citizen groups) to refashion their strategies for power and survival in the city, and the activities of these social actors have profoundly altered the urban space in parts of the capital city. They responded to the change of the political regime by refashioning the built environment within which they operated. Their responses, as I have shown in chapter 1, produced various consequences for the visual environment of the city. Matters concerning the urban space are now in the hands of mutually antagonistic citizens who take advantage of, and perhaps suffer from, the "looseness in the center." In these contestations over public space (by both the representatives of the state and citizen groups), there is the sense that the city has become an arena of multiple conflicts and a site for overcoming crisis in the ruling realm.

The discourses about "rights to the city," the reconfiguration of space by the urban population, and the city government's responses, as outlined above, indicated to Governor Sutiyoso the profound change that had taken place in the social environment and what he called the "behavior" of people in Jakarta. It was a shock to him since he was appointed during Suharto's reign, and he expected to perform just like his predecessors. Sutiyoso, however, never considered himself a failed governor. Instead, he believes that the critical responses he received from the public were caused by their traumatic experience of political transition in 1998. He categorized a large portion of the residents of Jakarta as *masyarakat traumatis* (traumatized people), and he saw himself initially as carrying out the task of curing and saving them and, if necessary, doing so by means of military prowess. "I am a Lieutenant General who can work together with the police and military apparatus to bring back security to the city."[3] However, the governor was also quick to realize that the idea of mobilizing the military apparatus was no longer an option since the Indonesian military had lost much of its legitimacy and popular trust.

After five years of his term as the governor of Jakarta, Sutiyoso realized that in his second term (2002-7) he had to play the game differently. He knew perfectly well that while he could continue to use the old techniques of militaristic force, such as forced evictions, he had to articulate urban projects that would allow him to gain social and political legitimacy within the various citizen groups. In other words, to regain some measure of control over the urban population and to restore authority after the collapse of an authoritarian regime, the governor had to come up with a populist project that was not only spectacular but also influential enough to make the residents of Jakarta at least share, if not take responsibility for, the violence that might be committed by the project. This effort can be further translated as the state's attempt to find legitimacy in the eyes of the public through an exemplary performance that would include all citizens. But such a mission demands an identification of the state with the collective desire of the public for a resolution to what members of the public themselves considered an "urban problem."

The busway project, as this chapter will show, can be seen as embodying the state's desire to remanage the urban population, many members of whom had been dreaming of a city free of traffic jams in addition to its social, economic, and political development. Indeed, it is by way of the cognate desires of the state and members of the civil society for an orderly city where transportation flows efficiently that we can grasp the specificity of the busway project. The busway has to be seen as conjuring up positions both outside and inside the sphere of state governance. Its operation involves practices of liberation (from the traffic jam), discipline, and regularity that constitute a form of governance associated with postauthoritarian Indonesia—a formation of power that I will discuss more toward the end of this chapter. As a project characterized more by desires than strategies, the busway is thus marked initially by ad hoc planning without a system, for presupposed here is a work that would show an immediate example of order, signs of recovery, and a sense that the city is dealing with problems. Such a project, which can be seen as based on a coalition of shared desires for a city free of traffic jams, nevertheless involves implementing a technique of representation associated with "shock therapy," as I will discuss below. I shall now turn to the question of why all social strata in contemporary Jakarta found the busway congenial and useful even though it was initially criticized as a flawed piece of infrastructure.

Traffic Jams and the Freeways

In 2003, as part of the celebration of the 476th birthday of Jakarta and in conjunction with the reappointment of Sutiyoso as the governor, the influential middle-class newspaper *Kompas* reported its findings on what Jakarta residents think about their city.[4] Polls were taken to allow the public to identify "urban problems" and voice their concern in response to the question: "What are the problems that most disturb your daily activities in Jakarta?" The research team reported that two "realities" received the most attention from the residents of Jakarta. The first is city traffic, which has become overwhelmingly chaotic (*semrawut*) — almost everywhere the streets of Jakarta (including the freeways) are often in a state of gridlock. The newspaper reported that respondents from all over Jakarta, from north to south, east to west, and the center all say that traffic jams are the most annoying problem in the city, far above crime (*kriminalitas*), the second source of concern. However, they are connected. *Kompas* reported that urban residents have been feeling unusually insecure. Urban thugs (*preman*) occupy the streets as well as the freeways of Jakarta. They extort money from drivers and passengers of cars, taxis, and buses. An urban observer pointed out that this "*pungli transportasi*" (unlawful extortion of transportation fees) has been on the rise since 1998.[5] Meanwhile, complaints over problems about public buses have also intensified. "The numbers of armed robbery and singing beggary have also gone up . . . all these have worried passengers . . . who have been hoping for a public transportation system that is safe, comfortable, inexpensive, and reliable time-wise. But this is only a dream."[6] The concern over safety on the public buses had reached such a point that the public's anxiety had been turned into the desire for a truly dependable means of public transportation, though this seemed be an almost impossible dream.

For some, the difficulty of turning the dream into reality was connected to the increase in unemployment and migration into the city. Newspapers often reported that no matter how poor and tough Jakarta has become and regardless of the policy of decentralization (which had given the outer regions more power to develop on their own to reduce migration to the city), Jakarta continues to be perceived as the political and economic center and a magnet for migrants from various parts of the country (or Java). It is reported that every year three hundred thousand (underclass) people from the surrounding regions come to Jakarta even though the city continues to expel thousands who do not have a city ID.[7] Many take up jobs as street vendors, and in the eyes of the middle class, "their presence has been extremely inflammable."[8] The street vendors are also present on the toll roads. Ir. Wiyogo Adiwasito, the director of Jasa Marga who manages the toll roads in greater Jakarta, observed that "lately in the areas of Serang, Banten, one could find more than a hundred kiosks and food stalls along the side lanes of Jakarta-Merak toll roads. . . . The number of such vendors has been increasing rapidly since the beginning of the economic crisis (1998/1999) in the nation. The problem of the vendors can thus be said as representing the problem of the nation."[9] The attention to the decline of national prestige and authority, the excess numbers of migrants, vendors, and the urban poor, the problem of traffic jams, and the desire for a safe public transportation system are both functional and symbolic.

In Jakarta, the conditions on the street indicate the status of the ruling power. Indeed, historically, they have been a barometer measuring the rise and fall of Indonesian political regimes. Elsewhere, I have shown how toll roads (and the flyover) can be seen as the embodiment of Suharto's New Order ideology of development (1966–98).[10] Through a particular politics of the street, intended to displace the political culture of the previous regime, Suharto's New Order linked the idea of progress and development to the construction of toll roads. Central to the construction of toll roads is the production of a new generation of middle-class Indonesians who ideally would avoid ground-level streets by driving on the freeways from the urban center to the new town at the outskirts of the city. Jakarta's freeways and the car-based middle class were key representations of "progress" and "stability" for the New Order "developmentalist" state. The fluidity of traffic circulation thus connotes the stable flows of social, economic, and political traffic.

John Sidel has written about the symbolic importance for the legitimacy of the New Order of the ease of traffic circulation (*sirkulasi*) in the city and the fatal consequences of the traffic jam (*macet*).[11] "Like the painted mannequin policemen standing watchfully at key road junctions in Surabaya to oversee the traffic, Suharto presided over the continuous flow of capital, labor, and commodities, and the regular rotation of military and civilian personnel. It was precisely this steady circulation (*sirkulasi*) . . . along one-way streets that kept Indonesia in motion as Suharto stood still, for more than thirty years."[12] Consequently, when the traffic did grind to a halt, one could safely (and anxiously) expect that the political realm was undergoing a deep crisis. In Sidel's words, "The cost and the limits of such *sirkulasi* were apparent to all who could sense the possibility of *macet*."[13] The notion of "traffic jam" (macet) thus refers to things beyond the backing up of traffic. It means the social, economic, and political components of the city and the nation are "at an impasse"; for *macet* means "to break down," "go dead," or "misfire."[14] It is associated with the stagnation of the national economy and the decline of discipline, disastrous social turmoil, and the possibility of, in John Pemberton's words, "an enormous political traffic accident."[15] In a macet circumstance, the state would normally be expected to step in to display its power to restore the flow and remove the blockage that is causing the standstill. This interplay between sirkulasi and macet on the freeway has been carried over to the post-Suharto era.

Today, when traffic is brought to a standstill, one would not simply think it is because of an accident, construction work, "big guys" passing through, or buses stopping irregularly; one would also think that perhaps rallies and demonstrations have closed down some streets or that vendors have taken over the streets and freeways. Yet now there is also a new component that has been added to the cultural meaning of the term *macet*, that is, an excess of private cars—the number of which has gone far beyond the capacity of the roads to carry them. Private cars, for the first time, are seen as part of "urban problems" rather than as one of its solutions. Since 2000, more and more images have been printed in the metropolitan press depicting the worsening condition of the streets and freeways caused by traffic jams. The proliferation of private cars is an excess brought about by the previous regime that privileged them.

The intermingling discourses of economic crisis, the excess of cars, popular desires for a city liberated from traffic jams, and, most importantly, the fear of a reoccurrence of an "enormous political traffic accident" could be said to have provided the grounds for the city administration's decision to remanage the streets and its traffic. They helped to create the conditions for the emergence of the busway as a new form of public transportation that would respond to the anxieties shared by the state, the ruling elites, and various citizen groups in the city. In other words, the busway arose in the context of these various discourses, which went beyond the developmentalist language of providing urban infrastructure. However, as a social artifact that embodied conflicting desires and fears, these same discourses, I will argue, returned to invest and challenge the meaning of the busway as it made its appearance in the streets of Jakarta.

As an apparatus that captured various discourses and emerged out of various anxieties and desires, the busway was thus both contentious and popular. We could say that the busway, as a machine for transportation, functioned as what Felix Guattari called a "collective apparatus of subjectification."[16] However, in contrast to the Foucauldian method of disciplinary practice in which subjectivity enters into the machine without much contradiction, the busway was intended to shock the city as it entered. Such an abrupt method deviates from the established norm of liberal governmentality, even though, after the shock, a process of normalization was expected to take over the process of subjectification. The busway played a therapeutic function; it was a kind of "shock therapy" for a city considered as suffering from contemporary "urban problems" and the trauma of regime change. I now turn to these techniques of treatment, which can be seen as a tactic of the present in coping with what Sutiyoso called the *masyarakat traumatis* (traumatic society). Yet such "shock therapy" has a rather specific history in the political culture of Indonesia.

Shock Therapy

We generally recognize "shock therapy" as a treatment for mental disorder through the use of an electric current. In other fields, it is associated with an abrupt strategy for economic or political recovery—a technique used by a regime to make radical change in society. Such an abrupt strategy displaces people for a while, but its effect immediately leads to, say, economic growth and then back to normality in social and political life.[17] In

Indonesia, the notion of "shock therapy" has often been used with a similar meaning, but at times the aim of such treatment was quite different.

In Indonesia, "shock therapy" can be seen as a form of political communication developed by the state in its attempt to recover from crisis by showing the public that power remains in the hands of the government. This idea can be traced back at least to the moment of early independence, in the 1960s, when President Sukarno directed that the main corridor of Jakarta be constructed in modernist urban form, a representation that the president believed would shock Indonesians and thus register a new time for the decolonized nation. Sukarno considered the display of the most advanced built form at that time as an important artifact to wake up the spirit of Indonesians who "have cringed too long." "Although Jakarta's alleys are muddy and we lack roads, I have erected a brick-and-glass apartment building, a cloverleaf bridge, and our superhighway, the Jakarta Bypass. . . . I consider money for material symbols well spent. I must make Indonesians proud of themselves. They have cringed too long."[18] Yet the construction of such a spectacular city came at a moment when the political and economic realm of Sukarno was in deep crisis.

The technique of shock therapy reached its most radical form during the reign of Suharto (1966–98). In the 1980s, at the height of his military power, Suharto ordered the killing of those who were identified as "petty criminals" of the urban underclass (the *gali*, largely military-supported gang members later pushed out of the state's patronage when no longer useful). After their killing, the bodies of the gali were displayed on both the streets and in the newspapers. Suharto called this method of representing the killing and the victim "shock therapy," a technique used to remind Indonesian citizens that they should behave properly and never act anything like the gali. More importantly, it reminded Indonesians that the state was there to protect and save them should they encounter, or began to act like, the gali. The president himself was fascinated by such techniques: "The corpses were left where they were (on the streets), just like that . . . this was for 'shock therapy' [in English] . . . so that the crowds [*orang banyak*] would understand that, faced with criminals, there are still some who would act and would control them."[19] Having people witness the dead body of the gali for a short while, the president believed, would soon lead them to normality and ensure that they would never go astray.

Such abrupt strategies (based on seeing an example charged with emotion) have been integrated into various techniques of governance in the post-Suharto era. However, unlike Suharto, who sought to use "shock therapy" to incorporate the power of the underworld (by controlling the fate of the gali), his successor seeks to release the inscrutable elements from the body of the nation. President Yudhoyono could thus proclaim that in the post-reformasi nation: "There needs to be some *shock therapy* so that the people know that this government is serious about corruption. . . . We want to improve the investment climate, starting with political stability, improved security, good taxation and economic policies, and legal certainty."[20] This may well be a presidential way of providing the ground for a neoliberal shock therapy to launch the new time, but the Indonesian type of shock therapy has many more varieties. According to Sofyan Djalil, state minister for communications and information, shock therapy "can be done in various ways."[21] It can take the form of "suddenly" exposing corrupt government bureaucracy as well as corruption in the private sectors. It can take the form of a military operation in Aceh and Papua. It can also take the form of sudden and spectacular raids on shanty towns, gamblers, prostitutes, and illegal migrants, as well as (as in our case) altering traffic flows to frustrate private car users in an attempt to encourage them to take public transportation. The aim of shock therapy however is not so much to solve problems as "to gain the trust of the people."[22]

Within the context of the "looseness in the center" post-1998, the main concern of "shock therapy" is to gain immediate popular attention and, ideally, the support of the public. As a result, an urban project initiated as a form of shock therapy should be identifiably spectacular, offering great impact on urban life, and resolutely controversial, one touching on the desire and sensibility of the public even though it is constituted with the aim of overcoming, at least temporarily, the image of there being a crisis in authority. The desired effect of such a project is consequently short-term even as it is promoted as comprehensive, long-term, and integrative. Like an electric shock, the essential focus of the project is to achieve a quick result with radical and spectacular effect, one that is practical but substantial enough to show instantly the commitment of the government to its citizens.

In post-Suharto Jakarta, such a project, while essentially imposed by the government, is also profoundly shaped by its broad appeal to the public in its overall conception of "good governance." The project should function, without privileging any social class, in a neutral, universal fashion to make civilians (after a quick wave of shock and return to normality) willing to share, if not take responsibility for, the violence that might be committed by the project itself. This collective subjectification by means of a populist project, conducted in and through "shock therapy," I would argue, suggests a form of governmentality that contributes to the formation of the political cultures of the post-Suharto era. We can even say that Indonesian political culture refashions the typology of "neoliberal states" that monopolize power "at the global level."[23]

THE BUSWAY: SPECTACLE, PEDAGOGICAL TREATMENT, AND THE RESTORATION OF THE "EXEMPLARY CENTER"

In response to what the governor perceived as "the multidimensional crisis" and "the change in people's behavior," the construction of the busway (see figure 6) involved some "shock therapy" techniques to cure the "masyarakat traumatis" (traumatized society) and uphold security, order, and normality. One example of this technique was to claim one lane from the three-lane motorway for the busway. The logic was that, with only two lanes open for other vehicles, traffic would become extremely crowded and heavily jammed, and this would frustrate car users to the degree that they would "wake up" and say something like: "I am not going out with the car anymore. I have had enough with it." One resident of Jakarta believed that creating such a consciousness was the intended effect of this "shock therapy." It was imposed by the government to deter the use of private cars: "Indeed [Emang sih], I believe that by taking away one lane for the busway, the city government intended to give a 'shock therapy' [in English] to the residents of Jakarta so that they will be too frightened [kapok] to use cars."[24] Such "shock therapy" techniques were not limited to law enforcement. The sudden installation of the busway and its shelters could also be said to have followed the logic of "shock therapy." A newspaper reported the first physical appearance of the busway on the most important street (jalan protokol) of Jakarta in the following manner: "In December 2002, suddenly [tiba-tiba saja] those who passed through Sudirman and Thamrin streets at the center of Jakarta found a new scene [pemandangan baru]. On one of the fast lanes in these important streets suddenly [tiba-tiba] appeared a series of boxes in red color. There was also a new traffic sign made of green aluminum plate with letters written in white: 'Special Lane

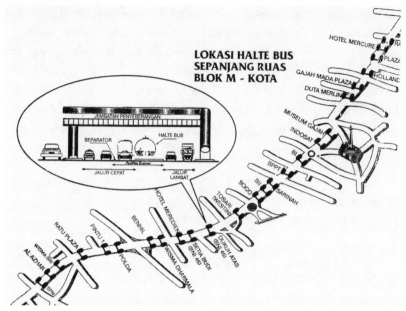

Figure 6 The busway route along Jalan Protokol that links the past and the present cityscapes with the National Monument (seen on the right), which was formerly designated as the central point for transit. Courtesy of *Republika*, 10 October 2002.

Bus Way' .... There was no conditioning [in English] at all about what the busway is and how it works."[25] Jakarta's newspapers reported that the city was awakened from its routine (*diusik*) by a program called the "busway." Decided behind closed doors, the program was initiated after the governor failed to lobby the central government for support of a more ambitious but indeed much-needed subway project. This failure seemed to be a blessing in disguise because the busway project has proven to be more practical, far less expensive, and visually more spectacular. Furthermore, it was quickly implemented to gain immediate effect during the tenure of Governor Sutiyoso, who wished to register himself instantly in Indonesian history as the "father of transportation" (overcoming thus his previous image as "the most maligned governor").[26] Unlike the subway, which would have operated invisibly underground, the busway runs above ground, thus creating a field of vision that immediately gains the attention of the passersby. Moreover, for the busway to operate successfully, visibly conspicuous measures of crowd control, discipline, and order in and around the field of operation had to be imposed, and this required the state authority to step in. Such a spectacular method of subjectification, based on seeing examples of disciplinary conduct in bus taking and riding, was mobilized not only to meet the ultimate need of resolving the acute traffic jams but also to restore the authority and legitimacy of the state in managing society. But first, the authority had to clear a space not only for the operation of the busway but also to ensure that it will indeed be the new visible, exemplary center of the city. Clifford Geertz describes the exemplary center as a microcosm that embodies political order.[27] The busway is such a system that integrates parts and constitutes an exemplary performance to signal political order.

The Ride, the Architecture of the Showcase, and the Disciplinary Mass Subject

To function effectively as an exemplary form of transportation, the busway not only had to operate by law and order but also to produce a system of practice that would contribute to the formation of a *culture* (of using public transportation). Indeed this was the mission that the governor had in mind. Yet to create such a culture in the perceived sea of disorderliness that marked the streets of Jakarta, a spectacle of order — in the form of an example — first had to be constructed. To play the role of an exemplary center, Governor Sutiyoso chose the "Jalan Protokol" (the important street) of Jakarta to be the first corridor of the busway — one that had to be perfected during his administration.

Historically, the Jalan Protokol has been the center that displays the rise and fall of state power. It was thus not surprising that Governor Sutiyoso began his busway in that symbolic center of power. He called it "Corridor Number One," and it ran from Kota (the center of the old colonial Batavia) in the north to Blok M in the south, where postcolonial modern shopping centers are located. Linking these two different times and spaces is the National Monument, which was originally designated as the main transit point. Corridor Number One runs along the thirteen-kilometer, north-south major thoroughfare of Jakarta. It offers passengers a panorama of the history of the city in the form of the changing visual environment, back and forth to the colonial past and the postcolonial present. Yet the busway not only serves as a vehicle that highlights the visual environment of the city along its route; it also shows itself as a new focal point for the city (see figure 7).

Divided at an interval of six hundred meters by some twenty-nine box-

Figure 7 The bridge to the busway shelter on Jalan Sudirman. Photo by A. Kusno.

like shelters, the busway makes itself visible to the residents of Jakarta. The bus shelter is about four by ten meters long. Set on a platform at the center of the boulevard, it offers itself to the public as a monument, a most visible object on the street. Lined up serially along the Jalan Protokol, the busway shelters compete with other national monuments as well as the surrounding international-style skyscrapers that stand along the thoroughfare. The busway shelters are an exact replica of those in Bogota (from where Sutiyoso got the idea), but the form seems to fit well with the surrounding cityscape of Jakarta. The modernist-functionalist style of its structure (made of steel, glass, and metallic elements) makes the shelter compatible with the modernist outlook of the buildings that stand on both sides of the Jalan Protokol. Covered by translucent glass wall and louvered panels, the shelter is a piece of transparent architecture that allows the inside to be seen from the outside and vice versa. From the outside one can follow the order of the architecture and the people it assembles. Staged as a platform, both the structure of the shelter and the people it organizes thus offer a spectacle of order and an example of disciplinary practice unavailable elsewhere in the city.

The shelter assembles the crowds, organizes their mobility, and channels them to different buses. It is true that such mechanisms of control are a necessary part of a terminal, but in this case, it is perfected by the participants themselves who ask for more rigid and efficient regulation. For instance, an impatient man who saw people jostling each other for space to get on and off the crowded bus grumbled: "Why don't they [the city] do something to handle the crowds? They could have installed some kind of automatic gate to manage the passengers, so those who want to get on the bus would have to wait for those getting off."[28]

Through the busway, a social order that demands a particular mode of behavior is constituted. Such a demand comes less from the government and more from the people themselves who ask for more regulation. This sense of order, control, and security depends not so much on instructions from the state but on the desire of the users who want to distinguish themselves from the unruliness of the city. Through the busway, we thus see a formation of culture that stems from a mutually constitutive relation between the state and members of society. Crucial to such cooperation is the ensemble of architectural elements that provide the setting for the expression of discipline. It is not surprising then that Sutiyoso was convinced that, in the context of Jakarta, the busway could be used as an effective tool to educate the public, especially the lower (middle) class, about how to properly use transportation (see figure 8).[29]

Yet such an urban pedagogy could not function merely through examples of commuters in business suits playing with mobile phones; it also depended on security guards. Governor Sutiyoso made it clear that he doesn't want to hear about "people waiting too long at the busway, and there should be no more pickpockets in the busway, and the busway has to be clean and comfortable."[30] Following the launching of the busway, the city government deployed some 560 security officers "to manage the traffic and ensure the security along the busway."[31] For the busway on the main corridor, measures were taken to ensure that there would be no crime onboard buses: armed and well-trained security officers were deployed as "bus marshals" on all the buses.[32] This was the first use of joint forces drawn from the police, the city Public Order office, and the transportation agency. Outside the shelters and the buses, some eight hundred personnel from the Jakarta Public Order Agency and two hundred staffers from the Jakarta Transportation agency were mobilized to monitor streets along the routes.[33]

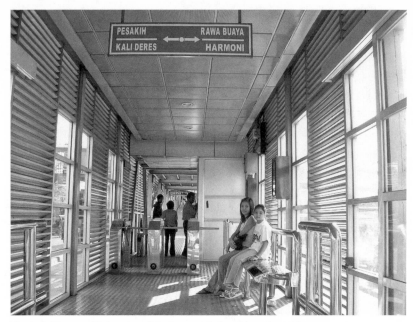

Figure 8 The metallic interior of the busway shelter. Photo by A. Kusno.

The spectacle of discipline and punishment alone, however, is not enough to form new exemplary subjects. The busway management company also launched a series of campaigns and activities to popularize the busway. Rude security guards, including those who were caught smoking in the busway stops, were replaced by "more friendly, trained officers." Starting in June 2005, the city government deployed "around 200 new security officers aboard our buses. They [were] specially trained to serve passengers quickly and efficiently in a more friendly way."[34] Meanwhile, the Trans-Jakarta Busway Management held a writing and photo competition for students and the general public with the theme: "creating a new culture of using public transportation."[35] To promote the idea of safe and efficient public transport, the company invited elementary school students to use the busway. A tour guide was prepared "to help children learn more about the transportation."[36] The function of the busway as an apparatus for the education of the public also attracted Jakarta's French Cultural Centre, which came up with the idea of displaying a video-art exhibition for two days at nineteen busway shelters to bring art into everyday life.[37] The busway thus became a platform for spreading culture around the city. The chairman of the Indonesian Transportation Society, Bambang Susantono, enthusiastically suggested that "it is very important that the design of the bus attracts passengers. . . . The bus should look futuristic, like the form of an express train, such as the 'Eurotrain' so that the busway will be seen as in the same class as the express train. Such a method would not make the upper class feel ashamed to ride a bus."[38]

Indeed the bus for the busway, called the TransJakarta, was designed to provoke a distinctive image. The buses for Corridor One use an eye-catching bright red color, which has the effect of strengthening the appearance of the busway as a monument and distinguishing the buses from their surroundings as they move unhindered along their exclusive drive lane, leaving other cars behind in their crowded lanes. The "joy of the ride" is more than just viewing the panorama of the city and enjoying the sense of being free from traffic jams. For most passengers, the capacity of the busway to liberate them from the gridlock of Jakarta traffic and the fear of the street offers them a sense of superiority and of being in a utopian (middle class) world of commuting in Jakarta. Tanri Yuliandini, a journalist, wrote about her "joys of riding the busway" in the following way:

> There was hardly anyone about that morning and I plumped myself down on one of the metal benches. Next to me was a man in a shirt and tie taking advantage of the *Media Indonesia* newspaper available to read there. . . . Another would-be passenger, this time a woman in a neat business suit, carefully coiffured hair and stiletto shoes, was standing nearby talking into a mobile phone. She would not have dared show her phone on a Metro-mini bus, I reflected, as I too took out my phone to SMS [text message] my friend, asking about her position. She was, unsurprisingly, still held up in front of Komdak, South Jakarta, in a traffic jam. The streets outside were already beginning to get congested, and I couldn't help but feel a little superior that I was not one of those stuck in the traffic.[39]

The busway fulfills commuters' dreams of a city free of traffic jams. Yet, as I have indicated, it also depends on various mechanisms of control and techniques of ordering space. "The joys of riding the busway" are sustained by various architectural elements visible from the street such as the bridge, the shelter, and the bus that structure the system of the busway as a whole.

The new techniques, procedures, and rules of conduct produce a kind of "citizen-subject." Both the microtechnology and the human subject constitute a form of rationality for governing the city.

The busway is thus about more than just alleviating traffic problems. It is about the restoration of order, discipline, status, and legitimacy of rule in the postauthoritarian regime of Indonesia. Governor Sutiyoso and his team are indeed aware that the busway alone will not be able to alleviate the severe traffic jams on the main corridor even though it is supported by the "3-in-1" traffic policy, which forbids all cars with fewer than three passengers on thoroughfares while buses and motorcycles must use the slow lanes. However, the governor knows that the busway will definitely produce the image that he is committed to providing good service to the public. The busway also gives him and the public some sense that the city, which has been suffering from "looseness in the center," now has some order and coherency. The busway not only offers speed, comfort, and a sense of superiority to its riders but also assembles the individuals and makes them visible as the body of the "self-regulated public," individuals who would otherwise disappear into the maze of unregulated flow of traffic. The network of the busway can be seen as an attempt by the governor to integrate dispersed power. It captures not only a particular class of body but also produces an exemplary "public body" as a whole. It transforms bus riding from what used to be a symbol of the underprivileged (in the city that prioritized private cars) into a symbol of power and honor. What used to be a mass transportation system for the lower middle class is now a transportation system for all.

Desire and Displacement

The integrative aspect of the busway contrasts with the displacement of buses and vendors caused by the "shocking" and "therapeutic" way the busway operates. As an apparatus for the production of appropriate behavior through exemplary practices, the busway also defines the boundary of what is included in and what is excluded from its field of operation. In this section, I show what the busway excluded and indicate how the displacement of other buses and vendors from the visual field of the new transportation system constitutes yet another side of urban governmentality in post-Suharto Indonesia.

To become an exemplary center, the busway demanded that other forms of public transportation either support or give way to its operation. Such displacement of the other buses could become effective only if urban problems were attributed to them. Indeed the municipality had for a long time identified the overlapping trajectories of several public buses that compete for passengers, especially in the main corridor of Jakarta, as a main cause of traffic jams. Owned by the state and private companies, these buses of various sizes each ran according to its own schedule and without coordinating with other buses. This created in the main corridor of Jakarta what Rustam Effendi Sidabutar, an officer in the Department of Transportation, called the problem of a traffic "spider's web" (*jaring laba-laba*).[40] The metaphor of the spider's web indicates that all the buses, no matter where they are coming from, lead to the center of the city and that the center, the Jalan Protokol, has been invaded, trapped, and paralyzed by disorganized elements. One way to overcome this invasion is to stop or restrict access of the unwanted vehicles to the center. The busway defined the boundary of other buses. It took over exclusively the Jalan Protokol and, through regulation, it prevented other buses from operating in the main corridor unless they ran as *feeders* for the busway. Only a select few were allowed to enter the center, and these were mandated to upgrade the services of their buses. As Mr. Sidabutar indicates: "There are buses that have become *feeders* (for the busway), there are also those that will stop operating because of natural selection. If the bus operators are incapable of providing better quality buses and services, they will lose customers (to the busway)."[41] Yet, it is clear that better service requires having full control over time and space, a condition met only by the high-profile busway. Through the busway, a neoliberal system of competition, exclusion, and selection was thus constituted for other buses.

The displacement of these other forms of public transportation shows that although the busway project could be seen as a way to enter into new alliances with populist interests, it is inherently open to contradictions and differing interpretations. The busway also displaced more street vendors as the idea of "clearing space for the busway" led to the eviction of vendors from the area of busway operation. For instance, in order to smooth the way for the busway corridor, the East Jakarta Mayor planned to remove some one thousand street vendors from the area and locate them in a traditional market with no compensation. The mayor was aware that "we had to announce the policy even though they (the vendors) generally refused the idea. *But there will be no arguing because the busway project must continue.*"[42]

This approach of harnessing the busway to legitimize forced eviction is not limited to the mayor. Instead, it has also become a framework for the upper middle class to remove unwanted elements from the city. A (middle-class) resident in Jakarta, for instance, complains about the proliferation of vendors in his area, and he harnesses the importance of the busway as an excuse to suggest the cleaning up of his neighborhood: "It is even hard for us to walk along the side of Kramat Jati market because illegal street vendors have occupied the area after dark. . . . The city administration should have cleared the area first before beginning the busway road construction."[43] In the process, the busway, which was constructed in response to the widely shared desire for an orderly city free of traffic jams, was used to justify the use of violence and authoritarian measures.

THE NEW GOVERNMENTALITY?

I have shown how the city of Jakarta, through its busway project, constitutes a site for technical intervention into society, especially at a time when the government needed to register a new time and restore the authority-image of the center in the aftermath of 1998. Yet, for technical power to work as an apparatus for the production of subject and subjectivity, it needed to engage the population in ways so that they too, through their exemplary performances, became part of the communicational circuit. I have indicated in this chapter the role of the busway in registering the authority of a postauthoritarian regime in which the desire and dream of the urban population for public transportation that is safe, reliable, and comfortable forms a crucial part of the legitimacy of the regime. Such dreams and desires, emerging in response to a large number of urban problems in post-Suharto Jakarta, were appropriated by the city government, which, unable to solve the problems comprehensively, launched the busway as a way to reclaim authority. What is striking, however, is that the entry of subjectivity into the busway, while engendered by a variety of popular desires, fears, and dreams embedded in the public life of Jakarta, was based on a technique of "shock therapy." It used the circuit of displacement and restoration to change people's behavior. The move from the "shocking" entry of the busway to the "joy of riding" was mediated by rules of operation, security guards, and the architecture of the shelters, all of which were staged as pedagogical artifacts for addressing both passengers and spectators. They were ensembles of tools for the performance of an exemplary center that produced results. As Sibarani Sofyan, a senior urban designer, explains: "The most powerful thing in Indonesia is showing examples. If it's built then, people will start to follow. Like the busway that Sutiyoso did. It is always the power of example."[44]

However, we should also note that the use of shock therapy and the power of example nevertheless reveal the limits of the Indonesian liberal form of governance at various levels. It shows, as I have indicated above, an exceptional disciplinary method of spectacle, in which the public was put through the shock of unfamiliarity to achieve a state of normality. Moreover, the shock therapy method shows not only a lack of transparency and public accountability in the decision-making process but also how the coordinating mechanism of the publicly supported busway could not be totalized. Regardless of the discourses of order and (self-regulated) discipline constituted by the busway, antagonism, subversion, and appropriation of the busway continue. For instance, the lane built for the Trans-Jakarta bus is often "hijacked" by motorcycles and even private cars (especially those associated with the political elites). Motorcycles sail through traffic jams by taking up the exclusive busway lane. "It is hard to get them to obey the road rules. Sometimes, the violators are even more steadfast than us officers."[45]

On a more specific level, the busway project is inseparable from the attempt of Governor Sutiyoso to regain legitimacy after a stormy start in his first term. He considered the busway as a strategic urban project that could also serve as a treatment for what he believed to be the social trauma caused by violent regime change. Defining Indonesians as a traumatized society, Sutiyoso saw himself as bearing responsibility for treating them not through military force but through urban projects such as the busway, in order to restore some coherence to the nation. During his second term (2002–7), Governor Sutiyoso learned the lesson of how to rule in what he called the "crazy age" (*zaman edan*) of postauthoritarian Jakarta.[46] He was at first heavily criticized for the busway project (it caused further traffic jams for private cars), but, as Sutiyoso recalls, "I remained calm, because I knew it would be like this [heavily criticized and ripped apart by the public undergoing the shock treatment]." Yet, once the project—the first corridor—was realized and some therapeutic normalcy returned through the joy of riding the busway, "those who protested against the project have asked me to add more corridors as soon as possible."[47] The governor of Jakarta feels that he has finally gained social and political legitimacy through his attempt to "bring into the consciousness of the public that the (busway) project is after all for the sake of the population at large."[48]

Sutiyoso's reflections indicate not so much that he was better prepared in his second term but that he should make his authoritative appearance in and through the critical voices of the public. Instead of undermining his authority, Sutiyoso suggested that the public opinions and debates that emerged after the first corridor was completed helped promote the busway and perfect its system of operation. They shaped the direction of its future program and helped define the governmentality of the city. In this sense, while the government might be held accountable for the project, the public too, through their desire for a city free of traffic jams, will be held responsible for the violence created by the project. The busway thus represents the emergence of a particular form of governmentality associated with postauthoritarian Indonesia. It produces a politics of subjection within the context of the erosion of the centralized state and the rise of democratic tendencies in Indonesia.

Toward the end of his term, it should come as no surprise that Governor Sutiyoso promoted initiatives associated with "sustainable environment," from the clean air and the "blue sky" program to greening the city and paving the sidewalks of Jakarta's main boulevards while evicting aggressively the urban poor from the center of the city. This initiative gives needed gravity to another unprecedented discourse of inviting the (upper) middle class "back to the city." At the end of his term, Sutiyoso was liked by the middle class not only for his busway project but also for welcoming private investments and contributing to "a spectacular decade of Jakarta property" and for returning the "rights to the city" to the middle class through a discourse known today as "back to the city."[49]

CHAPTER 3 "BACK TO THE CITY"
Urban Architecture in the New Indonesia

> Neoliberalism can be conceptualized as a new relationship between government and knowledge through which governing activities are recast as nonpolitical and nonideological problems that need technical resolutions. —ONG AIHWA, *NEOLIBERALISM AS EXCEPTION*

The spatial concentration of the busway and the spectacle of its disciplinary practices conjure up the sense of the restoration of the city's political authority, which had undergone "looseness in the center" following the collapse of the authoritarian regime of Suharto. It responded to the demand of the state for signs of having control over the streets and the population, engendering knowledge of power and political legitimacy. Built during the postauthoritarian "looseness in the center," the busway represents a technical return of the center through a pedagogical apparatus for the remanagement of the urban population who themselves were seeking some order and normality in the streets of Jakarta in the aftermath of 1998. To some extent, it cushioned the anxieties over the looseness in the center and constructed a post-1998 identity for the capital city. The busway thus could be seen as the government's aesthetic development project that responded to both the needs of the state and the urban population to register the appearance of the new Indonesia.

However, the highpoint in the integration of the busway coincided with the interests on the parts of developers to revitalize the urban center by bringing the middle class "back to the city." The cross-class infrastructure of the busway was rapidly incorporated into the network of the transportation system that was designed to prepare the ground for a class-based discourse of "back to the city." In this chapter, I discuss how the built environment of Jakarta is predicated upon a profound social reconfiguration associated with the mood of the post-Suharto era, which has given rise to the discourse of "back to the city." I look at some of the current architecture and urban design discourses, as an enterprise outside state forms of power, that help constitute a new regime of regulation and self-making in the new Indonesia.

SIGNS OF A NEW TIME

The sense that architecture and epoch are in some ways related naturally leads to the idea that "the new Indonesia" (whatever this might mean) should produce architecture appropriate to the mood of its era. This aspiration for the new nevertheless shares the idea that architecture is far from autonomous. Instead, it operates in the social formation within which it is embedded. We could thus ask: What role does architecture play in the social relations of post-Suharto Indonesia? To what conditions or opportunities has the "new" architecture responded? What kind of city design has been produced to accommodate and help constitute the new time? What cultural or political shift does it imply?

Perhaps a convenient way to start is by looking at some of the immediate responses of architecture to the aftermath of the 1998 riots. We do not know exactly the significance of the May riots in altering the subjectivities of Indonesian architects, but soon after the event, some architects pledged to make architecture sensitive to local cultures so that "it would be accepted by society and be able to socialize with the surroundings."[1] There was also a sense that the walls that divided the houses (of the wealthy) from their surroundings should be demolished. The sharp line between the haves and the have-nots would have to be altered through architectural design. The architects knew, better than before, that "harmony" cannot be achieved within the gated community no matter how well the architecture of the enclave has been designed. They also realized that the best-planned city will ultimately fail unless it engages with the surrounding communities. To be more concrete, we can say that the problem for the post-1998 architects was how to design a building that would promote a dialogue with its neighbor, namely the surrounding kampung and its the urban poor, so as to reduce social tension.

It is quite striking to learn that Kota Wisata, one of today's most exclusive and luxurious housing estates on the outskirts of Jakarta, declared in 2002: "It is very important [for people from Jakarta who have moved to live here] to preserve harmonious relations with local people living in the surrounding area."[2] The architects claimed that the interaction between the real estate and its surroundings had been articulated through a design of the site plan: "At the border area, the real estate housing is designed for lower middle-income consumers, and the line that divides the kampung and the real estate will be filled with a park [taman] where the two worlds can meet and socialize."[3] This "buffer zone," pretentious as it might sound for what is, after all, an exclusive community, still was a departure toward a "socially" (if not politically) sensitive spatial design. Although there are many opinions concerning what constitutes good house design, the designers of Kota Wisata, however, concluded that one criterion is certain: "A good house is a house that unites with its surroundings."[4] However that sentence is understood, it shows a change of consciousness if not architectural strategy of the architects in the post-Suharto era. Could we then say that the architectural and urban design paradigm of the new Indonesia is "contextual," one that aims at creating dialogue if not neutralizing conflicts with the social context within which architecture is embedded?

In any case, the Association of Indonesian Architects (IAI) shares this post-1998 design sensitivity. Budi Sukada, the chairman of the IAI at that time, indicated that "the sixth IAI Award cycle in 1999 (an award given every three years to meritorious architectural design) was worthy of mention because it signified a new movement in the discourse on Indonesian architecture."[5] The new movement, according to Sukada, rejects "building designs that were considered too artificial and over-the-top."[6] Instead, the 1999 IAI Award would be conferred on architecture that would "raise human dignity, be responsible to the social environment, sensitive toward the social context within which the building is embedded; not artificial, not relying on luxurious building materials; innovative, creative, modest but intelligent, educational and visionary."[7] With these design criteria, IAI hoped that architecture that was more suitable to the Indonesian context would emerge. Consequently, the 1999 (and 2002) IAI award program "did not recognize any project that incorporated the universal internationalism design approach." It also did not include any government institutions for "it seems that there was no government project deemed worthy by the IAI to receive an award at the end of the New Order's reign on power."[8] Instead, in 2002 (perhaps coincident with the reign of Megawati Soekarno-putri), the IAI honored, for the first time, Ir. Sukarno, the first president of Indonesia "for his concern toward architectural discourse in Indonesia" and awarded a project that conserved a historic building.

In short, from the outset of the new times, in 1999, the IAI began proclaiming its supposedly new mantra that "Indonesian architecture in the next millennium" will be "architecture that serves society."[9] No matter how utopian this architectural agenda might sound to us, it was not naïve. It was part of the ongoing struggle to find a way to engage with the city and to live in the multiple and decentered realities of the new times. At least the desire for conservation (after the destruction of the city), the aspiration for unity (in the figure of Sukarno), and the urgency to approach society through the redemptive power of architecture could be seen as some of the responses of architecture to social change in post-Suharto Indonesia.

Under such conditions, what are the new identifiable architectural features that have arisen in post-Suharto Indonesia? We can ask this question even though it is impossible to imagine a coherent aesthetic response to what are, after all, the multiple social conditions and discursive interactions within which architecture is embedded. It might be worthwhile to review recent architectural trends and analyze them as a general symptom of the new times. This chapter, however, has no intention of conducting such a review. Instead, it highlights some of the specific ways in which the architectures of the post-Suharto era try to engage with the historical and contemporary characteristic of the city. I show how the nation and the city are used as essential design tropes for the construction of an architectural narrative of social life in the post-Suharto era (even though such strategies are paradoxically marked by earlier practices and attitudes). I look at two types of urban architecture associated with the middle-class imagination (which architects share): the ordinary "private" house and the extraordinary "public" commercial building complex (for offices, entertainment, and shopping) known as the "superblock." I conceive them as representatives of attempts to come to terms with the conflictual realm of cities in the new Indonesia. I unpack the social meanings of the architecturally designed built environment; how the architectural styles and spatial layout of the spaces help maintain and redefine power relations. I also ask: In what ways does the sphere of the global market economy (which underlies the architecture of the superblock) appropriate nationalist discourse and offer thus a political rationale for the production of citizen-subjects of the new Indonesia? No doubt such reading has its own limitations for it only accounts for the architects' conception of the world. Yet such a study at least offers some insights into the making of the new Indonesia since architects are not only experts in their field but are also members of a particular social order. Through their works we thus can tease out some understanding of the urban governmentality of the new Indonesia.

I will start with the recent design of ordinary houses (for the urban middle class) that takes up the typology of the kampung (the poor urban neighborhood) even though such a strategy is no doubt a development out of the earlier attention to what was already called in the 1920s the "kampung question" (see chapter 7). I then move from this marginal practice to the dominant design trend in the central part of Jakarta by looking at the discourse of "back to the city" through the architectural design of the superblock. The relevance of this extraordinarily huge, privately funded project for us is that it takes up themes associated with the nation. I show the remarkable difference between these two architectural approaches to the city and address how the kampung and the nation are mobilized to engage (or disengage) with the "new" social environment of the city. I argue that the conceptual production of urban architecture represents a shift not only in design culture but also in the political economy of the city and the problematic nature of urban Indonesia in the post-Suharto era.

THE ARCHITECTURE OF THE KAMPUNG

Within the realm of the architectural sensitivity of the post-Suharto era, the works of Adi "Mamo" Purnomo are distinctive, if not representative, of the new attitude of architects searching for alternative formal and spatial expressions.[10] Known largely as an architect "who is friendly with nature," and who "considers the small plots of land in a metropolitan city as a challenge to create new spaces,"[11] Mamo, however, takes up larger social issues even though he has never explicitly stated them as part of his design agenda. The houses that I consider below belong to middle-class families in Jakarta who have "gone kampung" following the "monetary crisis" (*krismon*) that hit Indonesia after the end of Suharto's rule. The houses can be seen as examples of post-Suharto architecture that use the language of the kampung to address the urban life of the Indonesian metropolis. Through his architecture, Mamo seeks to constitute a culture of reconciliation for the city that has been deeply divided by the rich and the poor.

Let me first mention that, in general, Mamo's architecture is characterized by the creation of an inner courtyard in a small plot of land that serves as a microcosm for the interaction between human beings and nature (air, light, shade, and plants). The loosely enclosed inner courtyard allows components of nature to step into the interior space of daily life away from the hurly-burly of urban Jakarta. The courtyard, however, is more than a functional device enabling the daily interaction with nature. Instead, it is the central component in the whole design process since the courtyard organizes all the other spaces in the house. Consequently, with space determining form, Mamo's architecture often does not have a facade to show off. This is quite a striking departure from "facade-oriented architecture" that has dominated the design culture of Jakarta. Mamo's architectural strategy can thus be seen as a conscious move away from the facade-oriented building that governs the Jakarta housing market. It seeks to counter what Mamo himself calls the "major brand" (*label besar*) architecture that is characterized by an often expensive facade that wraps up the (often air-conditioned) massive volumes behind it.[12] The urban architecture of Mamo can be seen as an attempt to break away from this dominant trend.[13] Mamo conceives his work as belonging to an "independent brand" (*label indie*) architecture that promotes lifestyles of low-energy consumption, the use of nonindustrial local materials,[14] and perhaps more importantly, in the context of this chapter, the architectural language embedded in the local urban kampung fabric that characterizes the city of Indonesia.

The low-budget house in Tanjung Duren (2000) (which won the 2002 IAI Award), for example, employs the architectural language of the kampung for a middle-class residence.[15] Its exterior is fenced off by bamboo, and the interior projects an image of an alleyway in an urban kampung. The building material normally used for the exterior, such as cast concrete, is placed inside, thus blurring the boundary between the inside and the outside (itself a typology of the kampung). The house is built with used materials and fragments extracted from the banality of everyday life. The kitchen area is located at the front of the building, a technique that brings one back to the dwelling environment of the kampung (see figure 9).

The Tanjung Duren house thus exhibits the relationship of architecture

Figure 9 Interior of Tanjung Duren House (2000), designed to look like an alleyway. Photo courtesy of Yori Antar, reprinted from Tardiyana and Antar, *The Long Road Towards Recognition*.

to the typology of urban kampung. There is nothing nostalgic about the kampung, which still is a dominant feature of the urban fabric of Jakarta.[16] In mobilizing a "kampung style" and foregrounding it as "Architecture," Mamo is resisting architectural elitism. As the ordinary urban becomes an inspiration for a new architecture, there is no longer any ideological distinction between architecture and building, and thus between the city and the kampung. We should however notice that the elimination of such a gap is true for the middle-class family who still retains aspects of their middle-class lifestyle. The "kampung house" at Tanjung Duren is after all connected to the global world by the satellite disk mounted in the court-yard. This communication technology, like the courtyard, is a window to the outside world. It competes with the inhabitants of the house for an unobstructed contact with the sky. The kampung style that is built into Mamo's architecture thus represents a post-Suharto aesthetic sensibility among certain sections of the middle class who, in keeping with the lifestyle of their own class, incorporate the urban fabric of their lower-class counterparts.

Mamo's initial interest, if not passion, is to explore the possibility of different classes living together in an urban space. In an architectural sense, the house at Tanjung Duren and other dwellings he designs speak in different narratives, but they belong to the same inquiry, the question whether "the 'weak' and the 'powerful' can share a same room."[17] Mamo believes in the coexistence of the powerful and the powerless actors in the city as exemplified, as he points out, in the concept of *magersari*, which is a traditional patron and client relationship in which the powerful provide a space for the weak in order to promote the latter's self-growth and self-reliance.[18] No matter how problematic this vision might be in retaining the traditional power of dependency, it is presupposed here in the rejoining and reidentification of the excluded poor with the city. Mamo characterizes this interest most publicly in his design for a series of low-rise apartments for the urban poor in Jakarta—none of which, however, has been or will be built. The relevance of such design proposals for us is that they express a will to include the poor in the urban world.[19] They depart from that of Governor Sutiyoso who has sought to "relocate squatters living on river banks, along railway tracks, and under elevated express ways."[20] These spaces are in some ways attached to the public facilities of the city, but in Mamo's perspective, low-cost housing blocks for the poor should be legally allowed on those sites. His proposal counters the program of the city administration, which seeks to beautify the space under the freeway with parks, badminton courts, and soccer fields. With urban beautification rushing along in tandem with squatters facing eviction, the idea of keeping the illegal settlements by way of upgrading their appearances takes on particular urgency.

In a design competition for low-cost housing (1997, 2002), Mamo proposed a kind of self-sustained housing block of rental units (made of used materials) for the urban poor located under a freeway and along the riverside. He provided in the design a communal space for cooking and washing. Tenants are obligated to share responsibility for taking care of the facilities and the surrounding green space. There is rule and regulation in the use and care of the space. Yet, in Mamo's perspective, such disciplinary and pedagogical practices would, in any case, nurture a collective identity

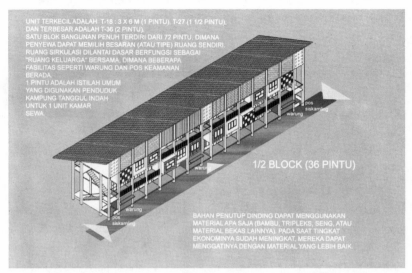

Figure 10 Riverside rental housing design for the urban poor. Courtesy of Yori Antar, reprinted from *Rusunawa, 2002* (Jakarta: Dirjen Perumahan dan Pemukiman, 2002).

and identification of the inhabitants with the place. Mamo also argues that the new building blocks should follow the formal characteristics of the shanty town on the riverside since over time such an image has already constituted a sense of place and forms a cognitive memory for the inhabitants (see figure 10).

Central to this idea is the obligation Mamo feels that architecture should come to terms with the typology of the kampung fabric and its cultural patterning. To nurture the relation between collective memory and the visual environment, Mamo constructs a facade composed of used materials and patterns them on what he imagines each user of the building might have done for him- or herself. Conceptually, the result is a facade of different mosaics of daily and used materials, stitched individually by the user as he or she occupies the space. As new tenants come in, the remnants of previous histories are supposedly still there to be seen, even as they change the pattern of the facade to fit with their own experience of urban life. Presupposed here is the idea of living space as an ever-changing social text (itself a development out of an earlier practice popularized by the late Romo Mangunwijaya in the 1980s in Yogyakarta).

Mamo's urban imaginary, which embodies collective memories, a sense of leftovers and scarcity, focuses on the problems of urban society today.

He attempts to orchestrate all those fragments of living marginally in the city and turn them into an architectural expression that, through practices of space and form, offers a kind of "citizenship" for the urban poor, even though this might be seen as constituted only at the symbolic level. For him, the kampung fabric is something to be endorsed rather than replaced. His architecture forces us to think about ordinary life and social text, social justice and public policy, urban activism and collective identities, and issues concerning the rights of the poor to find expression in the city. We do not know what the poor might think about Mamo, who designs on their behalf. They might find his representation problematic and resent his design as stereotyping the imagery of the poor community. Or they might consider that his architecture represents more the imagination of the middle class for it is still Mamo, rather than the poor, who find expression in the city. His architecture nevertheless forces us to reflect on the capacity of architecture to develop a new social imagination even though such imagination receives no support from the city, public policy, or urban social activism.

Yet, as I discuss below, Mamo's desire to develop a connection with the urban kampung fabric of Jakarta is dwarfed in comparison with a much larger and different desire of both foreign and Indonesian architects for megaprojects in the city. In the following section, I look at the design of several clusters of large-scale commercial and high-rise residential buildings of mixed function in the central part of Jakarta known as the superblock. The relevance of such projects for us is that they all take up the broad theme of the nation in order to express their own priorities. What kind of design strategies have been put forward (beyond those of Mamo) to help shape the contemporary narratives of the social life of the city and the nation?

THE SUPERBLOCK AND THE BRANDING OF THE NATION

In 2006, just a few weeks before the celebration of the sixty-first anniversary of Indonesian independence, the Building and Construction Interchange, a property consultant, published a report about the emergence of expensive, mixed-use development projects in the city of Jakarta. The report did not explain why and how such projects had become possible. Instead it shares its puzzlement with readers:

The property business today is facing high inflation, partly caused by the fuel hike last year, which has resulted in the steep increase in the interest rate and construction costs as well as a decline in the rate of consumption. Several market observers have also indicated the continuing oversupply of apartments and retail space. The Indonesia Real Estate Association has even issued advice to developers to stop supplying more space for the market. However, contrary to all these assessments and suggestions, several developers have launched megaprojects of values between 400 billion to quintillions of rupiah. . . . They seem to have been caught in competition with each other through several megaprojects, all of which show that they are indeed optimistic that today is the right time to build. Perhaps they hope that in five years time, when all these projects are completed, the economy of Indonesia will turn and offer them multiple profits. This 'competition' seems to be more than an attempt to show off power and money. Instead, they are also strategies to bring the Indonesian economy out of the uncertainty of the 1998 crisis, the effect of which has been going on for a decade.[21]

From this statement, we can appreciate that the analyst herself is surprised by the emergence of megaprojects at this time, but she nevertheless feels that such projects are strategies for overcoming the financial crisis and reinvigorating the economic life of the nation, and presumably, also the social life of the city. What has happened might simply be the operation of what David Harvey calls "the neoliberal state," the new Indonesia that centralizes capital in Jakarta as part of the logic of market-driven phenomena that operates in the world today.[22] Yet, it is not entirely clear how global capitalism operates in a crisis-ridden place like Jakarta (and other major cities in Indonesia), although it is clear to the consultant that one of the prime reasons for these investments is the idea that the recent construction boom would exorcise the ghost of the crisis and turn misery into fortune. What is also clear is that money and building are indeed coming "back to the city" with a vengeance. They register their presence through the construction of a series of enclaves of spectacular superblocks in the central business district of the city, which also contains the historic sites of the nation (see figure 11).

Encroachment into the national space of the city thus necessitates the superblock in order to come to terms with the historical narrative of the

Figure 11 Model of Epicentrum, the largest superblock in the golden triangle of Jakarta. Developed by the Bakrie family. Photo by A. Kusno.

nation. Yet in contrast to the national meaning of the sites on which many of the superblocks stand, none of them is coordinated with the aim of securing national autonomy. The superblock is a phenomenon of postcrisis Indonesia that no doubt is a further development of the neoliberal turn in the political economy of the country since the late 1980s. Once again, the very heart of the city becomes the arena for the consolidation of power, identity, and exchange values. The relevance of these megaprojects to us is that they not only constitute a discourse of consumerist "public-oriented space" that raises the question of what constitutes urbanity but also represent a new phenomenon in the city in the post-Suharto era.

The newly launched *Indonesia Design*, a glossy architecture journal of the post-Suharto era, is quick to highlight the spectacularity of the superblock. The editor characterizes the superblock as "a large space that contains several functions" for commercial and public services as well as for offices and residences.[23] The enormous microcosm (or better, macrocosm) seeks to include an entire world of an elite lifestyle within its safely contained cluster of buildings. One could say that the superblock is a compressed version of a self-contained elite suburb that has been repackaged to fit into an urban box. "Back to the city" however indicates nothing of the strength of the city (one could easily cast doubt on how a city could sustain such a scale of superblocks). Instead "back to the city" reveals only the fact that the superblock is taking advantage of the exhaustion of the city itself. Suggesting that the "suburb" paradigm (characteristic of the New Order's spatial politics) has fallen out of favor in the post-Suharto era, a developer of a superblock proclaims that people (the upper middle class) "would prefer to stay close to the working area where they do not waste too much time commuting. Efficiency will be an important issue in the future. People would now think twice to live on the outskirts of Jakarta."[24] Furthermore, as a contributor to the *Jakarta Post* indicated in 2007: "These days it is no longer only expatriates that occupy apartments. After the May 1998 riots prior to President Suharto's downfall, the majority of expatriates working in Indonesia returned to their home countries. Today, apartments are the choice of local businessmen and professionals, including artists and public figures who require privacy."[25]

Architects and developers have enthusiastically embraced such an opportunity to go "back to the city." Moreover, the superblock allows the staging of colossal designs in and around the sites that historically have been the showcases of national development. They harness the historic sites and the "golden triangle" of the city and register in them a new time. They allude to the spectacle of other cities in neighboring countries that have been launching their own megaprojects.[26] They compete with foreign architects in coming up with ever more spectacular designs. Together they seek "powerful architectural identity" or an "icon" to register their presence against each other "in order to survive the competitive nature of the Jakarta market."[27] Such projects include, among others, the Rasuna Epicentrum Superblock, the mixed-use buildings at Hotel Indonesia Circle, Senayan City, and the Archipelago Complex in Jakarta.[28]

It is not entirely clear how members of the surviving middle class might be able to be citizens of the superblock, but superblocks are meant to be not only showcases of the city's achievements and national development but also structures for the reproduction of a form of citizenship based on class. They inflect the older techniques of containment of what was perceived as the ideal dream world of the upper middle class that seeks to overcome the ever more complex macrocosm of the urban. However, unlike the mainstream discourse about gated communities, which calls for a fencing of the whole area, the superblock is subtler and perhaps less authoritative in its ordering of space. The underclass may enter the superblock, but they need to adjust to the norm and form of the new environment. They can become part of the "self-regulated public," as Foucault would assume, so long as they follow the script of what an architect calls the "good design" of the superblock. For instance, at the Rasuna Epicentrum, said to be the largest superblock, the designer of the project created a waterfront for the retail businesses where "people could dip their feet if they wanted to," but such facilities, the architect warns, should not be used for washing.[29] To ensure proper behavior of the (lower class) public, so the architect advises, "I have told my client that for the first three years, they have to invest in security, hiring security guards, not for keeping people away but rather for educating the public on how to treat public facilities."[30] The underlying sense of the impending tragedy that accompanies the architect's statement is part of the difficulty that architecture seems to encounter in its attempt to return to the city. A "good design," the architect urgently suggests, will not guarantee the production of a good citizen. Instead, some measures of discipline by security guards are needed. In the following section, I discuss the design of some of these superblocks and show the extent to which they contribute to the pedagogy of urban citizenship and how such participation is constituted, paradoxically, in the name of the nation.

Senayan City

Senayan City is said to be the first mixed-use superblock in Indonesia. This forty-eight thousand–square meters complex, which just opened in 2006, consists of a high-class shopping mall, apartment complex, and hotel and office buildings. Standing on the historic public space of Senayan built for the 1962 Asian Games under the aegis of Sukarno's spirit of decolonization, the Senayan City complex has already provoked some concerns for it exemplifies a kind of privatization of public space for commercial purposes. Back in the 1960s, Sukarno envisioned the Senayan complex (of some 279.1 hectares) as a center of physical and sports activities and a public space for the urbanite. Yet today, this recreational place, initially conceived as a center for the restoration of the national body, is considered to be a property too valuable for the uses envisioned by the first president (see figure 12).[31]

A strategic piece of the land has now been leased to Senayan City, which

Figure 12 Senayan City Mall. The sign reads: "Glorify Indonesia: A Tribute to Unity in Diversity." Photo by A. Kusno.

is owned by a consortium of developers under the leadership of the Agung Podomoro group. The investment is estimated to have reached 1.3 quintillion rupiah. This amount of investment seems too huge for the Senayan authority to resist. But the chairman of the Gelora Bung Karno has a way to comfort the public. He argues that we are not "giving up the historic place for private enterprise." Instead, the conversion of the Senayan land into a commercial high-class superblock is further enhancing the image of Senayan as the symbolic space of the nation. Indra Setiawan, the chairman of the Gelora Bung Karno Board, imagines a scenario in which the neoliberal private-public partnership can be harnessed to "develop the sports facilities to become more modern and multifunctional."[32] Mr. Setiawan is aware that the complex "is inherited from 1962, and where a certain part of it has already been encroached by commercial buildings in 1984 and 2002."[33] Yet in his opinion such development should be allowed to continue for it will help the city and the nation to overcome the crisis of 1998. The national health could thus seemingly be restored by way of consuming luxury goods. As a custodian of this public space, Setiawan nevertheless feels that he and his governing board have been careful in allowing such a conversion of land use. They would not simply give away the prestigious public space for just any private enterprise for this would downgrade the high status of the place. Instead, they will always make sure that the tenants are not coming from the lower class. "The selection has been tough. We only allow private enterprises of high-class caliber to enter the Senayan Complex. As for the middle lower-class (developers), there is no way that they can enter here."[34]

In the past Sukarno proclaimed that the spectacle of sports events was central to maintaining the spirit of decolonization and anti-imperial nationalism. Today, members of the business elite believe that Senayan City offers a spectacle of national recovery. This first superblock is seen as a symbol of the revival of the nation's economy. The chairman of its largest shareholder, the Agung Podomoro Group, has already been praised as "Maestro Pascakrisis" (Maestro of postcrisis).[35] Designed by DP Architects from Singapore (in collaboration with the Indonesian design firm, PT Airmas Asri), Senayan City consists of "5 floors of shopping malls, a 21-story office block, a 23-floor apartment and a 5-star boutique hotel with 255 guest rooms. All of these functions are packed inside a single main block of a shopping center and three towers on its sides."[36] The ensemble of different units constitutes an upper middle-class lifestyle, all framed in a coherent block—if not a castle flanked by three identically designed towers. Yet this is more than just an enclosure and a space of retreat from the unruliness of Jakarta. Presupposed here is a celebration of a new totality and, to appropriate Clifford Geertz's phrase, an "exemplary center."[37] According to the chief executive officer, Handaka Santosa: "We designed the mall with glass in such a way that visitors coming into the mall can be seen by others. They want to see and to be seen when shopping in Senayan City."[38]

Such a panoptic space is represented by the atrium, which also functions as an exhibition space, and the shopping arcade where "various famous brands gather as the main attraction to the customers."[39] The large transparent glass wall and the glamorous lighting in the atrium are expected to "bring out the retail hustle and bustle from the inside."[40] And where are the poor, the marginalized, and the disempowered in such an urban renaissance? There is a place for them too, as the manager is quick to point out: "visitors who have no such purchasing power, however, could hang around and do window shopping (activities of which) may still offer some satisfaction while they hope someday they will buy the items that now they can only dream of."[41] Senayan City thus represents an act of separation of the city from its kampung fabric, inhabited by those who have no such purchasing power, although such an act is meant to constitute an excitement for all to hang around—a narrative that recalls the spectacle of the 1962 Asian Games, where social and political conflicts were suspended, which in today's context, means the shared experience of a hot shopping festival. In acknowledging the fact that there are many more people who could only window shop, Senayan City seeks to create a theatrical forum that contradicts or seeks to exorcise the reality of the fallen city. It offers the urban poor a dream world of the elite—at least they can cheer at the festival—so that they too someday will be like the elite.

The "exemplary center" that Senayan City is advocating rests on the sense that the state of Indonesia has receded from leading the activity of disciplining and nurturing the public through the "power of example." The private sector, through the promotion of an elite lifestyle, has become the custodian of an urban pedagogy, which, with a great leap forward, presumably would lead to the formation of Indonesian subjects who can buy and consume. Many believe that using the built environment, along with the spatial practices embedded in it, as an example for people to follow is the right technique to make Indonesia move again. Sibarani Sofian, a senior urban designer of the noted San Francisco-based city planning firm EDAW that worked in Indonesia, puts this idea in a most exemplary way: "How to get (a city's vision) done, how to actually force everybody to go in one direction. What we introduced (in the city vision for Surabaya) is a special business district. Basically you try to define a very clear area and give it a different treatment—incentives or policies that apply to everything within that special pilot project district. Then, you can see real results. *The most powerful thing in Indonesia is showing examples.* If it's built then people will start to follow."[42] In the context of the superblock, the big box clustered over the central part of Jakarta is a testament to such "power of example." But as in Senayan City, such examples overlay the myth of the nation, in which everyone is embraced and asked at least to participate in witnessing national unity and the progress in the types of commodities and luxury lifestyles that are possible. In the following section I take up another example of the superblock that speaks the narrative of the nation in a more formalist way.

The Archipelago

If Senayan City wishes to drum up the spirit of shopping as a supplement to sports and in the earlier spirit of decolonization, the Archipelago, another superblock project at Senayan, takes in the abstraction of the nation in perhaps the most formalist way. The architects take up the theme of "our country's riches, with islands and oceans surrounding (our archipelago)."[43] They translate these facts about natural resources into a design "which has the analogy of turning the islands of our archipelago into an architectural component with separate and spread out construction" (see figure 13).[44] The translation is formalist in the strongest sense. The metamorphosis from ideas into built form is characterized in this fashion:

> The completed shape rules out geometric forms, nothing here comes in the shape of blocks but instead there are abundant flexible, dynamic and nongeometrical forms. The basic idea for the main block is a droplet of water, which is still linked to the initial concept — marine — closely linked to water.... Each design is a presentation and essence of the Indonesian tradition which is hoped to provide an abstraction of the modern side of Indonesia. This ambience is strongly represented in the pattern and shape of the mass.... Another idea for the design is the lofty tower used as both a hotel and an office block. The chosen shape also reflects the marine world — a lighthouse.... The hope is to turn this tower into a landmark of the area, similar to a lighthouse in the middle of the sea. The design of this building, which represents Indonesia and the maritime theme, is also represented in the office block which adopts a sail-like shape. It is expected that this project will become a landmark and [represent the] spirit of Jakarta from the architectural point of view. Just as Australia is famous for its Sydney Opera House, Jakarta should also be famous for its landmark, The Archipelago.[45]

The "dynamic form," the "separate and spread-out design," "the droplet of water," "the lighthouse," and the "sail-like shaped office block" are presumably abstractions from the Indonesian tradition carried over to the new time. Can we say that in the resort dedicated to the symbolism of water there is nostalgia for national coherence, gained through reintegrating the thousands of islands scattered in the archipelago? It is not clear, however, how one could possibly comprehend such a message in the spatial

Figure 13 Artist's impression of the Archipelago, with Sukarno's Asian Games stadium in the background. Reprinted from Urbane Indonesia, "Kontemplasi arsitektur kepulauan dan kelautan."

organization of the Archipelago. For sure, such a form could go anywhere even though the idea is said to be drawn from an ensemble of "Indonesian traditions." What is also striking (and questionable) is its take on the idea of technology—such as that symbolized by a BMW automobile "floating" in the building that is shaped like a droplet of water (said to represent the modern side of Indonesia). What seems clear is that the spectacular design of the Archipelago represents a desire for the superblock to break away from other centers by constituting itself as the center, a landmark for a corporate-lifestyle generation under the name of the nation.

Ridwan Kamil, the prominent young architect of the Archipelago, graduate of University of California, Berkeley, and founder of the architectural firm Urbane Indonesia based in Bandung, has indeed characterized his own initial interest in large projects for "their impact is greater."[46] "In large projects," as his fellow architect points out on his behalf, "the public can enjoy good design."[47] Yet, the public-oriented space that Kamil designed is privately owned. It seems consistent with the neoliberal idea that public space today can no longer be provided by the government. Kamil is following the paradigm used by global architectural firm EDAW with which he used to work. For members of this group, it is clear that "the government cannot do everything. It's really up to how the government stimulates private sectors to bring economic development."[48] In their projects in Indonesia (some of which Kamil and his Urbane Indonesia team outsourced), the EDAW regional director of economies, Chris Yoshii, has made clear that they want to create special economic zones or business improvement districts:

> It's taking a certain district with the support of government and local businesses to create this self-funding district that provides security and marketing, and they get some sort of benefit for streetside improvements, like street crossings. With this we are trying to establish an area that people feel safe to go out at night or on weekends. We are trying to create a certain district that has a nice character and safe environment and that helps stimulate other areas. It has a domino effect. Successful examples can be seen in Darling Harbor in Australia and Times Square in New York.[49]

We have seen this vision before. There is nothing more here than the fact that the design of the superblock of the Archipelago, like Senayan City, makes use of the older concept of an exemplary center — the spectacle of order and development through example. Indonesian architects and foreign consultants too seem to share the belief in this "power of example," that once a project is realized, "people will start to follow," although we should add, after some forms of disciplinary practice. Perhaps what makes each exemplary center powerful is precisely that there are many different versions of what is basically the same design — a collective replication of coordinated clusters of building blocks mobilized to create a unity of discourse to discipline the city.

The post-Suharto release of Senayan into the hands of private developers has thus opened up the possibility of the superblock and made such a large-scale urban pedagogy into a practical possibility. Kamil and his Urbane Indonesia firm have enthusiastically embraced this possibility in the grand designs for the Archipelago as well as the Rasuna Epicentrum project (in collaboration with EDAW) at the other corner of Jakarta's

Golden Triangle.[50] The relevance of such a project (which includes its urban pedagogy) for us is that it materializes, through "good design for the public," a will to include an entire nation within itself and to program citizen-subjects for the new Indonesia. Perhaps such a will suggests a kind of nostalgia for harmony in the tension-filled pluralist society of Indonesia — a (inter)nationalist wish that presumably could be realized, ironically, in the privately owned public-oriented superblock.

The Archipelago inserts multinational corporations into the heart of national space, but it does it in a way that makes one feel that it is the national culture (and the national subjects that still need to be educated) that have been raised to a global scale. Kamil himself recognizes such a condition for his architecture, as he points out, "one indicator of progressive architecture is international recognition."[51] His firm embodies the new international division of architectural labor as it receives outsourced projects from foreign consultants abroad to design master plans for projects in China, Thailand, Singapore, and the United Arab Emirates. The Archipelago, while using the idea of national culture as the framework for its design, at the core is not different from these other megaprojects elsewhere. Kamil and his team are operating within a larger environment of what Kris Olds has called the "global intelligence corps" of which the design cultures can never be other than those of transnational quality no matter how hard they try to localize.[52] What seems local then is the anticipation of how the space might be used and how its users can be adapted to the spaces of the superblock (for example, the need to invest in security guards). The superblock while celebrating freedom and creativity in the programming of everyday lives relies on an urban pedagogy associated with the disciplinary apparatus of the nation-state. By way of conclusion, let me end by discussing yet another superblock project which is located right in the heart of national symbolism: the historic Hotel Indonesia (HI) Traffic Circle, a monument of the Sukarno era.

The Grand Indonesia

While the Senayan complexes allude to nation and nationalism as a brand for consumerism, the Grand Indonesia project, designed by an architectural firm in Los Angeles (RTKL in partnership with PT Anggara Architeam of Indonesia), sees itself as carrying a mission to enhance the quality of yet another historic site: Sukarno's Hotel Indonesia (HI) Traffic Circle. The seven-acre site off the Hotel Indonesia traffic circle has been leased to a private company for thirty years.

> This is a project that will change the face of Jakarta, a project that is hoped to boost the value of Bundaran HI (Hotel Indonesia Round-abouts), as well as the architectural quality of the legendary Hotel Indo-nesia. . . . Expected to become a new icon for Indonesia, the new Hotel Indonesia will transform itself into Grand Indonesia, occupying the 7-acre golden spot in downtown Jakarta. Its original function as a busi-ness hotel is turned into a mixed-use complex with a 42-storey apart-ment tower, 41-storey rental office tower, a 6-star hotel in the old build-ing of Hotel Indonesia and an 8-storey shopping mall, with a total measurement of some 640,000 meter squares, in the midst of a lush urban garden.[53]

Designed as the latest landmark of the area, the new complex is, however, "a way to esteem the exterior of (the old) Hotel Indonesia." The new build-ing, designed in "international style," is obliged to come to terms with the old modernist monuments of the area and serve as a new envelope that mediates between the past and the present (see figure 14).

The frame that encloses the tower's facade is said to be a replica of the old Hotel Indonesia's facade for "the whole design of Grand Indonesia tries to adapt to the previous design of the old Hotel Indonesia by sympatheti-cally attempting to maintain the old design and develop it into a mixed-use complex."[54] The Sukarno era's Ramayana Room will be refashioned into an executive lounge. But the most explicit reorganization of time and space takes place in the shopping mall, which is hidden behind the old Hotel Indonesia. Over there, layers of spaces are organized horizontally and vertically according to themes that connote different times. They are decorated thematically and stocked with stylistic goods according to terms such as the "classical," the "modern," the "futuristic," and finally the "spe-cialty," which features "an elegant ambience with a soft lighting to bring back visitors to the early 1920s-era."[55] So the remnants of histories are still there to be seen. There is a form of nostalgia for unity and harmony implicit in this superblock.

The Grand Indonesia is anchored on historical ground, but it also pro-

Figure 14 Grand Indonesia under construction. The new towers over and envelops the old. Photo by A. Kusno.

duces a new category of its own. The mixed-use complex generates a new position but one that builds on the old desire to constitute a center for the display of urban imagery. The "residual" and the "emergent" are acted out thematically in the new layout to memorialize the nation, not in terms of decolonization, but as a brand or logo for contemporary corporate cultural life. In this sense, there is thus a question of whether the configuration of past-present is at all meaningful. This superblock reworks Sukarno's utopian idea. It brands Sukarno and his monuments and builds around them consumerism to provide a new syncretism for the nation. The super luxurious Kempinski Residences that tower above the superblock make this proclamation:

> President Soekarno inaugurated Hotel Indonesia in 1962 as the first international and luxurious hotel intended to accommodate presidential guests. With the Grand "Selamat Datang" statue adorning the roundabout aptly named after the hotel, it has thus been widely acknowledged as being the global entrance to Indonesia. Forty years later, its glory has been restored by Grand Indonesia as the new icon of an

exclusive lifestyle haven in Jakarta. Grand Indonesia continues to preserve the splendor of Hotel Indonesia's heritage as an original landmark enhanced with state of the art facilities, giving it a more modern appeal to suit the needs of today's world.[56]

We might say that the big block of buildings tries to develop a vocabulary that can respond to the idea of national rehabilitation. The buildings have, in any case, expanded the idea of architecture beyond a concern for permanent buildings (and their symbolism) to which the conservationist profession is normally dedicated. They too are committed to the idea of change within the old establishment and the idea of the city as an ever-changing social text. But the old symbolism and the new one are so combined that the latter seems to be blessed by the former, constituting thus the idea of not only overlapping time and space but confirming the legitimate presence of the Grand Indonesia in the present. There is thus a new narrative of history in this superblock. The present architecture invents its own past by completing the unfinished history of "state modernism" and its narrative of decolonization with the story of "market modernism."[57] Yet in such storytelling there is obviously a narrative of exclusion. In making people aware of the new social text of the city, the Grand Indonesia only addresses the public that is not found on the streets.

In this section, I have sketched some of the current architectural designs of various superblocks in the capital city. They represent a spectacle of commodity images, corporate cultures, and elite residential lifestyles above the ground that encroach onto historic sites, constituting thus a layer of urban palimpsest that seeks to overcome all that had gone before. What is striking is that they all exploit history by making connections with the historic site around which they articulate themselves. What is equally striking is that while all the architectures of these superblocks have their own narratives, they nonetheless tell the same stories in a similar fashion. The explosion of superblocks in the center of Jakarta is clearly a characteristic of the free market entertaining various narratives of the nation. We do not know to what extent the superblock expands such a consciousness of the nation's being hijacked by the market, but it does provide a sense that the nation has a new social life of its own in the post-Suharto era. If the nation can scale itself up to the level of the global and the market can bring Indonesia out of its current crisis, presumably then Indonesians too can upgrade themselves to become a unified subject of the superblock, and they would follow the "good design" of the superblock with or without the presence of security guards. Such a utopian vision however reveals less the optimism of the designer class in responding to the national crisis than it represents a profound uncertainty today about the status of the "middle class" (to which the architects belong) and its relations with the underclass. In such a moment of besiegement and estrangement, we might want to ask whether it is possible to resist such recomposition of the city and whether the architectural discourses of the superblock and their architectural technique of self-governing might be articulating an alternative form of sociality and citizenship.

THE TIME OF CRISIS

In this chapter, I started with the sensitivity of architecture toward the post-1998 social environment and showed how the architectural world has tried to tailor its design culture to the urban fabric of the city. I began with Mamo and showed how the kampung has been very important for the creativity of his architecture. He retrieves the kampung that many architects do not want to see even as it can be seen everywhere. He articulates an architecture of the kampung for a strata of the middle class who refashion themselves after the kampung following the crisis of 1998. In this context, the architecture of Mamo, in its rejection of spectacle and commodity conceptions of the visual, offers perhaps an alternative approach to the city even though we cannot expect that his architecture, by virtue of its architectural technique alone, will constitute any social change. Mamo's architecture is still for the urban middle class, who is living through the effects of economic and political crisis, and his architectural solution for the kampung is within the limits of a middle-class imagination of the urban poor. In order for Mamo's kind of architecture to make a different kind of statement, it must thus be grasped as a *symbolic act* that addresses the conflictual context of the city. We can only assess what the architecture of Mamo might mean for the politics of culture and what implications it might have on the kampung if his architecture is taken up by social movements that aim at securing a place for the kampung in the city. Mamo's architecture presents to the new urban Indonesia the problem of *whose* language architecture speaks and *what* public it is speaking to.

Can Mamo's architectural strategy be used to illuminate the very different attitude that superblock architecture takes toward the fabric of the city? Perhaps, if we consider that members of the middle class, as imagined by the superblock architects, are afraid that their class identity is in danger of being crowded out by the kampung class following the financial crisis of 1998 and the collapse of the Suharto regime that sustained them. Such fears conditioned the emergence of the new architecture of the superblock. In this case, the superblock, while intertwined with global cultures and contributing to the neoliberal competition between nation-states for capital, also reveals the growing uncertainty about the status of the middle class in Indonesia and thus its relationship with the underclass. Yet such a contextualism of the superblock displaces the context of city life today. Instead of critically engaging with the social and political histories of the site within which they are embedded, the aesthetic formalism of the superblock works to harden class positions by cultivating disciplinary space and standing against activities that it considers unruly in a public space. Their design strategies (which seek to represent the nation in the attempt to overcome the 1998 crisis) are governed by amnesia about the enormous tension that exists in the social life of the city and the nation today: the growing conflicts between circuits of poverty and luxury consumption, unemployment and the decline of state authority, evictions and urban violence, environmental degradation and the privatization of public resources. In a way, we can say that the superblock, by means of a powerful image of a new kind of urban form in the city, addresses the contested space of the metropolis by providing a microcosm for those who seek to escape from it. We can also say that their representations of commodity images and corporate cultures in turn bring the contradictory reality of the city into focus. In this sense, the superblock too reinvigorates urban life and registers a new Indonesia but in ways that dematerialize the reality of conflicts in the city. It too raises the question of *who* speaks in *whose* language and for *which* public.

Regardless of how we might want to respond to this question, both the kampung architecture of Mamo and the superblock of Kamil, together and separately, shape the city and engage in the struggle to search for norms of public life in the new Indonesia. Such struggle also represents a way of coming to terms, problematically, with the past, the memories of which seem to silently shape the spatial and architectural arrangement of the present. In chapter 4, I turn to another discourse about the built environment that deals more explicitly with the traumatic materials of May 1998, but one that finds expression less in the physical form of the city than in the minds of the urban population.

REMEMBERING AND FORGETTING

CHAPTER 4   **GLODOK ON OUR MINDS**
Chinese Culture and the Forgetting of the May Riots

"*Attack . . . attack . . . attack*" [*serbu*] the crowds [*massa*] shouted. Thus, hundreds of people spontaneously moved to the shops. Windows and blockades were destroyed, and the looting began. The massa suddenly became crazy. After the goods were in their hands, the buildings and the occupants were set on fire. Girls were raped. The wave of massa ransacked the whole city, but the Glodok area suffered the most. The festival ended in pain. So many materials are lost. Immeasurable are the pains that have been inscribed in the mind and feelings of the victims. Torn are the feelings of many of the children of the nation. This is just a small part of the story of the tragedy that took place on 13 and 14 May. Really! Those two days were the dreadful history that will never be forgotten for the rest of our lives, not until the end of the world. Three years have past. But is there any "justice"? No! All the investigations have ended in nothing. The promise to search for the masterminds has never been conducted. There seems to be an attempt to forget the tragedy of May. This is certainly not what the victims wanted, but they do not have any power to bring justice. Indeed, the tragedy of May cannot be illustrated through words [*kata-kata*]. — FAJAR, "TANGISAN MEI ITU MULAI DILUPAKAN" [THE TEARS OF THE MAY RIOTS HAVE BEGUN TO BE FORGOTTEN]

For a decade now, Indonesia has celebrated the May 1998 demonstration (known as reformasi) as a triumph of courage if not democracy in the nation. To the amazement of the Indonesian people, the authoritarian and repressive regime of Suharto was toppled by a bold group of students together with a provisional, loosely connected "coalition" made up of frustrated middle-class families, calculating military figures, opportunistic ministers and bureaucrats, street hoodlums, and the urban poor. Yet, in spite of such stirring success and solidarity, for many others the May reformasi remains a tragedy that the nation has forgotten. Riots, which took place over thirty-five hours and in approximately fifty locations throughout metropolitan Jakarta, involved the state's security apparatus as it sought to create a basis for the declaration of martial law as a "final" strategy for saving the collapsing regime. Thousands were killed in the ensuing disorder — including hundreds of poor looters trapped in ransacked lots — and hundreds of women and girls were gang-raped and tortured in these riots.[1] The violence was directed, both systematically and spontaneously, at Indonesians of ethnic Chinese descent, whom many (including segments of the Suharto regime) deemed responsible for the nation's problems. The burning and plundering of Chinese property, as well as the gang rapes of ethnic Chinese women, were carried out by certain military groups and ordinary Indonesians who were transformed into a violent mob, often at the incitement of the Suharto army itself.

The targeting of Chinese Indonesians has been attributed to the strength of their economy, the weakness of their political position, and the sense that Chinese Indonesians are not Indonesian enough — though few citizens would think of driving them out of the country entirely.[2] The ethnic Chinese, simultaneously admired and disliked by the Indonesians, have been a frequent target of rioting. Indeed, anti-Chinese riots have taken place since the formation of Indonesian nationalism in the early twentieth century under Dutch colonial rule, and perhaps even before.[3] Over time, they have become a familiar phenomenon, so familiar that the reason(s) for anti-Chinese riots have never been clear even to those participating.[4]

However familiar anti-Chinese riots may have been to Indonesians, the gang rapes of ethnic Chinese women in May 1998 were without precedent and went well beyond the recognizable framework of violence created by the long history of anti-Chinese activities.[5] The gang rapes introduced new, more extreme, and lasting violence into the vocabulary of anti-Chinese sentiment. Unlike with previous anti-Chinese riots, which were forgotten after a few days by returning to "business as usual," gang rape does permanent damage that cannot be erased, replaced (like commodities), or simply put out of mind (like other, more recognizable forms of Indonesian riots). Stories of rape, as Siegel points out, continue to haunt the public through narratives of the victims' depression, disease, suicide, pregnancy, and family rejection.[6]

Though the gang rapes have generated immense outrage and shame at all levels of society, Indonesians have not yet found a language to respond to or articulate this new mode of violence. Silence perhaps constitutes the only language for these events, thereby enacting still further violence through the suppression of the stories themselves. Siegel sees this silence as a form of national trauma, an effect of the failure of the national community to cope with its own barbarism: This "failure appears in the lower class people who raped and in the upper class elements of the political class who allowed them to do it."[7] Meanwhile, the majority of the victims still suffer from the event, and various new governments have kept quiet or denied its occurrence.[8] The state hopes that the nation will arrive at a condition of normalcy by stifling the violent memories of past horrors. In the words of former president B. J. Habibie, following his visit to the most damaged riot site at Glodok, a retail business center known as the Chinatown of Jakarta, two weeks after the riots: "We should all quickly get out of this problem. We are all Indonesians and live in the land of Indonesia. We do not discriminate against any race, religion, and ethnicity. We do not have to worry about that."[9] The rapes have profoundly shaped how the riots as a whole are understood, remembered, and forgotten. Rudi, a Chinese Indonesian whose shop in Glodok was burned out, indicated that it is "difficult for me to describe [the event] and furthermore, I don't want to remember what had happened. It is just too painful."[10] The nation's government, the larger populace, including Chinese Indonesians and the victims, are all variously involved in the suppression of trauma. They all share the difficult task of integrating the gang rapes that have inscribed the May riots into their own narratives of the past as well as the future.

This chapter centers on the relationships between memory and place, between identity formation and change of social consciousness. In this sense, it can be seen in terms of the growing interest in violence and collective memory. Over the past two decades, scholars in cultural studies in particular have focused on how individuals, groups, and nation-states have remembered catastrophe, genocide, and war through various forms of representation—for example, monuments, memorials, public spaces, and squares—as mnemonic devices that help to reflect on those events and regulate public memories.[11] Yet it is crucial to recognize that most of these studies have their particular focus on a specific material object, such as a monument or memorial, constructed under an explicit program and intended to represent events in the past. By focusing on the fact of commemoration, the studies in question rarely look at objects that were *not* built for a commemorative purpose but which are equally significant in registering, as well as forgetting, memories of past events. The everyday built environment, like monuments constructed for commemoration, enacts the dynamics of memory and forgetting, but operates often without demanding a state of spectatorial concentration to gain effect.[12]

It is precisely the everyday built environment, the changed cityscape of Jakarta, that brings the demands to represent trauma into visible relief even as it yields to the difficulty involved in such expressions. This chapter examines the spatial effects of the 1998 riots in the area of Glodok and the buildings recently erected to replace those that were ransacked and burned down. My objective is to delineate how these new spaces both represent and avoid this trauma, enabling a play of remembering and forgetting that contributes to the efforts of ethnic Chinese to retrospectively cope with the violent events in the midst of a changing political environment. I then turn to an illustrated novel by the Indonesian writer Seno Gumira Ajidarma that depicts the most extreme events of the May riots: the gang rapes of ethnic Chinese women. If the rebuilt spaces of Glodok engage with these acts by way of suppressing them, Seno's story concerns the effects of that suppression and how it opens up certain political possibilities. Set in the year 2039, the narrative construction constitutes a temporal response to the difficulty of coping with the trauma of the May riots. By examining both the power and the problematics of such representations, this chapter aims to show their role in reformulating traumatized time and space, in reimagining identities, memories, and political consciousness.

HOW TO DEAL WITH TRAUMA? HOW TO CREATE A NEW IMAGE?

On 26 May 1998, about two weeks after the riots had killed hundreds of people and destroyed over 4,500 shops in the Glodok area, President Habibie visited the site of destruction and met with the victims. The president's visit, according to Abdul Kahfi Bakri, West Jakarta's vice governor for governmental affairs at the time, was significant as an effort to show sympathy to ethnic Chinese shop owners who had suffered from the disaster.[13] It was hoped that the visit would generate trust among them toward the government. Habibie's government knew perfectly well that the first step toward reviving the damaged economy of Indonesia was to build up Glodok again. It was clear to Habibie that the way Glodok was to be treated would have an important impact on the economy and the image of the country.[14] Habibie thus remarked: "I suggest that we all work together to uphold peace, unity and work together to restore and upgrade the order of the economy that we had enjoyed before."[15]

In recommending that the country return to the previous, prosperous state, Habibie also maintained a persistent and problematic image of Glodok as simultaneously the place of the Chinese and the center of the well-being (or sickness) of the national economy. Such was the response of the Indonesian state. Yet what was the reaction of Glodok's residents to these proposals? "But how are we going to deal with the *trauma*, Mr. President? I don't understand how the looting could take place for two days in the daylight. We cried. But what we cried for was not even clear to us. The military commander and the head of the police had repeatedly said that they would guarantee security, but the looting still took place. How to build up a new image, a new economy in Glodok with an Indonesian spirit?"[16] There are at least two elements of this response that deserve attention. First, the word *trauma* is spoken in English, indicating its foreignness to the Indonesian language.[17] When used by this resident of Glodok, the term can be said to demonstrate the foreignness of the May riots and the unprecedented violence of the gang rapes that they contained. In this sense, *trauma* is also used to suggest the unrepresentable and incomprehensible suffering of the rape victims. Thus the voices that described the physical destruction of property lay a path for the expression of the violence of gang rapes, as *trauma* cannot be assimilated into the Indonesian language.[18] As I will show, this otherness, as well as the fear and confusion it causes, is registered in various modes of expression. The second element concerns an awareness that even the government, which traditionally had been relied upon for protection, could not guarantee the residents' security. Thus the ethnic Chinese community found itself in an uncertain and potentially vulnerable position. The state could not be trusted; the Indonesian middle class and the frustrated underclass could not be counted on. The residents give us a sense that, by simply reconstructing the previous economic order, the Chinese in Glodok would remain subject to attack and racial prejudice. Instead of following the suggestion of Habibie to restore the economic order "that we had enjoyed before," Glodok's residents looked for the creation of a new image. To understand what kind of image the Chinese Indonesians created to cope with the aftermath of the riots, we need to examine the buildings recently constructed in Glodok to replace those that were destroyed. How is space reconfigured to reimagine a time of trauma?

GLODOK PLAZA: DREAMING THE FUTURE, AND THE ARCHITECTURE OF REPLACEMENT

Glodok Plaza, then the largest electronics and computer center in Indonesia, was built in 1976, housing six hundred shops. It was torched on 14 May 1998. A reporter recorded the event in this way: "Glodok Plaza stands at the center of Jakarta's commercial district, Chinatown. Muladi, a security officer, watched as more than two thousand people walked to the plaza at 4:00 P.M. Some carried bags of stones, others with tools to pry open the gates. A few carried gasoline bombs. The police fired in the air, but the mob ignored them. Eventually the police stepped aside. Glodok Plaza was ripped open and burned out."[19] Chinese Indonesians remember the riots with an awareness that similar outbreaks might return. A year later, a small group of ethnic Chinese held a commemoration of the event at the ruins of the plaza. With white cloths tied to their foreheads and candles in hand, the participants laid down a long white cloth, bearing the words "we don't want to be victimized again," on the ruins of the building.[20] This, however, was the only act of remembrance that has taken place at the plaza.

At the beginning of 2000, Glodok Plaza was rebuilt in a manner that intimates the dynamics of remembering and forgetting after the May riots.[21] According to the general manager of Glodok Plaza, the rapidity of this reconstruction can be attributed to the name of Glodok, which is "already familiar in the mind of the people. Everyone knows Glodok locally and internationally. That is why, even though we have many new malls [in Jakarta], the prestige of Glodok has never faded away."[22] The area of Glodok is remembered not for its recent social and political violence but rather for its long-standing distinction. As a private enterprise remade to rebuild their businesses, Glodok Plaza reappeared in a new form to strengthen this image of glory and prosperity (see figure 15).

A new design was laid out to cover the remaining structure. P. T. Airmas Asri, the designer of the new Glodok Plaza, pointed out that the company won the design competition because it was able to give Glodok Plaza

Figure 15 Light from the future: Artist's rendering of the new Glodok Plaza, 2000. Courtesy of TCP Internusa, Glodok Plaza.

"a strong image of a center of electronics and computers in the new millennium."[23] The facade of the building projects this notion by way of decorative, colorful, and festive features made of steel, glass, and aluminum, all of which are visible from afar. Large billboards, facing the main street, exude a high-tech, transparent quality. The new facade is complemented by an inviting landscape that features greenery, fountains, and open spaces leading to the entrance.

The main challenge, however, is not in the treatment of the facade but rather in the task of designing "a new interior space within the existing old structure."[24] The new interior is guided by the principle of "brightness." To move the building, architecturally, from darkness to light is to open up the prospects for the future. This move, from the dystopian to the utopian, could be authorized, of course, only by a suppression of the past terrors embodied within the framework of its architecture. To eliminate the previous gloomy spaces, parts of the old structure were demolished, creating more internal open space and light. Several atriums were constructed throughout the building, allowing every shop to face an open atrium space and thus "erasing the impression of filth, darkness, and old and providing a sense of order. . . . The subsidiary atriums will enable visitors to enjoy the moment of shopping in every part of the building. The tenants will also enjoy the same spatial effect no matter where his [or] her shop is located."[25] These subsidiary atriums are all connected to an elliptical, main atrium at the entrance hall. Designed with careful attention to feng shui, this main atrium features a water fountain at its center to cool down the element of heat believed to be embedded in the area of Glodok.[26]

The conscientious concern for feng shui contrasts sharply with the attention granted to the commemoration of the riots. Indeed, what is remarkable about the design strategy of Glodok Plaza is the complete erasure of all traces of the old structure and, by extension, the memories of the riots. While the existence of the new building certainly resulted from the May riots, and while it was rebuilt from the remaining structure, the principal architectural concept allows for no mention of the unrest itself. What have been exposed are architectural features that supposedly enable consumers to identify the building with the electronic and computer age of the new millennium. Glodok Plaza ostensibly celebrates a future electronic festival, not a past traumatic event. The building shows itself as cheerful and inviting. It reaches out through its billboards. It tries to offer a dream of the virtual world instead of the memories of the horrific and very real past. There is optimism that technology will bring "light" to overcome the darkness of the past. The structure of the old building that carries the trace of violence is buried under layers of new materials and, ultimately, by electronic accessories. Overlain by the imagery of the present and the future, the trace of the old structure is gone, though it ironically still supports the new building.

Built on the burden of memories of violence are layers of computerized lightness that connect customers to new spaces. In addition, a so-called e-market place has become a component of the central facilities. As part of their leasing contracts, all the tenants have been given access to operate business-to-business transactions through the website.[27] The manager promotes the building as "the first internet-ready mall, which provides e-commerce through www.e-glodok.com and can be accessed by businesspeople from all over the world."[28] As "the first shopping center in Southeast Asia that brings together the fiscal and the virtual worlds,"[29] the plaza is not intended, therefore, to be a site of memory. In fact, all traces of the riots have been eliminated. One does not even need to visit the place to buy goods. There is now no emotional burden of visiting, seeing, and remembering the violence that was done there. The space of violence is reconfigured to imagine a future through bypassing the historical moments of trauma.

Figure 16 The new Pasar Glodok, built in the architectural style of the Indies.
Photo courtesy of Perkumpulan Fotografi Tarumanagara.

PASAR GLODOK: COLONIAL ARCHITECTURE AND
THE DISPLACEMENT OF PAST HORROR

First constructed in 1971, Pasar Glodok (Glodok Bazaar) was burned down during the riots. Completely rebuilt as a mall consisting of over 1,800 shops, the new Pasar Glodok—like Glodok Plaza—makes no reference to the violent events that led to its own destruction.[30] But if Glodok Plaza avoids these traumas through the language of a timeless and placeless future of information technology, Pasar Glodok enacts its own elusion by speaking of the area's architectural and political history. Built in what has been called an architectural style of the Indies, or Batavia, Pasar Glodok seeks to impress the public with its colonial heritage (see figure 16).

The president director of Pasar Glodok states that the design is consistent with the strategy of the city government to revive the architectural style of colonial Jakarta for tourism. The area of Glodok is located at the edge of the old section of Jakarta, where many Dutch buildings from the colonial time are situated. After the May riots, for commercial purposes, the city government decided to ease building permit regulations to rebuild Glodok as part of the revitalization project of Jakarta's colonial town.[31] The symbolism of Batavia is expressed at the exterior through the use of Ionic columns at the entrance, brown and orange geometrically corniced walls, curvilinear ornamentation on the gates, and the detailed building lines suggestive of what is known as postmodern classicism. In this sense, Pasar Glodok can be aligned with the architectural style of Batavia in its syncretic use of western classical and Indies forms. It endeavors to remind the public that Glodok was once part of Batavia and that the pedestrian spaces of Glodok will "attract tourists from various countries and the Jakartan who would like to enjoy the open air of Glodok."[32] Aspects of Dutch colonial architecture, once emblems of political authority, are transformed and given new meanings by virtue of their status as guarantees of a future city of tourism rather than one of an oppressive past. Soon, according to Sutardjianto, mayor of West Jakarta at the time, all warehouse spaces found in that area will have to stop their operations and be turned into tourist-related facilities such as hotels, restaurants, souvenir shops, cafés, theatres, and other amenities.[33]

The Indies architecture of Pasar Glodok, however, carries an ambivalent connotation. The syncretism of Batavian architecture is often an uneasy one, creatively awkward in its mixtures of Western, Betawi-Sundanese, Javanese, and Chinese elements. Yet, in Pasar Glodok, these various elements have been abstracted to such an extent that they blend seamlessly into one another and therefore constitute an architectural whole. This brings to mind disquieting thoughts. Is not the architecture of Pasar Glodok—in spite of its abstraction, in spite of its attention to the history and heritage of the location—a response to the situation of trauma, remembering, and forgetting for the ethnic Chinese? Is not Pasar Glodok the new image that was envisioned by President Habibie, who suggested that "we all work together to uphold peace, unity and work together to restore and upgrade the order of economy that we had enjoyed before?"[34] Does not Pasar Glodok express an aspiration of a harmonious community that—in the happy company of tourism—it suspend its memories of violence?

On 14 May 2001, three years after the riots, a group of Chinese Indonesians in white mourning dress carried black banners and photos of the May riots, commemorating the event right in front of the new Pasar Glodok. "We do this to remind the public, especially the Chinese Indonesians, to courageously speak up and demand that government respond to the violence of the May riots."[35] The commemorators carried photos that asked

Figure 17 Commemorators carrying photos of the May riots in front of the new Pasar Glodok, 2001. Photo courtesy of *Media Indonesia*, reprinted from *Media Indonesia*, 14 May 2001.

for an acknowledgment of what was *really* going on there. They retraumatized the space of violence in contrast to the new temporal imaginings offered by the spatial configuration of Pasar Glodok (see figure 17).

For some, the tragedy remains in darkness. It is hidden and muted, not least by the new architecture built on and over the site of the riot. If one walks behind the wall of the new Pasar Glodok, the remnants of the riots can still be found. As for the architecture of Pasar Glodok, while it speaks of old Batavia in ways that are somewhat crude, it also totally fails to address the violent history of the building's location. The commemorators, the photographs, and the ruins behind the building register its memories of violence. They break the architectural order that seeks to distance itself from the past horror.[36]

THE RETURN OF "CHINESE CULTURE"

Whether confirming Glodok's prospects for the future technological world or endorsing its historic past, the architecture of both Glodok Plaza and Pasar Glodok that I have described here draws overwhelmingly on non-Chinese architectural forms. Yet these forms developed in ways that are specific to the Indonesians (including the Chinese) who, in their attempts to cope with the May riots, produced this kind of amnesiac architecture that seeks to suppress, if not eliminate, the past horror. Glodok Plaza replaces memories of the riots by harnessing the high-tech futuristic language of architecture. Pasar Glodok, on the other hand, displaces the traumatized time and space by fulfilling the desires of the government to reinstate the coherent image of a peaceful colonial heritage town. The connections that these buildings have made to the future and the past are completely devoid of any reference to their recent histories of violence. If these architectures indicate a general need for *not* speaking Chinese after the May riots, other buildings both in and outside the Glodok area give frank and full expression to an ostensibly Chinese identity.

A building called Candra Naya, located about one hundred meters south of Glodok, served as the well-known house of the Dutch-appointed Chinese major in the nineteenth century.[37] This house, which is understood to be the city's largest and most complete building in the Chinese architectural style, has recently been the subject of a dispute.[38] While the municipality of Jakarta promotes the preservation of old buildings from colonial times for the sake of tourism, Candra Naya, the only surviving Chinese house protected under the city's historic preservation codes (Monumenten Ordonnantie), is strangely subject to demolition and relocation. For reasons that are not entirely clear, Candra Naya today is sandwiched between the skyscrapers of a hotel, apartments, and a shopping mall (see figure 18). The back section and the left and right sides of the house were demolished in 1995. The remaining front and middle sections of the house were then to be relocated to the Beautiful Indonesia in Miniature Park, a theme park on the outskirts of the city, often associated with Suharto's regime, which celebrates the diversity and development of Indonesia, though it totally ignores the Chinese contributions to the nation. The owners of the skyscrapers are Chinese Indonesians, and they are perfectly aware that they have violated (or been allowed to violate) the city's laws. But with Candra Naya in the way, they felt they could not make a profit because Candra Naya blocks the feng shui of the skyscrapers. To hide the controversy, security guards are employed to prevent visitors from viewing and even photographing the building. News of Candra Naya's situation spread beyond the confinement of the gate. It outraged activists and intellectuals of both Chinese and non-Chinese backgrounds. Their protest was sufficient to prevent the owners of the skyscrapers from getting rid of the house.

Figure 18 Candra Naya, a nineteenth-century house built in an Indo-Chinese architectural style, surrounded by a skyscraper. Photo by A. Kusno.

In post-1998 Jakarta, however, the process of demolishing Candra Naya is clearly understood as undemocratic. Several meetings have since been held, including a consultation with the spirit of the house, who is apparently very upset with what has happened to it.[39] At the meeting table were those who would like the house to be moved to a different site (for economic and practical reasons) and those who feel that it should remain (for religious, social, and political reasons). For the latter, Candra Naya was not only the house of a colonial Chinese major but also the headquarters of Sin Ming Hui, a social organization set up to serve and protect the rights of the ethnic Chinese during the early years of Indonesian independence, when many of them were abandoned, attacked, and killed.[40] Moreover, the propinquity of the house to Glodok has made it suitable as a site of commemoration for the May riots. Given this dual historical significance, this group feels that the building should not be moved. Instead, they want to save Candra Naya from the abuses of capitalism and reimagine it as a symbol of violated space that, when connected to the event of the May riots, could critically reflect on the traumatized space of Glodok.

Some of the most significant elements of Chinese architecture—the courtyard, the shape of the roofs, the engravings—are visible in Candra Naya but are no longer present in the homes of ethnic Chinese residents of Jakarta. Yet, the importance of Candra Naya lies not only in these architectural attributes as signs of a disappearing history but also in the symbolic value it has for both the present and the future of ethnic Chinese in Indonesia.[41] We might think that this awareness of the possibilities for resistance is enabled by a condition of postmodernity, but it is much more than that.[42] The attempt to make a connection between the nineteenth-century Chinese house and the identity of Chinese Indonesians today stems from the memories of the violence of the May 1998 riots. The appearance (as well as the disappearance) of Candra Naya in the consciousness of ethnic Chinese is fostered by the awareness of the nonexistence of "the *political site of memory practices*"[43] that would mediate the symbolic destruction of "Chineseness" during the May riots. With no site to commerate the 1998 violence against ethnic Chinese, Chandra Naya as a Chinese house that has been visibly violated represents a "monument" that inextricably raises moral and political questions.

If the struggle over Candra Naya represents the twilight of architecture that conveys a Chinese presence in Glodok, the Chinese temple with its visible elements of Chinese architecture continues to symbolize Glodok's rootedness in Chinese culture. During the 2001 Chinese New Year, Wihara Dhrama Bakti, an old temple in Glodok, attracted some two thousand people who came from various parts of the city to join in the prayer for peace, safety, and prosperity.[44] Meanwhile, the lion dance, or *barongsai*, a popular acrobatic dance performed with models of lions made of cloth and paper, suppressed during the time of Suharto for its alleged Chinese roots, has been staged widely on various occasions.[45] It attracted people (including non-Chinese) from various places.[46] The temple, the barongsai, and the Chinese New Year had all been "locked" indoors since 1967, by presidential decree.[47] The lifting of the law banning Chinese cultural expression in public has stimulated the revival of Chinese culture and language. Chinese characters have begun to appear in public spaces, and more and more Indonesian newspapers are printed in Chinese.[48] From the middle of the year 2000, some developers have incorporated explicit elements of Chinese architecture into the shops aimed at Chinese buyers. For instance, with the construction of shophouses promoted by Kota Wisata, one of the largest private housing companies in Jakarta, a shopping complex is turned into a Chinese village.[49] The shophouse evokes the image of traditional China but in a manner reminiscent of a modern picturesque theme park because of its overstated portrayal of Chinese culture. Its playfulness manifests the difficulties of constructing Chinese cultures other than those laid out in the image of the Orientalist.

Yet, along with the proliferation of architectural signs of Chineseness, there is also a sense that these signs might provoke an unintended response. The city wants to show the importance of the Chinese in the social life of the nation, to give them a prominence they deserve. But there is also a fear that representing Chinese identity creates a dividing line between the ethnic Chinese and the Indonesians that, for many, was one of the very sources of the May riots.[50]

This proliferation of signs of the presence of ethnic Chinese can be understood only in relation to the question of how Jakarta houses the memory of a people who no longer feel "at home" there. How can the city invite its ethnic Chinese citizens back into the nation after having alienated them during the riots? The nation tries to recognize the role the Chinese have played in the history and culture of the nation, yet the nation is also haunted by the possible absence of the Chinese economy. At the same time, from the state's perspective, the promotion of Chinese culture serves to redeem the violence done to the Chinese. The public declaration of Chinese culture is a byproduct of the May riots, given by the government to tranquilize if not erase the memories of the May riots themselves. For some Chinese Indonesians, the public performance of Chinese culture has, indeed, validated and affirmed a sense of cultural belonging. However, a sense of emptiness prevails in the recovering of Chinese culture, an impression that comes from removing Chinese culture from the context of its production: the violence of Suharto's time and the traumatic events of the May riots that most Chinese Indonesians are still living through.[51] Yet, as a case of "repressive silencing,"[52] this bypassing of "truth" has allowed the articulation of Chinese culture today.

For Chinese Indonesians, the promotion of Chinese culture, like the appearance of the new architecture of Glodok, if not redemptive nonetheless serves to overcome the overwhelming nature of the May riots. Avoiding the traumatic past by expressing Chinese culture and building amnesiac architecture on the sites of violence serves to neutralize the demands of trauma both to remember and to forget. In the face of violence and the threat against Chinese culture, the spectacle of Orientalist Chinese architecture might affirm a sense of Chineseness. Yet this type of architecture may also express the desire to forget the traumatized space and time through reimagining the supposedly timeless culture of the Chinese. It is out of this tangled web of forgetting and remembering violence that the recent architecture in Jakarta and the concomitant discourses about Chinese cultures have been produced.

The evasiveness of the state in dealing with the May riots, the nonexistence of any public memorial site, the appearance of an ostensibly Chinese culture, and the construction of amnesiac postmodern architecture in Glodok are all connected. They do not directly communicate the forms of physical violence, but they tell us about the traumatized spaces and the temporal response to such spaces. These reimaginings of traumatized spaces through discourses of "repressive silencing" of violence increase our understanding of the *effects* of what happened, but they do not tell us what *really* happened. They may increase our efforts to forget and to remember, but do they do justice to the extremity of the riots? What other mode of representation might do this?

JAKARTA IN THE STORY OF SENO GUMIRA AJIDARMA: THE FUTURE REMEMBERING OF THE PAST

If the spatial environment discussed so far bears no relation to the violent past, and the present provides no transcending ground to integrate knowledge and unify representations, perhaps a kind of "history of the present" could provide us with a possibility of seeing the story and its political potential, even as its narrative provides no escape from the here and now. It is most appropriate, then, to enter post-1998 Jakarta through a temporal narrative construction, regardless of how impossible it is to transcend the spatial environment of the everyday within which we are embedded.

Toward the end of 1999, an Indonesian writer, Seno Gumira Ajidarma, wrote a short essay entitled "Jakarta 2039" for the popular magazine *Matra*.[53] Eventually republished as an illustrated or graphic story, the essay is, as the book itself declares, "based on a true event told so that it will not happen again."[54] The novel *Jakarta 2039* can be read, like the architectural discourses portrayed above, in terms of the reconfiguration of time and space after the May riots. It differs from these reconfigurations, however, insofar as Seno makes gang rape a central component through which Indonesians of various backgrounds can reimagine the traumatized space by crossing time.

Jakarta 2039 is about the May riots as told "forty years and nine months later" by three people, each of a different generation. They have never known each other, but they are nevertheless connected and deeply shaped by the event that took place forty years ago in the city where they are all living today. The story is divided into three main sections, with each person telling a story about him- or herself and his or her own relationship to the event. Because each character is unacquainted with the others, it is only the reader who, having read all the stories, can comprehend the links between the individual experiences and imagine the story's coherence. In this sense, the story attempts to create an "imagined community" for the readers as residents of Jakarta who might be connected to (as well as divided from) one another by their private memories of what happened in May 1998.[55] The source of this imagining, however, is based not only on solidarity but enmity as well.

The story opens with heavy rain in Jakarta and a police helicopter chasing two rapists who run across the jungle of skyscrapers and the poor urban neighborhood of kampung in Jakarta (see figure 19). This scene has caught the attention of a woman at the window of her high-rise apartment. It triggers her to tell her story in front of her video camera. She tells how she traced her genealogy and discovered that she was born from a mass rape that took place more than forty years earlier. She discovered her history only after incredible efforts because no file or written record existed. It was, finally, the elderly people of the city who told her of her history. Those who witnessed the event kept it secret, and no institutional memory was made for future generations. Nor is there any memorial to recall the event. There is also no attempt to turn private memories into a public history. The city kept the woman's secret, and perhaps the city in fact has no secret to keep. Rapes continue to take place, and the poor and rich keep living side by side with each occupying different worlds. Violence becomes what is lived. Its real-life spectacle registers no active relation to the city's residents. There is hardly any response from people on the street as the two rapists are chased and caught by the police helicopter. The lack of reaction suggests that this is something people see every day. The city itself is a memorial to a violence that keeps reproducing itself.

If the city has no memory of violence since it continuously represents

Figure 19 "Keep running. The two criminals try to escape from the police helicopter. People on the street pay no attention to what is going on." Reprinted courtesy of Galang Press from Seno G. Ajidarma, *Jakarta 2039.*

violence, then what the woman discovers of her past is something that is both shocking and overwhelming. She will never know her mother who hates her. And her father could be any man in the city. Because of this, she has an enmity to her own past and to herself. It was only by chance that she learned the truth, a truth that she perhaps does not want to know. "Today is my fortieth birthday, I feel I am reborn with a curse." The video camera records her story. This technology perhaps records the first document of the unrepresentable memory of the riots that she had never experienced. This deep memory cannot find a place in the public space; she has to keep the burden of knowing within herself. *Jakarta 2039* is the Jakarta of today. The story shows no change in Jakarta's cityscape and its social stratification. Policemen coexist with the rapists, high-rise buildings stand side by side with the kampung, and the video recording joins with oral traditions. The normal pattern of the city's life continues alongside the hidden, broken, and strained relationship between communities, between avoidance and engagement with the traumatic experience. There is no social action from which the future generation can remember and understand what had happened to ensure "that the past horror will never return."[56]

The second story opens with the police helicopter flying over the city. The bodies of the two rapists hang suspended, fastened to the helicopter at the end of a long rope. This flying object serves as a Foucauldian spectacle of punishment to the residents of the city to remind them of the rapists' fate. An elderly woman watches the scene from her high-rise apartment window. It prompts her to write in a diary that she keeps in her laptop computer:

> Today is the birthday of my daughter. If she is still alive, she is forty-years-old. Where are you my child? . . . Forty years have passed, I have *tried to forget* what has happened to me but the curse keeps following me. Why do people have to have memory? Even forgetfulness fails to erase the fact that I was raped, tortured, humiliated, and abandoned. I really hate that I was born and I really hate that you were born. I was raped at 10 P.M. on 14 May 1998 in a building on fire and where the screaming of other women could be heard.[57]

This woman, an Indonesian of Chinese descent, is perhaps the mother of the woman in the first story. Like the nation that finds it difficult to incorporate the rape into its history, the woman finds it hard to integrate the horrible event into her own life. Yet, unlike the nation, she is not able to forget the event and the child to whom she gave birth. The child is connected to the event. The mother knows perfectly well that she could not keep the child who would remind her of what she seeks to forget. She has tried every way to forget. Yet within this commitment to forget, the mother remembers and still retains an ambivalent wish to see the child who is the result of gang rape. This is perhaps the significance of the May riots. Unlike what took place in previous riots, rape produces follow-up stories that cannot be contained in the past. The mother decides to stay in the city where she was gang-raped in order to reimagine the traumatized space as a space for possible reconciliation with her child, though she hopes that the child "will never know who she is."[58] Unlike those who see trauma as irreparable within the traumatized space of the nation, the mother stays, like the Chinese at Glodok, in order to reimagine it anew.

This second story asks: how do we deal with the effect of a trauma that demands representation yet refuses to be represented?[59]

The third story again begins with the police helicopter swinging the two bodies of the rapists from the rope, but now they hang right over the poor kampung neighborhood of Jakarta. The light of the helicopter illuminates the darkness of the area and brings down the shadow of the hanging rapists onto the thatched roofs of the shantytown. The next panel brings the reader to a house in a poor kampung. A young girl brings a glass of water to her dying father lying on the bed. She sees her father as a hard-working man who, in his relatively young age, looks old and seems to "carry with him a burden as heavy as a globe on his back."[60] Everyone has decided to leave him except her. That night her father asks her to stay at his bedside because he wants to tell her a secret he has been keeping for a long time. Closing her eyes the girl hears the story of the May riots that took place more than forty years ago in the city where they are living today. She hears the story of the looting, the burning, and the raping of many young girls, each by nine to twelve people. She pictures her young father, smoking a cigarette, calmly walking through the ruins until he spots a young girl crying and hiding alone at the corner of a destroyed building. Her father throws the cigarette away and, with eyes opened wide, approaches the girl and drags her to another corner and rapes her. His actions attract a crowd of people who then repeat the violation of the girl. Her father then lights a cigarette and calmly walks away without looking back. The old father ends the story with a note: "13 and 14 May, 1998, *they* write it down in history."

The young girl, hearing all this, pulls herself away from her father. She indeed remembers what her teacher told her (seemingly not from a textbook) in history class: "The riots on 13 and 14 May are the most humiliating event in the nation's history. Chinese women were gang-raped because they were Chinese."[61] Quietly turning her back to her father she says: "How could father do that kind of thing? Father has mommy, auntie, and now a daughter. I am also a woman, father. I feel the suffering of that woman. Father, I am so disappointed. How did this happen?"[62] "I don't know. Everyone was insane. Everyone did it. We felt that we were being led. None of us know how this happened. We have never talked about it. I have never wanted to meet those men again. When we met, we have never talked about it. We do not want to remember it."[63]

We can read Seno's story through a lens of skepticism and horror in the sense that everyone is involved in the making of the May riots, but there is no channel to unmake the event. Yet we should also ask how the memories of the woman in the first story connect to those of the second and the third. And what are the political implications of this connection with regard to the broader position of women in Indonesia? These three stories represent the ways in which the identities of these women have been permanently marked by the traumatic event. The three women depicted in the story, each representing a generation, recognized themselves through traces that go beyond class and ethnic identification. As the young girl in the last story indicates: "You have hurt me, father. That woman will never forget the event. Father will also never be able to redeem the sense of guilt. And now I have to live with this wound too, forever. If that woman had a child from the rape, she will be forty-years-old today. I have a sister somewhere."[64]

Seno uses his story to show that the basic feature of consciousness stems from the extreme event that has been suppressed by the state and its citizens. His narrative integrates the voices of the victims and, through them, constructs a national community. The question Seno raises in his story is not merely what the *effect* of the event is on the social and political consciousness of the city's residents, but whether it triggers the "collective" consciousness of city dwellers who have been numbed by the apparent commonplace of violence, rape, and poverty.

On the other hand, inserting this extreme event of the past into the present and the future contradicts the concept of development in the nation's history. Consistent with the erasure of history (by the state), Seno's story provides no historical context as to how and why the May riots happened. In this sense, his story might be easily incorporated into the state's denial of the gang rapes of ethnic Chinese women because it presents the event as one produced through "oral tradition" *without* any firm evidence. Nevertheless, through the story Seno engages the demand for a representation of the event. The story does not pretend to be adequate but teases out the repressed part of Indonesian history. In the narrative, the recollection has been blocked for decades by the state, which finds it difficult to domesticate the most extreme components of the May riots into its official history. Yet, this extreme past returns in the form of private narratives, passed on to new generations by the elderly who, though they have not forgotten the events, have preferred to suppress them.[65]

The younger generations, in turn, continue to carry the burden of these memories, keeping them off official records and confined to personal narratives and recording devices. The present and the future are continuously haunted by a past that is registered, not in any monument, but in the minds of the people.

CAN THE TRAUMA BE OVERCOME?

As I passed through West and North Jakarta, an area where the riots took place, I saw ruins of burnt or damaged buildings that have not been fully cleaned up. The fire-blackened walls of many ravaged shophouses and damaged homes that were plundered and set on fire are still evident. There are innumerable broken windows that have been covered over. Renovated buildings close to my neighborhood exhibit different facades. If, in the past, buildings were curtained with glass walls, they are now made of concrete with very small windows. Where glass walls exist, they are fully caged over by iron grids. These facades are part of the features used to counter the effects of rioting, but they are also ghostly objects that instigate fear and memories of violence. Some people still use damaged buildings, ignoring the gaping holes. Signs of deep social and psychological wounds that have yet to heal, these holes attract the attention of passersby only to return their gazes with a reminder of riots that might again occur (see figure 20).

High, sharp-pointed fences are now the main features of Jakarta's cityscape. These symbols of middle-class prestige were there before, but since the May 1998 violence the fences somehow appear different. They no longer seem to connote power. They do not have any real power to exclude. Rather, these enclosures signify defense, fear, and abandonment. They keep things inside, including the sense of personal wonder, trauma, and anguish. As many Chinese Indonesians have not yet been able to bring their trauma into the public light, some have given up their efforts to become "Indonesian." One can see from the street that houses are left empty and damaged. Perhaps the owners cannot afford to renovate their destroyed houses or shops, but some do not even want to recognize them as their own. For them, the trauma of the May 1998 riots cannot be cured within the space of the nation. As we have seen, these spaces bear no relation to the horrors that have taken place; they have instead been dehistoricized into spaces of exchange such as the modern mall or theme park. Like the cityscape of Jakarta, these spaces speak the silent language of the victims of the gang

Figure 20 Damaged shops in Glodok with the new Pasar Glodok and the skyscrapers that surround Candra Naya in the background, 2002. Photo courtesy of Perkumpulan Fotografi Tarumanagara.

rapes. The silence invoked by these buildings, as powerful as a voice, opens up the possibility of acknowledging the difficulties entailed in representing the gang rapes.

This brings us back to the question asked of President Habibie by the Chinese at Glodok: "But how are we going to deal with trauma . . . how to build up a new image . . . with an Indonesian spirit?" If trauma can be cured "with an Indonesian spirit" (supposedly then, within the space of the nation), perhaps it must involve not only the government's but also the perpetrating communities' feeling responsible for and *acting* on these memories. In the end, the "new image" imagined by the Chinese at Glodok may not be a single settled image at all—but simply a never-to-be resolved struggle over trauma that supposedly must be and can be overcome.

Jakarta 2039, the modernist architecture of Glodok Plaza, the postmodern expression of Pasar Glodok and other buildings that have taken up Chinese identity, and the ruins of the cityscape are all part of this unresolved struggle. Not unlike the victims of the gang rapes, they have tried (in every way) to forget, even as they acknowledge the difficulty of forgetting. They speak, even as their voices "cannot be illustrated through *kata-*

kata (words)." They speak, through the everyday environment, to a general need for an appreciation of the Chinese Indonesian experiences of violence and the difficulties entailed in representing them and for the creation of complex mediations that can overcome the trauma of the past by acting on Indonesians' unspoken desires for justice, forgiveness, and relief.

CHAPTER 5   **THE AFTERLIFE OF THE EMPIRE STYLE,**
            ***INDISCHE ARCHITECTUUR,* AND ART DECO**

"If [architecture] could speak, what would it say to us?"
— ROBERT A. BEAUREGARD, *SPATIAL PRACTICES*

In chapter 4, I presented the city of Jakarta and its architecture as if they could speak about the context in which they are situated. In some circumstances, for example, the aftermath of May 1998, architectural design features provide a means for reflection, creative intervention, and imagining possibilities. In other circumstances, the same properties of architectural design that provide such an opening are linked to a particular institutionalized pattern of power and authority. These different messages are often what are at stake in disputes about the meaning of architecture and its roles in registering the ways we live in the city. Yet, these messages are the result of an interpretation because architecture does not represent itself. Instead, it is the object of our thematic discourses that we construct to articulate a position that, like any other meaning-making mechanism, is inherently political. Whether architecture has politics thus is a question of perception, narration, and meaning construction shaped by the material conditions that form our existence.

In this chapter, I continue to speak for architecture by examining how the past is refashioned to cope with particular sociopolitical circumstances of the present. I analyze how the architectural styles of the colonial past have been appropriated within dominant discourses (of both the state and members of society) as well as reimagined by marginalized positions in the social context of a postcolonial society—an act that seems to be captured by the notion of "the past in the present."[1]

In the limited world of architecture, the notion of "the past in the present" can be seen as referring to a particular form of architectural expression that prevailed in the past and continues to remain powerful in the present. The prior form of representation reappears not in its "original" shape but in the imitation, quotation, and appropriation of it. Once things are quoted from the past, as poststructuralists remind us, they lose their original meaning. The distant past, once transported to the immediate present, generates a new meaning that is different from the one invested in the past.

While this transposition of the past to the present might be seen as largely an artistic and intellectual operation, the "the past in the present" also provokes another set of historical questions. It triggers issues about the relation between the colonial Netherlands East Indies and postindependence Indonesia. It raises questions concerning the sociopolitical and artistic relationship: What is being imitated, reused, transformed, and discarded after decolonization? What is being decolonized? What is being invested with new meaning and how and why?

These questions are also relevant to the discourses of architecture and urban design in the new Indonesia I have discussed so far and must be included in a national-cultural discourse. The architecture of the past in the present thus is not an issue of inheritance. Instead it is a symbolic act that helps construct a collective desire for a new time at the moment of crisis. These questions also lead us into an inquiry about the ideologies of architecture even though most architects prefer to claim that their architecture is beyond any ideology. Yet, architects are not only experts in their particular field but also members of particular social and political orders. The transcendental position they often adopt (as detached, professional formmakers) and the architecture they produce (as something beyond ideology) is in itself a form of cultural operation rooted in the social formation within which they are embedded. Drawing from this set of understandings of the notion of "the past in the present," this chapter explores the ways in which some of the key architectural expressions of the colonial time are appropriated (usually quietly) to cope with the situation of present-day (postcolonial) Indonesia.

The architecture of the past that I discuss in this chapter refers to the prevailing styles of the early twentieth century identified loosely if not uncertainly as "Empire style," "Indische architectuur," and the modernist "Nieuwe Bouwen."[2] The rationale for choosing these three prior forms of representation is not only that they have an ideological place in the historiography of architecture but they also left their traces in the form of contemporary "Indonesian architecture." I should note at the outset that these three architectural expressions, each in its own way, transcend local identities and identification. They are recognizably "modern" and, in the eyes of many Indonesians, clearly related to the "West." Their reappearance today, we could say, also owes much to the legacy of Dutch colonialism. However, this postcolonial connection to its colonial past is also mediated by the imagery of global culture that moves beyond the exclusive "metropole-colony" relationship.[3]

How do the architectural strategies in Indonesia today engage with Indonesia's colonial legacies? How do contemporary architects come to terms with the prior "colonial" mode of architectural expression? How do they make the architecture of "the past in the present"? I begin by outlining the situation that present-day Indonesian architecture came to in response to the late period of Suharto's New Order (1966–98) it helped to shape. This era is crucial not only because its cultural effects continue to the present day, but, more importantly, because the economic dislocation and rapid and fundamental cultural change of that era gave rise to various utopian and oppositional architectural discourses that have emerged from what are basically materials of the colonial past. Set in the long New Order period, this chapter brings the developments in Indonesia today closer to their earlier parallels in the making of new times. It brings today closer to the sphere of influence of previous encounters, events, and personages.

SHAPING THE CONTEXTS

Despite their strong sense of nationalism (set against Western imperialism), what Indonesian architects faced at the beginning of the postcolonial era was *not* the question of how to draw on existing architectural traditions of the past. The focus of attention in the early decolonization period was primarily on an imaginary future believed to be attainable through a continuing revolution. The architecture that caught the imagination of the ruling class was the modernist international style. This was understood, unproblematically, as embodying the spirit of revolution that was free from any "imperial" connection, either with the East or the West. The first president, Sukarno (who himself was an architect), for instance, strove for an architecture that moved beyond the vocabulary of the past and the limited space of the nation (see chapter 9). Sukarno and his architects had very little interest in developing the earlier modes of architectural representation even as Dutch professors of architecture, including the much-respected Vincent van Romondt, kept reminding them of the importance of Indonesia's own building heritage. Sukarno's interests in revolution forbade him from anchoring architectural expression in any foundation from the past.[4]

The question of how to draw on existing architectural traditions (of the past) started only at the end of the 1970s with a consciousness that emerged in tandem with the establishment of a political culture characteristic of Suharto's New Order (1966–98). The early 1970s saw Indonesia struggling to stabilize its economy and political system after the turmoil of 1965, when the nation's ideology changed from Sukarno's national leftist "revolution" to Suharto's own traditionalist blend of capitalist "development." The subsequent quest for identity in architecture thus stems from the vast change in the visual environment of the (capital) city, which was transformed even further in the late 1980s by the unleashing of neoliberal capitalism and the obsession of the state to ground those changes in a display of national culture and traditional symbolism. The concept of "development," while clearly derived from modernization theory, was compounded with the state's attempt to maintain its rule through a philosophy derived from Javanese traditionalism.[5] Wanting to achieve an integrated nation, Suharto's economic advisers propagated an apolitical developmentalism that was sustained by the traditionalist idea of familial collectivism under the authority of the "father." This seemingly contradictory impulse — "capitalist" economic development on the one hand and traditional authority on the other — worked together and found its expression in the title given to Suharto himself: "the father of development." Central to this title of "father" was the production of a generation of Indonesians who were expected to be apolitical in their outlook but fully committed to the tutelage of the father in achieving the material progress of "development." Indonesians were reminded that they should not forget that the country is "a bequest from the old to the young" and "authority is being delegated from the older to the younger generation."[6] In the minds of the power elite, the new generation needed to be reminded that material progress could go hand in hand with the preservation of "traditions." The members of this generation, known eventually as the "middle class" (to which architects and their clients largely belong), carried with them the burden of representing their identities vis-à-vis the state-father. Few things bring the negotiation between the "father" and his "children" into more visible relief than the visual field of architecture.

How did the middle class deal with the ideological inscription of the New Order? In various ways of course, but I will just point out one that relates to spatial and architectural representation. With land prices in the central part of the city driven up by the force of "development," the middle class in Jakarta (who were too late to enter the ex-European neighborhood of Menteng but eager to leave behind the urban kampung) were left with no choice except to purchase land in the periurban areas otherwise known as the suburbs where they could afford a house. These middle-class families who chose to live in the suburbs enclosed themselves in houses of various styles. They filled their housing tracts with designs obtained not through the national pedagogy of "tradition" but through (cable) television, magazines, and traveling abroad that brought in imagery of "global modernity."[7] In contrast to the state's cultural message of "tradition," they appropriated imagery foreign to the country and freely quoted Western architectural vocabularies.[8] They also alluded to the colonial Indies architectural style, (Western) modernist style, and the neoclassical Empire style. The past reentered the present, registering thus a condition of postcoloniality not so much through a political confrontation with colonial legacies but more through a contradictory engagement with the political culture of the state and the commodity imageries of global modernity.

How did architects respond to all this? The amalgamation of state and capital generates a self-contradictory field of force that shapes the architectural culture of our time. On the one hand, individual clients, ranging from the middle class to the nouveau riche brought architects ideas they had picked up from various representations of the past and the present. Most architects, even though they are dismayed by the taste of their clients, nevertheless are willing to fulfill their dreams. In the first part of this chapter, I will show how the neoclassical Empire style was revived to register the status of the middle class and the nouveau riche. On the other hand, architects who resisted commercial catalogues and mass production proclaimed their interest in cultivating a form of architecture that represented the call for tradition promoted by the state. This postcolonial patriotic quest for an "Indonesian architecture," as I will discuss in this chapter, re-enacts the earlier strategy of "Indische architectuur," which emerged under the colonial condition.

In between or above these two positions, there were also architects who believed that their work could be adequately independent of any ideological encroachments of both capital and the state. They held to the belief in the truth inherent in forms and styles. In the last section of this chapter, I will discuss this presumably avant-gardist position through the work of Budi Lim and show how his refashioning of art deco neither resists commercialization nor adheres to a nationalist viewpoint. Instead, through architecture, Budi Lim seeks to disturb the commercial circuit and twist the nationalistic aspiration even though his architecture makes no reference to any other social and cultural movements. His revival of art deco, while intended to create a "sense of place" for the main streets of urban Java, provokes a profound sense of displacement, which could thus be seen as a critical commentary on the contemporary "development" of Indonesian cities. In this sense, this approach is equally, if not profoundly, political and cultural.

In this chapter, instead of subsuming culture and consciousness under official nationalism or the logic of capitalism, I want to see all the different architectural positions (the commercial, the national, and the "avant-garde") as architects' imaginary responses to the problem and contradiction of the New Order and its history. These different architectural strategies, each in its own way, confront the dilemma and the question embedded in the establishment of postcolonial Indonesia. Few architectural styles have offered architects more strategies for grappling with the social and political conditions in which they are embedded than the three prior forms of representation associated with the Empire style, Indische architectuur, and the Nieuwe Bouwen. The reappearance of these styles in the postcolonial period constitutes an architectural discourse of "the past in the present."

THE RISE AND FALL OF THE EMPIRE

It is not difficult to imagine why the neoclassical style of architecture is termed the "Empire style" in Indonesia. The public recognize it as a building of Greek style (*gaya Yunani*) mixed with its memorable Roman columns (*kolom Romawi*). It refers to the rule of Governor General Marshall Herman Willem Daendels (1808–11) who first introduced this style to represent the formation of the colonial state in the Dutch East Indies, following similar architectural representations in Berlin, Washington, and his own Paris. The style visualizes order for it is, after all, based on a clear system of order. Nothing could be more perfect to represent the authority of a government that desired clear details and monumental appearance. Presidents and governors of Indonesia have all reused Empire style buildings to register their presence. The Provincial Government of Semarang, for instance, reuses an Empire style villa (once owned by a prominent Dutch family) as the seat of its government. An article on this building explains why the building survives the onslaught of time and politics:

> This building complex is the only governmental building with a European architectural style that combines the architecture of Greek and Roman classicism. The integrity of the architecture is reflected in the classical style of the Ionic column and the carefully crafted ornamental facade. The brick structure adds elegance to the building, which resembles a *villa* [in English]. The building creates a strong character for the main street of Jalan Pemuda. Moreover, it makes the whole complex of the city hall appear formal and monumental.[9]

We could say that the monumental appearance of, and the prominent position given to, the government building in the overall layout of the town made the Empire style a sign of authority, order, and prosperity. However, what we get from the comment is that the Empire style building actually gives a sense of place to its surroundings. The power of the style provides a context for the main street and the entire government complex. This aesthetic appreciation is ironically contradicted by the memories of decolonization signified nevertheless in the name of the street, *pemuda*, a term that alludes to the revolutionary youth of 1945.

As a powerful symbol capable of contradicting history and memory, it is no wonder that the Empire style has been a favorite among the Indonesian ruling elites since the nineteenth century. It was variously adopted by the *bupati* (the Dutch-appointed Indonesian regents who administered particular regions in Java) for their residences. An example of this can be found in the photo album collection of Woodbury and Page where the late nineteenth-century regent's house is built in the Empire style (see figure 21). Flanked on two sides by rows of houses belonging to the regent's subordinates, the regent's residence stood as a focal point in front of the square. This spatial organization created a perspective for the glorification

Figure 21 The regent's house in Tjianjur, 1874. Reprinted courtesy of KITLV from Steven Wachlin, *Woodbury and Page.*

of the regent who, nonetheless, was hidden behind the Greek facade. The Empire style has also found a place in key institutions in the economy such as offices, hotels, and banks. The Javasche Bank, established in 1827 and with several branches in the major cities of the Netherlands East Indies, adopted the Empire style as its official trademark. In Surabaya, Liem Seeng Tee, a tobacco businessman, took over a neglected Empire style building in the early twentieth century. Liem kept the Greek facade but innovatively wrapped the Greco-Roman columns with the giant image of Jie-Sam Soe cigarettes. Ordinary Indonesians might have mixed feelings about the Empire style, but they too embraced images of authority and connections to the source of colonial power. The central piece of the Empire style — the Greco-Roman columns — could also be found in the houses of Indonesian lower-ranking civil servants. Josef Prijotomo has shown that in the 1930s, many houses in the kampung where Indonesians lived were built with the image of the Empire style in their minds.[10] We could even speculate that a network of Empire style buildings was sporadically formed according to a hierarchical relation within the patrimonial sociopolitical system.

However, with the introduction of the Ethical Policy at the beginning of the twentieth century, the Empire style was marginalized.[11] The new colonial politics based on a desire to emancipate (or better pacify) the colonized demanded a different form of architectural representation. The cohort of Dutch architects arriving in the Indies at the beginning of the twentieth century embodied such a change. Sharing the critical mood of the new century, these architects found the Empire style both too rigid and too old fashioned to represent the new age of technology and the new political culture of the state. For these architects, the Empire style not only represented the whole ancient regime saturated with feudalism and exploitative imperialism but was also a stumbling block for progressive change.[12] Unlike Mr. Liem, the tobacco king of Surabaya, the Indonesian bupatis, and the kampung elites who continued to refashion Greek columns, Dutch modernist architects trashed them altogether. Distinguishing themselves from the bureaucrats (who still favored the Empire style), the new cohort of architects sought to dismantle the earlier forms of representation in order to put a new colonial culture in place.

The new mood of the time gave rise to two distinctive architectural movements: Indische architectuur and the Niewe Bouwen. Their significance lies not only in their originality in appropriating the contemporary zeitgeist but also in their dissociation from the Empire style. In this sense, the Empire style acted as a negative catalyst for the new design movement, one that came as an imaginary resolution for the Ethical Policy. Since that time, the Empire style has continued as a kind of outdated, residual style of architecture. It has found its restitution more than half a century later in the hands of the new postcolonial middle class, especially since the 1980s. The postcolonial resurrection of the Empire style no doubt results from the attention given to it by Indonesian elites during the colonial era. Today, we find the Empire style in modernist floor plans, in the facades of middle-class housing, and in the kampung neighborhood. Such popularity might be attributed to the continuing aesthetic appeal of classicism, but its continuity is also related to the sociopolitics of the place in which it is embedded. Let me now turn to our own time.

THE EMPIRE STRIKES BACK

How and why did the new rich and middle class find the discarded Empire style a viable architectural form for their emerging class identity? A simple answer is that the formation of the Indonesian middle class is inseparable from the political culture of the state. The classical (which evoked the image of government even as it is foreign to the vocabulary of "tradition") provides a language for the middle class to express its architectural identity. Moreover, in contemporary real estate development, the Empire style is eminently marketable. The signifying of money (for example, the bank building), the connection to the state, and access to the classical West are all interconnected. And, since its formation in the social field of the New Order, the Indonesian middle class has long been searching for an identity that would best represent itself as close to but different from the national culture. Members of the middle class have also been trying to find a style that allows them to differentiate themselves from their "lower-class" counterparts. The Empire style might be seen as a radical move away from the national culture, but members of the middle class continue to invest it with the idea of modernity, prosperity, and power. They believe that this past and provocative form is capable of providing a significant context to their surroundings, endowing the places where they live with culture, authority, and a sense of being well off.

Middle-class homeowners mobilize the architrave, Ionic-Corinthian columns, and the grand staircase as elements of their houses and organize them from the interior to the fence. Others refashion the Empire style and "modernize" it by simplifying the ornamentative order with "a touch of French elegance." This kind of stylistic mutation has occurred in various new towns where the Empire style continues to proliferate. For example, Ciputra, a major real estate developer, while organizing its spaces around different individual styles and names, offers the Empire style though it is conceived as "classical-modern."[13] For the new town, the Empire style certainly does not belong to the past and neither is there need to mark a difference between past and present. What is at stake is the revival of the "old," which in turn gives power to the "new."

Yet, the capacity of the classical to permanently perform its timeless values through various mutations ironically undermines its original meaning. As more (if not all) houses are designed with a similar style, the monument loses its singularity. Duplication in proximity runs against the capacity of the Empire style to unite perspective (see figure 22). "Classical-modern" style on the other hand conjoins Indonesia past and present without memories of conflict, with a sense of irony, and without historical consciousness. It also erases memories of colonialism to which the original style is attached. Perhaps we could say that the reference here is not to the colonial past, but to the Disney-like global world that enters Indonesia in tandem with the spread of consumer culture. With "classical-modern," there is in fact no difference between Disney-like architecture and the colonial-infused Empire style. We could say that the "classical-modern" of the new town ignores specific memories of colonialism by creating the

Figure 22 The return of the Empire Style: A house in North Jakarta. Photo by A. Kusno.

sense that the Empire style belongs not to the Indonesian past but to an ahistorical world. By doing so, it turns past-present relations into a new kind of relationship, unrealizable in the modernist tradition of the early twentieth century. If the Dutch architects at the turn of the century saw no space for reconciliation with the Empire style, its present revival offers the possibility of bringing the past and present together in a single framework. Given the intellectual tradition of architecture in Indonesia (and its memories of countering the Empire style at the beginning of the twentieth century), it comes as no surprise that the revival of the neoclassical by the new town is largely despised by architects of the postcolonial generation.

Repressed from the modernist architectural tradition for several decades, the Empire style can now be seen as returning with a vengeance. It reassembles fragments of architecture associated with "Western" civilization and expresses them as a living (instead of colonial) heritage of Indonesia. When we see the proliferation of Corinthian columns, Greek temples, and Roman features in upscale real estate, middle-class housing, and also the kampung neighborhood, we begin to understand that the Empire style of postindependence Indonesia is the best representation of the nation's paradoxical history. It is a representation engendered by its experience as an independent country whose expression, however, is intimately linked to Western representations of status and power. If there is anything authentic in the revival of Empire style that goes beyond the simplistic notion of postmodernity, it lies in the subconscious acknowledgment of Indonesia's paradoxical history.

The path that the Empire style revival takes is thus different from that of the conservationist. Instead of resorting to the preservation of the past monuments, the middle class engages with the monument by refashioning it, not for the sake of the past, but for the strengthening of its own present authority and class identity. We might say that the "classical-modern" points to the prosperity of the (post)colonized and their capacity to become equal with the West. However, in all its stylistic mutation through the Disney-inflected world, it also reveals the colonial legacies of the Indonesian state that the nationalists sought to suppress. It makes visible the contradiction of development and provides the site for the struggle over class and power at the symbolic level.

THE GHOST OF INDISCHE ARCHITECTUUR

In 1982, in the relatively quiet royal town of Yogyakarta, miles away from the center of the Empire craze, the governor of Central Java issued a decree that all government buildings in his region should use the "Joglo"—the traditional roof of a Javanese house—as a symbol of nationalism. This decision was related to the fact that the governor had been offended by the design of a hospital near his office that had adopted the Empire style for its facade. The governor proclaimed: "We have Joglo architecture which is more beautiful, why use foreign architecture? . . . Is it appropriate for this foreign architecture to be juxtaposed with the existing statue of our national hero? . . . In essence, no matter how much it would cost [to replace the Greek facade with a Joglo one], I will be the one responsible, because it is very important for the pride of the nation."[14] To placate the governor, the facade of the hospital was reconstructed, resulting in a Javanese look with a Joglo roof. The governor's iconoclastic decision against the Empire style came in the 1980s, at the height of the traditionalist turn in Indonesian official nationalism. The controversy over "Indonesian architecture," which I will discuss below, relates in some ways to this event in Central Java, which itself can not be separated from the sense of prosperity and the speeding up of development in the 1980s, compounded by the insecurity felt by the New Order state and the need to restore authority by using traditionalistic cultural imagery.

By the end of the 1980s, with economic growth at around 6 percent for fifteen continuous years, the state confronted, for the first time, a middle-class generation that was both supportive and critical of its regime. This middle class, while sharing with the state its fear of "communism" and the "underclass," also aspired to democracy, the rule of law, and human rights. In 1974, a riot took place in Jakarta, which signaled, for the first time, the contradictions of "development." A series of student demonstrations in 1978 and 1979 convinced the regime that the nation was going through a period in which it found itself confronted by the generation that had grown up in its own cradle. Several authoritarian measures were taken, such as the imposition of strict controls on universities, mandatory education on national ideology, and turning into law the principle of unity (*asas tunggal*). The youth, according to the state, had gone astray, misled, in part, by the insidious forces of globalization and urbanization. To remind the younger generation that "Indonesia is a bequest from the old to the young," President Suharto ordered the reeducation of the public, especially the youth, on the ideology of the New Order. Here I just want to emphasize that the basis of national ideology is the traditional village family, believed to embody the authentic identity of "Indonesia."

By the 1980s, the state had begun its campaign for order, harmony, and authority, qualities that were assumed to be embodied in a "traditional" village. Suharto indeed identified himself with the village and often emphasized his own rural origin. The perceived stability of the village was seen as challenging the unpredictability of the city and as a reminder to the youth of their origins, where they had come from and where they should return. The village embodies "our ancestors' way of life." It is deeper than history. "Our ancestors' way of life dates back to before the arrival of Hinduism, before Buddhism, before Islam, before Christianity and before the arrival of ideology. . . . Thus if we want to be convinced of the truth, why should we reach for other ideologies, be they socialism, communism, Marxism or even liberalism and religion. . . ."[15] This allusion to history sidesteps historical phenomena as powerful as Islam, colonialism, and modernity. The reference to the village is also not generic, but Java-centric. The world's religions and ideologies are great and powerful, but their intermingling with Java strengthens the latter. Java has been absorbing historical phenomena instead of being displaced by them—so the story goes. The "ancestral way of life" is beyond history and ideology. The transposition from Hindu to Javanese Hindu and then Indonesian Hindu indicates the absorption and the transformation of Hinduism as it enters into the sphere of Java, the core of Indonesia. Within this logic, it's surprising to see the minimal identification with the West in the cultural formation of "Indonesia" as if the history of the Dutch in Indonesia took place only at the periphery if not at the margins of Java.

To return to the event in Central Java, the rejection of Empire style and the allusion to "traditional authority" as exemplified by the governor of Central Java could be seen as part of the discourses of the New Order coping with the contradictions of "development." In a more general way, this contradiction is the dilemma to which "Indonesian architecture" responds as an imaginary resolution. The discussion about "Indonesian architecture," mobilized under themes such as "traditional architecture," "toward Indonesian architecture," "the role of cultural identity in architecture," "Indonesian traditional architecture," "the architecture of Pancasila," "Asitektur Nusantara," and "Indonesian tropical architecture," can be seen as an attempt to grapple with the dilemma in the 1980s.[16] Yet no one seems to have a satisfactory answer to the question as to "what Indonesian architecture actually is." There is also no clear answer as to how far and to what degree architects under the New Order related themselves to the maintenance of official nationalism. What is clear, however, is that many architects and academics strongly disagreed with the parochial Javanese nationalism of the governor of Central Java. In many respects, architects of the New Order avoided the trap of ethnocentrism by conceptualizing "Indonesian architecture" in a broad sense, even though they could not come up with a clear idea of what that thing called "Indonesian architecture" really is.

In the middle of the passionate discussion on, and confusion over, issues about "Indonesian architecture," at least one building proclaimed itself as articulating a language for an "Indonesian architecture." The University of Indonesia (see figure 23) was designed by a consortium of architects teaching at the faculty of Engineering.[17] The significance of this building lies not

Figure 23 Citing vernacular building concepts: The typological approach of the rectorate tower of the University of Indonesia. Design by Gunawan Tjahjono and the University of Indonesia design team. Photo by A. Kusno.

only in its name, which bears the national identity, but also in the attempt made through architectural form to negotiate with the political culture of the state. First, the university, located on the outskirts of the city, clearly contributes to the politics of control of campus-based activities. But the university also offers a design that seeks to avoid or counter ethnocentric nationalism. Instead of privileging one culture, the architecture of the University of Indonesia incorporates fragments of various cultures and synthesizes them to create a broadly based imagery of "Indonesia." It calls on various types, elements, and spatial concepts and manages them in ways that would prevent any one image from dominating. The spatial layout constitutes a decentralized cluster of faculties. These multiple centers are effective in limiting the concentration of crowds, but they also dissolve the idea of the center and unity in the Javanese concept of power. The University of Indonesia thus could be seen as a statement of "Indonesian architecture," one that responds to the questions posed by the ethnocentric nationalism that prevailed in the 1980s.

The framework of the architecture of the University of Indonesia was

Figure 24 Bandung Institute of Technology, designed by Henri Maclaine Pont.
Photo courtesy of Iwan Sudradjat.

undeniably innovative and arose from a specific context of political negotiation, economic dislocation, and cultural change in the 1980s. But it also
recalls an earlier strategy of architecture in the early twentieth century
identified loosely as "Indische architectuur" in which Dutch architects
such as Henri Maclaine Pont played a major role.[18] Like the architects of
the New Order, Maclaine Pont responded through his work to a situation
of change in the political cultures of his time. The Bandung Institute of
Technology that Maclaine Pont designed could be seen as an imaginary
answer to the Ethical Policy. Like the architects of the New Order, Pont
was conscious about using things associated with the idea of tradition,
but he synthesized vernacular forms to create a new kind of architecture.
Like the architects of the University of Indonesia, Pont too quoted architectural elements from various places and composed them to make a new
statement that did not privilege one element over the other. His architecture, like the architecture of the university, thus transcended the cultural
context to which the elements belonged. He elevated them to a metalevel,
constituting thus the idea of the translocal "national" culture of Indonesia
(see figure 24).

Can we then say that the New Order architects (unconsciously) picked
up the architectural strategy of the Indische architectuur for a building

that bears a postcolonial national identity? Like Maclaine Pont, architects of the New Order rejected mindless copies of Indonesian architectural traditions, but behind their objection was a desire to maintain a firm relation with these traditions. Like Maclaine Pont, Indonesian architects also use the principle of synthesis and don't just copy the symbols of a particular place or ancient regime. The synthesis presumably creates a broadly based idea of Indonesia.

During the time of Maclaine Pont, modern architecture became not only a symbol of cooperation between "the East" and "the West," but also took part in guiding Indonesia into the modern world. In a similar way, architects of the postcolonial times were challenged to come up with an architecture of order, harmony, and authority to guide Indonesia through the developmental world. If the new colonial policy in the early twentieth century demanded a form of architectural representation that was different from the Empire style, the New Order of Suharto suggested cultivation of an architectural representation that was based on the way of life of "our" ancestors.

If these parallels make sense historically and aesthetically, the architecture of the University of Indonesia could be seen as drawing on Indische architectuur. The stylistic affinity between Indonesian architecture and Indische architectuur indicates that the latter is by no means a closed historical issue. It has now returned in what we call "Indonesian architecture." Both "Indonesian architecture" and "Indische architectuur" rejected a simple copy of the local and the global. And they were mutually interested in finding a subtle way of countering the Java-centric regimes promoted by both the colonial and postcolonial states.

THE ZEITGEIST OF ART DECO

Architectural historian Donald Langmead points out that Holland's architectural debate through the 1930s was "between the Nieuwe Bouwen — Modernism, Internationalism, Objectivity, Functionalism — and the Delft school."[19] In the colony, a site that is completely overlooked by Langmead in his account of Dutch modernism, these two opposing views expressed themselves in Nieuwe Bouwen and Indische architectuur. The dialogue between them however was inseparable from the new colonial state's ideology of development.

As we have seen, the Indische architectuur of the early twentieth century claimed a "representation of reality" status for its attachment to "local" vocabularies, even as the expression attained a translocal status. Nieuwe Bouwen, on the other hand, shared a common claim with the modernist tradition that it was somehow more "formalistic," more "autonomous" and "universal." Yet, both Nieuwe Bouwen and Indische architectuur shared the thrust of overcoming the Empire style—the symbolic remnants of the nineteenth century's colonial feudal world. Both represented the new colonial society, which by then was ruled not merely by the state and its bureaucrats but also by the power of the market and the wealthy families as well as the increasingly prosperous private citizens (including the middle *orang partikuler* class) (see chapter 6). The claim of the new aesthetic to fashion a progressive strategy for the colony therefore cannot be separated from the maintenance of the social "distinction" and the establishment of the "middle-class" in the colonial milieu. What did Nieuwe Bouwen mean in Indonesia in the past (1930s) and in what ways does this architectural strategy inform the present?

The strong economic resurgence in the 1920s created the need to build professional offices, trading companies, banks, and corporate headquarters, as well as new towns for the European colonial "middle-class" such as the Gondangdia area in Batavia, the New Tjandi in Semarang, the Gubeng and the Darmo areas in Surabaja, and the Polonia in Medan. The expansion of this urban economy in the colony demanded identifiable codes and signs in the cityscape. Few things expressed the sense of the new times more clearly than the buildings recognized as of "*moderen*" style, which by the 1930s had lined the main streets of the major cities in Indonesia (see figure 25).

In Semarang, Liem Thian Joe reported in the early 1930s: "Once we arrived in the urban area where offices and warehouses were located, there were rows of office buildings for banks, shipping companies, exporters, importers, brokers and lawyers. There were various kinds of buildings that were built in modern [moderen] and healthy ways. All these indicate the progress [kemadjoean] of the city. . . . People can see this immediately once they pass through this part of the town."[20] We do not know exactly the stylistic reference of *gedong moderen* (modern building) that Liem encountered, but for these "economic" types of edifices Nieuwe Bouwen supplied the architectural language. Unlike Indische architectuur (which was implemented mostly in buildings related to governmental and public institu-

Figure 25 The face of the main street in Surabaya, designed by Ir. Th. Van Oyen in the 1930s. Notice its climatic considerations. Reprinted from G. H. von Faber, *Nieuw Soerabaia* (Uitgave NV Boekhandel en Drukkerij H. van Ingen, 1934).

tions), Nieuwe Bouwen was far more popular and widespread among the "middle class." Nieuwe Bouwen registered itself largely in buildings associated with capital (such as companies, shops, restaurants, movie houses, and the residences of the middle class). In the Indies town, the most popular version of this style is art deco. By the late 1930s, the city of Bandung was already seen as joining Bombay and Shanghai as one of the major sites of art deco architecture outside Europe and America. Stylistically complex, art deco is also known for its allusion to historicism, even as the past vocabulary is subject to a playful formalist abstraction. So attractive was this style that by then, the Preanger Hotel (in Bandung), one of the oldest hotels in the Indies, and the Javasche Bank (in Semarang) found it necessary to refashion themselves in art deco clothing, leaving behind their previous Empire style facade.[21]

The new offices of the prominent ethnic Chinese businessman Oei Tiong Ham in Semarang also followed the spirit of the time. Designed by Liem Bwan Tjie, the new art deco building of Oei's office is significantly different from his previous building, which was a prototype for what could be called an Indo-Chinese shophouse.[22] The radical difference between "old" and "new" architectural forms (see figure 26) marked the sense of a

Figure 26 An old building (on the left) contrasts with a new office for the Oei Tiong Ham Concern, designed by Liem Bwan Tjie, 1930. Reprinted from den Dikken, *Liem Bwan Tjie* (1991–1966).

coming of a different time, one that would permanently push out not only the past but also the malaise that hit the Indies in the late 1920s.

Fredrick Jameson suggests that the 1930s was an era that entertained a kind of contradiction between "a wealth of images of the modish, of high styles and fashions, night clubs, dance music, roadsters, and art deco" and "the seamy side of the real, in the form of the great Depression and of gangsters and their saga and characteristic raw materials."[23] The coexistence of these two contradictory modes and the attempt to deal with their differences were expressed in the aesthetic mediation of art deco. Jameson also indicates that as a stylistic expression, art deco — in its fascination with new technology — has also been a style that is most easily pirated by the state and society — by the Soviet Union in the form of socialist realism, by Central Europe in fascist art, in the United States, by Hollywood.

Similarly, in the late colonial society of Indonesia, art deco was available for appropriation by both colonizer and colonized. Rudolf Mrázek has written about this moment of fascination with technology and modish style as characteristic of late colonial Indonesia.[24] Both Indonesians and the Dutch were subjected to the operation and promise of technology even as they shared very different social and political positions. What Jameson characterized as constituting the contradictions of the 1930s, modish fashions, dance music, and gangsters, could all be found in the Indies in the form of night fairs, gramophones, dandies, and fantasies of liberation. In the Indies, art deco represented enthusiasm for technology and new economic and political possibilities. Yet all these enthusiasms were also contained in a normalized situation in which people in the Indies were given a sense that life was good and becoming better (a feeling that coincided with the regime of surveillance and political suppression conducted by the colonial state to ensure the permanent death of the urban popular radicalism of the previous era, on which see chapter 7). The stylized form of art deco thus acted out the struggle for upward mobility among members of the middle class who were trying to come up with new possibilities for what was expected to be a "normal" life.

THE RUINS AND MEMORIES OF ART DECO

How relevant is the art deco style for the architectural strategy of postcolonial times? If in the 1930s, art deco gave images of the modish, what has it turned into fifty years later? This question seems to be answered by the architectural discourse of Budi Lim, who has been practicing architecture since the 1980s. Budi Lim did not experience the modish normalcy of the 1930s, but he did capture the spirit as well as the ruins of art deco in the postwar development of the major cities in Indonesia. Over the course of fifty years, the urban Indonesia where he grew up has undergone a major transformation that has profoundly changed the image of the city. For Budi Lim's generation, the change of the 1980s seems to match that of their parents' in the 1930s. The two eras were both revolutionary in making one feel that the old has been swept away for good.

Yet, just as the old was about to be completely wiped out, Budi Lim took a trip by road in the 1980s to see the major cities of Indonesia and observe the buildings that lined the main streets. In between the ruins of the past and the new developments, he picked up what he identified as the building typology of the prewar main streets (perhaps the series of "gedong moderen" that Liem Thian Joe remembered in his chronicle of Semarang) and reimagined it anew. In the manner of Robert Venturi's and Denise Scott Brown's venture in the main street of Las Vegas, Budi Lim strolled along the main streets of cities in Java. He constructed in his mind a building typology of the Indies towns of the 1930s and 1940s as they appeared to

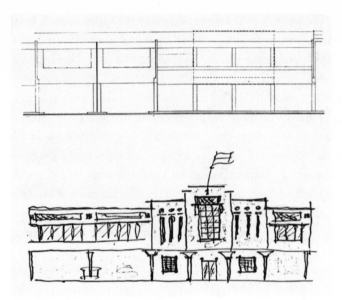

Figure 27 Sketch by Budi Lim for the Bank Universal Wahid Hasyim Branch, Semarang. Photo courtesy of Budi Lim.

him in the main streets of the 1980s. The buildings, he argues, still carried traces of the past. The strongest impression remaining from the Indies towns of the 1930s, he concludes, is of the buildings in the art deco style (see figure 27).

For Budi Lim, these buildings, mostly in decay, should have constituted a kind of cognitive image for the urban population. The deterioration of the buildings should have produced an even stronger feeling that they should be preserved in mental life. Budi Lim seems to believe that once an image has been formed in mental life it will not perish, and in critical circumstances, it can again be brought back to life. Urbanites too, he believes, have become—perhaps subliminally—familiar with the architectural forms they have experienced even though they would not be able to name the forms' styles. Budi Lim is convinced that urbanites recognize and remember certain images (or vocabularies) of the buildings that surround them even though they do not know exactly what the style is or the overall grammar of the art deco building. He believes that people of his generation continue to remember the art deco buildings of the 1930s that once characterized the Indies towns even though many of these buildings have changed their original forms.

We do not know exactly how buildings structure memory or how memory works in relation to buildings, but their linkages are sufficient enough for Budi Lim to create a series of office buildings and shophouses along the main streets of contemporary cities in Java that resembles, or at least reminds passersby of, the (fragmented) image of the prewar Indies town. It is this imagery of past streetscapes, erased by the adverse conditions of wartime and postwar urban development, that Budi Lim, through his architecture, aims at retrieving. As the moment of the 1990s (when most of his works emerged) sped up, a return to the 1930s began to look increasingly like a relapse to colonial times. With development rushing along, bringing the destruction and disappearance of more and more colonial buildings that were then replaced by functionalist boxes, the idea of slowing down and looking at the past seemed to take on more substance. The retrieval, however, was far from simple revivalism. There was no attempt to copy a particular building of the past. What was retrieved in Budi Lim's architecture was only the effect of déjà vu in which the form of the new building would supposedly trigger the memory and imagination of the past townscape (see figure 28).

Consistent with the spread of this Indies art deco style of the 1930s, Budi Lim disseminates his architectural style in major urban centers of Indonesia, thus constituting a form of translocal architectural identity based on the local typology of the main street. The Universal Bank project is perhaps the most characteristic form of his production. Its effect lies in the streets and the spaces with which the building seeks to communicate. The building (small compared to other buildings of its type) is often lost in the large spaces of the main street. Yet it is precisely what is lost in the large main street—like the dream image of the past—that has made Budi Lim's architecture attain its characteristic form.

How can we classify the work of Budi Lim, which offers us another sense of the past in the present? Do any of the stylistic architecture repertoires that we know, including the one Budi Lim himself identified as art deco, seem appropriate for his buildings? Budi's architecture, signified by the asymmetrical composition of solids and voids with masses united by a tower and the corporate logo, is the emblem of art deco architectural strategies generally. Yet, Budi Lim's interest in and appropriation of the typology of the streetscape of the main road of the Indonesian town has made his architecture more than a replica of the international art deco

Figure 28 Bank Universal Wahid Hasyim Branch, Semarang, 1991.
Photo courtesy of Budi Lim.

style. The typology of Budi Lim's architecture is derived from the remnants
of the Indonesian townscapes of the 1930s, even though the latter makes
references to Amsterdam, the Hague, or Shanghai. The architectural language of art deco (available as it is) gives Budi Lim the means to bring
back, in a different and new expression, the "hidden typology" of the past
Indonesian townscape. His decision to return to an earlier form is clearly
driven by some formalistic considerations (as it is for every architect), but
this formalism is also constituted within the social, political, and cultural
contexts of postcolonial Indonesia, which has a collective architectural and
urban memory.

Since it was produced in the 1980s and 1990s, when the ideology of national development had been consolidated, it is tempting to see the "retro"
art deco of Budi Lim as taking part in the construction of the sense of prosperity and progress generated by the state discourse of "development." The
series of buildings he designed for the Universal Bank testifies to the economic boom and hopeful financial future of "development." He brought
back the Indies art deco and reinvested it with a meaning appropriate for
his own time. Perhaps the sense of a new temporality, generated by "development," serves as a kind of gloss on Budi Lim's own interest in art

deco. Budi Lim states that his interest in the urban typology of the 1930s and 1940s is not so much about the stylistic expression of art deco itself. Instead, he is more attracted to the spirit of the time and the energy of optimism that the art deco style of the Indies town seemed to embody. The facades Budi Lim put on for the main streets of the 1980s could thus be said to participate in the optimism of the 1980s as well as repair the decay of the visual environment and the contradictions of "development" itself.

There is, however, another more profound displacement. Seeing this urban form of the 1930s as the embodiment of progressive energy and spiritual optimism that fits well with his own sense of the 1990s, Budi Lim might be seen as producing a form of architecture that is resolutely post-colonial. The irony of looking back and finding a parallel in the colonial past displaces the nationalist historiography. The colonial and the post-colonial share similar architectural signs and codes even as the latter belongs to a radically new age.

Finally, there is yet another displacement, and this reveals the limits of the contemporary discussion about "Indonesian architecture." At the time when Budi Lim was constructing the building series of the Universal Bank, the architectural world of Indonesia was discussing ways to imagine the nation. The source for this imagining was largely confined to "indigenous-vernacular" architecture. This mode of thinking, while drawn critically from official nationalism, might be seen in part as a project for criticizing the transformation of the social and spatial order by the unprecedented forces of commerce. It could be seen as a response to the proliferation of a commercially generated style of architecture.

We do not know if Budi Lim felt the pressure of this debate about "Indonesian architecture." He is, however, mostly fascinated with the urban architecture of the shophouse and the small-scale commercial build-ings that line the main streets, all of which are associated with economic activities in many cities of prewar Indonesia, though these are the activities of small traders and not large corporations. These shophouses were the main feature of the Indies town in the 1930s and 1940s, and they remain dominant in the major cities of postindependence Indonesia even though they are largely ignored or criticized—by the world of Indonesian archi-tecture—for their association with the utilitarian world of the economy. In the discussion of "Indonesian architecture," perhaps the suppression of buildings associated with shophouses should be understood as the situation in which Budi Lim's reinvention of main street art deco came as a strategic intervention.[25]

THE POLITICS OF STYLISTIC MUTATION

In this chapter, I have aimed to show how Indonesian architects appropriated the architectural language of the colonial era for their own creative use. We might read the mobilization of the past architectural paradigms and references to address the contemporary situation as an effort to come up with alternative forms of representation. In some ways, we could also see this appropriation as an attempt to decolonize colonial cultures. Yet the question remains as to just how far Indonesian architects were politically conscious in their appropriation of the colonial forms of representation. The appropriation (or better, displacement) of colonial forms might be seen as merely a transparent, functional, and convenient architectural strategy, with none of the political connotations implied in the term "decolonization." In the architects' own reading, their architectural strategies might have nothing to do with politics even as their architecture, as I have shown, imagines communities both with and against the grain of the "national" interests.

What then have we learned from architecture in contemporary Indonesia? First, the colonial forms of representation continue to be valuable sources for the creativity of the present.[26] But what is more important is that when we examine the reappearance of past styles in contemporary times, we begin to understand that the architecture of postcolonial Indonesia *does* constitute a reflection of the nation's colonial legacies even though such a reflection is expressed through a suppression of the connection. If we find anything authentic in "postcolonial architecture" that goes beyond the label of "westernization," it lies in the architects' unacknowledged acknowledgment of Indonesia's paradoxical history. The true achievement of the architecture of Budi Lim, the displaced Empire style of the new rich, and the architecture of the University of Indonesia is that each in its own way gives visible form to the colonial legacies of the postcolonial state— a knowledge that official nationalism of the state has sought to suppress. Each of them assembles fragments of colonial history and gathers them up in its own private practice before releasing them (somewhat unconsciously) from the nationalist confinement into the public spheres of the university, the bank, the shophouses, and the private residence. In doing so, they represent to the eyes of the public the historical contradictions of postcolonial Indonesia.

In the second place, the colonial styles are opened up for appropriation because their paradigms fit historically with the idea of "Indonesia." What is significant about the three architectural styles that I have discussed is that all of them (art deco, Indische architectuur, and the Empire style) show no commitment to a single particular culture. This aspiration to transcend a particular ethnic culture links the colonial architecture of the past to the idea of Indonesia as a nation. In one way or another, these architectural styles are all hybrids and subscribe to references outside "Indonesia" even as they are connected to local vocabularies. Marked by the trans-local imagery unavailable in the rigidity of ethnic and place-bound architecture, the art deco of the Universal Bank, the Indische architectuur of the University of Indonesia, and the Empire style of the houses of the new rich could be said to be involved in an experiment associated with "Indonesia" — a category marked by an open-ended heterogeneity and looseness as well as the overcoming of a particular ethnic identity.

In this sense, the architecture of Indonesia confronts its colonial past less by evading it than by appropriating it. Part of the reason for the lack of interest in the preservation of the old (namely, colonial buildings) lies in the sense that the old has already been dealt with by quiet appropriation, displacement, and refashioning for the architecture of the present. The engagement with the colonial past, however, did not ask questions of "colonial legacies" and "decolonization." Instead, the reception of "colonial legacies" goes something like this: colonial legacies, in the form of Empire style, Indische architectuur, and art deco, offer Indonesia varieties of choice unavailable in its own local repertoire. Colonial legacies here are accepted with a mix of gratitude and irony as they are displaced to the postcolonial times.[27] In this sense, the way Budi Lim and his contemporaries have appropriated the past allows them to overcome questions of colonial legacies.

Finally, how can we see the appropriation of colonial forms as a critical engagement with power and authority? In one way or another, the architecture of the University of Indonesia was subject to the New Order's authority (which imposed strict controls leading to a long period of decline in campus-based critical activities). The Universal Bank owes its existence to the network of capitalist oligarchy characteristic of the time. The new town and its neo-Empire style contributed to the status consolidation of the middle class and the new rich. In this sense the present architecture of the past, while critically constituting Indonesian history, is vulnerable to the domination of existing power relations. Perhaps this weakness prompts the forgetfulness of "colonial legacies," the subjection to the control of capitalism, and the official nationalism of the state even as the various architectures of the past in the present could all be seen as challenging the authority within which they are embedded.

REMINISCENCES

CHAPTER 6 **COLONIAL CITIES IN MOTION**
Urban Symbolism and Popular Radicalism

> In fact, urban experience and in particular the struggle for the city (for
> its preservation and restoration, for the freedom of the city) provide the
> setting and objectives for a number of revolutionary actions. —HENRI
> LEFEBVRE, *EVERYDAY LIFE IN THE MODERN WORLD*

In chapter 5, I showed how Budi Lim's formal reference to the art deco of
the colonial Indies town operates as a commentary on both the past and
the present. For Budi Lim, the crucial thing about art deco lies not only
in the disappearing imagery of the colonial townscape that the styles of
art deco represent but also in the modernist spirit of the colonial age that
speaks through them. The strategy of taking up a symbol of colonialism
and reinterpreting it in postcolonial Indonesia suggests that perhaps, at
one point in Indonesian history, some aspects of modernist colonial architecture had already allowed for the resistance of the Indonesian population to colonial rule. It raises the question of how colonial architecture
of the early twentieth century might have helped shape the formation of
alternative identities for the Indonesians under Dutch colonial rule. In
this chapter I show how and why the new visual environment of the early
twentieth century contributed to the formation of political consciousness
in Java. The historical question for such an inquiry is why did popular radicalism and modern political consciousness first emerge in areas around
the centers of traditional authority (in the royal towns of Surakarta and
Yogyakarta) and not in the center of modern colonial cities such as of Batavia or Bandung?

In 1924, two years before the Indonesian Communist Party launched

an abortive revolt against the colonial government, Mas Marco Kartodikromo, a young radical who had moved around the urban centers of Java,
observed the city of Surabaya with an eye on what it was like before:

> Now if a person came back to Surabaya after being away for seven or
> eight years, he or she would certainly be amazed at the changes in this
> great city.... The gas and electric lights lining the street lit the place up
> like daylight.... Even at midnight the main streets are still busy—not
> all that different to the daytime. Horse carriages, cars and all sorts of
> vehicles still sped along the roads, sounding their horns loudly. Cine-
> mas like the Royal, the East-Java and dozens of other large cinemas in
> the main market had just finished showing films to audiences of thou-
> sands, who were now streaming out of the "flicks," waiting for taxis or
> other vehicles. Why were the people still waiting even when the film
> was over ... ?[1]

The impact of new urban life and the change in the visual environment
of the city in the early twentieth century had indeed provided the inhabitants of the colonial city of Java with new ways of conceiving both time
and space. Mas Marco was clearly fascinated by the new urban life and
the change in the visual environment of the city. He was a product of the
development of the urban popular "mass" cultures of the early twentieth
century. Mas Marco, however, was also one of the urban radicals charged
by the Dutch colonial government as an agitator of the Indies social order,
and he had to be completely removed from the city in the aftermath of
the communist revolt in 1926. The universe of Mas Marco could be said to
have been opened up by the change of the social and visual environment
such that he then conceived himself as interrelated with the larger world
of the city. This consciousness relied on a sense of being both "urban" and
"modern," a new subjectivity that carried an ultimate political implication:
a sense of anticolonial nationalism, among others.

This chapter concerns the change in the visual environment of the colonial city and how it helped to shape political imagination. What kinds
of architectural and urban spectacles were constructed and what role did
they play in contributing to the formation of alternative identities for the
Indonesians under Dutch colonial rule? How could the colonial city be
understood less as a "form of dominance" and more as something that was
appropriated by the colonized to produce unintended consequences that

contributed to the undermining of colonial power? The focus of this chapter is thus the political implications of the visual environment of the colonial city. I rely on literature and a range of discursive visual representations in documenting how the material city was experienced in its wider social political context. Yet what can we expect from the visual environment?

THE VISUAL ENVIRONMENT

The question of how the visual environment helps constitute the collective subjectivities of the urban population is a persistent challenge to scholars working on the material environment of the city. In the limited world of architecture and urban design, the works of Kevin Lynch on the cognitive image of the city have popularized this question.[2] Various scholars have taken it up including Marxist cultural critics such as Fredric Jameson who expands the concept to the realm of the political (which Lynch ignored).[3] The notion of "cognitive mapping," for instance, raises the question about the difficulty (as well as the possibility) of forming a collective political consciousness in a city seized by the ever-changing forms of capitalism. What sort of understanding do people bring to the nature of their involvement with the visually perceptible built environment? How can we account for the role of the built environment in helping to form collective identities and a changing political consciousness when various and often conflicting meanings can be invested in a single image, form, or object?

Visually perceptible forms (such as buildings and their symbolic elements) can be seen as not merely expressing a social and political system but also as helping to constitute the subjectivity of the people who live in and through them. However, we cannot fix the meaning of an urban form nor can we assume full knowledge of a subject's actions embedded in physical space. An object, a building, or an environmental form like a street may invite many different interpretations from many different people, and some interpretations may be labeled misinterpretations. Yet, it is precisely the fragmentary, multiple, incomplete, and imprecise nature of the experiences of the visual and spatial environment that has made the interpretative reading of the image of the city so important. It may be that some idiosyncratic misinterpretations (on the part of those who experience the city) are actually teasing out aspects of spatial experience that otherwise might remain unarticulated or unstated.[4] It is thus possible to argue for the power of the visual environment in registering subjectivity insofar as that power is seen as merely contributing to rather than determining the experiences of people.

This chapter suggests the importance of keeping alive the interpretation of the visual environment even as the experience of the city is subject to multiple interpretations. I seek to unpack the social meanings of the built environment and indicate the acts of interpretation that Indonesian people (might) have made of the visual and spatial environment created by or for them during what Takashi Shiraishi identified as the early twentieth-century colonial "age in motion" (zaman pergerakan). I interpret some discursive events, visual materials, and accounts from recollections and works of fiction in order to explore the implications of the changing visual environment on the development of popular radicalism in the early twentieth-century urban Indies.

In order to account for such discursive relations between society and space, let me first trace some cultural expressions of urban popular radicalism in the early twentieth century. In their studies of late colonial cultures of Indonesia, Rudolf Mrázek, James Siegel, and Takashi Shiraishi have argued that there was a profound engagement of Indonesian social and political movements with the urban environment of the city.[5] From their studies, we can now be sure that changes in the urban environment of the early twentieth century can be seen locally (if not globally) as a political catalyst. To give Shiraishi's formulation of the "age in motion" a spatial context, we can say that it was in the city that "'natives' moved ('bergerak'), in their search for forms to express their new political consciousness, put in motion ('mengerakkan') their thoughts and ideas, and confronted the realities of the Indies in the world and in an age they felt to be in motion."[6] In this chapter, I draw on insights from the studies of Shiraishi and Mrázek, but I pay more attention to the ways in which the visual environment of the city interacted with the urban population and explain how and why the emergence of political consciousness first took place in the Javanese royal centers such as Surakarta.

I also discuss some aspects of the changing urban symbolism of the royal town of Solo (the capital city of Surakarta in Central Java) and consider how the new visual environment might have provided the cognitive framework for social processes of consciousness change. Why and how did popular radicalism and modern political consciousness in Indonesia first emerge in areas around the heart of traditional authority (in the royal towns of Surakarta and Yogyakarta) and not in the centers of colonial cities such as Batavia or Bandung? I then explore the general development of the visual environment of the Indies town in Java and raise questions concerning the connection between changes in the visual environment and the emergence of popular radicalism in early twentieth-century colonial cities. I begin by calling attention to some cultural fragments of anticolonial political consciousness that found expression in the urban spaces of the early twentieth-century colonial town.

THE URBAN GENERATION AND THE RADICAL "AGE IN MOTION"

As was mentioned in the introduction, on 3 April 1920, someone named Doelriadi called attention to the dilemma and leading question of his time. He wrote, perhaps to his own astonishment, a short statement entitled "Zaman baharoe" (The New Time) on the front page of *Persatoean Hindia*, a newspaper based in one of the once relatively sleepy royal towns of Central Java:

> The notion of "moving" [bergerak] not only means "striking" [pemogokan]. It also refers to what in Javanese is called "change" [obah]. Ten years ago, the movement [pergerakan] of our nation [bangsa Hindia] was marked by the desire [kemaoean] among young people to obtain a job in the government. . . . Now the era is asking for a different thing. It is no longer interested in the notion of honor. Instead it honors money. Our young people will go where there is money [mengejar wang]. . . . Recently however, the movement has gone in yet another direction. Besides the pursuit of money, people are looking for "human rights" [hak kemanoesiaan] and freedom [kemerdikaan]. In this era, virtually everyone in our nation, young and old, men and women, are chasing freedom and human rights. These two words are their favorite [buah bibir].[7]

Doelriadi could not help but notice that something in the life of his social environment had gone awry. He however embraced the change as inevitable and was convinced that the new time (zaman baharoe) had everything to do with the push and pull of money that came in tandem with the consciousness of freedom and human rights. He preferred to leave to the mystery of history the question of "who is moving us so." He was more interested in pursuing the political implications of the combined energies of money, human rights, and freedom that were associated with the desire of having both individual and collective accesses to urban modernity. Ignoring the advice and wishes of their parents, Doelriadi and his friends (from both high and low) could be said to belong to the urban generation that defined modernity as a condition (a zaman) that provoked struggles for money, individual rights, and social justice. Members of his generation seemed prepared to consume what the city could offer (through pursuing capital), struggle for their rights to the city (according to human rights), and liberate themselves from colonialism (to achieve freedom).

The connection between political consciousness and urban modernity seemed to be widespread. It moved to various urban centers in the Indies and was expressed through the notion of "movement" (pergerakan), which took on a literal and metaphorical meaning. In Sumatra, Hamka (a Sumatran religious scholar and a leading figure in the struggle for national independence) was also moved by the new times. In 1924 he prepared for his first trip to Yogyakarta to see for himself the Sarikat Islam (SI) (the first large-scale modern Indonesian political organization), which was on the rise. But there was something more to his trip. Hamka was particularly interested to see Tjokroaminoto, one of the charismatic leaders of the SI, of whom he had heard so much. People in Hamka's kampung spoke very highly of Tjokroaminoto and referred to the leader as "tjermin auto" (the mirror of an automobile) because "his brain is said to be as clear as the mirror of an automobile."[8] The transposition of Tjokroaminoto's name to an automobile part indicates a profound integration of the Indonesian political world into the popular culture of the modern city. This sense that the city was on the move, as if riding in an automobile, had affected people's self-identity and identification. The idea of seeing oneself "in the mirror" and "as a mirror" connoted the particular consciousness of one's appearance in the public associated with urban modernity—how one thought about oneself as one was constituted as a new subject of the city.

As Hamka was preparing to witness for himself the mirrorlike brightness of the SI leader, Mas Marco had already described the emergence of a new type of urban Indonesian in Java who made his appearance in the city as if he was seeing himself in the mirror. In 1924, Marco described this mutually constitutive relation between the city and self-fashioning in his short story titled "Tjermin boeah keroyalan" (The Mirror of Living Royally). Mas Marco described his protagonist in the following way:

There was a young clerk from a trading company in the crowd who was walking about at the Boeloeplein intersection as if he was waiting for someone. Now and then he would look down at the tips of his newly polished shoes — perhaps because they were getting dusty again. He was wearing a newly laundered white shirt and trousers, which he thought made him look smart. The rain coat he held in his left hand and which he had recently borrowed at a small cost from an Arab in Kampung Melayu also added to his good looks. His newly cut hair was covered by a grayish white boursaline hat. A silver watch chain hung on his chest and was threaded from his top pocket to his button hole, even though he had no watch. This really gave him a stylish appearance.[9]

This young man was not rich, Mas Marco told us, but "he did not want to be left out while others were out on the town having fun. . . . Although he had just been paid that morning, he really didn't have enough to pay for a meal. For him though that was nothing."[10] He was a new type of man in the Indies, one that despite not having much money would not want to be left out from an engagement with the city. Rudolf Mrázek refers to these young men as the first Indonesian dandies, "ex-natives," new subjects who could not be adequately classed as "natives" for there was no recognized space yet known in the Indies to fit them into. One of them was described by the police as someone who often appeared "with a peculiar skullcap on his head, yellow shoes on his feet, colored eyeglasses on his eyes, and several pens and pencils in his vest pocket."[11] In the eyes of the colonial state, this "modern" man raised a troubling question. For the Dutch "those natives who borrowed Dutch clothes to place themselves in the modern colonial society . . . clearly . . . were not genuine natives. [They were] the new breed that clearly did not fit into the Dutch category of the native."[12] Dutch authority however perceived them as a problem even as the state was largely responsible for their emergence.

Indonesian "dandies," as Mrázek calls them, indeed were one of the results of the Dutch attempt to accommodate the expansion of private businesses and state activities. They were the educated and skilled labor needed for the "modernization" of the colony. Some of them liked to read, write, and exchange books. They belonged to the emerging strata of the orang partikuler (those businessmen or salaried men who worked for private companies). They were never true Javanese aristocratic officials or civil servants of colonial Java. They were not *priyayi*, the nineteenth-century pseudofeudal ideal of the refined, cultivated, leisured, upper-class Javanese. Instead they were independent orang partikuler who were invariably contemptuous of much of the traditional sphere in which their parents had been brought up. They were members of the new times (zaman baharoe in Doelriadi's definition), members of the urban generation who engaged in the unpredictability and freedom offered by the city, which in turn allowed them to play the role of critical observer of modern life. Such men (and they were almost always men) often used clothing to register the new mood of the time, match the interior of the modern office where they worked, and differentiate themselves from others. When they wrote novels (as did Mas Marco), they took the city as the site for their stories.

Yet, the urban modernity of the early twentieth century created not only a different type of person but also implications for the political order of the Indies. These new selves built up by the colonizer to cope with the economic demands of the modern age had returned (in the manner of Homi Bhabha's colonial mimicry) with a threatening gaze.[13] By the 1910s, many of them were haunting the orderly Indies by taking part in street demonstrations, strikes, political rallies and finally, by revolting against the colonial state. Many of them were practitioners of Islam, but they were neither fundamentalist Mohammedans nor messianic proponents from the countryside. Instead they were urbanites who could be described as resolutely "modern."

In his study of the rise and fall of popular radicalism in Java, Takashi Shiraishi describes how the meetings of Sarikat Islam, the first large-scale modern Indonesian political organization, were conducted:

> Here the merry festive mood of the rally and the sense of power and solidarity felt by the SI members are recreated by the visual image of tens of *andong* with the SI flag, (and) the sound of music — probably "Het Wilhelmus" (the Dutch national anthem). . . . This was the rally, the occasion of merry, pleasant festivity. And here every speech was greeted with great applause. But this was not an ordinary festivity to which the Javanese were accustomed. For one thing, the rally was distinctly modern. Music and not *gamelan* sounded. Photographs were taken. People came to the place dressed as they liked — Javanese, European, and "Turkish" (Arabic).[14]

We can appreciate the striking modernity of the scene, but we might also wonder about the process by which the rally came to rely upon urban culture for its authoritative position and how the leaders of the SI came to use a modern medium to mediate their relations with their followers. The rally took the form of a festival, like a theatre performance that included things that were "modern." The scene was also resolutely "urban." The keywords that supported the festivity such as "politics" (*politik*), "organization" (*organisasi*) and "rallies" were all as new as "music," "photographs," and "fashion" to the world of Java. The modern spectacle involving new visual images, the sound of music, and the opportunity of dressing "as they liked" sustained the power of the rally and represented the relative sense of moving in an unpredictable direction characteristic of city life.

The change in urban life was indeed a fundamental aspect of the process of social transformation. Between 1900 and 1925, the population of almost all the major cities in Java grew by more than 100 percent as did the growth of the members of political parties. They were matched by the growth in the number of commodities and different modes of representing them. In figure 29, we see a "new advertisement from M. J. Mohammad," perhaps a distributor, that depicts new commodities dropped from the sky by colonial aircraft.

These commodities were not produced in the colony. Instead they were dropped into the Netherlands East Indies by the "wind of Progress." Nevertheless they were expected to be greeted with astonishment and excitement by Indonesians who would then consume them. One could argue that providing these commodities was a form of cultural imperialism, but it also moved the Indies in a most unpredictable way. The motion of commodities moved the time forward by promising if not generating new possibilities for one's self-representation even though this often had quite varying implications. M. J. Mohammad claimed to be advertising new products. The advertisement appeared to address everyone who had the right to consume and a freedom to choose. These dandies must have encountered such advertisements for in them we can discern the contours of a modern urban community. They were awakened by the commodities that accompanied the increasing participation of Indonesians in a modern urban life associated with politics. Their explicit outcry in the form of "urban social movements" (such as rallies, strikes, and later the revolt)

Figure 29 Advertisement from *Bintang Hindia*, 1924 that states: "New Kind of Advertisement from M. J. Mohammad," showing new goods arriving by airplanes. The Indonesian "awakening" was accompanied by the consumption of both capital and commodities. Reprinted courtesy of publisher from James T. Siegel and Audrey R. Kahin, *Southeast Asia over Three Generations: Essays Presented to Benedict R. O'G. Anderson* (Ithaca, N.Y.: Southeast Asia Program Publications, Cornell University, 2003).

could be said to be a contingent product of these visual representations, although it struck the Dutch as the "native awakening" in the Indies in the first quarter of the twentieth century.

Yet, for the city to be felt as awakening and moving, it would need to be compared to something considered as "still" and "unmoving."[15] To see how the city might be considered as on the move, we need to look at a comparative moment at work in the visual environment of the city in the early twentieth century. This will also explain why popular radicalism first arose most profoundly in the centers of "old" Javanese power such as Surakarta and Yogyakarta and not in the capital city of Batavia or the "European" cities of Bandung and only later in the port cities of Semarang and Surabaya.

The popularity of western fashion, automobiles, and movies among people in Java reflected not only new forces at work in society (a new zaman as in Doelriadi's report) but also a crisis in the representation of traditional power. Earlier, it made sense that the realm of Java, in a metaphysical sense, was seen by many as embodying the equilibrium between the outer and inner states of mind, for Java is considered as *"jiwa"* — the depth and soul of a human. But during the age in motion, the order of things had become very different.

Benedict Anderson has observed that three of the four rulers in contemporary Java held a title that indicated the centrality if not the fixity of their position as the sustainer of equilibrium — Paku Buwana (Nail of the Universe), Hamengku Buwana (Sustainer of the Universe), and Paku Alam (Nail of the World).[16] This was also expressed architecturally, as Clifford Geertz pointed out: at the center and apex, stood the king who fixed himself as the axis of the cosmos; around him and at his feet, the palace; around the palace was the capital composed of reliable and submissive members who lived in the relatively self-contained royal compounds; around the capital at the periphery were the bondsmen, "getting ready to show obedience," whose dwellings were made of impermanent building materials; and finally the imagined world beyond Java that constituted the outer circle of the political realm. This configuration of space depicted the structure of society.[17] The supreme ruler, his capital, his administration, the artisans, and the commoners must therefore occupy a space that perfectly represents the workings of the universe as a whole.

Politically, the ideal layout of the *kraton* (palace) expressed the position of the king vis-à-vis his subjects. The king was at the center, and everyone else, including his family members, occupied a hierarchical position based on his or her relation to him. Other social norms, governing everything from dress to manners, were also grounded in this hierarchy. Those who were connected, even tangentially, to this structure would be seen as above the masses, even if some member of the latter was far wealthier, financially, than any of those attached to the king. In traditional Java, money was a worldly thing; trade was a worldly occupation and traders were marginal if not outside the hierarchical structure of the kraton. We can thus understand the declaration of Doelriadi, as indicated above, and appreciate the profound transformation he felt in the social life of Java in the early twentieth century when the pursuit of "money," "human rights," and "freedom" had displaced the old attachments and became the prime focus of the new generation.

By the early twentieth century, the architecture of traditional society had indeed been displaced. The royal town of Surakarta, which historian Kuntowojoyo called the "macro-cosmos of the big universe," had been filled with contrasting images that destabilized its position.[18] In regard to the visual environment, tensions had developed around the positions of new buildings that clustered around the kraton complex. Earlier, the office of the kepatihan (Javanese court), the Sanggabuwono stage (the platform of the cosmos), the Grand Mosque, the Bondholumekso (the Javanese pawn house), the Taman Sriwedari, and Taman Balekambang were all understood as forming a synchronic part of the larger kraton complex. However, by the early twentieth century, this set of buildings was countered by another set of buildings associated with the power of the Dutch. The office of the Dutch Resident was counterposed to the office of the kepatihan; the Vastenburg castle to the Sanggabuwono stage; the Purbayan Catholic Church to the Grand Mosque; the Volkscreditbank and Javaschebank to the Bondholumekso. The entertainment places, such as Taman Sriwedari and Taman Balekambang, were also countered by the Schouwburg and the Societiet buildings.[19]

These "countermonuments" formed a paradigmatic ensemble that constituted a system of opposition between the "new" and the "old" power. Along with this, the new syntagmatic linkages of the transportation system and the road network contributed to the undermining of the traditional orientation of the Javanese cosmos. This change in the spatial configuration and visual environment of the city altered not only the cosmological coherence of the royal town but also the city inhabitants' cognitive mappings thus resulting in a new sense of time. From the perspective of Java, the diachronic relations between the two different styles of building were considered locally as disturbing the equilibrium of Java for their presence had pushed away the centrality of the court. Mulyadi et al. report that the Dutch buildings stirred up controversies and were considered locally as undermining the old symbolism and thus engendering a sense of disharmony in Java.[20]

Figure 30 The susuhunan of Solo with a Dutch resident of Solo, emerging from the traditional *pendhopo* sustained by Greek columns. Photo courtesy of Leo Haks, reprinted from Leo Haks and Steven Wachlin, *500 Early Postcards* (Singapore: Archipelago Press, 2004).

The juxtaposition of the two different sets of monuments came to represent the declining authority of Java. The new visual regime recalls the image of the Susuhunan of Surakarta walking on the arm of a Dutch resident of Surakarta. They emerged from the traditional *pendhopo* whose roof by then had been supported by Greek Corinthian columns. The glory of the diminutive king could be maintained only under the guidance of the taller Dutchman. The sense of impotence prevailed even as the ruling class tried to conceal the reality (see figure 30). To return to the urban form of Surakarta, the juxtaposition of monumental buildings represented a state of dependence of the Javanese ruling class on the colonial government. It also offered to the viewer a comparison between what had come before and after the decline of Javanese power. The "disturbing" juxtaposition of different powerful monuments created in the visual environment a new set of coordinates. It created disharmony for the "old" power and displaced its stability, but it also generated new possibilities such as helping to form modern political consciousness.

The visual contradiction embedded in Solo is of particular significance as the mood of restlessness had been growing rapidly at the turn of the century. By 1900, Surakarta (the Javanese center of the universe) had undergone an unprecedented change. The "quiet" Indies town had been filled with sights, sounds, and smells of a "modern" commercialized town.[21] In Kuntowijoyo's words, "the skeleton of the city remained the same, the environment had become entirely different."[22] This change had a lot to do with the circulation of popular culture and the increasing importance of money. Such change intricately challenged the existing configuration of power, status, and identity. Earlier, access to governmental positions (for example, being a civil servant of the Dutch-Javanese colonial regime) was considered paramount in Javanese culture, but now working outside the governmental sphere and having money to access the new aspects of urban culture was considered a far more important enterprise. The pursuit of money (*wang*) and the engagement with human rights (hak kemanoesiaan) and freedom (kemerdikaan), as indicated by Doelriadi above, had created not only tension with the traditional authority but also entailed a rupture of the existing colonial order.

CONSUMING URBAN MODERNITY

A year before Doelriadi proclaimed the arrival of the new times (zaman baharoe) to his fellows in Central Java, Indonesian radical Mas Marco published *Student Hidjo* after it was serialized in his journal.[23] Student Hidjo is a young Indonesian who embodies the new times. He likes to wear a jacket and tie, with pens in his vest pocket. He belongs to the new urban milieu. Marco described him as crossing the border to Holland and, later with his girlfriend, consuming modernity in the urban centers of the Indies. They survey the urban landscape of the Indies town, identified as "PANORAMA" (a word written in capital letters). They engage in picnicking (*plesir*), riding the tramway, exchanging jokes in English and Dutch, and moving in and out of theatres, movie houses, hotels, restaurants, and the milieu of the regent and Dutch officer as if the divided world of the colony is nothing but a single space in flux. The different worlds are flexibly intertwined. Human relations too, unlike in the past, are far more unpredictable, including Hidjo's own relationship with his lover(s). With them he consumes lemonade, exchanges fashionable words in Dutch and English, and wears highly priced clothes from the store. Behind their consumption however, there are attempts to turn the hierarchical order of the

Indies upside down. At one of the novel's climaxes, Hidjo and his friends celebrate their being together by driving around in a car and honking the horn in the royal town of Java as if to wake up the colonial-sponsored ancient regime.

The urban modernity of the early twentieth century provided not only an escape from traditional bonds but also a space for the criticism of that order and the larger colonial-feudal cultures embedded in it.[24] For Marco, the fascinating thing about the city was its invulnerability to the order of antiquity. The possibility of wandering around and engaging with the city and having the flexibility to go by *dokar* (two-wheel buggy), tram, taxi, or simply on foot was in stark contrast to the inaccessibility of the palace and the ritualized performance of the court. Unlike the fixed order of the buildings of the kraton and the Dutch government offices, the commercial buildings (of shops, restaurants, hotels, theaters, and movie houses) allowed experiences to slip along lightly. The visual configuration of the cityscape filled with hotels, restaurants, movie houses, and offices along the main roads was in no particular order except that they all tried to interpellate the passerby through various building styles and billboards. The street scenes composed of the cafes, hotels, restaurants, and theatres were attractive to members of the public who could pay; their attraction stemmed from a sense of detachment from the order of "home" and the old way of life.

As a way of distancing the old, Marco's stories bring together the traditional order and the new, blending them so that the earlier world loses its authority. In this sense, the order of the "Dutch-Javanese town" described above was seen by Marco as a problem to which his urban novel came as an imaginary solution. The hierarchical realm of the court and its declining power (as represented by the presence of Dutch authority) had encouraged an invention of a different and more independent subject position. Through Hidjo and his friends, Marco showed how urban modernity had productively undermined the hierarchical rigidities of colonial Java and helped loosen the urbanite from the grips of both antiquity and colonial order.

Student Hidjo is about not only urban modernity in the colonial context but also the colonial world turned upside down and the imagining of the new world of equality and solidarity. It could be seen as a prose version of Marco's 1917 poem "Sama rasa sama rata" (Solidarity and Equality), which called for a new world and an end to the old hierarchy sustained by both the Dutch government and Javanese aristocrats. Marco's newfound stance against traditional authority (sanctioned by the colonial state) can be seen in his poem that sought to lead his readers in a different direction (against the traditional north-south axis).

> Trust me my brothers
> Orient yourselves only to the east
> Where lies the light [*tjahja*]
> Which will illuminate the world
>
> We call it the sun
> That gives light to the earth
> It lights the day, and hides at night
> Bright and dark are now clear
>
> If you walk on the road
> To the north and south
> You will certainly feel cold
> And mindlessly fall to sleep
>
> You will end up in a place called "Pool"
> The endless sea
> If you try to pass through it
> You will be destroyed
>
> Your body will be frozen
> Like the rigid iron
> Tools of the factory of the sugar plantation
> Steamroller that exploits your people-nation [*bangsamoe*]
>
> Walking to the east will allow you to move around
> Reaching the west you will find
> So you will make another around [*berkitar kitar*]
> Because the world is round [*boendar*][25]

EAST- AND WESTBOUND: THE RAILWAY JOURNEY

The poem of Mas Marco Kartodikromo represented a movement in a different direction. Being east- or westbound (which allows people to "make another around") was constructed to contradict the traditional north-south axis that for centuries had governed the orientation of Javanese traditional authority. Marco perhaps had the map of Java in his mind. Given the shape of the island, there were indeed more things to see if one travels east or west. Marco's consciousness however could also be seen as being informed by the change in the visual environment of the city. By the early twentieth century, the royal town of Surakarta was already known for or symbolized by its "restaurant Doehne, Hotel Slier, Hotel Russche, Restaurant Djiran, Office of Javasche Bank, city tram, *ruituig*, bicycle, horse racing, cars from Cadillac and Oldsmobile, . . . while electricity was already lighting European quarters and main roads."[26] Developed along the main roads leading to other towns in the direction of east and west, Solo was already seen by its residents as merely a part of a larger administrative and commercial network. The expansion of communication and transportation networks had made the "earlier" center only one center among others. Solo and Yogyakarta, the two royal towns of Java, were only stop centers in the chain of railway stations leading to other centers such as Semarang to the north, Surabaya to the east, and Batavia and Bandung to the west. While the Javanese palace had fortified itself with walls as thick as four meters and fixed its orientation to the north and south, the railway and the main street of Java (opened up by the Great Post Way, Groote Postweg) had pulled the orientation of the town in the opposite direction of the east and west, thus drifting the soul of Java farther and farther away from its center.

Mas Marco's poem "Solidarity and Equality" might be seen as belonging to the age of the train, which by then had fully realized the fast track east-west connection.[27] Nothing indeed could more explicitly represent time in motion than the train, especially when the locomotive moved across the countryside. Tan Malaka, a veteran Indonesian communist and a top wanted man by the colonial police, once wrote, as he confronted the new locomotive that pierced into his Minangkabau world (*alam*):

> Just look at this machine! How hard it works! The smoke of its breath is puffing out! I feel the heat of its sweat. Listen to its whistle warning: Step aside! Step aside! I am running! Don't get in my way! How many thousands of kilos of goods I am carrying as I speed on my course! How many hundreds of souls ride behind me! Men, women, girls, boys, children and babies! Step aside, step aside, I cry again. Your danger is my shame! I am responsible for your safety; I must keep to my promise.

One minute late destroys my reputation. My brother the mechanic is directly responsible. James Watt was my grandfather's name. Fast, sure and safe is my slogan. Perfection is my future.[28]

The movement of the locomotive, going in and out of his Minangkabau "world," had made it virtually impossible to make an easy definition of what is inside and outside. His ancestors had been changed, and his alam turned inside out. The locomotive, a prime symbol of the modern age, was taken over by Tan Malaka who was also simultaneously possessed by it. The strong moving object left him with political knowledge and masculinity, a sense of liberation and hope, as well as the burdens of discipline, promise, and responsibility. Yet, his body owed as much to the mechanic and electrician as to the surrounding with which he interacted. They created in him a sense of self. His mobile traveling body, like the locomotive, did not occupy a privileged center of perception. Instead, Tan Malaka and his locomotive embodied each other. This extraordinary mutual embodiment transforms the locomotive from an agent of colonial exploitation (for railways came to colonial Indonesia first to transport goods from plantations) to a vanguard of liberation. Such mutual embodiment between the train and Tan Malaka suspends the binary opposition of the colonizer and the colonized. In his mind, the locomotive conjures up an image of progress (running with full speed), nationhood (carrying many thousands of kilos of goods and many hundreds of souls), and a desire to take over the present (for a perfection of the future). We no longer need to know how and why the locomotive got there in the first place, a condition that paradoxically had allowed it to become an object of dream, fantasy, and the desire to break away precisely from the condition that determined it.

Like Marco, Tan Malaka too belonged to the age in motion. For these radicals of the early twentieth century, the idea of house or home, or the axis of a cosmos that symbolized permanence, posed no attraction. In fact, in most of the Indonesian novels of the early twentieth century, the train was never portrayed as a vehicle used to return to one's "hometown." In Indonesian fiction, the train was often featured as the arena for the comparative world, the imagined future, the revelation of truth, the making of important decisions, and ultimately, the crystallization of political consciousness. It offered a direction to the future no matter how unclear that would be or how one might go astray as one follows the railway.

Moving with the train (in the east-west direction) signified liberation not only for men like Tan Malaka but also for women. Marco told such a story in his *Mata gelap* (The Blind Eyes).[29] The protagonist, Retna Poernama, a somewhat liberated young Sundanese woman, had finally decided to leave her family after an unsuccessful affair with her sister's husband. "Yeah, so be it! Let her [my sister] be angry, but I am not afraid of her. If I were to be expelled from my parents' house because of what I did, I can immediately go to Batavia, Semarang or Soerabaja—in short, to places where I will have no trouble to survive."[30] She wasn't sure of her future, but she felt certain that the train was going to bring her to a city where no one would recognize her and where she could find her new self. From the beginning, the railway journey already offered her such promises. "Although Retno Poernama takes the lower-class compartment, she feels content. What she is seeing in the train makes her happy, and she forgets all about her parents, her relatives, and her hometown."[31]

Retno Poernama didn't know the cities she had in mind but felt sure that she would be able to survive in the urban setting of Batavia, Semarang, or Soerabaja—all major cities in Java. She took a midnight train from Tjirebon (West Java) to Soerabaja (East Java). Not only was Soerabaja the last stop on the train, but it was the farthest point, a place where no one could recognize who she was. Retno Poernama expressed her subjectivity through the train and the city. She was determined to live in a city for the city was a new place that offered her the possibility of not "being known by relatives." The city in fact did not offer her any stability or security for, like the train, it was also on the move. There were, however, various possibilities for her to become someone in the city. At the worst, she thought she still could choose to be a "slave" or a *nyai*.

The city indeed promised possibilities, many *or*s as well as many *and*s. Upon her arrival in Semarang (where the train halted), Retno Poernama was already visited by choices she had to make immediately. "It is so crowded here. I have never seen such a fine [*bagoes*] place. But where should I stay? My sister's servant used to say that there are many hotels around here: Hotel Hindia, Hotel Soerabaja, Hotel Slamet Datang, etc."[32] There were choices as to where one could stay while on the move, just like there were possibilities to become one thing or the other. Behind the encounter with the city and the advertisement of hotels, we can discern the contours of a modern urban community radically different from the one known to Retno Poernama.

ADVERTISING AND URBAN COGNITION

When Retno Poernama was informed that there were many hotels in Semarang: "Hotel Hindia, Hotel Soerabaja, Hotel Slamet Datang, etc," she was, in fact, being visited by advertisements. By 1917, the population of the Indies town had grown "so crowded," and there were many more people like Retno Poernama who were new to the town and needed to be told where they could stay. Hotels were not for locals. They needed to be advertised in order for them to become visible to potential visitors before they arrived. In fact, in the newspapers' advertisement sections, hotels in one city were often featured along with those in other cities: "Hotel Tengger in *Bromo*, East Java at the height of 6,000 meters above the sea; Hotel Toegoe in *Jogyakarta*; Hotel Jansen in *Malang*'s Alon-alon; Hotel Lans in Rembang *Semarang*, and Grand Hotel Noiless & Metripoly with five floors in *Soerabaja*."[33]

The image of the "Alon-alon" (the traditional "piazza" in front of the palace compound) and the image of the grand "five-floor" hotel (presumably one of the highest buildings) were made parallel and equal, both represented selling points of the hotels, and they contributed to the creation of an image for the city where the hotels existed. If advertising commodities brought in the landscape of the world, it also brought to the public the streets where the shops and the hotels were located, thus creating an imagined and cognitive map of the city. Like the train schedule that projected stops at several towns before reaching the final destination, advertisements connected cities and roads and arranged them in a readable format. Lined up in the advertisement section of the newspaper was thus a whole realm of representation that was not only marketing commodities and services but also making the city imaginable. Urbanites were supposed to read into the advertisements a process that created an image of the city as "the city" (see figure 31).

Historian Bedjo Riyanto points out that between 1897 and 1914, *De Nieuwe Vortstenlanden* listed shops in Surakarta and Yogyakarta in a manner that featured the same shops in other cities. "Toko Pianelli Frebes, *Soerakarta* and *Semarang*; Toko Midden-Java, *Djogja, Bandoeng, Solo* dan *Tegal*."[34] The intercities connection represented by the advertisement con-

Figure 31 Advertisement for a chain of pharmacy stores in Weltevreden (Batavia), Soerabaja, Medan, Semarang, Makassar, Djogja, Bandoeng, and Soekabumi, circa 1920s. Reprinted from the advertisement pages of *De koloniale roeping van Nederland* (The Hague: Dutch-British Publishing Company, 1930).

veys the impression that Indies towns are all more or less the same. Such a representation constituted a sense that one's city was merely one city among many others. There was no axis of the cosmos in such a network of cities. There was only a series of nodes that offered passersby another round of moving to yet another city—"so you will make another around," as suggested in Mas Marco's poem. With this sense of unbound seriality, Retno Poernomo was not much concerned about the difference between Semarang and Surabaya.[35] What was important for her was that they were cities that contained different livelihoods such that even in the worst case she could still choose one or the other, an activity similar to picking a hotel from an advertisement.

In the early twentieth century, images capable of being detached and circulated apart from their immediate settings were particularly powerful. They catalyzed the concept of "movement and moving" and extended the field of urban experience by allowing people to see a world they could not immediately apprehend. In Pramoedya's *This Earth of Mankind*, the young

Minke was stunned by what printed photographs could offer: "pictures of landscapes, august and important people, new machines, American sky-scrapers, everything from all over the world—I can now witness for myself on these sheets of printed paper."[36] The images brought together the otherwise unconnected worlds. Seeing the world condensed on printed pages demanded a capacity to make a connection between the objects represented. Yet advertisements were more unsettling than photographs. Readers knew that the worlds presented by advertisements were subject to change and enlargement. There were more to come though always on a provisional basis. While moveable and constantly moving, advertisements arrived as a readable text to be observed with some expected reception. This however also invited a sense of agency. The capacity to consume visual images, such as advertisements, constituted an experience of mastery, even though one had to learn to read the code in order to participate in such a visual world.

In Pramoedya's story, Minke, the pioneer of Indonesian nationalism, could be seen as a product of advertising. It might not be too far-fetched to suppose that advertising contributed to rather than distracted him from the formation of his political consciousness, a consciousness feared by the colonial state. Before becoming a journalist and anticolonial nationalist, Minke created advertisements and short articles for the auction papers. Since Minke wrote and read advertisements, we could expect that he found himself participating in the world-in-motion. In the early twentieth century, when writing and reading was still a new form of practice in Indonesia, it seems that advertising had an unexpected power to draw people to act and imagine themselves anew. For Minke, participation in the world of advertising might have contributed to his habit of arranging his experiences into a readable representation.

Similarly, when Mas Marco composed his urban novels, we could imagine him wielding the visual environment of the city in the manner that Minke organized his reading of printed images. Both were finding ways to explore the authority and community built into the urban life of the early twentieth century. The relation between representation and the city is vividly expressed in Mas Marco's short stories written in 1924. In *Semarang hitam* (The Dark Semarang), Marco wrote about the experience of an orang partikuler reading the city in and out of the newspaper: "A young man turned the pages of the newspaper . . . all of a sudden he came upon an article entitled: PROSPERITY: 'a destitute vagrant became ill and died from exposure on the side of the road'."[37] In dismay, the young man went off to stroll around the city. What he saw there (in another short story about Surabaya) revealed more about the unevenness of the colonial city. Marco's protagonist turned himself from a subject who read the newspaper into a subject who evaluated the city and revealed the hidden truth of the injustices of colonial life. What is also striking is the way in which Marco organized the intersection between realities and representation in a format readable by countless and nameless other "dear readers":

> Yes . . . dear reader! Things are like that. In the big cities of our Indonesia, it is quite common for streets to be called the Heerenstraat—a name which has its roots in the capitalist spirit which divides social classes. If all things were fair, for every Heerenstraat, there should be a Kinderstraat (Children Street), shouldn't there? . . . Usually Heerenstraats are busy, wide and have shops and large tiles along them. It is of course apt that such streets are called Heerenstraat, for along this street in Surabaya are many grand restaurants, like the Simpang Restaurant—establishments whose expensive prices stop any ordinary worker having a drink there. You have to be one of the rich *tuans* (Europeans) to go in there. . . . If we compare the Heerenrestaurant on the Heerenstraat with the Tjap Krusek Warung on a narrow, smelly kampung alley, the capitalist 'caste system' becomes most obvious. . . . In one place people are happy, in another they are sleeping in the rubbish of those drinkers. . . . If you don't have the ability to study high-flown theories from foreign books, it is surely enough to understand the practical realities of everyday life. Comparisons show up injustices, don't they?[38]

Though the unevenness of the colonial city was hardly a surprising item of news, and though Marco's dramatic rendering of his discovery emphasizes the significance of the everyday built environment, his experience alerts us to the role of representations in forming the experience of the city. Before the era of print, news about the ill, the poor, and the dead were available only in oral forms, but in the era of the urban generation of Mas Marco, the oral transmission of such news came only after it was printed in the newspaper.

There is another feature of Marco's reading of the news from the newspaper that brings us back to the visual environment of the city. The physical setting of the city was made into a legible landscape to address political concerns. The streets marked by restaurants and shop fronts each displaying signboards of various kinds became a sight to be read as part of the phenomenon of a larger force of colonial modernity working on the city. If the advertisements, like the rail track, annihilated the spatial distance that connected the whole of Java (and the world), then the main road too brought the world closer to viewers, allowing them to locate themselves within a larger setting. Unlike advertisements, the actuality of urban space quite often stood in contradiction to the imagined fullness of representation. Advertisements and the main street offered the possibility of mastery to consumers, but it was also one combined with despair. While they triggered the sense of "collective consumption," they also heightened feelings of inequality and urban life's inaccessibility.

While Retno Poernama in *Mata gelap* could not help admire the prosperity and fine places of Semarang as she left behind her own town, in *Semarang hitam*, Marco's protagonist reveals the contradictions of the colonial city: the prosperity and the destitution. The unequal order of the urban space was read comparatively to organize a new field of vision so that one could better position oneself within the urban space. Marco made the visual environment of the city readable in a format similar to that of the advertisement that connected images that were otherwise unconnected. However, unlike advertisements, the city was read cognitively, alongside the signs of inequality for in practice the urban form also revealed much of the colonial structure of injustice. In the juxtaposition between different street scenes, Marco put himself in the position of an observer who looked at himself in the urban world. For Marco, the visual environment of the city offered not only promises for a better future where everyone could consume what was advertised but also the injustices of the colonial city.

THE VISUAL WORLD IN MOTION

This chapter is intended less to explain the socioeconomic bases of popular urban radicalism in the early twentieth-century Indies town than to show the visual and spatial mediation of political consciousness. The change in socioeconomic interests and state policies were of fundamental importance. The international political ideologies and global modernity that had circulated in the region by then clearly had a powerful impact in promoting restlessness—just as anticolonial movements were developing at much the same time elsewhere. What I am proposing is that the change in the visual environment of the city played a role in the change of consciousness. It provided a contrast and comparison necessary for a criticism of Indonesia's own ancient regime. In this regard, the princely towns in Central Java (where urban radicalism first began) played a historic role. Given their conservatism, most vividly expressed in their architectural and urban symbolism, the traditional royal town nevertheless provided the grounds for comparison that, in turn, put in motion the radical age in Indonesian history.

I have also argued that the dynamic relations between the railway journey, the print culture, and the visual environment of the city shaped the experience of the urban generation of Mas Marco. In a way, Mas Marco's writings on the city used some aspects of the traditional town as rhetorical devices to underline some striking qualities of modern urban life. His protagonists, dandies, and liberated women in the colonial world showed traces of the importance of space, place, and setting in conditioning as well as mediating and shaping their social and political consciousness. They also called attention to the centrality of spatial and visual mediation of urban space in forming political consciousness even though they were also often quite uneasy about their positions in the physical landscape of the city. Yet, the urban experiences that taught Mas Marco the art of criticizing the city could not be said to constitute a simple binary opposition between the colonizer and the colonized. Mas Marco was clearly fascinated by the visual environment of the city—images of traffic, street signs, building, lighting, people, and so on were regularly mentioned in his novels even though he pointed them out in relation to the unevenness of the city. The spectacle of the city captivated Mas Marco, which in turn opened up a desire to engage with them in a political way. The fantasy of liberation from the colonial world thus came through a simultaneous identification with and rejection of colonial spatial practices. By the mid-1920s, the colonized had appropriated various aspects of the spectacle of the city, the urban culture, and the movement of trams and trains, and incorporated them into the more popular and radical ideas of "human rights" (hak kemanoesiaan) and "freedom" (kemerdikaan). These "keywords" became the catchwords for political parties that organized strikes and protests with increasing intensity.

By way of closing this chapter, I will briefly discuss some of the responses from conservative nationalists to the age in motion. For some conservative Javanese nationalists, the moving world of Marco, Minke, and Retno Poernama posed a threat to the social order that had secured Java for centuries. While acknowledging the problem of colonial order, these Javanese nationalists were fearful of disorder and fragmentation. Some of them found comfort in imagining the precolonial times when the mighty Majapahit kingdom established an influential realm marked by peace, order, and prosperity. Javanese nationalist Soetatmo depicted the "age in motion" in the following manner:

> In the meantime, the Indies are experiencing chaos, a hell; men cannot distinguish friends from enemies. The government plays double roles, now of friend, then as enemy, now progressive, then reactionary. Men fight against friends and go along with enemies, while they are definitely confident that they are fighting enemies. Nobody knows the right end and struggle breaks out everywhere: nobility against nonnobility, kromo against ngoko, capital against (wage) labor, ruler against ruled, government against the people; the society is upside down and totally out of joint. Such is the present picture of the Indies.[39]

For Soetatmo, the chaos provided the opportunity to retrieve the wisdom of the great Javanese civilization of the past as a vehicle to overcome modernity and reconfigure colonial society. Only through Javanese past wisdom, he argued, could the urban chaos be put back into order. For Soetatmo, the age in motion had mostly affected the youth who saw their world differently from that of their parents. Overwhelmed by the age in motion, Soetatmo recalled the upbringing of Indonesian youth in his parents' time. Two generations earlier, boys (and only boys) reaching a certain age would be sent by their fathers to a *pandita* (always a man) who lived an ascetic life in the mountains. Under the care of the pandita the boys were supposed to learn how to control themselves and know their place in the order of "nature."

In Soetatmo's own time, however, the notion of the pandita had been lost in the past. The mountains had been replaced by the city, and this attracted the youth who in turn became conscious of the social injustices of colonialism. Soetatmo, while acknowledging the problem of colonial relations, was trying to find a way to control the outburst of anticolonial urban radicalism. He saw Javanese culture as still having the potential to bring order to the present chaos. To domesticate the incendiary "sama rasa sama rata" (equality and solidarity), Soetatmo retrieved the Javanese concept of family and state. "Equality and brotherhood . . . are also preached by the wise; but not the quality of democracy, which speaks of equal rights, but equality in the family, where the eldest son plays a more important part in carrying domestic burdens and duties, and so enjoys more rights than his younger, still playing-around, brother. There are no equal rights in such a family and yet among the children there rules equality and brotherhood in the fullest sense of the word."[40] By calling on the past proper upbringing, the urban radicalism expressed in Marco's "equality and solidarity" (sama rasa sama rata) could thus be domesticated and turned into something sustaining rather than threatening the order of the day. However, the world in motion could not be fully contained. Instead it evolved finally into party politics. Shiraishi points out that, by the middle of the 1920s, "parties started to suppress first-person voices in the name of organization and discipline."[41] They organized strikes and protests with increasing intensity.

In 1926 the Communist Party launched a revolt against the colonial government. The movement was soon crushed and the era of urban popular radicalism met a violent death, along with its dandies and Marco.[42] A new type of urban and social environment was eventually constructed, one that promoted a sense of normalcy. For the first time there were efforts made to improve the physical environment of the Indies town in order to resolve tensions and conflicts in the city and overcome memories of the age in motion. The new Indies town coincided with the colonial regime of surveillance and political suppression that was mobilized to ensure the permanent death of urban popular radicalism. We do not know exactly how the urban space of the Indies town contributed to the rise and fall of social and political movements, but after the death of urban popular radicalism, Indonesians lived in a social environment of relative peace and order until the revolution of 1945–50. In the next chapter, I turn to the construction of this physical environment, which, I argue, contributed to the appearance of order and normality in late colonial Java.

CHAPTER 7   **URBAN PEDAGOGY**
The Appearance of Order and Normality in
Late Colonial Java, 1926–42

There should be no misunderstandings at this point; Urbanism will
emerge from revolution, not the revolution from urbanism. — HENRI
LEFEBVRE, *EVERYDAY LIFE IN THE MODERN WORLD*

On 10 October 1931, about a year before he died in the penal colony of
Boven Digoel, Mas Marco Kartodikromo started his "prison note-
book" with the following remarks:

When we first heard that all the communists in Indonesia would be
exiled to Boven Digoel in Nieuw Guinea, we (exhilaratingly) whispered
in our heart . . . in this land of exile (for the first time) we would be able
to organize ourselves according to the ideals of the communists that
we have been talking about for years in the meetings, newspapers and
books. . . . But in our heart we also asked ourselves what if the purpose
of putting all the communists together in one place in Boven Digoel is
for the colonial state to learn the [*ilmu*] science of communism aspired
to by the Indonesian Communist Party [Partij Komunis Indonesia] and
the People Council (Sarekat Rakjat)? What if there are spies [*spion*]
sent by the government to create conflict and division between us? . . .
For sure the tumult would be announced in the newspapers. The government will then be able to say: Have a look, Indonesian people! The
communists in Boven Digoel could not even organize and get along
among themselves. So, Indonesian people should follow the leadership
of the existing Dutch government.[1]

This note clearly summarized the question and dilemma not only of Marco
and his comrades but also of Boven Digoel, which first appeared in his

mind as the utopian space of the communists, then the laboratory of the colonial state, and finally the disciplinary showcase in which the Indonesian people could watch the downfall of the revolutionaries. What is even more striking is that all of these changes in perception worked themselves out in the cautious imagination of Marco himself. He was an observer watching himself being watched by both the state and the Indonesian people who saw him and his comrades as objects for the self-regulation of their imagined public—a fatal consciousness that had turned the revolutionary into his or her own negation.

After the destruction of the Indonesian Communist Party in 1926/27, the pergerakan (the urban-based popular radical movements for a new and free (trans)national world) as a whole met its violent death. In its place, as Takashi Shiraishi points out, the Indies government installed "an extensive and effective surveillance apparatus ever watchful of and ready to crush any 'subversive' movement."[2] Central to this apparatus was the urban space and the ways in which the imagery and legibility of a particular place created a self-regulating perception among the public of what is normal and abnormal, legible and illegible.[3] First, I will discuss the construction of "normality" or what is legible by one of the state apparatuses experienced by Marco, the "penal colony" called Boven Digoel, whose invention had profound consequences for the disciplining of the post-1926 urban space of Indonesia.

Boven Digoel was the first mass internment camp to be located in the center of malaria-infested New Guinea. After crushing the communist revolts in 1926/27, the Dutch colonial government institutionalized Digoel for people involved in "subversive" movements. Digoel, however, was in fact neither a penal colony nor a concentration camp but a place for all the troublemakers "to live a normal live under abnormal conditions."[4] The colony led a "normal" life in the sense that all the internees enjoyed—in the words of the Governor-General in 1928—"the same rights and are subjected to the same obligations which law under normal circumstances demands from and bestows upon other free persons."[5] These "free" prisoners were supposed to (re)create for themselves a life that would eliminate their revolutionary past. Central to this attempt was the creation of a self-styled harmonious community life akin to that of a village in which every internee could become a "normal" villager.

Rudolf Mrázek and Takashi Shiraishi have analyzed in detail the social

and political contradiction of this strangely "normalized" life of the internees in Digoel.[6] What I would like to emphasize is that this construction of
"normality," however, was "abnormal" because no such "village community"
could be created except in a stagelike manner. J. J. Schrieke, the government representative for general affairs at the Volksraad, was one of those
who was most aware of the artificial quality of Boven Digoel. He pointed
out that Digoel was "a special place of residence, on an island that is un-
inhabited (or whose population has been evacuated), not unhealthy, not
too big, situated in the deep sea, easy to guard, offering space for about
one hundred families, without a post office—where each internee can be
provided with a hut and a plot of land for his permanent dwelling."[7] This
isolated "colonial showcase" implies a theatre-like setting that involved an
audience who watched from afar the internees in the colony "dying, going
insane, or being broken."[8]

The camp was thus not meant for any improvement in the life of the
internees. Instead, it provided a spectacle of punishment for the gaze of
people *outside* Digoel. The colonial administration regularly released news
in Malay newspapers reporting the condition of the people in Digoel, often
accompanied by internee's letters to their relatives and friends. This discourse of transparency included Marco's own psychological report on the
"social intercourse of exiled people in Boven Digoel."[9] Indonesians were
thus provided with an image of the abnormality of the "normal" life of
Digoel.[10] In this sense, the main target of Digoel was not the die-hard
revolutionaries (who had already been contained) but other Indonesians
back home who might still have the dream of reviving radical movements
against Dutch rule. The fearful image of the detention camp, circulated in
the mass media, would make people (outside Digoel) know their place,
behave, and stay away from anticolonial movements.

We don't know how effective the image of Digoel was in taming Indonesians' fantasy of liberation, but there were various responses to the image
of Digoel. Shiraishi reports that, in 1933, Sukarno was "so terrified at the
thought of living in Digoel, away from his mother and perhaps without
his wife," that he preferred cooperation with the colonial government.[11]
Meanwhile, Indonesians who lived through the 1930s measured themselves
up as "normal" against the "abnormality" of Digoel. They would perhaps
say something like: we are "normal" compared to those who are living in

Digoel, and we will remain normal as long as we prevent ourselves from being taken to Digoel. The image of isolation and the strange life of Digoel served not only to reduce anticolonial movements but to create a sense among people that they had been living "normally" for they did not and will not, after all, find themselves in the penal colony.[12] So pervasive was the image of Digoel, that Indonesians remembered the 1930s as "zaman normal" and the period of 1927–42 as the age of Digoel, "for the normalcy in the Indies in these years was constituted fundamentally on the phantom world of Digoel."[13]

Shiraishi's study encourages us to go beyond his analytical concern. Take, for example, the efforts of the city government in creating the image of a "normal" town by way of organizing buildings and creating order in the appearance of the urban space. If we bear in mind this Digoelian politics of social control, we might be able to consider some of the post-1926 urban design paradigms as a conscious or unconscious articulation of the visual order of the zaman normal. In the time of zaman normal, urban space functioned as a mirror for an identification of what is "normal" and what is "pathological." Central to the architecture of zaman normal is thus the way urban space had become not only a symbol of power or a representation of the authority but more like a mirror for the viewing subjects to reflect on their own subjectivity. The following is an interpretative reading that aims at making sense of the politics of spatial representation and the cultural code of late Dutch colonialism in Indonesia.

THE NEW REGIME OF SEEING

In 1937, the Committee for the Decentralization of the Netherlands Indies held its congress in Batavia. The Congress was rather special that year for it displayed a series of photographs depicting the change in the cityscape of the Netherlands Indies over the past twenty years. After a tour of several cities, some of the photographs were finally published as an album for the occasion of the twenty-fifth birthday of the Sociale Technische Commissie van de Vereeniging Voor Lokale Belangen.[14] The purpose of the publication, according to Engineer Ir. Lemei and his colleagues of the Sociale technische commissie, was to make the general public (more) aware of the new visual and (implicitly) social changes in the urban environment.[15] Ir. Lemei and his colleagues understood change as the demand of time, however, they were worried about the current visual quality of the city. They considered many of the new buildings as damaging the environmental character of the Indies town (*karakter der omgeving*). More specifically, Ir. Lemei lamented the disappearance of plants and vegetation, which for years had given character to the "tropical town." Meanwhile Ir. Lemei's colleague, the prominent town planner Thomas Karsten, noticed an unprecedented tendency in the colony, that is, the appearance of order and ordering (*ordening*) in the urban environment.[16] He also seemed to recognize that this tendency toward order stemmed from the colonial government's new obsession with order and rule in the late 1920s.

The new regime of order, observed by Karsten and Lemei, could indeed be discerned in several photographs exhibited in the Congress. For instance, in a pair of photographs entitled "Semarang, Sociëteitsbrug, Groote Huis en Bojong: ca 1920 and 1937," two pictures taken at different times (see figures 32 and 33) offer a scene that represents the emergence of a particular sense of order. The caption reads: "The widened bridge, the heavy pillars for lanterns and the architectural detailing make the bridge look heavy; The landscaping of the Big House [then the Governor Office] and the new Javasche Bank at the end of the street. Some trees remain."[17]

The disappearance of plants and trees has indeed made the buildings in the area look more substantial and visible. As buildings made their appearance by displacing the trees, a visual regime based on order and ordering began to rule the city. We do not know who took these pictures, but we can make something out of the quality of communication in the photographs. The camera that took these two pictures was set above the ground. It surveyed the street. It caught the disappearance of trees and the increasing visibility of the buildings on both sides of the street. The buildings and the street, in turn, created a frame for our eyes to locate the human figures on the bridge. These human figures, however, are not significant. The presence of tiny human figures is meant more to show that they were following the layout of the city space: the strollers on the sidewalks, the automobile and horse carriage in their designated lanes, all moving along the direction set up by the street. We, the viewers, find it easier to identify ourselves with the order of the city than with anyone on the street. The street and its surrounding architecture have appropriated the human figures. There is a quality of policing in the photograph, where the human figures are con-

SEMARANG, SOCIËTEITSBRUG   1920

Figure 32 Before: Sociëteitsbrug in Semarang, 1920. Reprinted from Karsten, *Het Indische stadsbeeld, voorheen en thans.*

1937

Figure 33 After: Sociëteitsbrug in Semarang, 1937. Reprinted from Karsten, *Het Indische stadsbeeld, voorheen en thans.*

trolled by the grid of the urban space. We, the viewers, become the police, or we could become the human figures in the picture under the surveillance of the camera. The picture structures our way of seeing. It invites us to place ourselves within the designated urban space. In fact, there is a policeman in both pictures, but the policeman, like the other human figures, is secondary, for he too was placed inside the camera even as he contributed to making people know their place. The symbolism of the city in these pictures lies not in the monumentality of the buildings or in the monument of the powerful but in the spatial arrangement for the proper placement of the human figure who has become the object of representation.

What does the scene in *Het Indische stadsbeeld* lead us to? It does not lead us to satisfaction over the improvement of the colony as was—perhaps—intended. Instead, it leads us to understand that by the 1930s the urban space had become a pedagogical apparatus or a heuristic device that, through its organization of space, attempted to create an obedient "public." The scene of Semarang, Sociëteitsbrug represented the "glass house" of the colonial government that, since the anticolonial revolts in 1926, had begun to monitor the urban life of the colony through the optic of urban design.[18]

Indeed, the visual environment of the 1930s was different from that of the 1910s. The photo albums, which juxtaposed images of these two periods in the manner of then and now, suggested a watershed in Indonesian urban history, one that had given rise to a new form of power based on order and visibility. This new order, I suspect, was not only a response to urbanization and public health but also a move to make use of urban space to further the effective surveillance of the Indies population. The challenge was not merely how the state could impose legibility by law and order on particular sites for particular people but more importantly how, through the use and perception of urban space, people in the Indies could be involved in creating a proper image for themselves. To go back to the image of the Sociëteitsbrug bridge in Semarang, one could project oneself walking across the bridge, following the path, and moving within the frame of the camera. One knows that one is behaving well, knowing one's place in the grid of the city, and thus appearing "normal." Both the photograph and the urban space normalize the scene while serving as a medium for the disciplining of the daily experience of the city.

THE STREET AND THE NEW MARKET

The prominent architect and urban planner Ir. Thomas Karsten once declared that the Indies city "was the center of order [ordening]" and that the market was "a necessary element in the ordering of economic life" to transform the "primitive agrarian" mentality of the population to an "urban-ordered" mentality.[19] Karsten, however, did not only create order but was also aware of the centrality of the visual environment as the site of signification. Karsten formulated the colonial town as an "organism" that, he believed, can be coordinated visually on the ground as well as from above. The town can be seen as an organism, organized around "the interrelationship between the various sections, centers, important buildings, and other sources of traffic."[20] The most critical part of this formulation is not only how to connect various elements to constitute the whole but also how to govern the parts that would otherwise refuse to be incorporated. The challenge of urban design during the zaman normal was to coordinate and integrate the unruly parts so that they would become components of the "normal." Under the regime of order and visibility, the sight of unruliness would have to be removed or given a place in order to guarantee the presence of the "proper." A modest illustration of this can be found in the creation of the city market seen as a proper place for the street vendors who, by the 1930s, were no longer allowed to move freely on the streets. It has been a phenomenon of the Indies town, Karsten said, that instead of going to the pasar,

> the small-scale trader, who is usually Native, tries to find his customers in the street, either keeping on the move most of the time or else, if he can, finding a more or less fixed spot, often at or nearby an intersection. . . . The objections are the sometimes gross pollution of the streets, the nuisance to the public and/or to the houses along the street, the unsightliness. . . . The Western authorities, particularly, often find it intolerable that these typical, and usually rather unpretentious, forms of Native economic life manifest themselves in 'European' sections. Indeed the disorderliness usually accompanying such economic forms is out of place, and hence is a nuisance objectively as well as subjectively. . . . The warungs [food stalls] are disfiguring the urban scene with an unsightly structure generally having an extensive appendage of benches, awnings,

screens, and cooking utensils. Properly such *warungs* should be located only at well-chosen and well-equipped points. . . . Such things need to be given full consideration in drafting the street plans and neighborhood plans."[21]

The basic frame of reference here is order, place, and visibility, which, by the 1930s, were considered paramount to the well-being of people in the Indies town. The unruly warung, the nomadic vendors, and their customers were to be contained and their movements framed by walls. Accordingly, toward the end of the 1920s, many city markets were built in order to stop the free movements of the small-scale traders so that there would be no crowds on the streets.

These ideas were put into practice.[22] In Semarang, in 1910, there used to be only eight acknowledged bazaars, but by 1936, the number had jumped to sixteen. To further contain the mobility of small-scale traders, several bazaars were brought together to form a central market. In Semarang, for instance, the Pasar Djohar, Pedamaran, Beteng, Djoernatan, and Pekodjan were all blended together to form the Semarang Central Market. The city markets were generally built in two-story form of concrete materials with light and ventilation. They were fully enclosed, clean, and spatially organized according to the classification of goods. They were located strategically at the center of the city, near the *alun-alun* (the square associated with the indigenous palatial compound), and close to other shops. Once placed within the neighborhood plans and contained in a building complex, the nomadic traders and customers became part of the domestic scene. We can see this ordering in another set of photographs exhibited in the Congress. "The Pasar in Malang" depicted the scenes of the new market in the 1930s. The picture is taken from above the ground. It points straight to the clock at the entrance tower of the bazaar (see figure 34). The effect is similar to that of the bridge of Semarang. Human figures move according to the movement provided by the clock and the spaces of the buildings. No one seems to be outside the grid of the market space and the regulated time of the clock. With the creation of the new market, street vending became "out of place." Vendors became wanderers and *liar* (wild), while their activities were considered pathological to the economy of the city market. The point here is about not only the order of the city and the "taming" of the street vendors but also the effects of the city market and the impression it makes

1937

Figure 34 A central "disciplined" market in a city of Java, 1937. Reprinted from Karsten, *Het Indische stadsbeeld, voorheen en thans.*

on the street vendors. The displacement of the street vendors provided a new sense of "normalcy" to the sellers and buyers who found themselves in the designated space of the city market.

With the establishment of the city market, urbanites were more able to perceive urban order and disorder. It is no coincidence that the Indonesian novelist that we have encountered, Mas Marco, took up the city market in Surabaya in 1925 as a setting for one of his short stories.[23] Marco was clearly impressed by the discourse of order around the city market. His detailed description of the policeman directing traffic in front of the Main Market of Surabaya indicates the newness of the regime of order. When the protagonist of the story and his friend "got to the Main Market they stopped a moment at the edge of the road, for something had caught their eye. Even though it was almost midnight, there was still a police officer on duty, directing the continuous flow of traffic to both left and right. . . . When the policeman held up his hand in one direction, telling the traffic to stop, traffic in the other direction would go. While this was happening, traffic in the other direction built up, waiting for the policeman to give them the 'go' signal."[24]

The Main Market, however, is not merely a place for police to ensure the bounds of the established form. The formal functioning of the market itself marked territories and subjectivities. Marco himself was affected by the practice. After visited by "order," he was consumed by the "disorder" outside the wall. Other transactions, uncontainable by the police and the order of market, feature in Marco's story. "Not far from where the policeman was standing keeping the peace, two sailors could be seen in the doorway of the new concrete market building. At least seven neatly dressed women were swarming about them, laughing loudly and pulling occasionally at their sleeves. Quite obviously they were the 'flowers of the night'—busy, modern and famous Surabaya's 'decorations'."[25] There was more energy circulating around the building than normal. Marco despised this "pathological" circuit of energy. However he himself embodied such energy. Seeing both sides of the wall, Marco finally found himself in Digoel. There, he felt he was being watched by the government, its spies, and the Indonesian public.[26]

THE AESTHETIC OF THE NEW KAMPUNG

By the 1930s, the performance of *belanja* (shopping in the market) had been normalized by the clock and kept indoors by the new market. Belanja is no longer simply a nomadic street activity but a functional element of a site plan coordinated in relation to the police station, town hall, mosques, theatre, sports stadium, and recreation facilities. In the meantime, the image of the urban kampung had become more disturbing for the urban planners of the zaman normal. With the growth of European settlements and the concomitant demand for what was considered a healthy environment, the urban reformers had to incorporate into their urban vision the huge space and hardly known areas called the "kampung." Yet the adherents of modern planning had great difficulty in organizing this extensive space because they had no complex categories for the kampung world. As the population in the area had grown extensively even Indonesians had difficulty in imaging the world of the kampung.[27]

There were indeed many different kinds of kampung realities but, in the eyes of the colonial state, none was as worrying as the potential for the kampung to become a source of social unrest. In Karsten's view: "Considering the great significance of the home to the Indonesians, such a (poor kampung) situation cannot help call into being strong feelings of dissatisfaction and social inequality, with all their political consequences."[28] In 1926, the pharmacist-reformist entrepreneur H. F. Tillema, who was also an "engineer of health and hygienist,"[29] referred particularly to the relations between rebellion and sanitation. He asked the government to "consider that wormseed oil is a good medicine and strap oil a bad one, that the injection needle and the lancet are definitely better and more humane tools of civilization and pacification than the bayonet and the chopping knife."[30] The tools of pacification take the form of a built environment necessary for the production "urban-ordered mentality."[31]

Most of Tillema's works (1913–26), however, belonged to the age of pergerakan—the time of the "natives awakening" and "popular radicalism" that generated "disturbances, irregularities and confusions" especially in the urban centers of Indonesia. As if envisioning the coming of the new age of normalcy, Tillema worked exclusively to improve the Indies town and published his works privately. He was perhaps the first to see the affinity between the visual and the social order and provided thus a paradigm for the zaman normal. His work opened a path for Thomas Karsten who, by the end of the 1920s, was convinced that [the traits of a] town's beauty are "outward signs of an inner order and harmony; they testify to the character of the town's society in the same way facial traits testify to the character of the person."[32]

Karsten's phenomenology ends in the revelation that the appearance of the town conveys a particular meaning. It plays the role of a face that not only represents the soul but also affects the way a viewer would interpret the facial expression. When the kampung has a character of an aesthetic harmony, so the story goes, it holds everything together and controls the unity needed for the well-being of its inhabitants. Karsten's strong sense of environmental determinism convinced him that "a people forced to live in disorderly and unfriendly towns will be encouraged in a tendency towards social discontent and unruliness. Hence the degree of aesthetic harmony and beauty in the Indies town . . . has a very concrete, in fact almost a political significance from the realistic point of view."[33]

The simplest but most exciting way to achieve inner order and harmony would be to build a new kampung, for "the old city remained an unhealthy place in spite of all improvements and would be best thrown to the ground."[34] This was the view of Tillema, the protagonist of the "new" urban kampung and the first modernist in the Indies. Unlike Karsten, Tillema was convinced that the urban kampung could not be improved unless it was built anew. His vision of a normal city is just incommensurable with his knowledge of the kampung. He collected photographs to illus-

Figure 35 The model *kampung*, designed by Tillema. Reprinted from Tillema, *Kromoblanda; Over 't vraagstuk van "het wonen" in Kromo's groote land.*

trate the poor conditions of the kampung, and he used the knowledge of hygiene to plan his new kampung. He recommended the creation of a new town oriented in the direction of major winds, with wide streets lined with trees and houses around open space adapted to tropical heat and humidity (see figure 35).[35] He considered the city that did not fulfill the demands of hygiene, ventilation, and lighting as abnormal. He drew comparisons with nineteenth-century discourses of public health in Europe. His *Van wonen en bewonen, van bouwen, huis en erf* drew cases from British colonies and built up arguments from literatures concerning environment and health that brings us back to the "garden city" movement in Europe.[36]

The colony, however, is not a metropole. The Indies is a different place where security and control are at stake. Even so, for Tillema, the ordering of space is not merely for the sake of security and control. His model does not provide a wall or a gatehouse, and there is no watchtower around the compound, although his well-organized buildings would ensure functional and visual surveillance, and the provision of facilities and well-ordered space would guarantee the self-regulation of human behavior. The new kampung he proposed includes a complete set of infrastructure and ser-vices such as systems for drainage, rubbish removal, sanitation, and water supply as well as facilities for sports, bathing, playing, and landscaping. All these facilities were carefully placed to ensure order and visibility. The new visual order served as a symbol of urban modernity and represented a ritual of living that is "normal," controllable, and predictable. It also antici-pates a new era if not a culture of the zaman normal.

In the zaman normal, the norm of order and visibility was not only intended for the colonized but was also applied to the regulation of the privileged. In the last section of this chapter, I will consider the design of the Koningsplein (the King's Square) to see how the authority planned to "normalize" the public. The design challenge of Koningsplein during the zaman normal, I believe, was filled with questions not only of political symbolism but also of signification that involved the visibility of both the "king" and his subjects.

KING'S SQUARE (KONINGSPLEIN)

In the early 1920s, the famous Dutch architect and the "father of modern architecture," H. P. Berlage, visited Indonesia. In 1923, he found that Batavia, the capital city of the colonial government, was on the move. "The city is on the railway," he said, uncomfortably.[37] And in general, cities in the Indies "were built as floating."[38] Berlage's unsettling comment seems to indicate his awareness that Indonesia was caught up in the radical "age in motion" in which even the relatively controlled city of Batavia was filled with a sense of instability. Perhaps as a way to end this uncertainty, in 1937 the Koningsplein, whose reconstruction had been suspended in 1923 due to the time of malaise, was opened for redesign. The Koningsplein was expected to be the center that would bring a sense of normalcy back to the Indies. This was obviously a big challenge. Between 1936 and 1939, the redesigning of the Koningsplein was the leading feature of such technical journals as the *De ingenieur in Nederlandsch-Indië* and *Locale techniek*. Photographs of the models and sketches were presented, and they invited debate (see figure 36).[39]

By the 1930s architects knew that the best way to control the city was to create a miniature of it. For the first time the design of the Koningsplein was imagined through models. From the model and, the site plan, we see a large empty square divided by a grid pattern on which were laid out buildings, streets, and pathways. There is a railway station, a museum, a stadium, a telephone office, the office of the resident, and, at the center, the Raadhuis. Set in the vast square, all these buildings however are impressively small, if not cute, especially in their miniaturized form. The large empty square further reduced the scale of the buildings, especially the Raadhuis, which looks quite small. It appears as a tiny building protected by a row of trees. More than one plan was made for the Koningsplein, but they all proposed that the Raadhuis be at the center, visibly important but protected by not wall but space. The only element that makes the Raadhuis appear monumental is the approach to it. In one model, the boulevard is

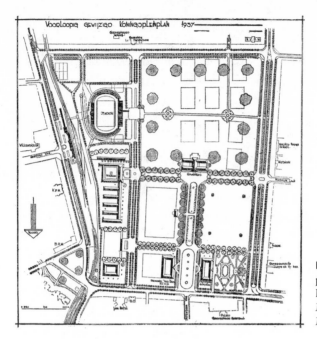

Figure 36 Konings-
plein plan, 1937.
Reprinted from
*De ingenieur in
Nederlandsch-Indië.*

lined with trees, and in another, with a row of buildings on both sides.
At the center, the Raadhuis commands the surroundings. It looks out as
much as it is watched from everywhere. It is not surprising then that a
most intensely debated topic concerned the visibility of the Raadhuis in
the square. Some people were concerned that the series of trees might
block the view toward the buildings in the square.

The 1937 plan for the Koningsplein recalls the ethical politics of Dutch
architects and reformers. The pharmacist-entrepreneur H. F. Tillema in
his magnum opus had proclaimed that any building for Westerners in the
Indies (and wasn't the Raadhuis essentially for the Westerners?) "should
be designed modestly, and also otherwise adjusted to the Eastern circumstances."[40] Thomas Karsten, one of the designers of the new Koningsplein,
was fully aware of the importance of Tillema's dictum of the "Eastern circumstances." Karsten wrote:

> Though historical information on the subject is scanty, there is sufficient
> evidence for this point in the well-planned and systematic design of
> several large Native towns, many medium-sized and smaller ones, and
> the often excellently laid-out rural kampongs. . . . The town-planning

implications of these Native attitudes need to be considered here. Their social implications are vast, since they indicate that Native society is in principle quite willing to submit to guidance and planning for the general good, as long as such guidance and planning are in keeping with Native traditions . . . such as the orientation of dwellings facing approximately north and south, and the arrangement of the village around the alun-alun and the important buildings clustered about it.[41]

Looking at the site plan of the Koningsplein, one cannot avoid seeing a synthesis or contextualization. The buildings in the Koningsplein not only form relations to one another but they construct an aesthetic of zaman normal—a gesture of reconciliation, of returning to a normal state in which the cosmos and the relationship between the ruler and the ruled is in order. The means of unification however was not to go back to the past relations but to look for the present shared responsibility and propriety that would ensure traditional order, harmony, and peace. The architectural reference for this vision might have been drawn from various sources, but I would like to draw our attention to a domestic one.

The new Koningsplein recalls the prototypical map of the "layout of an average regency seat" made under the supervision of Dutch geographer H. Ph. Th. Witkamp to represent what one might "reasonably expect to find in a (peaceful) Indonesian town."[42] Witkamp brought into visibility as many as 174 items, buildings, and spaces, and listed each of them in the key to the layout map. There is a precise quality of policing, naming, and seeing things that used to be unseen (see figure 37).

To ensure visibility from above, trees were imagined as absent. Referring to the map, Tillema reminded us that "it might be pointed out that the vegetation is usually denser than is indicated: it has been underemphasized on the map in order to accentuate the location of the various buildings."[43] With the vegetation in the background, everything it used to conceal is opened for view. "They are all there: the regent, the assistant resident, the photographer, the president of the district court, the kampong head, the Chinese noodle vendor, the pedlar, the salt-supply administrator, and all the others."[44] They are all connected, especially by the matrix of the built environment. The map has in its center the alun-alun (the square), bordered to the north by the dwelling of the (Dutch) assistant resident and to the south, the ("native") regent. Surrounding them are "the mosque,

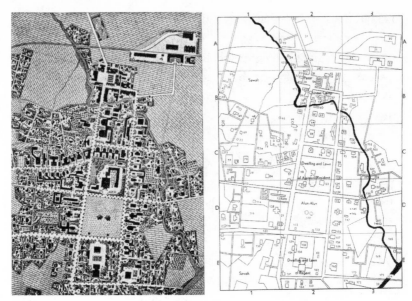

Figure 37 Map of a regency. Reprinted from Wertheim, *The Indonesian Town.*

the barracks for the military police, the house of the police chief, the guest house, and the boarding house." Round about the center dwell the "Europeans who are not in government service, the Javanese, and further away, the Chinese." The list continues, "everything has found a place."[45] Witkamp's layout created an order for the town that would otherwise be hidden under the trees. The visibility of the buildings on the map evaded the sense of unruliness on the ground. One need only follow the surveyed plan and go down with one's camera into the most private section of the kampung, such as the latrines. In fact, this technique of seeing from a birds-eye-view and down to the field was what Tillema did for his *Kromoblanda.* With camera and maps, he created a sense of order for the reality on the ground.

Karsten's plan for the Koningsplein played out, in a way, the map of Witkamp, but Karsten's square is much more abstract, pure, and standardized. The average regency seat of Witkamp had been further "normalized." Karsten followed the "traditional" north-south orientation, but he did not cut the vegetation. He did not imagine that the vegetation was not there. Instead, he organized the plants in an orderly manner. As the naturally grown trees in the late Indies cities "were becoming something of a sign of imperfection,"[46] Karsten transplanted "display trees," ones that "grow

Figure 38 Housing in a new town, circa 1990s. Reprinted from Sarwoko et al., *Pembangunan perumahan dan hunian modern di Indonesia.*

fast but not beyond the guidelines of the plan."[47] The 1937 Koningsplein provided such a display of trees for they were there to help bring normalcy to the capital city. The 1937 design of the Koningsplein could be seen as a replica of Witkamp's plan in which the synthesis among elements would help maintain the cosmic balance that had been displaced by the "age in motion." However, unlike Witkamp's plan, there is no need for the police house in the Koningsplein for there is no place to hide in the empty square where the buildings are small and subject to the gaze of eyes from all sides. The well-placed buildings give no space for any unruly development or behavior. The site plan and the birds-eye-view of the models give no time to anyone to move in without being seen. The site plan, if realized, would be sufficient to generate propriety and normal behavior essential for building up a culture for the zaman normal.

THE LESSONS OF ZAMAN NORMAL

In a way, all the different spatial politics that I have sketched relate to the history of zaman normal. Of course, the urban discourses of the zaman normal are marked by inherent tensions. They carry with them the implication of disruption, as the appearance of urban order becomes not only a location of control but also a repository of energies to install different orders and different rationalities. Moreover, there is always more than one blind spot in the city. Those who have done research on the urban life of zaman normal would be able to tell us different stories as well as provide different perceptions and interpretations of Indonesian activities and behavior during the appearances of urban order at that time.

What I would like to emphasize in conclusion is that the urban discourses of the zaman normal have enormous consequences for the spatial politics of the postcolonial *zaman Order Baru* (New Order of Suharto). Most notably they were born from the crushing of radical movements and the implementation of surveillance by an apparatus of suppression. And for both periods, ideas about order, stability, and normalcy are central. These two regimes of order have also been haunted by their memories of violence, which demanded that they create a sense of "normality" for the present. It would be useful to compare the colonial zaman normal and the postcolonial Order Baru. In this conclusion, I can only suggest that to a great extent what the city and urban life was like during the Order Baru can be best understood in relation to the zaman normal. Let me end by discussing the image of a new town of our time (see figure 38).

This photograph is taken from a housing promotional handbook published in the 1990s by the Indonesian government and a housing business group.[48] It is captioned "healthy housing environment." There is nothing particularly unusual in the image (except perhaps for its "normality") for it has become part of Indonesian daily life today: the houses, a few human figures — children, mother or perhaps housemaid — the cars, a small park with almost no trees except some newly planted ones for "display" only, and, most importantly perhaps, a security post with a guard in it at a strategic location of the compound. Yet this image embodies a larger set of unresolved issues that have been the subject of this chapter: questions concerning order and control; visibility and surveillance; social exclusion and legibility; harmony and identity. It represents the normalcy of our time, but what we also observe, however, is that we are back in the flow of history to the era of the zaman normal, the dream world of Tillema, and the age of Digoel.

MENTAL NEBULAE

CHAPTER 8

"THE REALITY OF ONE-WHICH-IS-TWO"
Java's Reception of Global Islam

> The main difficulty is in fact to transcend the heaviness of regional, colonial and then nationalistic histories which have strongly partitioned off the historical space. — DENYS LOMBARD, "NETWORKS AND SYNCHRONISMS IN SOUTHEAST ASIAN HISTORY"

In chapter 7, I started with a commonplace approach that conceives of architecture as a form of dominance and a political strategy of colonialism and ended by teasing out the scene of reification and the appropriation of a colonial politics of space under postcolonial conditions. Setting up a diachronic mode of analysis, in the end I sought to show the present moment as a construct related to events of the past, a return that marks, ironically, the arrival of a new time. The migration of the past to the present indicates that the issues of pacification, surveillance, and containment are also major components in the political life of the new establishment. On the other hand, the politics of space indicate not only ties to authority but also signs of modernity, political consciousness, and fantasies of liberation traceable not so much to street demonstrations but to cultural practices such as memoirs and popular novels.

As was mentioned in the introduction, in the era of "peace and order" characteristic of the zaman normal of late colonial Indonesia, when societies were pacified through urban design and practices of everyday life, major cities in Java and Sumatra witnessed a proliferation of the dime novel (roman picisan). Roman picisans were extremely popular, not only because they were inexpensive and entertaining, but also because they offered stories of patriotic adventure and political intrigue that undermined colonial authority and the environment of zaman normal. Of all the fictive characters that appeared in roman picisans, none seems to be more popular than detective Patjar Merah (The Scarlet Pimpernel).[1] The different volumes in the *Patjar Merah* series were written by various authors with the most famous titles written by Hasbullah Parindurie (pen name Matu Mona), published between 1938 and 1940. Matu Mona borrowed Baronesse Emmuska Orczy's character, the Scarlet Pimpernel, a savior of French aristocrats during the French Revolution, and refashioned the hero into Patjar Merah, an anticolonial patriot from his region.

Patjar Merah was in fact a character modeled on Tan Malaka, the real-life anticolonial nationalist wanted by the colonial state.[2] As Patjar Merah, Tan Malaka was depicted as capable of taking on the appearance of any nationality and he spoke the languages of the countries through which he traveled: In Thailand, he was Vichitra; in China, Tan Min Kha; and in Palestine, Ibrahim al Molqa (Tan Malaka's own childhood name). Under different names and roles he moved from one stage to another, from one part of the city to another, and in the process his identity was transformed and thus was uncontainable by colonial authority.

I have explored elsewhere the real-life Tan Malaka (1897–1949) and the theme of resistances that ran beneath the material order of zaman normal.[3] I showed how Tan Malaka's adventures in Shanghai in 1932, when the city was engulfed by the conflict between China and Japan, shaped his political consciousness and articulated a mnemonic practice that eventually informed his understanding of Jakarta in the 1940s under Japanese occupation. His journey was as much about the claims of comparability of colonial cities as it was about these cities' emancipation and rights to sovereignty and independence. The emergence of Tan Malaka's anticolonial consciousness intersected with the variety of urban forms he encountered in Shanghai. In a time when the city had either been colonized or come under the threat of Western (including Japanese) powers, the city came to embody political authority and thus became a symbol of sovereignty.

Yet the voyages that taught Tan Malaka the importance of transnational imaginings intersected with a persona created for him by writers of roman picisan at home. His geographical experience of Shanghai entwined with the imagined description of him in the popular fiction about Patjar Merah. In the calmness of zaman normal, minds were set free to imagine reality as fiction and fiction as reality, both profound features of resistance against the colonial environment of order and peace.

Through the figure of Tan Malaka, I argued that Indonesian modernity emerged out of a series of citations, and the modernity of the nation could be seen as relying on the quotations of images of the world. By juxtaposing Shanghai and Jakarta under Japanese occupation after the end of Western colonialism, I found a way to overcome the difference between the problematic categories of East and West and pointed instead to the mutually constitutive relations between them and to the tensions and coalition among elements internal to the East.

In this chapter I engage with this theme using architectural discourses, looking at the ways in which the global spread of Islam was received by the state and the religious elites in Java. I focus on the subtleties of inter-Islamic tensions by examining the relationship between Islamic architecture and the Javanese culture of Indonesia.[4] While continuing the study of the relationship between architecture and the intertwined histories of different cultures and powers, I will show how certain developments in Islamic architecture in Java can be made more understandable if we approach them differently. Instead of focusing on the global spread of Islam and its effect on Islamic architecture in Java, I will consider the way Java conceives of and responds to the cultural flow of global Islam. I will show the way in which architecture became the site of negotiation, or the point of articulation, between the global pan-Islamic Islam and the Javanese world. From this, I will raise some larger issues concerning history and agency, religion and politics, architecture and ideology.

Using the form of the mosque, this chapter thus shows how architecture is imagined differently by people at various times. Such imaginaries however demand an introduction of the setting and some terms and concepts that often appear as an unspoken framework of this chapter even as they have come into view in the previous chapters.

The *place* is Java, the most populous island of the Indonesian archipelago, where the capital city of Jakarta is located, and which was also the principal colony of the Netherlands through a greater part of the modern era. The island of Java has long been a place where various civilizations have met, and for centuries it was the seat of both the Javanese dynasty and the Dutch colonial government. It was the place that stirred the first anticolonial nationalist sentiments in the early twentieth century and since then has been home to the majority of the key players of Indonesian politics. It was also the birthplace of the Indonesian state and the control center by which other islands in the Indonesian archipelago were coordinated. As shown in previous chapters, Java is an island of modernity, but it is also a place that has witnessed virtually all of the worst violence that has occurred throughout the life of the nation. It is thus not surprising that Java has become the center of Indonesian history and provides the repertoire for the retrieval of the memories of the nation. In this chapter *Java*, by virtue of its power over Indonesia, is read as interchangeable with *Indonesia* even though this assumption is problematic. Java, at least since the establishment of Dutch modern imperialism in the late nineteenth century, has been stretching its culture to cover the vast space of the Indonesian archipelago.

I treat the *time* as discursive, moving back and forth between the precolonial (1498), colonial (1830s), and the postcolonial (1970–99) eras, but I prefer to think of the time period less as a chronology than as a moment of return, reconfiguration, and shifting of culture and identity. By moving culture across time, I do not assume that there are somehow unchanging inner values that encapsulate the essence of Java unaffected by historical phenomena as powerful as Islam, colonialism, and modernity. By loosening time, or suspending it, I merely hope to show how Java, through incessant attempts to accommodate, adapt, and resist historical phenomena, transforms itself even as it acknowledges the difficulty of the transformation, the expression of which, quite often, is the essence of Java itself. When we loosen culture a little from the grip of time, culture emerges as the representation of the ungrounded that yields for the cosmopolitan, but more often, alas, the essential.

As shown in this book, *architecture* refers to not merely a reflection of the culture of a society but also the unsettling negotiations of culture and identity. When we place architecture in a particular place and time, people in Java, for instance, begin to identify with and speak for as well as against not merely the architecture but also the sense of place and the time within which they are embedded. *Culture* can be understood as an invented tradition, used and abused by social actors to achieve particular political and ideological ends. Yet culture also refers to a way of life in which the invented tradition is practiced in nonideological, customary, and quite often religious ways. This chapter, while acknowledging that culture is always already political, shows the power of culture in the second sense in order to illuminate certain aspects of architectural discourses in Java.[5]

Islam, like *Java* (or *Hindu-Javanese culture*), is a term that cannot be fixed even as it is spoken clearly in the island of Java. In Java, claims have been made that one can find Islam in Java as much as one can find Java in Islam. In fact, the ungroundedness of the terms *Java* and *Islam*, the contestation over the boundary between them, and the question of their unresolved conciliation express this chapter's undercurrent. For analytical purposes nevertheless, this chapter refers to Islam more as the global and Java as the local, even as this formulation is problematic as indicated by the expression: "the reality of one-which-is-two." Islam, like Java, is both local and global at the same time. The chapter therefore seeks to understand what Islam and Java mean to each other as they communicate through architectural discourses.

The imaginaries of *Java*, *Islam*, *architecture*, *culture*, and *time* require us to look at specific episodes in the past as well as present tales of the island.

HISTORY AND AGENCY: JAVA WAR OR ISLAMIC WAR?
COLONIAL JAVA, 1825–30

Sufi Islam as filtered through India in the thirteenth and fifteenth centuries entered Java "on the heels not of conquest but of trade."[6] This mode of encounter allowed this particular form of Islam to develop first in the commercial strata in the coastal area of Java before it was absorbed into inland Java and became the religious order of the Javanese kingdom in the fifteenth century. This gradual incorporation, over a long period of time, allowed Java to identify its own tradition within the type of Islam it encountered.[7] Among Javanese Muslims, this interaction has produced various styles of discourse and practice of Islam in Java and constituted in Javanese Muslims a sense of double identity that moves between Islam and Java. Only in the last quarter of the nineteenth century, with the opening of the Suez Canal in 1870 and increasing direct contact between the Middle East and Java, was a real challenge to the traditional elements of Javanese culture developed. However, despite the effort to discard the non-Islamic element and to modernize Java through Islam, a large portion of Islamic followers remained within the framework of traditional Java. This divided loyalty has manifested itself in two major Islamic groups: the pan-Islamic "modernists," known for their attempt to discredit the non-Islamic component of Javanese culture, and the traditionalists whose discourses and practices of Islam are embedded in the heterodoxy of Javanese culture.[8] In between these two extremes lies the majority whose members identify with one of these two major groups but are usually unable to take sides.

Perhaps the best illustration of the shaping of this double identity, which involved Dutch colonial rule in Java, is the legend of Diponegoro, a Javanese prince who led a war against the Dutch colonial government in 1825.[9] This war shocked the Dutch because, for the first time in the history of Dutch rule over Java, a "rebellion" was organized under the banner of Islam. Haunted by this war and the capacity of Islam to mobilize Javanese against the colonial government, the Dutch began to discredit Islam in various aspects of colonial discourses. In the mind of the Dutch, with this event Islam had taken over the normally peaceful Javanese. For the Dutch, one way to bring peace back to the Javanese, and with it, the colonial order, was to suppress Islam and promote Javanese culture as something essential and more valuable than Islam. It is this colonial construction of Javanese culture that has separated Java from Islam.

However, what is crucial to us is what Prince Diponegoro himself thought about the conflict. What was Diponegoro's point of view concerning the Java War? From his perspective, while conducted under the banner of Islam, the war was a reenactment of an episode of war in Indic Javanese mythology. In other words, in Diponegoro's mind, the Java War was a symbolic expression of his own tradition's aspiration to conquer Java and not to liberate the island (as the Dutch would have thought).[10] It seemed Islam had no importance for him except insofar as it related to his Javanese culture. What stems from this story is a conjuncture of two different historical perspectives that brought into being the idea that Java is not merely part of Islam but that Islam is also part of Java.

This sense of duality as seen through the lens of Diponegoro (of seeing Java as part of Islam but not quite, for Islam is part of Java) is eventually captured under the notion of "Javanese Islam." This is what I will refer to in this chapter as the "reality of one-which-is-two."[11] The importance of this story lies in the condition in which this reality of one-which-is-two circulates across the barrier between precolonial, colonial, and the postcolonial Java. Today, the Javanese are still living through this ambiguity. Few things bring this ambiguous identity of Islam in Java into clearer expression than architecture.

"I Don't Feel Comfortable with the Form": Java, 1980s

In 1986, the Islamic community of Central Java was seriously offended by a research report of a team of architects. The report indicated that the Menara Kudus (Kudus Tower), a monument reputedly built in the seventeenth century and recognized popularly as a symbol of Islam, was originally a Hindu-Javanese monument (see figure 39).[12] In response to this disquiet, the architects who were involved in the research quickly explained that the focus of their research was the architectural form (the stylistic expression), and this formal architectural analysis had nothing to do with the history, politics, or the rituals surrounding the monument.[13] The journalist who reported this incident made an assessment that the spread of Islam in Central Java had been carried out through the local Hindu Javanese culture, and so it was perfectly logical that a trace of local culture could be found in an "Islamic" monument.

This dispute over the identity and representation of Islam in Java returned two years later in another event. This time it was in a debate over the design of a university's mosque in Jakarta.[14] The rector of the university (Universitas Nasional), Mr. Sutan Takdir Alisyahbana, proposed a design that was based on an ancient Hindu-Javanese monument in Central Java (see figure 40).

The rector's proposal might simply be one of the expressions of enthusiasm in Indonesia in the 1980s concerning the promotion of indigenous architecture. The traditional mosques in Indonesia have three-tiered roofs, and since about 1975 many architects and also government policy promoted this supposedly original Indonesian architecture.[15] Yet, outside the architectural circle, the rector was confronted by responses such as: "I don't feel comfortable with the form, because it doesn't provide you with a sense of a mosque. Maybe I am conventional and Mr. Alisyahbana (the rector) had a creative idea. However, there is no Islamic character in the building."[16] After receiving other strong criticisms from various Islamic communities and a report that potential donors (especially from abroad) were not happy with the style of the mosque, the rector gave up his idea. He finally approved, albeit reluctantly, a new design that included a tiny pan Islamic dome on the top of a three-tiered Javanese roof. Gone from the mosque also was the monumental Hindu-Javanese proportions (see figure 41).

Figure 39 Kudus Tower, with a tiered roof in Hindu-Javanese style, from the seventeenth century, Central Java. Reprinted courtesy of Tata Sastrowardoyo from Tjahjono, *Indonesian Heritage*.

TAMPAK MUKA

Figure 40 The initial design of the mosque of Universitas Nasional, 1988. Reprinted from *Tempo*, 7 May 1988.

Figure 41 The revised design of the mosque of Universitas Nasional, Jakarta, 1988. Reprinted from *Tempo*, 7 May 1988.

Behind these architectural events lay a long disquieted history of Islam in Java, a history that was composed of an unending tension and reconciliation of the reality of one-which-is-two. Questions concerning Hindu-Javanese culture on the one hand and the pan-Islamic Islam on the other, the tension between the polytheism of Hindu-Javanese culture and the monotheism of Islam, and most critical of all, the increasing sense on the part of a certain Islamic community in Java that un-Islamic components have long been part of Islam are all caught up in a dispute over the globality, identity, and authenticity of Islam in Java, a contestation over the reality of one-which-is-two.

It might be useful to note that the codification of the dome as the architectural style of global Islam is inseparable from the Dutch colonial discourse of distancing Islam from Java and that this style emerged perhaps only in the late nineteenth century. Work still needs to be done on the origin and the spread of the style of domed mosques. We know only that the Dutch, in the course of pacification following the bitter conquest of Aceh (a province in the most northern part of Sumatra) in 1897, built a new mosque to replace the one that was burned down several years earlier during the conquest. The new mosque, known as the Great Mosque of Kutaradja, adopted a Middle Eastern (Orientalist) style with an impressive central dome and pointed arch windows. A clock, like those found in European city halls, with Arabic numerals, hung above the entrance. This style was in remarkable contrast to that of the destroyed mosque with its tiered roofs.[17] It was intended, in the words of the then-Governor General I. W. van Landsberge, to be "aesthetically pleasing, well built, (and) suitable for the requirements of the Islamic religion."[18] If the Dutch found it important, politically, to contest the reality of one-which-is-two, they perhaps also realized the deep formation of this double consciousness that had taken place long before their arrival.

The First Mosque: Localizing Global Islam, Java, 1498

Let us thus go back to fifteenth-century Java as it may be helpful to take into consideration an earlier confrontation between Javanese and Middle Eastern Islam prior to European colonialism, especially when the negotiation in that now-distant clash is today quite clearly visible.

I will take the case of the Demak Mosque, which is known as the oldest great mosque since it was built to mark the first Islamic Kingdom in Java in the fifteenth century. This part of my discussion is drawn from the work of Nancy Florida who translated and interpreted a Javanese manuscript written in the nineteenth century about a sixteenth-century history called *Babad Jaka Tingkir*—The History of Jaka Tingkir.[19] *Babad Jaka Tingkir* is an epic history that concerns the emergence of Islamic power in Central Java, and it is written as a prophetic script for the future. In it there are prophecies and fantasies of resistance and intervention to everything that was considered conventional in nineteenth century Java when *Babad* was written. In the *Babad*, there is a chapter on the construction of the Demak Mosque (see figure 42). The unknown author of the *Babad* tells the story of how, in the late fifteenth century, the Javanese Islamic saints (the Wali who brought Islam to Java) invested the structure of the mosque with the Javanese symbolism of power in order to make Islam part of the Javanese world. The author of the *Babad* narrates, in the form of poems, an intricate dialogue between the Middle Eastern Islam and the Javanese religious cosmology and demonstrates how these two worlds were brought together after intricate negotiation. What is interesting is that the negotiation between these two worlds was inscribed in the form and space of the Demak Mosque. It would need a lengthy description to properly represent these processes of cultural negotiation; I can show only one part of Florida's rich interpretation about the way the Demak Mosque became the site of nego-

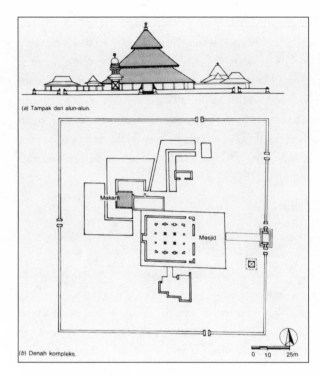

(a) Tampak dari alun-alun.

Makam

Mesjid

(b) Denah kompleks.

0   10   25m

Figure 42 The front elevation of the Demak Mosque, fifteenth century, Demak, Central Java. Reprinted courtesy of P. T. Gramedia Pustaka Utama from Wiryomartono, *Seni bangunan dan seni bina kota di Indonesia.*

tiation between the authority of Middle Eastern Islam and the power of Javanese culture.

One of the stories was about the orientation of the mosque (*kiblah*) after it was built. (Unlike in our architectural tradition today, the author of the *Babad* suggests that at the time of Demak Mosque the problem of the building's placement came after the whole structure was completed!) As we know, according to the standard Islamic building code, the mosque, no matter where it is located, should orient its direction (*adhep*) toward the Ka'bah of Mecca—the spiritual center of global Islam.[20] If we look at the standardized map of our time, the building orientation of Demak Mosque (see figure 42) is approximately to the west (or northwest). Architecturally, from our perspective, the location of the *mihrab* (a niche within the wall facing Mecca) is indeed more or less oriented toward Mecca. However, the issue of orientation is much more complex in the text of *Babad*. In this manuscript, one finds that the Demak Mosque (almost having a personality!) would not kiblah. In other words, the mosque, which embodied the society of the new Javanese Muslims who constructed it, did not want to orient itself to the Ka'bah of Mecca! It may be important to point out that the Javanese word for *kiblah* means "to face Mecca" and "to obey." For the Demak Mosque, it seems like it is fine to face Mecca but to obey is another thing. The Demak Mosque, while accepting Islam, did not want to submit to the authority of Islam's Meccan center. Instead, it seeks to define its own version of Islam and set itself up as a center of power from its position at the margins of the Islamic world.[21] The clash between two authorities thus took place in the building itself:

> But all the Wali eight
> Of vision still did clash
> The mosque nudged to right and left
> Swinging to and fro from north to south
> Still never came to rest

It was only when the Wali intervened that the mosque was put to rest. The author of the *Babad* indicated that the Wali negotiated with both the Meccan Ka'bah and the Demak Mosque to coordinate an axis of power that would bring the two centers together into an alignment, producing what has since been known as "the reality of one-which-is-two."

> Allah's Ka'bah did his right hand grasp
> His left hand having taken hold
> Of the uppermost peak of the mosque
> Both of them he pulled
> Stretched out and brought to meet
> The Ka'bah's roof and the peak of the mosque
> Realized as one being were
> Perfectly straight strictly on mark[22]

Mecca, the focal point of global Islam, was brought home to Java only after Mecca was seen as a center but not the only center of the Islamic world. From the point of view of global Islam, the Demak Mosque may seem to represent the power of the new faith in Java, but from the Javanese perspective, Islam has been localized and incorporated within the larger cultural framework of Java. This process suggests that not only is Java part of Islam, but Islam is also part of Java or Javanese life.

This act of negotiation and other uncanny happenings related in the

Babad Jaka Tingkir also reveal the loss of the full coherency of the Javanese world. With the establishment of Islam in the fifteenth century, Java
was no longer "the center of the universe." The encounter with the Other
(Islam) made Java aware of its own limits and that its own "self" was to be
shared and a new boundary to be drawn.

The process of localizing global (Islamic) culture in traditional Javanese
symbolism in a different but not radical way is a story about controlling
Islamic expression for Javanese religious ends.[23] Was this effort political?
Perhaps, especially since this mosque was built in the period that saw the
transition from the ancient Hindu Javanese regime in East Java to the beginning of the Islamic regime in Central Java. However, this process was
not just a struggle for political power but was also a struggle between the
Javanese religion and the spreading of a particular version of Islam. Most
importantly, the process of localizing Islamic culture was part of a gigantic enterprise on the part of the Javanese to meet the challenge to Java's
own religious framework caused by its encounters with the plurality of the
global world in the fifteenth century. The new Javanese Muslims wanted to
encompass the new experience in such a way that the Javanese world would
maintain its religious balance and that its own center would not have to
shift radically. By localizing Islam, the coherence of the Javanese world was
retained, though in a somewhat compromised form: the reality of oneness
in Javanese culture was transformed into "the reality of one-which-is-two."
This transformation from "one" into "one-which-is-two" shows how, in the
fifteenth century, the old Javanese cosmology lost its absoluteness when it
confronted a new social environment. To survive, the Javanese belief system appeared in Islamic form. The tradition of a "one-which-is-two" per-
sists until today.

Decentering Islam: The Old Way Is Still Valid . . . , Java, 1970

In 1970, five centuries after the establishment of the Demak Mosque, the
well-known Javanese architect Mintobudoyo designed and built a small
mosque for the Javanese royal family in Central Java in the Taman Sari
Royal Garden complex. The mosque has a single column at the center.
From this column four Javanese master pillars branch out, supporting four
corner beams of the upper roof. It seems to me the intention of this architect was to construct a focus, a vertical center that represents the unity of
the Javanese and the Islamic worlds. The vertical column pays tribute to

global Islam, and the horizontal spread of the four Javanese master pillars confirms the existence of the local power. However, Mintobudoyo makes it clear that Java is at the center of the whole negotiation between Javanese and Islamic elements. The mosque orients itself to the east, away from kiblah. It was reported that Mintobudoyo would rather have resigned and given up his job than allowed his mosque to be directed toward the kiblah: "To [Mintobudoyo], a Javanese mosque should face East, any deviation from this direction for a mosque would violate the Javanese rule."[24] The commissioner finally accepted Mintobudoyo's position, and the mosque was built accordingly. It is not clear whether Mintobudoyo consulted the tale of the Demak Mosque for his design, but he reminds us of the symbolism of the Demak Mosque. The mosque of Mintobudoyo also embodies "the reality of one-which-is-two." What Mintobudoyo also reveals to us is a remarkable architectural way of saying to the global world (of Islam) something like: the old way is still valid, our perception of the order of things is still true.

I am conscious of the fact that by arguing for the power of local culture (instead of the hegemony of the global), I seem to be proposing an argument for local specificity. However, what I want to point out is that global Islam, like other hegemonic forms of European modernism, should be seen as a part, not as a whole, of the many existing cultural centers. The interest of thinking about the multicentricity of our world lies in the way a particular culture determines the content, form, and the status of its cultural expression, a determination that involves competitions of interest and the marking of, and contestation over, boundaries of cultural practices.

The example of the Demak Mosque shows that the form the mosque took was not given. Its form was not the result of an act of pure invention of one culture that then became an important point of reference for subsequent mosque-builders. Instead, the Demak Mosque was made up, reproduced, and rearticulated, along with other practices, products, and discourses demarcated over time in Javanese society.

POLITICS AND RELIGIOUS FAITH: SECULAR OR RELIGIOUS NATION-STATE? INDONESIA, 1960S AND 1980S

Today, the Demak Mosque still remains a powerful force in Javanese governance. President Suharto (1966–98) saw the restoration of the mosque

Figure 43 The standardized mosque promoted by President Suharto, circa 1980s, with the Arabic epigraph for *Allah* enclosed in a pentagon attached to the lightning rod at the apex of the roof. Photo by A. Kusno.

as part of an effort to build up the nation's spiritual capital.[25] Launching the renovation of the Demak Mosque in 1987, Suharto reminded Indonesians that it was the only piece of royal heritage left behind by a Javanese king who was exiled by the Dutch colonial government. The press, citing the eighteenth-century king of Surakarta, Susuhunan Pakubuwana I, continued: "Demak Mosque [and the Kadilangu grave] are the only heritage of absolute value [that we have left] and should not disappear from Java."[26] The president went as far as to promote replicas of the Demak Mosque that were to be used nationwide, in a standardized form, in every province of Indonesia (see figure 43).

The style of Suharto's mosque, as we recognize, is a revival of the legendary Demak Mosque. But this cross-reference to the ancient past is not just a statement of a postmodern regionalist paradigm. Instead, it indicates the way Suharto, as a Javanese, dealt with global Islam. As architecture critic Hugh O'Neill points out, this negotiation between the realms of Islam and Java (the nation) is most explicitly shown in the lightning rod installed at the apex of the roof.[27] Attached to this rod is a hollow pentagonal frame that encloses the Arabic epigraph for *Allah*. This pentagonal frame represents the five principles of Indonesian nationhood, *Pancasila* (a Sanskrit word indicating the embodiment of Hindu-Javanese culture in the nation-state). Putting the Arabic inscription *Allah* within, not above, the five-sided metal frame is a way of saying something like: No, we are not being absorbed. Islam is only part of Indonesia. We are not seeking Islam to transform our society, but we seek a transformation of Islam to fit with our own (or old) national Javanese concept of life which is (still) true.

The first president of Indonesia, Sukarno (1950–65) dealt with Islam in quite another way. His strategy is not clearly expressed in the Istiqal Mosque that he built during his reign.[28] However, if we read carefully what Sukarno, the patron of the mosque, said about the building, we find the extraordinary remark that since Indonesia is an Islamic nation, it should encompass the greatness of all mosques in the world.

> What! Would we build a Friday Mosque like the Masjid Demak, or Masjid Banten [these are all mosques founded in Indonesia]. I'm sorry! What if I approached Masjid Banten! When it was built, it was already great. But if erected today, what would it rank, technical colleagues? . . . It is my wish, together with the Islamic community here to erect a Friday Mosque which is larger than the Mohammad Ali Mosque [in Cairo], larger than the Salim Mosque. Larger! And why? We have a great nation! My wish is to build with all the populous, one Indonesian nation which proclaims the Islamic religion. We are always amazed! . . . Why can't we build a mosque which is larger and more beautiful than [all the existing great mosques]?[29]

This style of talking is characteristic of Sukarno, the great orator, however it also makes sense if we understand the content through the cultural framework of Java. In other words, this statement can be adequately understood only if we place Islam squarely within the cultural framework of Java. For Sukarno, it is not just that Islam is a global religion, but that the globality of Islam could or should be absorbed by the cultural framework of the Indonesian nation. The Istiqal Mosque, being international in style, not least through its pan-Islamic dome,[30] shows a successful absorption of the larger Islamic world by Sukarno's national (or better Javanese) regime. The remarkable statement that Sukarno repeatedly made that his Istiqal Mosque (see figure 44) should surpass all the great mosques of the

Figure 44 Istiqal Mosque, Jakarta, circa 1960s. Reprinted courtesy of Tata Sastrowardoyo from Tjahjono, *Indonesian Heritage.*

world he had visited shows the power of his Javanese culture cast in the national form.[31]

What we have in these two cases is how the architectural representation of Middle Eastern Islam was altered, rearticulated, and transformed to fit with the Javanese cultural framework now cast in a national form. We might argue that the discourses of mosque building by these two presidents show that politicians necessarily use culture for political ends. In this case, the internationalist style of the Istiqal Mosque in Jakarta, promoted by Sukarno in the 1960s to symbolize his nation building, was eventually countered by the local (Demak) style of the mosques sponsored by the Suharto regime in the 1980s. We might argue that this competition to construct a proper religious expression and invent a symbol of authority through architecture was clearly for political ends, and therefore these discourses should be understood through a secular, not a religious, rationale.[32]

Yet, I am inclined to read the discourses of mosque building under the regimes of Suharto and Sukarno differently. What would the discourses of mosque building be like if we see the two ex-presidents of Indonesia not merely as secular politicians but as Javanese who lived in and through the changes of their own cultural milieu? How did they reconcile the competing demands of their cultural milieu and the secular nation-state, local Javanese culture and the global structure of Islam? What would it be like if instead of seeing Java as part of the Islamic world we take a different perspective and view Islam as part of the larger world of Java?

From this inverted perspective, these two national mosques, each with its own style, are not making the statement that "Indonesia is an Islamic country," but quite the contrary, they state that Islam has been absorbed (or incorporated) into the world of Indonesia. One might argue that these are the political acts of a secular nation attempting to mark the boundary of religion, but they are also religious acts to encourage Islam to join the recognized Javanese culture embodied in the nation-state.

There is a contestation, negotiation, and mutual absorption between Java and Islam that plays out, in political terms, the religiocultural "reality of one-which-is-two." If we think of both Sukarno and Suharto less as politicians and more as Javanese, we will see that the impulse behind the contestation over the styles of the mosque is more than political. Instead it is part of a deeper Javanese cultural enterprise that seeks to encompass the new experience of living in a social life of nationhood. In other words, the goal of these Javanese presidents was not just to increase their political power but also to create a particular religiocultural faith. What we have in them are therefore subjects composed of "the reality of one-which-is-two" — the reality of being both a secular politician and a religious Javanese — which makes their politics of mosque building irreducible to political functionalism.

ARCHITECTURE AND IDEOLOGY:
"ARCHITECTURE IS NOT ONLY PHYSICAL"

By way of conclusion, let me explore a little further the remodeling of the Javanese self through contemporary architectural culture in Indonesia. If we think that architects are not only experts in their field but also members of a particular social and cultural order, then we will perhaps encounter professional subjects composed of a "reality of one-which-is-two," as was the case with the ex-presidents. The consciousness of Indonesia's own globality manifested in the "reality of one-which-is-two" could be seen through the long struggle, continuing to the present day, in the intellectual culture of architecture over what constitutes "Indonesian architecture." One powerful resolution can be found in the expression of something like an "inner traditional concept" and an "outer modern expression." This development is very often demonstrated by striking architectural innovations. One can find in a modern building all kinds of functional elements and high-tech structure, but behind them is an intangible inner concept defending a cultural faith. The modern structure is the outer circle protecting the unity of the inner circle. We can see this sense of coherence in a famous and well-received phrase among postcolonial Javanese architects that "architecture is not only physical."[33]

At various national conferences on "modern architecture and Indonesia" or in discussions about "Indonesian architecture," we might see the circulation of a (shared) proposition that the ideas of modern architecture are at bottom the ideas of a Javanese building culture and that the ideas of Vitruvius, Frank L. Wright, and the much-loved Dutch architect Henri Maclaine Pont, and so on, were all to be comprehended or absorbed by the larger framework of local culture.[34] (This is not peculiar, because we also, a lot of the time, use our own universal modernist architectural framework to understand the strange and the incomprehensible.) It is thus not surprising that the all-absorbing words in search of a totality such as *Arsitektur Pancasila, Arsitektur Indonesia, Arsitektur Nusantara, Arsitektur Tropis* gained their currency among architects because they underline the encompassing power of the hidden concept to cover different architectural expressions, no matter whether they are from East or West, old or new.

The unprecedented debates on "architecture and identity" since the 1980s, I suspect, are more than just a sign of professional insecurity in the age of free-market globalization. They are also part of an enormous effort to come to terms with inner concepts and are thus a defense of a cultural faith. This is perhaps why many Indonesian architects do not seem to focus much attention on the ideology or politics of architecture. It is not that they do not think about the link between architecture and politics. They are actually interested in politics and concern themselves much about the power of politics. However, of more importance to these architects is the conviction that architecture embodies the permanent inner values that could always overcome politics. This awareness that the core of architecture is cultural (if not religious), while its political life is something that can be taken or left, has made architecture, in the eyes of these architects, irreducible to political functionalism.

Some might argue that architecture and urban design are always political and we should look at architecture in Indonesia, Islam, and Javanese culture and understand them with reference to the secular framework of politics. Yet, as I have tried to show in this chapter, there is a need to find a way to talk about what lies beyond our own existing framework for understanding the politics of architecture. This problem also applies to the nonpolitical perspective used by many Indonesian architects in Indonesia in the sense that they too have incorporated what we thought to be a politics of representation into their own nonpolitical framework.

Through a series of architectural cases, I have explored the remodeling of the self associated with the emergence of the "reality of one-which-is two" in Javanese culture in its long engagement with global pan-Islamic Islam. The formation and transformation of Javanese Islam and the architectural form it has taken is inseparable from the context of social and economic change in Java. Each of the architectural cases explored needs to be contextualized, but this chapter is intended less to explain the socioeconomic bases of the "reality of one-which-is-two" in Java than to show the formative roles architecture managed to play in the struggle within those contexts and processes.

In the following chapter, I will continue the discussion of the changing political form of architecture in relation to the transformation of social life in the nation diachronically across different times. The object of my inquiry is the gatehouse, an artifact that is far from monumental, but, as I will argue, plays a significant role in defining governmental strategies, regulating public memory, and assembling techniques of survival that over the course of a longue durée produce a normative practice for individuals and society. The key force for the reproduction of gatehouses is the inhabitation of politics in everyday life, which constitutes what Denys Lombard called the *mental nebule* of Indonesian society. The gatehouse, like the mosque in this chapter, embodies a culture of crossroads deeply marked by the interaction of several traditions even as it is represented as having an autonomous history of its own.

CHAPTER 9 **GUARDIAN OF MEMORIES**
The *Gardu* in Urban Java

> The basic problem ... is ... somehow to convey simultaneously both
> that conspicuous history which holds our attention by its continual and
> dramatic changes—and that other, submerged, history almost silent
> and always discreet, virtually unsuspected either by its observers or
> its participants, which is little touched by the obstinate erosion of time.
> —FERNAND BRAUDEL, *THE MEDITERRANEAN*

Unlike the "intelligent cities" of Southeast Asia, Indonesian cities have
not yet surrendered the realm of discipline to the policing technology
of security cameras. Instead, the gatehouse (known popularly as the gardu)
is still the prime resource for community defense, state policing, and surveillance. The reason for the proliferation of gardus in the urban landscape
lies not only in the incapacity of the city to provide alternative security
systems for its residents but also in the active role the gardu still plays in
the modality of urban life.

Indonesians who have lived in urban Java would recognize the gardu
as a place where (mostly) men gather to conduct night patrols or watches
and engage in such leisure activities as gambling and gossiping. Many of
them would recognize the variety of forms gardus have taken. The minimal
one (generally found in rural areas) is often made from bamboo, wood
planks, and a thatch roof. Usually on stilts and measuring about two by
two meters, it is open on the front side (with or without a door) (see figure
45). In cities, the gardu is often a more permanent construction. It is like
a tiny house made of brick, often with a sofa or chair inside or beside it.
Those who conduct the night watch, the prime practice of the gardu, are
armed with hand weapons, which include long bamboo sticks with their

Figure 45 A *gardu* at the entrance to a *kampung* in Surabaya, circa 1920s.
Photo courtesy of KITLV.

heads shaped like forks, wooden sticks, and sometimes knives or mache-
tes, but no firearms. Their key instrument, however, is the *kentongan*, a
hollowed-out tree branch with an opening line down the middle that produces sound when it is struck with a stick. Hung on the doorway of the
gardu when not in use, the kentongan is used by members (adult males) of
the *ronda* (the night watch) on patrol to alert the community to the state of
neighborhood security. In the new towns of major cities, gardus have occasionally been fashioned in elaborate styles with high Baroque motifs and
Javanese architectural elements. They are visible at almost every junction
in major cities in Indonesia, especially in the urban centers of Java. They
are placed sporadically as well as strategically over ditches and at sidewalks,
junctions of streets, entrances to kampungs, gates of commercial buildings
and housing complexes, as well as fronts of houses. During the period of
national election campaigns after the collapse of Suharto's rule, they were
painted in the symbolic colors of certain political parties and adorned with
the party's banners, stickers, and slogans. At the celebration of Independence Day, they appeared in red and white, the color of the national flag.

Indonesians would thus recognize the gardu as an artifact that represents security and order with connections to both the state and local power. Profoundly visible after the May 1998 riots, gardus (especially for the ethnic Chinese) also trigger memories of chaos, disturbance, and insecurity. Soon after the collapse of Suharto's government, the gardu was also harnessed by the then-oppositional party, the Partai Demokrasi Indonesia-Perjuangan (the Indonesian Democratic Party for the Struggle for Freedom, PDI-P), to mobilize supporters and to retrieve memories of Sukarno, the father of the party's leader, Megawati.

This chapter is about the interplay between urban memory, monuments, and symbolic struggles over identity and place. Benedict Anderson, who was perhaps the first person to recognize monuments as an important form of "symbolic speech" of Indonesian political cultures (rather than simply an expression of the state's ideology), points out that few observers "have recognized that monuments are a type of speech, or tried to discern concretely what is being said, why form and content are specifically what they are."[1] Anderson suggests that to understand the intention and context of a particular culture, it is important to analyze the form and content of its monuments even though we cannot fully account for the role of these monuments in forming and transforming collective identity. A single object can indeed be invested with various meanings. Yet it is precisely the fragmentary and imprecise nature of the experiences of monuments that makes the interpretative reading of the object so important. By looking at the signifying practices of gardus, this chapter aims at connecting work on the spatial dimension of community identity with study of Indonesian monuments and forms of memorialization.

However, it is important to recognize that gardus are a form of "symbolic speech" that are intended neither as monuments nor as memorials even though in some cases (as this chapter will show) they perform such functions. As a tiny construction located at the margin of "monumental" structures, the gardu is often neglected by urban conservationists and researchers of the city. Like other urban artifacts that have become part of "normal" everyday life, the role of the gardu in registering public memory has usually been overlooked. As part of everyday structures, the gardu however is as significant as a "monument" for it plays a crucial role in expressing political views, regulating public memory, and defining territory and collective identity.

This chapter examines the political roles and the changing meaning of gardus, genealogically, from our own times back to the past. It shows how the gardu has continued to be a visual medium through which collective memories are both formed and transformed across different historical orders. Instead of showing the gardu as merely a symptom of a recent global urban form associated with the rise of disciplinary society and gated communities worldwide, I aim to reflect on the gardu as an institution that embodies specific histories, ones that over time have shaped the collective memories of people who have lived through those histories. Such a tracing of the history of gardus necessitates an ensemble of discursive moments and various signifying practices connected to the experience and territorial defense of ethnic Chinese, the Javanese concept of space, the territorial politics of Dutch colonialism, and the discourses of neighborhood watch under Japanese occupation as well as the political communications of Indonesia during the revolution and postindependence era. How does this everyday institution and artifact function as a mnemonic device that plays a role in registering public memories?

MEMORIES: THE POSKO OF MEGAWATI AND THE PLATFORM OF SUKARNO

In 1998, on the eve of his resignation, President Suharto said quite bluntly that he had no problem with leaving office, but if he were to step down immediately, chaos or maybe even bloodshed and civil war would be the outcome, a situation that no one, not even his handpicked successor B. J. Habibie, would be able to overcome.[2] Thus, without Suharto and his military governance, Indonesians would find themselves in an uncertain and potentially vulnerable position. Suharto's statement delineates the condition in which Indonesians would find themselves had he stepped down and been replaced by the new era. Suharto was forced to resign, but his "prophecy" that chaos, bloodshed, and unrest would follow has in a large way come true. Soon after the riots in May 1998 that caused the death of hundreds of residents of Jakarta, in East Java approximately 120 people accused of witchcraft were killed between December 1998 and the end of February 1999. In East Timor, massive violence took place, involving elements of the Indonesian military. Serious political violence and killings also occurred in many different parts of Indonesia, Aceh, Borneo, the Moluccas, and Western New Guinea, and several bombing incidents took place at major cities on the islands of Java, Sumatra, and Bali.

Figure 46 A *posko* of PDI-P at Tubagus Angke Street with the shape of a *pendhopo* roof and the image of Megawati and an angry bull. Photo by A. Kusno.

Perhaps as a way of coping with this state of chaos and the fear that riots and killings might occur again, the residents of major cities in Java and Sumatra built, at their own expense, gardus at almost every street corner.[3] This sense of urgency was particularly felt by the ethnic Chinese. They built fences and gardus for their neighborhoods and participated in night watch schemes. They also hired police and local hit men to watch over the streets from the gardus. In less than a year, the number of gardus and gates multiplied, becoming permanent features of the cityscape.[4]

This community response to the time of chaos, however, was soon appropriated by the political elites of the country in their aim of winning the attention of the public. In 1998, the political leaders of the then-opposition party, the Indonesian Democratic Party (PDI Perjuangan), chaired by Megawati Soekarno Putri, mobilized the construction of gardus, known popularly as *posko* (*pos komunikasi* — that is, "communication posts"), at various places throughout the country (see figure 46).[5]

In response, Jakarta's governor ordered that all the poskos be demolished for they worsened the cityscape of Jakarta, but the PDI-P paid no heed and continued to disseminate poskos not only in the capital city but also in other cities across Indonesia.[6] In the urban center of Solo alone, the PDI-P built 262 poskos in less than six months. The construction of poskos at street corners coincided with the aftermath of May 1998, when Indonesians, especially those of ethnic Chinese background, protected themselves by constructing more gardus. In a way, the followers of Megawati harnessed ethnic Chinese Indonesians' fear of more riots in the city. The poskos offered the urbanite a sense of order and protection even though they also reminded passersby of violence and the possibility of violence recurring. According to Slamet Suryanto, one of the PDI's leaders in Solo, the posko contributed to the creation of order and security in the city after it was badly hurt by burning, looting, and killing during the May 1998 riots. "Since the construction of poskos in almost every street in Solo, the condition of the city has cheered up. If the post-May riots had made Solo a dead town with very few people on the streets, now (as a result of the poskos) there is a sense that life has begun again."[7] From the posko, the party also donated money and distributed aid packages to poor residents. Roy Janis, one of the leaders of the PDI Jakarta branch, considered the posko as a structure built for the purposes of "overcoming criminalities in the city, preventing students fighting on the streets, and helping the distribution of foods to the urban poor . . . Poskos (thus) belong to the public while they can be used for the party's political campaign."[8] In the minds of the PDI elites, the presence of the posko suggests the party's care for the public and symbolizes the willingness of the political elites to communicate with the populace. As a form of what Anderson has called "symbolic speech," the posko moves between the ideology and practices of everyday life.

There are various reasons behind choosing the posko as the symbol of the party's campaign. One of the leaders of the PDI-P indicated that the posko is "a symbol that could mobilize crowds [massa] at any moment. It is also a sign of power."[9] To other members of the PDI-P, the posko, scattered all over the city, often with no attachment to any particular neighborhood, represents the "homelessness" of the PDI-P after its headquarters was raided and destroyed. This sense of homelessness is well conveyed by the semipermanent structure of the posko, which can be torn down and built quickly in other places.

However, there is something more to the posko. For Megawati, the posko was not merely a gardu post for communication, a kind of mouthpiece of her political party, but also a structure that represented the public image of herself and her father, the first president, Sukarno (1950–65). Megawati urged the members and sympathizers of her party to safeguard

Figure 47 A *posko* of PDI-P at Surabaya Street with a painting of Sukarno on the door. Photo courtesy of F. Prihadi.

the posko, use it properly as a center for education, and avoid any action that would damage its image.[10] In the eyes of her supporters, Megawati embodied the posko. They called every posko "the headquarters of Megawati Sukarno Putri" and displayed photos and drawings of both Megawati and Sukarno as if they were standing on the platform of the posko addressing the audience. The images of Sukarno and Megawati in the posko were also drawn from history for they depicted a Sukarno whom Indonesians admired. The drawing of Sukarno pointing his finger recalls the well-known image of the first president standing on a podium delivering speeches to a mass audience (see figure 47).

We do not know precisely if Indonesians at large remember the podium as an embodiment of Sukarno, but the podium did symbolize free speech. In 1996, as a statement of protest against the reinstallation of Soerjadi by the Suharto government as the leader of PDI-P, the followers of Megawati set up a "free speech podium" outside the PDI-P headquarters in Jakarta.[11] Placed outside the headquarters, the podium supposedly reached out to the Indonesian public, but it also sought to recall the image of Sukarno delivering his spirited speech. For weeks, this free speech podium became the arena for speakers to routinely denounce the government until it was finally smashed to pieces on 27 July 1996. The posko could thus be seen as an object that sought to commemorate the violence done to the PDI-P, the "free speech podium," and the symbolic position of Megawati–Sukarno.

In this sense, the adoption of the posko and the image of Sukarno giving a speech could be seen as a form of commemoration. It sought not only to remember the violence that had been done to Megawati's political party but also to reconstitute the historical figure of Sukarno as the embodiment of "free speech." The followers of Megawati also invoked the image of Sukarno because they believed in the power that the podium seemed to possess to concentrate the attention of the populace. The connection between Sukarno, the podium, and the people was in fact emphasized in one of Sukarno's speeches. In 1964 during his Independence Day speech, he proclaimed:

> For me, this podium—the podium of 17th August [Independence Day]—is a podium of people [*podium rakyat*], a podium of revolution, a podium that orients the determination of our nation! I use this podium as a space for dialogue between Sukarno, a person and Sukarno, the leader of the revolution. I use this podium as a space of dialogue between Sukarno, the leader of the revolution, and the Indonesian people who are undergoing the revolution. . . . This is a podium where we form a dialogue. It is a place of communication for 103 million Indonesian people. . . . That is why every time I stand on this podium of 17th August, I am not only talking to the revolutionary people of Indonesia, but also to all human beings undergoing revolution.[12]

From the podium Sukarno gathered support from his audience who, from a distance, could in fact hardly see or hear him. It was only the podium that they saw and remembered clearly. Pramoedya Ananta Toer, for instance, recalls President Sukarno addressing the Indonesian people. Pramoedya however could hardly remember the messages or the facial expression of the president, but he could not forget the things around the leader, especially the high platform, the watchtower, and the loudspeaker that provided the setting for the event.[13]

The attraction of the leader appearing on a platform as both a seeing

Figure 48 A *posko* of PDI-P at Wijaya Street, located above the alleyway to a *kampung*, that recalls the image of a podium. Photo courtesy of F. Prihadi.

object and an object to be seen is inseparable from the changing modality of "seeing power" in traditional Java. Before discussing the mutual gaze between objects considered powerful and their audiences in traditional Java, let me mention another interrelated dimension of Megawati's posko. Poskos were constructed on every street corner of the city in order to contact people and to tell them something like: we are here to protect and serve you, and our presence should allow you to see the authority and the benevolence of our leader (see figure 48). Often constructed on a location without the consent of local residents, the posko assumes the position of a vanguard by claiming, through banners, the territory on which it stands, such as "this is the territory of Banteng (a black "angry" bull, an icon of the PDI)," "PDI is the party for young people (*anak muda*)," and "you are entering the territory of PDI."[14] For the followers of Megawati, what matters most in the placement of the posko is not what it claims, but that the posko, wherever it is located, should radiate its influence outward, reaching as far as possible to the outermost territories.[15] For them, the dissemination of poskos is a political maneuver aimed at maintaining and expanding their sphere of influence (and the destruction of poskos by political rivals is also a political maneuver aimed at curtailing their sphere of influence).

The poskos and banners of Megawati not only compete with those from other political parties but also with billboards and advertisements that are widespread throughout the city. Political ideologies are thus set up alongside the ideology of market capitalism as both claim the right to the city. To the territorial claims of Megawati's poskos that attempt to increase her sphere of influence, we must append an older political tradition. Note that many posko adopt the roof shape of the pendhopo for this shape manifests most clearly the "old" Javanese concept of power and authority.[16] The posko, with its messages and its mission "to help residents to overcome various problems that have emerged as a result of recent political situations,"[17] recalls an older tradition of spatial politics in Java in which the representation of the pendhopo and the competition for power and influence were at stake.

Pendhopos and the Boundary of Traditional Power

The pendhopo is a pavilion-like structure that stands in front of a Javanese housing compound. It is visible from the street and accessible to people (mostly males). Standing in front of the *Omah* (the inner structure of the Javanese house), the pendhopo mediates the ruler and the ruled, the inner and the outer circle, by integrating the latter into the former's sphere of influence. As a symbol of traditional authority, the pendhopo can thus be seen as spatializing the Javanese concept of power. Members of Javanese society often associate the pendhopo with an umbrella (*payung*) or a banyan tree (*waringin*) for it shelters people and offers a space for them to come together.[18] By virtue of its spatial capacity to draw people into its domain (the practice of *mengayomi*), many Javanese believe that the pendhopo represents the power and authority of the owner of the house. They also assume that if the owner is powerful, he ought to be able to absorb everything from everywhere into his pendhopo. Because of this emphasis on the power of the pendhopo as a symbol of the center attracting the surroundings, there is no need in the traditional polity to mark the boundary of the ruler's territory, a demarcation that would limit the centripetal forces of the center. In the competitive field of power, the higher, bigger, and more encompassing the pendhopo, the more it would attract followers.

In this sense, the posko of today's political parties replays in some ways the function of the pendhopo, where people were supposed to find power, protection, and security. Entering the pendhopo, one becomes part of its sphere, an act that is similar to people going to the posko for help and assistance. It is also similar to passing through a gate where one's identity is (temporarily) transformed from being an outsider to an insider. It is striking, but logical, that many poskos use the roof shape of a pendhopo to increase their influence and incorporate members (see figure 46).

In precolonial Java, the importance of the pendhopo, however, lay not only in its capacity to invite and absorb allies but also in its ability to conceal the king behind the walls of his residence. In contrast to the open pendhopo, walls enclose the residence of the king. His invisibility and inaccessibility guaranteed his power. He only appears on particular occasions through a rigid ritual of a procession passing through a series of gates and the pendhopo in order to further sustain his inaccessibility. His grand pendhopo is all that people could see of him.

This old symbolism, however, collapsed—at least visually—when Sukarno appeared on the podium. To the thousands of commoners, the appearance of Sukarno on the high open platform meant that the hidden power had been displaced or had finally emerged and offered itself to them. No other form of communication could more convincingly prove the newness of Sukarno's gesture. Sukarno's near-modernist white suits and his spontaneous speech were all in stark contrast to the heavily ritualized procession of the king hidden behind or under the pendhopo. In the eyes of the commoners, Sukarno embodied a power that is visible and was a new leader who had (to a remarkable degree) freed himself from the grasp of traditional symbolism.

What I am suggesting here is that the fragmented images of the past lingered on. Sukarno's podium gained its power from displacing (if not replacing) the image of the traditional pendhopo. Yet both Sukarno's podium and the king's pendhopo in turn have provided precedents for Megawati's posko. There are however some significant differences between Sukarno's mode of communication and that of his daughter. Sukarno's audience was indeed the people (rakyat), and no matter whether they understood his speech or not, it was through them that he gained political legitimacy. Megawati's audience, by contrast, was the "middle class" who feared the people (known in her time as the massa) whom the elites had been trying to avoid and control.[19] If people gathered outside to see Sukarno, the person, on a singular podium, the "people" of Megawati saw only her replicas, in the form of the many poskos available on every street corner. If the podium of Sukarno symbolized the mobilization of the masses to continue the revolution, the posko of Megawati called for power, security, and order. Megawati's call for stability, however, was also historically based for it recalled the long-standing disciplinary discourses of Megawati's political enemy and predecessor, President Suharto (1966–98).

Pos Hansips and the New Order

What was the posko before Megawati? Before this, in the social environment of Suharto, the gardu was called a *pos hansip* (post for civil defense). The term *posko* was also used in Suharto's time, but it referred to a post for military command (*pos-komando*), a control center temporarily set up by Suharto's military units in unfamiliar and untamed terrain. The presence of the "military posko" in what was considered as unruly grounds delineated the interaction between the army and the surrounding areas it sought to control. *Posko* in the Suharto era was thus a term for combat in a "battleground." Poskos were used to control aspects of social and political life in the field to assure order and security. It might be important to note that Suharto's army men spent most of their careers in nonurban settings, such as rural and jungle areas, since "communism" was believed to be playing a vigorous role in rural consciousness. I believe it was in those areas, outside the city, that the term *posko* was first used. We can find the term *posko taktis* in the program of *Abri Masuk Desa* (military joining the village),[20] which started in the 1970s, and the term was also probably used in the annexation and pacification of East Timor and the other outer islands. As a structure for controlling and pacifying unfamiliar and "dangerous" terrain, the posko can be seen as a symbol of menace and insecurity.

Toward the middle of the 1980s, the army intelligence envisioned a change in their terrain of operation. For years to come, according to army intelligence, security threats would no longer come from Aceh, East Timor, or the Irian but most likely would come from urban regions. As units of the military were regularly discharged from East Timor and the villages, many returned to urban Java and picked up security jobs with the police that had been created for them in the city. The surplus labor of the army contributed to the militarization of urban space. Some ex-soldiers preferred to operate on the streets and organize urban thugs. Others found themselves involved in pos hansips in various neighborhoods, banks, shopping centers, and new private housing complexes, as well as in the houses of the elites. The owners of these sites either agreed or had no choice but to accept that Jakarta was not a safe place and gardus in the form of pos hansips were needed to combat threats from the streets. Many of these "homecoming" army officials, however, worked through state institutions and registered their presence by making the city their official combat zone.

Thus by the 1980s, one of the tasks of Suharto's army was to transform the village-based military posko into the urban-based pos hansip. In other words, the army had to change the unfamiliar territory of the city into a familiar place by first ousting all imagined and real threats and then installing in strategic places pos hansips as part of the urban-based community. To function effectively as an apparatus of the state, the pos hansip was immersed in the everyday life of the community by facilitating night watch schemes and providing a space for socialization and the monitoring of public life. The transformation of the military posko into the pos hansip was crucial to Suharto's politics of space. It was as crucial as his transferring the spatial basis of the military operation from the village to the city.[21] A most poignant but perhaps unconscious indication of this transfer of the site of operations was the billboard depicting the "development" of rural areas of Indonesia (see figures 49 and 49a).

In the billboard we see a gardu. It represents the order and security of the presumably prosperous village of Cianjur. The gardu also represents the leadership of Suharto who is depicted as giving instructions over the radio. Suharto often associated himself with rural origins (orang desa) even though, as president, he was located at the center of the city. What is peculiar about this billboard is that while it depicts the scene of the village, it was intended for the urbanite. Placed in the central part of Jakarta, the billboard carried with it the rural and urban continuum. It was staged in the mid-1980s, a time of prosperity, which came in tandem with the establishment of standardized security measures in the city.

The city was a relatively new setting for Suharto's army. It became the major site of military operations only after East Timor, the villages, and the outer islands had been pacified. Nevertheless, since the early 1990s, residents of Jakarta occasionally saw units of army men (such as the sapu bersih) in black uniforms (whom Jakarta residents called "ninja") flying down ropes on the skyscrapers in the business district of Jakarta. As the ninja skillfully surveyed the new terrains and impressed the urbanites, the military officials established poskos for, according to the intelligence reports, the city, unlike the rural areas and the jungle, was far more complex in the

Figure 49 Billboard displayed in Jakarta by the Department of Education. Reprinted from Paul Zach and Gretchen Liu, *Jakarta* (Singapore: Times Edition, 1987).

Figure 49a Detail from upper left of billboard in Figure 49, showing a village *gardu*.

sense that "it is hard to identify the enemy combatant in the city."²² The military poskos stationed in villages and East Timor were thus transferred to the city of Jakarta. From the poskos, the military units gathered information, surveyed movements, and monitored the cleaning up of the city from any potential threats.

Suharto indeed built his regime using the idea of cleaning up (*bersih*) the nation from the imagined threat of communism. This obsession with bersih was expressed through the terms used for various military missions.

The army unit responsible for urban warfare, for instance, was called sapu bersih (sweeping).[23] The military also established bureaus, which aimed at screening citizens to ensure that they were all from a "clean environment" (bersih lingkungan) and that they had no relationship to the social environment of communism. To qualify for a job, citizens were required to obtain a certificate of good behavior from the neighborhood where they were living as evidence that they did not need to undergo "self-cleaning" (bersih diri) from communism. It is logical therefore that the "clean environment" registered itself, most visibly, in the discourses of kampung improvement projects, the new towns, and the setting up of pos hansips in every neighborhood, for few representations could express so clearly the discourses of cleanliness than the control of the built environment itself. The streets and the kampungs of Jakarta were constructed as "less clean" in contrast to the sanitized new towns, the discourse of which was inseparable from the attempts to create a new depoliticized Suharto generation and to forget the image of Sukarno standing on an open podium in a public space, concentrating the masses and stirring their passion for revolution.[24]

The famous governor of Jakarta, Ali Sadikin (1966–75) was instrumental in fulfilling the objectives of Suharto's regime.[25] One of his main tasks during his tenure was to prevent the retrieval of Jakarta's past as a space for the mobilization of revolutionary masses. Several important moves were made, one of which was to categorize people seen as potentially threatening public order such as the "illiterate and unskilled cheap laborers from the countryside, trishaw drivers, construction workers, vendors, the homeless, beggars, and prostitutes."[26] According to the governor, they were among the poorest 60 percent of the population of Jakarta who lived in the kampung, a term seen as "no longer suitable with the order of the city for it reminds people of a backward society."[27] Throughout his tenure, the governor attempted to control the kampung and its inhabitants through "the environment security system" (Siskamling). "For the easier process of monitoring and servicing, I need to limit the number of RT [administered neighborhoods] to forty families and each RW [district], fifteen to twenty RT."[28] Through this program, the governor transplanted the "traditional" norms of cooperation (gotong royong) between members of a community to "humanizing the environment."[29] In his memoir, Sadikin reported that in the 1970s, the Ministry of Defence institutionalized the neighborhood watch (ronda), and by 1977, 16,718 persons were trained as officers of civil defense (hansip), and for the purpose of ronda, about 2,280 gardus (pos hansips) were constructed throughout Jakarta.[30]

This disciplinary discourse was not limited to the kampung, for the privileged too were subjected to surveillance. The governor also formed similar community organizations for the upper middle-class neighborhoods. Real estate housing, which started to grow only in the late 1980s, began to make security a major component in the selling of new houses.

The grand and intimidating gateways, pos hansips, and security guards have since then become the first structures built for the marketing of the new towns. By the 1990s, with the discourse of security and order registered in the minds of the urbanite, the pos hansip, attached to buildings and neighborhoods, had become a familiar urban feature for the residents of Jakarta. It became the symbol of security and order connected to the power of the regime. No matter how different the style of one pos hansip was from that of another, in the minds of the public they were all connected to one source: the state. Many Jakartans, including recent residents, recognized them as "gardus of the regime." The meaning of this expression is associated with capital, private corporations, and the prestige of the "middle class," as well as their fear of the streets (see figure 50).

Many Jakartans who live in the new towns are aware that the pos hansips, widely distributed and attached to particular neighborhoods, have become the eyes and ears of the state brought home to survey the daily life of the streets and the inhabitants of the city. Yet, for the middle class of Jakarta, it is through the state that their security and social hierarchy are supposedly guaranteed. In fact, the new towns where they live have spatialized such social order. Through the pos hansips, both social and physical boundaries have been created for the neighborhood. Those who live behind the pos hansips are the "insiders" as opposed to the "outsiders" who are wandering on the streets. At the pos hansip, one can often find a notice: "guests that stay for more than twenty-four hours are expected to file a report," or "scavengers cannot enter," a strategy to discourage unwelcome visitors and wanderers. This disciplinary method has never worked in practice. People are always capable of finding a way in and out of the checkpoint without being noticed, and no one seems to bother reporting his or her guests to the pos hansip. Nevertheless, with the installation of networks of pos hansips on the streets, there is now less of a possibility for the unauthorized placement of platforms for the mobilization of crowds.

Figure 50 The Bali-Sanur *gardu* for a gated community in Jakarta.
Photo courtesy of F. Prihadi.

In the time of Suharto, the gardu was indeed a post for command and not the place for communication between "Sukarno and his revolutionary masses."

However, although the gardu has become part of the political apparatus of the state, it also provides ways in which national populations can conceptualize their own defense, especially when the state turns against them. With the absence of security apparatus during the riots of May 1998 (which many believe was part of the state's strategy to terrorize the populace), various communities (especially Indonesians of Chinese background) barricaded themselves around the pos hansip in their neighborhood, and from there stood up against the invading mobs. The collapse of the Suharto regime crumbled the network of the pos hansips, but the structure persisted and has been reborn with new life. It has been placed in the hands of communities and individuals and used to safeguard their own properties. Increasing numbers of gardus and gates are now being built but without the authorization of the state.

In this sense, the poskos of Megawati exploited the mixed sense of empowerment, fragmentation, and insecurity in the public following the overthrow of Suharto. Through her poskos, she replayed the idea of restoring order and security in the neighborhood, a discourse that was ironically derived from the previous regime against which she had come to power. The gardu provided a vocabulary for Megawati to integrate fragments of the past (the precolonial pendhopo, Sukarno's podium, and Suharto's militarism) and the experience of ethnic Chinese into the consciousness of the present.

TRACES

The gardu I have been discussing until now looked simultaneously in more than two directions. Today, it is part of a global cultural form and, as part of the realm of "gated communities," unites much of the contemporary urban world. Yet, it is also part of a specific history of Indonesia. The last two centuries of European colonialism contributed greatly to the signifying practice of today's gardu. Its coordinated use suggests to us a clear territorial demarcation, the origin of which can be traced back to the spatial politics of the Dutch colonial state. The gardu represented the emergence of the colonial state in nineteenth-century Java, a state that was marked by the reorganization of space in both the city and the village. To this acknowledgment of the colonial state's contribution to the practice of using gardus, I must also add the observation that the historical experiences of ethnic Chinese living through periodic violence against them also played a decisive role in the discursive formation of gardus in Indonesia. This section thus deals with the earlier forms and practices of gardus associated with Dutch colonialism and the experiences of ethnic Chinese.

In two valuable works, Joshua Barker has studied the spatial dimension of neighborhood security in the construction of communal identities in urban Indonesia.[31] Examining the institution of neighborhood security, Barker shows the intertwined relations between the state strategy of surveillance and the local practices of security watch. He illustrates how the state and the local community mutually constitute and contest each other in defining criminals, foreigners, and insiders (as well as those who are in between). This contestation is marked by a sense of territoriality that is profoundly unsettling. But Barker's critical observations of the intermingling of state and local power encourage us to look at the earlier discourses of territoriality that involve Dutch colonial power and the spatial strategy of ethnic Chinese. How did the earlier discourses of territoriality overdetermine the present strategies of the state and the local communities?

In their studies of the rural politics of colonial Java, historians Jan Breman and Onghokham traced the complex processes by which a bordered *desa* (village) came into being in the nineteenth century. Their accounts are instructive because the territoriality of the urban neighborhoods investigated by Barker could be seen as coming out of the colonial discourses of the bordered desa. The gardu is thus intimately connected to the spatial politics of Java under colonial conditions, and it was part of the apparatus for the structuring of community identity. The studies of Barker, Breman, and Onghokham lead us to understand that gardus are tied to a particular territory. Their studies, however, also prompt us to consider the ways in which gardus could lead a life of their own and move across time and space. At one point, it serves as an institution of the state and particular neighborhoods, and, at another point, it works as an artifact for memorialization.

If the meaning of the gardu has changed over time as it has been made and remade for social practices and political legitimacy, its origins are even more obscure. I believe it owes much to the emergence of various sites including that of the cross-regional highway, the political construction of the "village community," the formation of city police in early twentieth-century Java, and the experiences of ethnic Chinese in Indonesia. What social, political, and other effects did the spatial politics of the Dutch have on the institutionalization of gardus in the landscape of Java? To respond to this question, let me first pay tribute to the Javanese concept of space and show how such a powerful system could not by itself generate the tradition of the gardu. Such a tracing is necessary to dispose of the orthodox belief that the much-loved and much-hated gardu is really a product of a single culture inherited from "our" ancestor.

Space in Flux

As indicated earlier, in the eyes of the Indonesian public, gardus have been associated with informal gatherings (of men) and information exchange and are connected with ideologies of security, discipline, and the spectacle of power. An inquiry into the "origins" of gardus requires being sensitive to diverse functions and the different signs a gardu once symbolized. It also involves being aware of the dependency of those functions and signs on changes in the social and built environment within which they are embedded.

It is reasonable to believe that gardus were already in existence in Java

Figure 51 Sketch of guards guarding the *kraton* (palace) of Yogya. By A. de Nelly, one of Johannes Rach's pupils, circa 1771. Reprinted from Peter Carey, *The British in Java, 1811–1816: A Javanese Account* (Oxford: Oxford University Press, 1992).

before European colonialism. They could be found at the entrance to the compounds of the nobility or the notables. However, precolonial gardus were neither for the purpose of demarcating territory nor for defense and exclusion. Instead, their presence was to show the power of the king as a center of the cosmos. For instance, the nine guarded gates of the Yogyakarta palace refer to the existence of the king's body (the nine "cosmic" holes of the king's body) rather than the territorial stretch of his kingdom (see figure 51).[32]

Benedict Anderson, Soemarsaid Moertono, and Oliver Wolters have written about the nonexistence of the concept of the boundary in the Javanese polity.[33] They emphasized the permanent state of flux and the instability of the traditional polity. Similarly Anthony Reid and Kathirithamby-Wells have demonstrated the difficulty of defining the "city" of Southeast Asia in terms of its boundary for there is no clear division between compounds outside the king's palace and no explicit physical differentiation between what is inside the town and what lies outside it.[34]

Historians of the rural politics of Java, such as Jan Breman and Onghokham have also shown that there is a similar tendency in rural areas. The domains of both the local notables and the peasants were not demarcated territorially. Instead they were spread out over various settlements and underwent regrouping according to the prestige and the prosperity of the notables and the up-and-down fortunes of the reservoirs of agricultural producers. The degree of instability was intensified by the notables' constantly competing to win the favor of the higher authority as well as the subservience of the peasants. The consequence of all this was that the degree of success of a notable was determined not by the extent of his territory but by the number of people he could draw into his circle. An extract from a survey report of a district in West Java dating from the end of the nineteenth century provides us with the colonial state's adverse reaction to such a state of flux:

> Until the reorganization of 1870, the desa [village] boundaries were never clearly delineated. The desa was a conglomeration of persons, falling under the jurisdiction of one loerah [headman], with the consequence that, at any time, everyone was free to renounce their obedience to him and had the option to place themselves under the authority of another chief. The land, no matter where it was situated, always went with the person, so that there could be no question of a demarcated desa area: "tjintjing di mana, ngawoela ka mana soeka," *"live where you like, serve whom you will"* — is an old proverb which retained its force until 1870.[35]

Without going in detail into the political basis of rural organization in precolonial times, it is sufficient to indicate that the organization of the Javanese countryside, like its urban counterpart, was always in a state of flux. Had there been gardus, they would have been merely sporadic and would never have constituted a system that would help systematize the notions of bondage, territory, and boundary. The idea of territorial demarcation and community formation defined by boundary is foreign to Java.

In what follows I will show how the emergence of gardus as demarcating territorial boundaries in the Indonesian village and town is connected with the decline of sultanate power and the rise of the colonial West in Java. Let me start with the rural area of Java in order to indicate the political creation of boundaries and the establishment of the "village community" of which gardus were a crucial part. The erratic principle of village boundaries underwent a process of change in the nineteenth century, most notably under the rule of the French "Napoleonic" Governor General Daendels (1805–11) and the rule of Governor Raffles during the English interregnum (1811–15), and during the period of the Cultivation System (1830–70). The intermingling of these different regimes of power gave rise to a territorial consciousness and, as I will show, the gradual formation of an attachment to gardus. This was not merely a discourse of security but also involved the representation of power, territory, and identity.

Guarding the Road

The most significant change in the morphology of the Javanese town occurred when Herman Willem Daendels, the French Governor General of the Netherlands Indies, ruled Java (1805–11). From the outset, it is quite possible that the gardu and its institution of day and night watches (ronda) began on orders from Daendels. The Indonesian word *gardu* might even come from the French word *garde*.[36] In any case, Daendels was the first person to use territorial demarcation as part of a strategy to rule Java. He institutionalized the idea of the boundary by dividing the Dutch territories in Java into sharply demarcated spaces called "residencies."[37] He then connected these residencies by a thoroughfare built in 1808 called the Grand Post Road (Jalan Pos Besar in Malay or The Grote Postweg—in Dutch), which ran across the coastal and inland area of Java (from the west coast of Anyer to the east coast of Banyuwangi). This massive project, which caused the death of thousands of Javanese forced laborers, stemmed from the need to improve communication between the "residencies," expand trade, and, perhaps most importantly, pacify the uprisings in certain areas in Java.

Peter Nas and Pratiwo have studied the layout of the original Grote Postweg and its later development.[38] One of their important findings concerns the effect of the thoroughfare on the urban symbolism of the Javanese town. The new road stretching along the island of Java in an east-west direction disrupted or undermined the spatial orientation of the Javanese "town," which had been traditionally laid out on a north-south axis. This change of spatial orientation contributed to the undermining of the traditional authority of Java, which had been in decline since the eighteenth century.[39] Besides the spatial disruption, there was also another symbolic displacement of Javanese authority involved in the building of the Grote Postweg that will bring us back to the discourse of gardus. As part of the

Figure 52 Changing horses in a *pendhopo* guardhouse on the Great Post Road in Java, nineteenth century. Photo courtesy of KITLV, 1994.

transport system of Grote Postweg, a series of posts, which were essentially guardhouses, were installed along the road at particular intervals for travelers to change horses (see figure 52). Steven Wachlin, the editor of the photo collection of colonial photographers Woodbury and Page, describes the image of the Grote Postweg in this way:

> Changing horses in a pendhopo in Cisokan, on the Groote Postweg near Cianjur. In order to facilitate traffic, pendhopo were built every nine kilometres along the Groote Postweg, the Great Postroad stretching from west to east along the whole length of Java. Travellers rode in special carriages drawn by four to six horses which were operated by entrepreneurs who obtained concessions from the government. A journey from Batavia to Surabaya lasted about nine days.[40]

This pendhopo was essentially a gardu. In other words, the gardu adopted the roof shape of the pendhopo. The pendhopo, which previously was attached to the housing compounds of the Javanese elite, was displaced to the Grote Postweg. It appeared as a freestanding structure guarding the road every nine kilometers. We could say that the Grote Postweg pioneered the commercial use of the pendhopo and inaugurated the Dutch as the new authority of Java. But why was the pendhopo adopted for regulating traffic on the Grote Postweg? One reason might be that the pendhopo was associated with "traditional" power and protection. Another might be that, in the Orientalist eyes of the Dutch, the roof had a picturesque quality. The Grote Postweg appropriated the symbolism and function of the pendhopo to gain attention and influence in Java. By detaching the form from the body of the Javanese "royal" residence, the pendhopo was displaced and reborn as the first commercially administered gatehouse.

It would be valuable to find and study the perceptions of the public as well as the Javanese court of the construction of the Grote Postweg with its pendhopo gardus along the way. European travelers in the late nineteenth century identified the gardu of the Grote Postweg as a kind of "resthouse."[41] In one account, they indicated that "twice we found busy passersby going on in groves beside these rest-houses—picturesque gatherings of men, women, and children (and) the main road was crowded all the way like a city street, and around these passers-by the highway hummed with voices."[42]

The road, while gaining people's attention, however, also invited robbers. A historian of Semarang, Liem Thian Joe, reported the frequent appearance of bandits and attempts at robbery along the Postweg, which forced merchants and travelers to hire martially skilled guards on their journey.[43] Regardless of its popularity and the danger the road posed to travelers, it became a focus for the inhabitants around the area. The thoroughfare and its pendhopos reoriented the patterns of settlements and the subjectivity of the populace along its way. A new center in the form of a road that filled people with anxiety and yet offered a new form of mobility was thus created, competing with if not displacing the centrality of the sultans' court. Travelers saw "rows of open houses on each side of the highway" and "along every bit of the road were posted the names of the kampungs and estates charged to maintain the highway in perfect condition."[44] With security at stake, a routine of day and night watches (ronda) was first institutionalized to guard both the kampung and the estates as well as to help provide security for the Postweg. Henri C. C. C. Brousson perhaps was right. The French word *garde* was transformed eventually into the Indonesian word gardu (*rumah jaga*), an unconscious tribute to Daendels's contribution to the life of the gatehouse.

The "Village Community"

The English interregnum (1811–15), while brief, contributed much to the formation of territorial consciousness and boundary policing for it introduced a tax system based on landholding, which had never been a tradition of Java. The land-based tax system, appropriated perhaps from British India, required a concentrated and permanently settled population. At least the mobility of the population would have to be calculated and each member of the settlement registered.[45] To the state's need to secure peace and order along the Postweg was added the need to patrol the movement of people in and out of the registered land. Along with this, a master plan was made to group the scattered homesteads into a concentrated unit of settlements. In his study of rural West Java, Breman helpfully included the master plan, which deserves a closer look (see figures 53 and 54). Figure 53 shows "the plan of a desa as it presently exists." There is no clear boundary or territorial demarcation on which one could base an argument for a "village community." The houses are scattered, and they are connected by unconfigured pathways. In contrast, the master plan in figure 54 shows the layout of a new village that was fenced off, leaving only one guarded entrance from the main street.[46] The layout of the old village was fully altered to achieve the Cartesian order of a disciplinary space. One could argue that the gardu at the entrance from the main street provided a coherence to the "village community."

This systematization of rural communities reached its peak after the Java War (1825–30) in the form of state plantations operated under what is known as the Cultivation System (1830–70). Onghokham indicates that by then, for the first time, "the whole of Java was divided into villages, each with its own territory, and one bordering on another, so that there was no administrative vacuum in Java."[47] These colonial state plantations brought together scattered settlements and formed what we know today as "village communities."[48] The boundaries between them thus formed were sustained ultimately by a network of gardus.

With the creation of the "gated community" came the idea of insiders and outsiders, the normal and the pathological. In *Hikayat Siti Mariah*, a romantic novel written in the years 1910–12 about semivillage life in the late nineteenth century, the author Haji Mukti began his story with a kampung guard shouting from a gardu: "*Horda!*" (from the Dutch "*wier daar*"

Figure 53 "The plan of a *desa* as it presently exists," with a *gardu* only for the house of the notable. Reprinted courtesy of Jan Breman from Breman, *The Village on Java and the Early-Colonial State.*

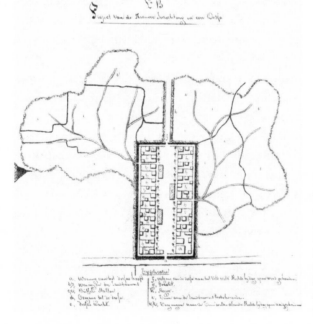

Figure 54 The "plan of the new establishment of a *desa,*" with a *gardu* for the whole village. Reprinted courtesy of Jan Breman from Breman, *The Village on Java and the Early-Colonial State.*

meaning "who is that?") to which a reply came from the other side: "*Prin!*" (friend). With a secured space and a guard operating with a standard speech code, a disciplinary procedure was established to identify the threat posed by those who were wandering around and were not the "friend" of the community. With the establishment of the gardu and the "village community," the state was finally able to arrive at a set of fixed beliefs about the "wandering class." "They are not to be depended upon. They left often for the most trivial of reasons and just as unexpectedly as they had come. Their number remained consistently unstable and uncertain. These roving folk usually had a lower moral standard than the settled population. It has been said of them that they found their greatest delight in 'gaming, the seductive dancing girl and poisonous opium'."[49] With the physical space firmly in place, knowledge and power proceed with clarity. By the 1870s, the government had already found a tool to cope with the increasing size of the "wandering class" and the activities of the organized *kecu* (thugs) that "disturbed" the order and peace of the village. Dutch Resident Zoutelief, who controlled the residency of Surakarta, Central Java, was using the method of the night watch (ronda) at his "gated communities," where an order could be given to "close the door to the village compound."[50]

While clearly "seeing like a state,"[51] it would however be misleading to think that the Dutch had a complete hold on the everyday governance of the Javanese village and town. Quite to the contrary, the colonial state did not monopolize the control of social life nor did it impose a standardized law applicable to everyone under its authority. Instead, the colonial state allowed local authorities substantial power to rule and govern as long as the interests of the state were not disturbed. Onghokham has written about this division of power established by the Dutch to manage Java through the state plantations. Onghokham shows how the Dutch, after taking over Java in 1830, delegated authority to the native regent (*bupati*—local lords), who organized thugs, known as *jago*, to maintain order and security in both rural and urban Java.[52] This hierarchy of power is known to historians as the Dutch dualistic principle of organizing its colony. While the colonial state upheld the political order by privileging the rights of the powerful, it allowed the local authorities to possess substantial power to construct their own ways of maintaining order as long as the position of the state was not threatened. In this sense, to the members of these colonial "plural societies," gardus (being part of a localized practice of community watch and surveillance) might have been seen as symbols of local autonomy even as they were tied to the politics of the state. The territorial demarcation and the dualistic power hierarchy introduced by European power could thus be said to have given rise to a tradition of gardus.

On the other hand, with the increased interest in the culture and civilization of Java in the last half of the nineteenth century, the gardu began to be portrayed as an expression of Javanese culture—an object of menace and desire. The gardu since then has become an object of study. For instance, in 1893, a long article was devoted to the study of gardus. Its author, H. A. de Groot, discussed gardus (*wachthuizen* in Dutch) in relation to the possibility of establishing a police system in the colony. The context for the discussion of gardus was a profound sense of insecurity created by kecu (rural thugs) in the villages and periurban centers of Java.[53] In a way, we could say that the gardu represents the reluctance of the colonial state to impose a more overarching system of police. Had the colonial state implemented a unified security system such as an overarching police organization, perhaps the neighborhood gardu would not have come into existence.

In this section I have tried to delineate how the gardu came to be formed under the spatial politics of the colonial state. Yet, to explain how the gardu came to be imagined by the Javanese as part of the cultural traditions of local communities in Java, we need to return to the city and examine the discourse of security during the radical "age in motion" and the concomitant formation of a unified police system.[54]

Urban Radicalism and the Police Station

In the photo album of Woodbury and Page, a gardu stands at a prominent place in Masteer Cornelis, by then a "grey area" between the city and the rural area (see figure 55). The gardu was made of permanent building materials and carefully crafted to appear like a monument that could be seen unobstructed from a distance. What also seems clear is that gardus were prominently represented in the late nineteenth- and early twentieth-century urban centers of Java.

Like Woodbury and Page, the journalist H. C. C. Clockener Brousson was also impressed during his trip to Batavia at the turn of the century by the gardus that were "placed at a particular interval along the street where people lived."[55] By the early twentieth century, the imagined unity of a

Figure 55 One of a series of *gardus* on the road between Weltevreden in Batavia and Meester Cornelis, before 1880. Photo courtesy of KITLV.

"village community," conceived using the image of the gardu, had been fully materialized in the city.

As far as the discourse of the gardu is concerned, the order of things was not very different in the city. Like its rural counterpart, in the urban center of Java the colonial state allowed the non-Europeans to maintain the security of their own quarters. What is significant about the city, however, is that the urban center consisted of people from various ethnic backgrounds. The powerful colonial institution responded to this multiplicity of cultures by preserving racial privileges and segregation even though unofficial ethnic clusters had already been formed before Europeans came to the archipelago. The different population groups thus lived more or less separately in the town according to differentiations in ethnic classification.[56]

Before the emergence of the city police (which I will discuss below), the Dutch "protected" the people of the Indies by delegating power to the elites of the ethnic groups, who often hired urban thugs to safeguard their quarters in strategically placed gardus. The Chinese quarter thus had its own head and security guards. The European neighborhoods also had their own gardus organized by the local governors. The Chinese and Arab inhabitants handled their own neighborhood security, and the indigenous kampung took care of its own neighborhood, guarding it like a desa. The formation of urban gardus is thus connected to the spatial segregation of colonial space, which consisted of the European enclave, the Chinese kampung, the kampung for Arabs, the kampung for Malays (*Melayu*), and Kampung *Keling* for Indians, among others. Using the gardu, each quarter organized its own day and night watch schemes. In fact the practice of the night watch was the basic form of security for the segregated neighborhoods in the urban center.

It is however important to acknowledge that one of the characteristics of neighborhood security embodied in the gardu is that it is a passive form of defense. The watchmen would only stay in the gardu or patrol around their compound with the kentongan. They would not patrol the streets beyond the designated territory of a kampung.[57] However, by the early twentieth century, this rather passive form of security watch sustained by the gardu was considered outdated. As Java underwent the popular urban radicalism known eventually as the "age in motion," the overall safety and well-being of the colony was considered to be in danger. At the beginning of the twentieth century, different security measures were deemed necessary. The newly established city government issued an order that the gardu system was to be replaced by a centralized police system.[58] Central to the new system was that the police force would patrol the streets in propinquity to the kampung.

The initiative for change was prompted by several developments. The most important factor was the increasing number of European families staying in the urban centers of the colony. As most European families lived in the city, the social unrest in Java at the turn of the twentieth century made them feel unusually insecure. Meanwhile, the growth of the urban population blurred the distance between the safe European enclave and the "native" kampung. The task of the twentieth-century police was to keep the city as a safe haven for the Europeans. Safety, as historian Marieke Bloembergen points out, was "a specifically European problem."[59]

The first professionally organized city police was formed only in 1914. The number of recruits needed to safeguard the city increased over the years, with Europeans at the top rank and Indonesians at the subordinate level. In Surabaya alone, as Bloembergen indicates, the number of police increased from 297 members in 1905 to 1,358 in 1917.[60] In 1918, alerted by "the rise of [political] consciousness of the people in Java following their counterparts in East Asia," the Dutch colonial government expanded the security measures to the outskirts of big cities. Soon, some three thousand civilians (including Indonesians) were recruited and trained as field police (*veldpolisi*) to safeguard the outskirts of the big cities in Java. These professional police "spoke the native language and understood local culture, but they were not allowed to police the areas from where they were originally from."[61] This had an important consequence, which I will indicate below, but it suffices to say that since the police could not take care of the area that they were from, a distance was created between the police and the community.

As far as methods of security are concerned, what seems to be new in the early twentieth century was the display of police presence on the streets. The visibility of police on the streets was deemed necessary to the success of street surveillance and to ward off potential threats. At the beginning of the twentieth century, police houses (*politie posthuis*) were built at strategic nodes encompassing different neighborhoods, with, of course, a concentration in the European neighborhood. At the beginning, the police house appeared similar to the village's gardu, but unlike the watchman of a gardu, the policemen made themselves distinctive by wearing a uniform.

Soon, the police fully emancipated themselves from the world of the watchman by occupying officelike buildings. This type of building was placed at strategic locations related to European interests, such as near the post office (*posthuis*), government buildings, and big private offices.[62] At first, it was thought the new *politie* would be able to replace the watchmen of the gardus. Orders were in fact given to clear out the gardus from the city.[63] Yet, this intention to centralize the security system under the watch of the police was never fulfilled. There might be many reasons for the failure of the colonial state to impose a unified security system. The economic and financial considerations are obviously of fundamental importance, but one of the crucial reasons, I think, is that by the turn of the century, the members of the colonized (who were infected by the age in motion) identified with the gardu as a symbol of their culture, one that could be mobilized to challenge the authority of the state's police. The gardu thus continued to exist. It remained a local institution but one that had become somewhat hostile, at least symbolically, to the "national" police.

Since the emergence of the new police house, the gardu increasingly had been seen by Javanese sociopolitical organizations, such as the Syarikat Islam (SI), as a symbol of local power, one that could be mobilized to represent a form of resistance to the colonial state. Historian Marieke Bloembergen indicates how the Syarikat Islam installed several gardus to guarantee the safety of workers in Surabaya as the latter engaged in a dispute over revenue against a landowner. For the members of the SI, the installation of the gardu was both functional and symbolic. The staging of gardus could be seen as a sign of the SI's support of the cause of the workers in Surabaya. Considered "illegal" by the colonial state,[64] the SI nevertheless continued the practice. The SI regarded gardus as not only providing public safety and support for the underprivileged but also challenging the authority of the new police and consolidating power for the organization. The gardu symbolized this form of power struggle, an event that reminds us of our own time—the discourses of posko in post-1998 Jakarta that I discussed at the beginning of this chapter.

The gardu represents competing claims for authority, but it also expresses the sense of the colonial society that gives it meaning. And yet, the meaning of the gardu changes constantly. In different social environments, it is involved with different practices of signification. What I have tried to indicate in this section is the process by which the gardu came to be conceived and appropriated. I have also indicated the "newness" of this supposedly old practice. Only at the turn of the nineteenth century did the gardu find its territorial "community" and come to be imagined as a "local tradition." Under the Ethical Policy at the beginning of the twentieth century, this "village-urban community," along with its ethos of mutual help (gotong royong) and ronda, was promoted by Dutch scholars and the Javanese elite class as the archetype of Javanese tradition.

The Chinese Experience

As far as the discourse of the gardu is concerned, the experiences of ethnic Chinese are of particular interest and importance largely because the idea that the gardu either belongs to the discourse of Dutch colonialism or is the cultural property of Java has dominated much provincial Dutch-Javanese thinking about the gardu. There are two reasons to consider gardus in the context of the ethnic Chinese experience. First, the ethnic Chinese have been subjected to various social unrests since (if not before) the early formation of colonial power. Their continuous experience as a customary target must have sensitized them to come up with coping strategies, ones that might have led to the institution of the gardu. The territorial practice of the gardu might have been drawn from the experiences of this community. Second, gates, walls, and guards have always been endemic to the Chinese townscape. If Denys Lombard is right, we might want to consider his suggestion that the Chinese system of spatial defense based on neighborhood watches known as the *Pao Tjia* system (said to be invented in around the tenth century) might have been implemented by ethnic Chinese in the coastal areas of Java long before the arrival of the Western powers.[65]

In any case, let me make a start by considering the experiences of ethnic Chinese through the spatial segregation of colonial cities. We know that colonial spatial divisions ethnicized urban space, but we have not yet seen how the segregation of space also made possible spatial defense, which in turn contributed to the formation of the "ethnic" community. The practice of placing communities in ghettos along ethnic lines prepared the ground for such tactics of self-defense as barricading the segregated space with a gardu at the gate in order to prevent attackers from entering during situations of chaos, riot, and war.

Liem Thian Joe, the chronicler of the city of Semarang, points out that "matters concerning guards (*djaga*) and guardhouses (*gardoe*) had already started since the era of the Company [the Dutch East India Company (voc) — Vereenigde Oost-Indische Compagnie]."[66] The first institutionalized racial segregation of space in the Dutch East Indies indeed took place after the massacre of Chinese people in 1740, following the competition for trade and land in the emerging Batavia. Initially, an area, known today as Glodok, had been set aside for the Chinese people.[67] Liem indicated that in 1741, a year after the massacre of the Chinese in Batavia, the Chinese in Semarang decided to build a barricade around their neighborhood.[68] They "built *betengan* (barricades) made of strong timbers and boards in front of Chinese kampungs which during that time were clusters of open space surrounded by rivers. . . . Headed by the *Kapiten*, the Chinese populace patrolled the barricades day and night."[69] From this bulwark of resistance too, the Chinese in Semarang eventually waged war against the Dutch East Indies with the help of ethnic Chinese mobilized from other regions. This event was clearly significant, and the method of defense was unprecedented as the local populace remembered the barricaded areas as a bastion (betengan — in Malay or *phangshia* in Fukianese).[70]

We could problematize Liem's account by indicating that gates and walls have always been part of the Chinese townscape. However, the point here is that by the nineteenth century, the ethnic Chinese in Java had learned that they would be the usual target in any conflict involving Dutch authority and the sultans of Java. Since then, barricades, gates, and guardhouses have become permanent features of the Chinese quarters. A rumor of conflict would be sufficient to generate an alert and create a sense of threat and uncertainty, which would lead to the construction of additional gates and guardhouses. For instance, during the war between Prince Diponegoro and the Dutch in 1825: "So the rumors (*kabar-kabar angin*) spread in Semarang. Some say that one of the (Javanese) kings is fighting against the Dutch government; others believe that the latter is having a war with a foreign country. Quite a few think that thousands of bandits have been raiding everywhere. All these have created confusion in Semarang."[71] As a response to these "rumors," Chinese communities in Semarang constructed gates and gardus around their kampungs. "The gate was made so strong. It was reinforced on its two sides by a very thick wall, so it would be very difficult to break in. It closed at dark. Every night, grownups guarded the gates. Inside the gates, women and children are moved to the temple from where everyone will fight to the end. For months, the gates were guarded every night for dangers might come unexpectedly."[72]

The gates were left intact after the war (1830) for "who knows, if the '*gegeran*' [turmoil] returns, the gates will provide security for the Chinese kampung."[73] Liem recorded that by the 1840s the practice of night watch (ronda) had become regular, with one chief heading each kampung. The chief of the night watch was called *kepala tontong* (the head of the "tontong," the instrument that produces a sound when struck with a wooden stick). By then the Chinese community in Semarang had also incorporated several words into the technical vocabulary associated with the night watch in the village, including the exchange of the exclamation we saw in the village: *horde* and *vrend*.

A gardoe and a kentongan are required at a junction or entrance to a street [*moeloet jalan*] or to a village [*moeloet doesoen*]. Every Chinese man who lives in the city as well as in smaller places could not escape from patrolling the night. Those who couldn't fulfill this obligation are allowed to hire someone to replace him. Every gardoe is required to have two guards: one watches from evening to 1 am; and the other from that time until morning. They are not there just to watch, but also to move around the neighborhood [ronda] with a special weapon. If there is a killing, the guard will strike three times on the kentongan he brought with him; if there is a fire, he has to strike four times so that everyone knows where the danger took place. If he sees someone [especially strangers] after 9 pm, he has to shout: "who is there?" The person then ought to reply: "vrend" [friend]. Otherwise the guard has the right to catch and bring the suspicious person to the police.[74]

So far I have only seen sources that talk about gates and gardus in the experience of the ethnic Chinese such as that of Liem's account of Semarang. The fact that Liem's *Riwajat Semarang* is filled with stories centered around guarding and the gardu is not surprising given the continuous experience of violence against this group in the urban history of Java, especially since the eighteenth century. It is much less clear if other quarters shared the experience of guardhouses in their respective communities.[75] It is also not clear whether the night watch scheme was first practiced in the ethnic Chinese neighborhoods of the urban center and then exported by the colonial state to the village before it was imported back to the urban center. In any case, the history of gardus in Indonesia is intimately connected to the experiences and collective memories of ethnic Chinese. It cannot be separated from the responses of ethnic Chinese to the threats and violence they were exposed to during periods of social unrest.

In the following section, I pick up the account of Kwee Thiam Tjing, an ethnic Chinese journalist who volunteered as a city guard (*stadswacht*) during the time of "revolution."[76] Kwee's account is instructive for it shows us how matters concerning guarding and gardus are inextricably bound up with the experiences of ethnic Chinese even as this community found themselves in the era of "decolonization." Kwee also shows how his subjectivity as someone who observed and participated in *Indonesia dalem api dan bara* owes everything to his experience as a guard of the city.

Guarding in Indonesia Dalem Api dan Bara

On the eve of the Japanese occupation, the Dutch, desperate for manpower to defend the Indies, promoted a program that trained volunteer civilians as city guards (stadswacht). This proved to be the first mobilization of civilians by the colonial state to safeguard the city. Chinese Indonesian journalist Kwee Thiam Tjing volunteered as a city guard in Malang where he lived and reported his experiences in a remarkable book titled *Indonesia dalem api dan bara*. Kwee did not use the word *gardu* for his post. Instead he used the term *wacht*, which has an association with *gardu* in Dutch (*wachthuis*). This in itself indicates a conceptual and political difference between the meaning and practice of gardu (with its local association) and the stadswacht (a city guard program initiated by the colonial state). The imagery of guarding and the guardhouse occupies a substantial place in his book. We could even say that Kwee's subjectivity was formed and transformed by his position as a guard of the city.

From the beginning of the book, Kwee sketches the relationship between the guardhouse and a change in his consciousness. After he volunteered to guard the city, he saw guardhouses (wacht-wacht) everywhere, "at the junction of various streets especially those on the way to the city,"[77] but in his eyes, the presence of the guardhouses and guards like him were a mockery for the collapsing Dutch. He knew that the training of the city guards and the proliferation of guardhouses on the eve of Japanese occupation were a last resort by the Dutch to display its authority by mobilizing colonial subjects to defend their own "motherland." Yet the more guardhouses and guards Kwee saw around him, the more hopeless he felt, for the visibility of the guardhouses did not represent the strength of the colonial state. Instead, people saw the proliferation of guardhouses as a sign of the collapsing government, for no one, not even the most ignorant of the colonized, respected or were empowered by the existence of the guardhouses. Kwee felt that even though he had already been equipped with all kinds of military protocols, uniforms, and weaponry, as well as a guardhouse, no one seemed to look up to him no matter how much he had done to remain respectful and dutiful to his job. "Our rifle is created to be mute. The only order we were given is to remain calm, calm and calm like Buddha when he was in Nirvana . . . the passersby could have put some flowers [out] and burned incense for us."[78] At the guardhouse Kwee and his fellows were even bullied by children and mocked by adults who thought that Dutch power had already gone to the point of no return.

> While we are sitting at our guardhouse [wacht], a group of Indonesians walked in our direction. From their clothes and manner, we know

they are from the village. While they get closer to our guardhouse, one of them asks his friend, following the style of villagers talking in such a loud voice that everyone on the street can hear. — "Brother, what are they doing?" "Don't worry! They are just Dutch soldiers [*serdadu Londo*]! What else could they do? The Dutch have already lost!" They talk just like that, while passing in front of us as if we are not there. They think we are just like wind.[79]

Deprived of its enabling political network, the symbolic authority of the guardhouse disappeared. Yet, Kwee Thiam Tjing represents how the power of the guardhouse is defined not only by its appearance but, more importantly, by how it shapes him and the social relations within which they are embedded.

Indonesia dalem bara dan api starts with the experience of Kwee as a volunteer city guard even though he was never fully convinced that it would do any good for the collapsing regime. Nevertheless, his job as a guard of the city allows him to construct his subject position as someone who is both observing and participating in what happens to his city. Kwee witnesses the unfolding events in Malang, but what he sees owes much to the sense of being a guard who is watching over the city. His position as a guard of the city allows him to narrate from the position of an observer seeing as well as remembering more than others what his fellow Indonesians have done to each other. No wonder he starts his account with his experience as a guard and ends with his eventual sense of failure to become one.

At a deeper level, Kwee Thiam Tjing indicates a profound ambiguity of ethnic Chinese toward gardu and its whole practice of guarding. The gardu is a structure that members of the ethnic Chinese community rely on, especially at a time of unrest, even as they are always worried about their dependency on the gardu. Volunteering as a city guard, Kwee was in fact attempting to conquer this fear. He even moves beyond the standard form of community defense associated with the Chinese neighborhood that Liem Thian Joe of Semarang had earlier delineated for us. Kwee could have helped by organizing a neighborhood watch for the ethnic Chinese by creating betengan or phangshia around the Chinese neighborhood, but Kwee saw his commitment as lying beyond the confinement of a particular community, a conscience that presumably could be heeded only by becoming a guard for the whole city where he had been living. But *Indonesia dalem api dan bara* shows precisely the horror of such a commitment. In the end, Kwee goes back to his own neighborhood and finds no one at home. After an incredible search he finds the killing field at Mergosono and the remains of many ethnic Chinese, including his friends and family members who had been brutally killed by the Indonesian mobs (the *Djamino* and *Djoliteng*) under the guise of revolutionary *pemuda*.

> At that time, my heart was in terrible pain and I was mad with anger. I left the Ang Hien Hoo [one of the Chinese associations that did not seem to care about what had happened], and went to the [Dutch] *Troepen Commandent*. I told him that I am an ex-city guard [stadswacht] and I would like to be a volunteer (again) to mobilize friends to find the killers. I asked him to lend me the weapons and I will do the revenge. I don't need to be paid. I don't mind if I died for I am doing this for my Chinese [*Tionghoa*] community.[80]

Indonesia dalem bara dan api could be read as a story haunted by a sense of horror, disappointment, and guilt that as a guard (trained by the supposedly powerful colonial state and committed to safeguard the city), Kwee could not stop the massacre of persons from his own community. He in fact did not know who he was guarding against. At the time of unrest, the enemy was both internal and external. Guarding and failing to guard haunt the pages of *Indonesia dalem bara dan api*. Like the guardhouse that marks the boundary of territory, Kwee saw himself as the guardian of human conscience who, however, saw with his own eyes humanity's limits in defending itself against the brutality of time (*zaman pantjaroba*).

RETRIEVALS

In the previous section, I showed how the gardu and its territoriality could be traced back to the earlier territorial strategy of the ethnic Chinese in coming to terms with continuous social and political unrest in the city. I also showed how Dutch colonialism was involved in the formation of gardus in the late nineteenth and early twentieth centuries in Java. Having traced how the gardu was constituted under Dutch colonialism and how it was formed and perceived in the Chinese community, it is no longer possible to say that the gardu was a product of a single culture. Instead, the gardu was constituted along with other cultures over time in Indonesian society. In this process, the Dutch and especially the Chinese played a decisive and historic role.

Nevertheless, as both an object and subject of social practice, the gardu can redirect cultural memory and can be subjected to a different narrative of the past. How was the gardu reinvented during the Japanese occupation of Indonesia? How did it synthesize practices of the past and how did the gardu under Japanese occupation affect Indonesians in the long run? In this section, I will show how, under Japanese occupation, the discourses of gardu and its institution of neighborhood watch received its signification as part of the Indonesian cultural tradition. What was the process by which the gardu, under Japanese occupation, came to be imagined as part of Indonesian cultural heritage?

Japan Incorporated

Toward the end of the Asia-Pacific War, Mohamad Hatta, the first vice president of Indonesia remarked: "What matters above all other values [brought by Japanese occupation] is that people's minds have been liberated from their sense of inferiority. In contrast to the Dutch, the Imperial army [of Japan] has taught us to be brave and to recognize ourselves on our own merits."[81] Nothing of the discourses of the gardu and the perception that it is part of the cultural tradition of Java can be grasped without understanding the impact that the Japanese occupation had on postcolonial political elites as well as the Indonesian public.

Japanese military administration in Indonesia, while only lasting for three and a half years, was significant for its style of governance, which, as Hatta pointed out, was in complete contrast to that of the Dutch. If the Dutch preferred an indirect hierarchical rule where divisions were constructed between colonial subjects, Japan, with its ideology of Pan-Asianism, eliminated the divisions by integrating Asians as "brothers" under its rule. Central to Japanese occupation indeed was the mobilization of civilians, especially the youth, for the Asia-Pacific war. Japanese historian Goto Ken'ichi indicates that in a short period of time as many as "37,000 young men in Java alone received a strict military training and ideological education under the banner of 'defense of the fatherland,' a programme that would have been unimaginable under Dutch rule."[82]

This war mobilization was in stark contrast to the Dutch quest for "peaceful" colonization in the Indies. If the training of the city guard by the Dutch produced only scarecrows who were afraid of aircraft and ghosts, "the training course of Japan for Indonesian youth was designed to instantly turn them into cruel beings who would follow order."[83] If Kwee Thiam Tjing found no one paying attention to the city guard in the city he was living in, under Japanese occupation, people were instructed to stop and pay respect to the city guard. If the city guards under the Dutch were trained with disciplinary protocols, the Japanese "little brothers" were treated with corporal punishment. "Even a small mistake would receive slapping, kicking and hitting."[84] R. Joesoef, a high-ranking police officer, observed in a brief report that in a short period of time, many Indonesians were appointed as policemen and very soon "everyone knows very well how to march properly."[85]

Changes were taking place not only at the level of government. The everyday life of Indonesians was restructured through participatory work that would lead to a meaningful target—the liberation of Indonesians from Western imperialism. One of the most important apparatus used to bring together Indonesian people of various backgrounds in order to run an occupied region (against the "European colonizer") was the *tonarigumi* (neighborhood association). Imposed in both urban and rural areas, ten to twenty adjacent households were organized to share community work, which was programmed to ensure both order in that community and loyalty to the government.[86] This technique of community subjectification was perhaps developed first in the Japanese colonies in Korea, Manchuria, and Taiwan before it was imported back to Japan in the late 1930s for the preparation of Japan's coming war.[87] In the Japanese occupied territory of Indonesia, the neighborhood was parceled into several units and communal life was institutionalized in order to help Japan win the war in Asia. Aiko Kurasawa reported that "the total number of tonarigumi for the whole of Java was 508,745 and the total number of households was 8,967,320. These figures mean that there was approximately one tonarigumi for every 17 to 18 households."[88] Some twelve households in each cluster would become "a big family with mutual love and help just like in one's own family" with father(s) as the head even though the tonarigumi "was mostly taken care of by women."[89]

Central to the tonarigumi was the security organization called Keibodan whose members were inhabitants of the neighborhood. The job of Keibodan, according to Aboe Djamal, one of the community leaders from the island of Madura, was basically policing. "The task consists of some secrecy in order to combat espionage, check the circulation of goods, watch over security, help combat air raids, increase the production and delivery of paddy and other crops, and observe suspected people, especially those along coastal area."[90] This community vigilance was strengthened by the imposition of collective responsibility for the behavior of their fellow members. Everyone in the community had the task of preventing espionage, antigovernment activities, and undesirable ways of thinking and undesirable lifestyles in their neighborhood. They were also asked to contribute financially to run the operation. The Japanese military administration made steady use of Keibodan and co-opted the neighborhood chiefs of the town and village in Java to coordinate the operation of tonarigumi. Above all it made use of the gardu to coordinate mutual household surveillance (see figure 56).

The Japanese military government was very careful in harnessing the practice of the neighborhood watch. Members of Keibodan were portrayed as working together, in the spirit of mutual help (gotong royong) with the kampung guard (*pendjaga kampong*) of the neighborhood. For the Japanese military government, the gardu was a symbol of the cooperation between the state and the neighborhood. The gardu was not merely the representation of kampung security but also served to stimulate a stronger "spirit of mutual help (gotong royong)" between the state and the community.[91]

If the policemen under Dutch colonial rule were seen as belonging to the realm of the outsider because they "rarely entered the kampung but carefully patrolled the asphalt roads that encircled them,"[92] the Keibodan ruled the kampung from within, working hand-in-hand with the pendjaga kampong of the neighborhood. In Japanese colonial magazines, pictures of the gardu were taken from *within*, signifying at once the embodiment of Japanese military practice in the daily life of a neighborhood. This kind of shot would not have been taken by the Dutch who, for reasons delineated above, could only see the gardu from a detached exterior. The *Sinar Baroe* newspaper wrote: "Every kampung resident has contributed as much as they could by becoming part of the Keibodan, which is the key institution that watches over matters concerning security. Today, gardus [also

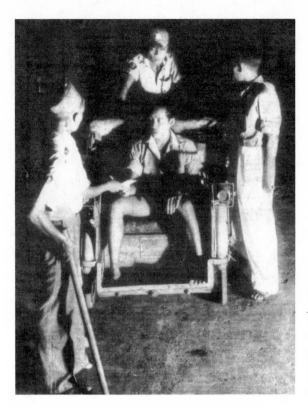

Figure 56 During the Japanese occupation, members of Keibodan measured the state of security on the street. Reprinted from *Djawa baroe* 16, 15 August 1944.

called *roemah djaga* during this time] have been built at various places, and every night members of the Keibodan have been guarding the community. The public knows how useful the night watch is. So don't hesitate to contribute financially for the construction of more [roemah djaga]."[93] We can say that the Japanese abolished the dual (or plural) system of Dutch colonial administration by creating the institution of Keibodan to bridge the separated worlds. Through an identification with and involvement in the gardu, the Japanese military government replaced the Dutch colonial governance with a centralized system based on direct state intervention in community life.

In a matter of a year, the Japanese military government in the occupied region of Indonesia had already institutionalized the culture of the gardu. In Solo, *Sinar Baroe* reported that "all the kampung people [rakyat] have been mobilized to watch the security of their kampungs. Regulations have been imposed without any difference for the rich and the poor. As the rear guard supporting forces at the frontline, every inhabitant in the kampung is obliged to watch over the security of his or her neighborhood. Those who resist will be punished and, if necessary, expelled from his or her kampung."[94]

The gardu coalesced with communal memories and forced aspirations. Yet, it is with this mix of politics and everyday life that the gardu played a significant role not only in commanding and maintaining order at a local level but also in serving as a symbol of Japan's ideology in Asia, that is, the unification of all the colonized in fighting against "Western powers." The practice of collectively guarding one's neighborhood had this aim of bringing together people from various ethnicities and classes. The *Sinar Baroe* reported instances where Indonesians, Arabs, Chinese, Indians, Malay, and Javanese cooperated in the gardu in their cosurveillance of each other's communities. The practice of night watch cut across differences in class and status. "Even an aristocrat (*bangsawan*) or a prince would fulfill the obligation of night watch together with his clerk or servant of his palace."[95]

Perhaps in order to live with this new institutional requirement of communalism, S. P. Pakoealaman, one of the princes in Central Java, had to suppress the power hierarchy of his realm. He proclaimed that the spirit of tonarigumi could indeed be found in the *Kedjawen* (a belief system of the Javanese) and it should therefore be valued as part of the heritage of the nation (*pusaka tanah air dan leloehoer*). Pakoealaman declared: "I hope tonarigumi will spread the feeling of care for all people in our nation as well as reviving our belief system in order to cast away the [individualistic] slogan of: 'who you are, and who am I' [*sopo siro sopo ingsoen*]."[96] Through the practice of cosurveillance, the gardu supposedly brought together people from various ethnicities and classes, all on the same platform watching as well as being watched. Despite the projection of Japan's military values, the gardu engaged in making claims for both a new future—the liberation of Indonesians from the subjection of Dutch colonialism—and a continuation of an age-old gardu tradition inherited from "our" ancestors.

By conceiving the gardu as the embodiment of the imagined past and future Indonesia, a culture was thus created for Indonesians. Once the gardu was institutionalized, Indonesians began to conceive the institution of the gardu as a form of empowerment for their cultural practices. Yet, culture does not operate in a vacuum. There were instructions published in the state-sponsored popular media, such as *Sinar Baroe*, to remind Indonesians to think of this "invented tradition" as their own and to explain how to practice it. As pointed out earlier, the Dutch (especially through its Ethicial Policy) did contribute to the discourses of the gardu, especially the idea of gotong royong and making the gardu an archetype of Javanese tradition, but details of how this invented culture could be systematized, organized, and popularized for the efficiency of social and political control can be found only during the Japanese occupation.

Yet, from what perspective was it possible for the Japanese military administration to view gardus and the security watch as embodying an age-old tradition of Java/Indonesia/Asia? There are at least two conditions that turned the practice of gardu into a "traditional" institution. First, as part of the discourses of liberation from the West, Japan encouraged Indonesians to identify themselves with cultures that were supposedly "non-Western." The urge to differentiate Asia from the West turned the institution of gardu into a tradition of the East.

Second, and perhaps more important, the tonarigumi was in fact derived from the Chinese technique of spatial defense known as the *Pao-Tjia* system (protecting the home), which was known since the Song dynasty. Denys Lombard has even suggested that the *Pao-Tjia* system might have already been implemented by ethnic Chinese in the coastal areas of Java long before the arrival of the West.[97] Having traveled across Asia, and with three Asian colonies to govern (Manchuria, Taiwan, and Korea, as well as its own territories), the pan-Asiatic eyes of Japan had no trouble seeing the existing practices of gardu and night watch as the embodiment of Eastern culture. In other words, when the Japanese military administration arrived in Java, the practices of neighborhood watch and the gardus formed a repertoire that the administration conveniently retrieved, repacked, and redistributed in the form of tonarigumi to every part of Java and Indonesia. What Japan did was formalize the practice by empowering the supposedly cultural tradition of the colonized in the campaign against the West.

By the end of the Japanese occupation, Indonesian youth, unlike Kwee Thiam Tjing, already felt equipped to guard the city, which by then had entered the era of revolution. How did the gardu and the practices of guarding under Japanese occupation affect Indonesian subjectivity in the immediate era of revolution?

The Gardu Effects: Pemuda in the Time of Revolution

After the surrender of the Japanese military government and the declaration of independence, the time that Indonesians recognize as their period of revolution, much of the country was plunged into bloodshed and violence that claimed many thousands of lives. The official combatants—the new Republic of Indonesia and the returning Netherlands Indies Colonial Administration (NICA)—were incapable of restoring order. They fought against each other while taking advantage of unofficial militias in the political violence. Each side, however, was also perfectly aware of the importance of order and security as the basis for the consolidation of power. The country was divided and engaged in the discourses of order and disorder as violence continued, especially at the "neutral" but shifting lines dividing the two forces.

Efforts were nevertheless made to ensure security and order. In Jakarta, for instance, the British Military Police, which served as a temporary neutral group, soon formed police forces to end the political violence in the city.[98] Following the Dutch system of plural government, each ethnic group was delegated the task of safeguarding its own neighborhood. Meanwhile the Dutch military commanded a system of territorial control by issuing military passes for those who traveled along main roads (*hofdwegen*).[99] It also announced in newspapers the security zones and listed the boundaries under its protection.[100] The Indonesian National Military (TNI) established "commando posts" in villages and at the border to ensure security and order.[101] Travel documents were marked by dates. The "commando posts" served as checkpoints as well as markers of the boundary of the state. Outside these official measures, various communities took the initiative of forming their own security organizations, especially in the secondary cities and smaller towns where rampages and killing by unofficial militias went unchecked. Chinese Indonesians too, as a group that was often targeted, found no other option except to form its own security organization such as the Pao An Tui.[102]

The time of revolution was thus marked by patrols and neighborhood watches (ronda) in the city as well as in the countryside. It was also a period in which political identities and identification and ways of expressing them in the public space were critical. "Outward appearances" were crucial not only for navigation and a sense of orientation but also for survival.[103] Signs were inscribed on buildings to mobilize identification and indicate affiliation. Of particular importance was the right combination of colors (red and white symbolizing the national flag of Indonesia, and red, white, and blue symbolizing the Dutch). Out of this struggle for independence and identification, a peculiar type of person (known eventually as pemuda — those with a young spirit and ready to fight for independence) emerged in the urban centers of Indonesian territory.[104] What is important here is that the pemuda considered themselves as the guard of the nation.

In 1951, Pramoedya Ananta Toer wrote *Di tepi kali Bekasi*. Pramoedya shows the formation of a new type of Indonesian (the pemuda) who, after experiencing the war mobilization by Japan, emerged as freedom fighters for the Republic of Indonesia. Young Farid, the protagonist, is an admirer of Japan's military units, the *barisan jibaku* and the *pasukan kamikaze*, especially the willingness of these special troops to crush the enemy and fight to the death. Farid admires, even as he can't understand, the forces that created such forms of sacrifice. Nevertheless he realizes that the "national consciousness of Indonesians was awakened by the Japanese. . . . The Dutch gave only a colonial mentality to Indonesian people . . . to the old man in front of him."[105] Farid considers himself a new man. He is the type that the pretty Nanny admired, "the young, strong and vigorous man. His bravery, perseverance, and sacrifice for the nation are just like those of Amir [her late boyfriend who had died in the Revolution]."[106] Through the eyes of Nanny, Pramoedya constructed a type of man known then as pemuda, a type that was peculiar to the time but was born out of the Japanese occupation.

In one way or another, Indonesians were both fascinated and terrified by their experiences during the Japanese occupation. It was however this mixture of feelings that most powerfully formed their new subjectivity. Almost a year after Japan's surrender, the *Kedaulatan Rakjat* newspaper recalled one of the last impressions of Japanese occupation: "All the Japanese detainees, from soldiers to high officers, saluted by bending their bodies in front of our troops standing in the guardhouse at the camp."[107] The time of revolution can indeed be understood through the lens of the identity formation of Indonesians, an identity shaped by the discourses and practices of guarding the city. Central to the issue is the struggle over the identity of the pemuda who represented themselves, consciously or unconsciously, as the guard of the nation.

Figure 57 "Where is your letter of reference, *bung?*": *Pemuda* guarding the city. Reprinted from Soedjarwo, *Lukisan revolusi rakjat Indonesia, 1945–1949.*

One of the ways to discuss the subjectivity of the pemuda as the guard of the nation is by looking at a photograph (figure 57) taken in the early revolutionary time. In this photograph, considered as "a typical image of the revolutionary era," we see a group of young men standing in front of the camera.[108]

With their hands on rifles and weapons, they posed as the guards of the city. Looking at this image, we could probably say that the practice of gardu during the Japanese occupation had spilled over to the time of revolution. The pemuda marked their presence in the city with the spirit of a guard that one could find under Japanese occupation. They might belong to the Indonesian national army (the TNI) or to one of the unofficial militias (the fighting groups called *laskar*), but their stylistic formation (at least in the photograph) recalls the image of the security guards standing at the gardu. It is an image one would confront as one approaches the entrance to a guarded neighborhood. These youth represented the city (in ruins) behind them. They considered the city as under their guard and saw themselves as the protectors of the city as well as the destroyer of things associated with the enemy. They considered themselves as the vanguard of the newly liberated world of the Indonesian masses (the rakyat). They patrolled around the city in a self-styled uniform. They took the urban space as their gigantic canvas on which they inscribed writings, slogans, and flags associated with the new time and identity. They saw themselves as the embodiment of order and security even as many of them participated in political violence and acts of destruction.

In the early outburst of revolution, there was at least a half-dozen or more of these different fighting groups consisting of pemuda. Clothed in different styles, they did not associate themselves with any particular political or ideological position. While sharing a similar vision of struggling for independence, they were also involved in competitive, intricate, and shifting alliances. Political identity was at stake in the time of revolution. The uniforms, as William Fredrick argues, allowed for differentiation, identification, and group formation.[109] Yet, for those who lived in the city or areas under the influence of the pemuda, a most important way to communicate their political outlook was the right response to the frequently asked question: "Where is your *surat keterangan* (letter of reference), *bung* (brother)?"[110] Like the guard in the gardu, the pemuda too checked the political identity of the people they met and decided whether the person was an ally or an enemy.

The pemuda however were not common guards one would encounter in a gardu, nor were they policemen controlled by the state. Instead the pemuda were guards that did not recognize boundaries. They were often seen fully or partially armed, patrolling across the city and the countryside. The pemuda did not respect the officially agreed-upon boundary between the two main forces.[111] Instead they blurred the boundary by moving around claiming territories. They went as far as to the outskirts of the city and the villages and checked the neighborhoods in the area to find out the political affiliations of the inhabitants. Imagining themselves as the guard of the new revolutionary society, the pemuda spread their political influence to the village even as the villagers were mostly afraid of them.

Securing the State and Becoming Tradition

The pemuda, the returning Dutch colonial administration, and the Republic of Indonesia struggled to consolidate power by offering different safety measures. We do not know if the gardu was used or inscribed with marks of identity and identification like the poskos of the PDI-P, but each of these constituencies was involved in the maintenance and expansion of their sphere of influence by projecting values. These struggles for territory and identity came close to the end only after Indonesia gained its sovereignty. In 1949, the TNI announced that on the matter surrounding security, "one should not act on his own but should follow the law initiated by the authority of our nation."[112] Yet, as the new Republic of Indonesia gained its full authority, some of the laskar groups continued

Figure 58 Troops departing from the *gardu*. Reprinted from Sekretariat Negara, *30 tahun Indonesia merdeka, 1945–1955,* no. 416, p. 353.

to see themselves as the guardians not merely of a city or a kampung but the country as a whole. Seeing themselves as participants in the change of the time, they felt responsible for the future of the country and acted on its behalf by fighting even the newly formed Republic of Indonesia. One such group was the Darul Islam, which sought to bring the new republic under the banner of Islam. To achieve this end, it identified the republic as its enemy. In turn, the republic conceived Darul Islam as *gerombolan* (wandering rebels). Unlike during the time of revolution, after the transfer of sovereignty, particular political and ideological positions became an issue among Indonesians. Within the force field of order and security, so crucial to the legitimation of power of the new republic, the gardu made its appearance. Perhaps the best way to indicate this is by looking at an image found in the official photo album of the "30 years of Indonesian Independence" (see figure 58).

In figure 58, we see "the troops [*pasukan*] of the New Republic marching down the field to conduct operations [against the Darul Islam] in January 1951."[113] A gardu is in the background, marking the safe territory of the republic. In the gardu are children and women looking at the camera. The troops are marching to an unknown destination, presumably into the untamed areas where they might find the "gerombolan Darul Islam." The camera makes the gardu appear as the point of origin from where the troops are departing and to where they are supposed to return. It is the home with children and women waiting for them to come back. As the "home" of the republic, the gardu not only indicates the territorial identity of the republic but also is an index of security as several guards are standing around it. However, unlike the marching troops, they appear relaxed and at home. The gardu and the troops delineate a territorial identity demarcating thus areas of the known and the unknown.

The caption of this image does not make any reference to the gardu. Instead it brings to our attention only the forces of the republic. The gardu is a familiar structure, so familiar that no comment is needed. We don't know whether it was built by order of the republic or was part of the structure of community defense harnessed by the pasukan republic. We know however that it represents order and security as well as threat. In the picture at least it belongs to the republic. Can we say that the gardu animates subjectivity? Can it be seen not only as acting for people but also acting upon them? How does the gardu affect the formation of culture and tradition?

Thirty years after the Darul Islam event, Edi S. Ekadjati, a Sundanese intellectual, recalled the security system of the gardu (*garduh* in Sundanese) as belonging to a system of traditional defense of the Sunda land. Ekadjati remembers the village of Karangtawang in West Java during the time of war with the Darul Islam. Knowing that the pasukan republic was still incapable of fully protecting the village, several initiatives were taken by the inhabitants of the desa. Ekadjati reports that members of the village community fenced the whole village with bamboo two meters high. They also organized a security watch (ronda) among themselves and built several gardus, each of which was equipped with a *khokol* (the kentongan — the sound-bearing instrument).[114] In addition, the village also conducted periodical mass praying and even mobilized the magical spirits of the village (in the forms of *jin* and tigers) to safeguard the neighborhood.[115] Since these practices were part of their tradition, no difficulties were recorded in setting them up and in mobilizing community participation. Every member of the village community seemed to know this traditional defense system. Like cultural practices understood as tradition, the gardu and its practices have thus been registered not primarily in written documents but in the minds of the people.

Dispersed Receptions

We have seen in this chapter that the gardu not only moves across orders but also touches various grounds, including the realm of the state and the domain of daily life. It is not only an outward sign of a social and political phenomenon but also an institution of everyday life that actively constitutes the norm and behavior of people who live in and around it. Yet, the truth of the gardu cannot be known for certain, but as a tradition, it has gained a life of its own, one that does not need to have a history. It brings together various memories even though one does not know where they are coming from. Like all traditions, once initiated, they mark simultaneously all-time and no-time with no intention of representing the past or the future. To return to our post-Suharto scene, Mangara Siahaan, the vice secretary general of PDI said in 1999 that the posko was "a symbol that could move people [massa] at any time. It is a symbol of power . . . [and] when we set up the idea of posko, people [masyarakat] were enthusiastic."[116] Perhaps precisely because of the ahistorical nature of tradition, the gardu is seen as possessing a power of its own. For Ekadjati and Siahaan, the gardu could be easily retrieved. It might be invested with various meanings, but it continues to retain its power. And as a traditional practice, it seems to be capable of performing multiple social roles and moving easily across time and space.

The experience of guarding the neighborhood and the nation has been transmitted from one generation to another. It has been carried over to postcolonial times. The beating of the kentongan during the night watch continues to the present. The gardu, the ronda, and the codes of the kentongan have been carried over to other times and have become the structure of everyday life today in both the city and the village of Indonesia.[117]

Yet, like many other urban forms of the contemporary world, the gardu in Indonesia can also be seen as part of the gated-community phenomena, in which private security, community surveillance, and state power intermingle. Here, the gardu absorbs into its sphere images of other times and spaces while isolating them in the dreamworld of Disney-like cosmopolitanism (see figure 59).

In this isolated world, it stays as a reminder to the developers and consumers of real estate housing of the threats of urban violence. In urban Indonesia this global impulse of the gardu has intertwined, often unnotice-

Figure 59 Selling property, selling *gardu*: The Parisian classical baroque gatehouse of Lippo Karawaci. Reprinted from the brochure of Lippo Karawaci, obtained in 2002.

ably, with particular trajectories of precolonial, colonial, and postcolonial histories. In this crosscut, it seems that older modes of representation have returned to the present as cultural resources while new trajectories have been opened up.

In the student uprising across Indonesia in 1998 that led to the fall of Suharto, many gardus of the state (the pos hansips) were taken over by students and became important gathering points nationwide. In 2001, in Papua, a major island in the eastern part of Indonesia, the emergence of the proindependence protest movement against the Indonesian state was marked by the construction of poskos on which were displayed the movement's morning star flag. As a response, the state launched a series of co-ordinated raids on the poskos.

Closer to home, the appointment of a new head of the neighborhood (RT) where my parents are staying was marked by the construction of yet another gardu at another corner of the street, increasing the collection of gardus in the area. Written on the wall of the gardu is a new term: *posko-hansip*, bridging thus the era of Suharto and those of the chosen ones after him. The newly elected RT, who is a civilian, quite spontaneously felt that the election of a new RT "should be marked by the building of a new gardu" regardless of the fact that there were already six guardhouses within a radius of thirty meters. One of the residents of the neighborhood told me, humorously, that it is "through the gardu that the Pak RT (chief of the neighborhood) will be remembered." What then has happened to the old gardus? Some of them have become the house of the guards (*Pak hansip*) in which one can find a pantry and a bed. The size of the gardu has been extended with an old sofa laid outside. As the gardu grows deeper and becomes more like a tiny house, the interior has grown darker, and yet from there the eyes see without being seen.

Gardus have also been the subjects of talk shows. In 2004, Anwar Hudijono, a newspaper commentator, published his work in a small book titled *Gardu*. In the introduction, Anwar explains why he chose this as the title of his book. "[My] writings are light and relaxing, just like chatting in the gardu. Talking in the gardu has no order and direction, unlike discussion on TV or in a seminar. Everything can be talked about with ease [*ngomong ngalor-ngidul*]. What is important is participation . . . spontaneous . . . and egalitarian."[118] While light and relaxing, the gardu of Anwar is also meant to be a guardian for "social change towards a more democratic life . . . With *Gardu*, we will be able to reflect on various events and ultimately act on them for social change."[119] The gardu is less what it looks like than what it does. In Anwar's mind, it is a monument by virtue of its capacity to evoke chatting and even social change. It is a modest way of transforming the world. His gardu, like those of Megawati, Suharto, Kwee Thiam Tjing, the Dutch, the Chinese, the Japanese, the pemuda, and Pak RT has become a medium for the projection of aspirations, values, power, fear, desires, and of course, tradition.

Today, the gardu remains instrumental for the symbolic spectacle of the state's (as well as personal) power even as its appearance often means, in the minds of the public, the decline of the state's authority. It continues to register class status, prestige, and of course "man-power." Yet, especially among ethnic Chinese of post-1998 Jakarta, it triggers memories of anti-Chinese riots. It keeps alive the culture of rumors, the practices of the night watch, and the surveillance of the streets. For most men in Java, it remains an enjoyable place for drinking, chatting, and gazing at women who are walking on the street. For many women, the gardu is highly gendered and it is based practically and historically (if not also theoretically) on excluding women. It continues to be an unsettling place that is domi-

Figure 60 All men: Where have all the women gone? Cartoon depicting men (only) chatting at a *gardu*. Reprinted courtesy of P. T. Gramedia Pustaka Utama from Benny Rachmnadi and Muh. Misrad, *Lagak Jakarta: Reformasi* (Jakarta: Kepustakaan Popular Gramedia, 1998).

nated by men. For other members of the society, it awakens urban militarism, Sukarno's street-based populist politics, and communist threats. As a whole, the gardu integrates these different memories into the consciousness of the city (see figure 60).

FINALLY . . .

The gatehouse (gardu/posko/pos hansip) has complex roots in Indonesia. I have shown how it survived in many different forms, operating as the artifice for memorialization as well as the construction of spatial identity. I have traced its "origins" in the spatial politics of Dutch colonialism and the experience of ethnic Chinese and shown how it was eventually institutionalized under Japanese military administration and mobilized in the postcolonial era as an autochthonous tradition. Over time the gardu finds its place in the collective memory of Indonesians, which can be retrieved at any time and under any condition.

I began with an image of PDI-P's posko and its symbolic elements. I then pulled them apart into smaller pieces and reassembled them back with fragments of Indonesian histories and memories. Throughout the process, I teased out some recent memories of the gardu and flashed those memories back to the past to trace not only moments that have contributed to the formation of gardu but also instances that have indicated its affective power in shaping subjectivities. I problematized the generally held belief that the gardu is inherited from Javanese culture and from time immemorial. Tracing the artifact across orders confirms the sense that the gardu is not the result of an act of invention of a single culture. Instead, it is reproduced and reinvented together with other practices and discourses delineated over time in Indonesian society.

I have taken a long circle, cast in a sequel, suggesting the interdependence of various sites and the historic roles of ethnic Chinese and Dutch colonialism. I have also integrated different memories and many modes of representations that affect the meaning of the gardu. I have shown that each experience of the gardu is to some degree affected by the historical experiences of other times that have been transmitted across generations through the recurrence of the gardu itself. This interweaving of experiences across time and space is crucial for an understanding of the persistence as well as the proliferation of gardus in contemporary urban Indonesia. Showing the importance of memory-crossing in understanding the reiteration of gardus, my effort in this chapter has been to make gardus visible, to think their publicness, visualize their power, and question the formation of subjectivity in urban Indonesia. Yet, as with other attempts to trace social memories and the change of subjectivities, there is no ending to this story. The life history of the gardu, like other forms of life story, remains discursive, fragmented, and incomplete, but it seems to me the spatial and temporal circle offered in this chapter (as well as in this book) has been completed.

NOTES

Introduction

1. Doelriadi, "Zaman baharoe," *Persatoean Hindia*, 3 April 1920, 1. My translation from Indonesian.
2. Shiraishi, *An Age in Motion*.
3. The recollections of the past pose a desire to open up an expected future. For a discussion on Javanese ways of writing history, see Florida, *Writing the Past, Inscribing the Future*; and Gouda, "The Unbearable Lightness of Memory."
4. The literature on space and power, especially in the context of colonial and post-colonial architecture and urbanism, is by now too extensive to be listed here. For a discussion on the recent theoretical debates on the topics, see King, *Spaces of Global Cultures*, chaps. 2–4. For a recent discussion on architecture and memory, see Crinson, *Urban Memory*.
5. Williams, *The Long Revolution*, 9.
6. Escobar, *Encountering Development*.
7. Prakash, "The Urban Turn."
8. I appropriate Ben Highmore's explanation of everyday life as a domain that has often become "the unknowing host for the return of traumatic material." See Highmore, *Everyday Life Reader*, 2.
9. Nordholt and Samuel, *Indonesia in Transition*.
10. Zurbuchen ed., *Beginning to Remember*.
11. Nordholt and Samuel, *Indonesia in Transition*; Wessel and Wimhofer, *Violence in Indonesia*.
12. Robison and Hadiz, *Reorganising Power in Indonesia*.
13. See Foucault, "Governmentality."
14. For a discussion of the suburbanization of Jakarta during the Suharto era and the role of developers, see Leaf, "Building the Road for the BMW" and "Suburbanization of Jakarta." See also Firman, "The Restructuring of Jakarta's Metropolitan Area."
15. Forty and Kuchler, *The Art of Forgetting*.
16. In the study of architecture, the question of social memory has been asked since

the 1960s, most notably, with the publication of Aldo Rossi's *The Architecture of the City*. Rossi's book is basically a critique of orthodox modernist architecture for its denial of a place for memory. It suggests that the denial itself is a form of acknowledgment not only of the existence of memory but also its suppression. The book raises the issue that the city, along with its whole corpus of objects and places, embodies the collective memory of its people. Architects and builders, Rossi argues, should develop new forms of visual environment based on the study of existing urban architecture for it is this that stores such a collective memory. The attraction of Rossi's thesis to architects is that, for them, it adds another mission since they can now see themselves as not only guardians of the existing urban architecture but also of the people's collective memory. It also confers on architects the responsibility to come to terms with the particular histories and memories associated with the city and to "transfer" them, by means of their architectural design strategies, to the form of the new buildings they design. Yet it has never occurred to Rossi and his followers how buildings could adequately stand for memories. They also ignore the plurality of memories and the question regarding just whose memories are stored and transferred. Moreover they forget to ask what lies just beyond those memories—things that cannot quite be recalled not only because of the official politics of suppression but also because people do not want to remember them as they remake their life. See Forty, "Introduction," in Forty and Küchler, *The Art of Forgetting*, 1–18. For other explorations, see Crinson, *Urban Memory*; Boyer, *The City of Collective Memory*; Huyssen, *Present Pasts*.

17. Recognizing the limits and the arbitrariness of buildings' ability to represent collective memory does not however eliminate the mnemonic potential of buildings. The built environment, be it architecture or buildings of everyday quality, can still be seen as a medium in which individuals and societies remember and forget. For a discussion on how the mnemonic capacities of medieval storytellers were dependent on the degree to which they were able to read the real and imagined physical environments, see Yates, *The Art of Memory*. For a discussion on the relations between memory, place, and historical narratives that have given an "environmental memory" to a Palestinian village, see Slyomovics, *The Object of Memory*.

18. See Walkowitz and Knauer, *Memory and the Impact of Political Transformation in Public Space*.

19. Olick, "Collective Memory."

20. Yeoh, "Postcolonial Cities."

21. For a discussion on "specific intellectuals," See Rabinow, *French Modern*.

22. Yeoh, "Postcolonial Cities," 461.

23. The conference, which took place on 23–25 August 2005, was organized by the History Department of Airlangga University in Surabaya in cooperation with the Netherlands Institute for War Documentation (NIOD). Papers presented at

the conference have been published in Colombijn et al., *Kota lama, kota baru*. The week-long workshop on "Street Image: Decolonization and Changing Symbolism of Indonesian Urban Culture, 1930s–1960s" took place in late August through early September of 2004. It was organized by professor Bambang Purwanto of the Centre for Southeast Asian Social Studies, University of Gadjah Mada, Yogyakarta in cooperation with the Netherlands Institute for War Documentation. For a discussion on urban symbolism, see Nas, *Urban Symbolism*.

24. AlSayyad, *Forms of Dominance*.

25. See among others, Ai, *Text and the City*; Frederick, *Visions and Heat*; Harootunian, *Overcome by Modernity*; Karl, *Staging the World*; Lee, *Shanghai Modern*; Mrázek, *Engineers of Happy Land*; Robinson and Shin, *Colonial Modernity in Korea*; Shiraishi, *An Age in Motion*; Thongchai, *Siam Mapped*.

26. Mrázek, *Engineers of Happy Land*.

27. Shiraishi, *An Age in Motion*.

28. See Lynch, *The Image of the City*. See also Jameson, "Cognitive Mapping."

29. Oshikawa, "'Patjar Merah Indonesia' and Tan Malaka."

30. See note 25.

31. Anderson, *The Spectre of Comparisons*.

32. See Kusno, "Tan Malaka, Shanghai and the Politics of Geographical Imagining."

33. Chakrabarty, *Provincializing Europe*.

34. Lombard, *Le carrefour Javanais*.

35. Ibid.

36. For a discussion on "history of the present," see Foucault, "The Subject and Power."

Chapter 1: Whither Nationalist Urbanism?

1. The centrality of Jakarta comes from the discourses of Sukarno, the first president during early independence, as well as from Dutch colonial urban history. The concept of the center is also derived from the traditional polity of Java. See Kusno, *Behind the Postcolonial*, chap. 2. For a planning history of Jakarta see Silver, *Planning the Megacity*.

2. "Arsitektur kedaerahan atasi kesenjangan" [Regional Architecture Overcomes Social Gaps], *Bisnis Indonesia*, 28 July 1999.

3. By the beginning of 2003, the city had witnessed full-scale forced evictions of illegal migrants, shantytown dwellers, and street vendors. This display of municipal authority was concomitant with the discourses of antiterrorism after the Bali bombing, the sending of troops to Aceh, the strengthening of military positions in the civilian government, and the formulation of policies concerning the decentralization of the country. See chapter 2 for an analysis of urban governmentality in the second half of Governor Sutiyoso's rule.

4. Goenawan, "City."

5. Pramoedya, "Letter to a Friend from the Country."

6. Ibid.

7. Goenawan, "City."

8. Ibid.

9. Ibid.

10. Indonesian writer Ajip Rosidi remembers that he was disappointed with Jakarta when he first came to the city. Yet he also found himself losing his sense of comfort in his home village and finally acknowledged that, "I love you Jakarta, because you are the city of my second birth," cited in Abeyasekere, *Jakarta*, 195. The centrality of the city can be clearly observed in the annual spectacle of millions of people leaving Jakarta every Idul Fitri, followed by the equally incredible scenes of their returning to the city.

11. Minister Sarwono Kusumaatmadja in 1996 as cited in Heuken, *Historical Sites of Jakarta*, 17.

12. Seno, "Dari Jakarta," 19.

13. Kusno, *Behind the Postcolonial*.

14. Seno, "Dari Jakarta."

15. Ibid., 19.

16. Ibid.

17. Ibid.

18. Pramoedya, "Letter to a Friend from the Country."

19. Seno, "Dari Jakarta."

20. On assuming power, the governor confronts a formidable political and managerial task. He has to negotiate a multitude of economic interests and political aspirations and is under great pressure to support the desire of the commercial real estate enterprises, the needs of large corporations and small entrepreneurs, including those of vendors, and the influx of people from the countryside searching for employment in the city. Historically, however, governors of Jakarta have never conceived long-term plans to facilitate consistency or followed through on programs started by their predecessors. Instead, Jakarta changes according to the vision of the current governor. According to one politician, "Urban programs in Jakarta can be easily changed following the taste of the governor." See "Jakarta tidak mempunyai rencana strategis" [Jakarta Does Not Have Any Strategic Plan], *Kompas*, 24 June 2002.

21. The legacy of targeting the "underclass" can be traced back at least to governor Ali Sadikin (1966–75) who categorized the "illiterate and unskilled cheap labourers from the countryside, rickshaw drivers, construction workers, vendors, the homeless, beggars, and prostitutes" as potentially threatening public order. They were among the poorest 60 percent of the population of Jakarta who lived in kampung, a term seen as "no longer suitable with the order of the city for it re-

minds people of a backward society." Sadikin, *Gita Jaya*, 160, 168, 112. For histories of, and stories about, the life of the urban poor in Indonesian cities, see, among others, Murray, *No Money, No Honey*; and Jellinek, *The Wheel of Fortune*.

22. Some exceptional cases include the massive protest against the planning of the Beautiful Indonesia in Miniature, known as "Taman Mini," in the early 1970s.

23. Bresnan, "The United States, the IMF, and the Indonesian Financial Crisis," 88. See also Firman, "Indonesian Cities under the 'Krismon'."

24. The Urban Poor Consortium, a nongovernmental organization, indicates that in 2001 the number of people unemployed amounted to four hundred thousand even though the official estimate stood at only one hundred thousand. According to police data, "An average of 21 armed robberies took place every week.... About 12 cars and motor vehicles were stolen weekly and two dead bodies with stabbed wounds were found every week. Most crimes occurred in public places, like on the streets, on public buses, at bus terminals, intersections and shopping malls. ... There have also been regular bomb blasts." See "Capital Continues to Flow out of RI," *Jakarta Post*, 18 September 2002.

25. "Capital Continues to Flow out of RI."

26. A. Matin, "Bintaro Jaya: Kota taman dan kota toko" [Bintaro Jaya: Garden City and the Town of Shops], *Kompas*, 29 March 2000.

27. In this book, the notions of "urban poor" and "underclass" are used interchangeably. For a genealogy of such social categories as the "middle class" and the "underclass," see Siegel, *A New Criminal Type in Jakarta*.

28. "Jakarta mirip kota kaki lima" [Jakarta Resembles City of Vendors], *Kompas*, 12 June 2000.

29. Ibid.

30. Governor Wiyogo indicated in 1989 that one of the reasons why he was not enthusiastic about constructing more pedestrian walkways was that vendors like to make use of sidewalks. For a discussion on pedestrian walkways during the Suharto regime, see the special issue of *Kota* 2 (March–April 1989).

31. "Public Don't Trust Leaders," *Jakarta Post*, 6 August 2002.

32. Ibid.

33. "Assembly Members Make Me Sick," *Jakarta Post*, 3 August 2002.

34. "Belum efektif, penanganan pedagang kaki lima" [Still Ineffective, the Handling of Vendors], *Suara pembaharuan*, 12 August 1999.

35. "Jakarta mirip kota kaki lima."

36. "Belum efektif, penanganan pedagang kaki lima."

37. There are two hundred political parties currently registered with the Ministry of Justice and Human Rights. See "RI Strives to Find Ideal Number of Parties," *Jakarta Post*, 9 September 2002. The city has also witnessed the formation of various human rights organizations, such as the Urban Poor Consortium, Indonesian Institute for Democracy Education, Jakarta Residents Forum, among others. A

group of pedicab drivers has also planned to establish a new political party. See Damar Harsanto, "Pedicab Driver Plans to Establish New Party," *Jakarta Post*, 5 August 2002.

38. "Warga tak perduli pada dekrit" [Citizens Ignore Regulation], *Kompas*, 21 July 2001.

39. Editorial, "Nyanyian moralitas para politikus" [The Morality Songs of the Politicians], *Media Indonesia*, 16 September 2002.

40. As cited in Damar Harsanto, "Jakarta's Poor Urged to Resolve Their Own Problems," *Jakarta Post*, 14 September 2002.

41. Bertrand, "Inhabiting Jakarta."

42. Ibid.

43. See Barker, "State of Fear"; Siegel, *A New Criminal Type in Jakarta*.

44. "Polisi mendukung pengerahan massa" [Police Supports the Mobilization of Masses], *Suara pembaharuan*, 31 August 2002.

45. Cited in "Sutiyoso Blames Public for His Failure," *Jakarta Post*, 19 July 2002, emphasis added.

46. Cited in "Sutiyoso: Most Maligned Governor?" *Jakarta Post*, 11 November 2002.

47. Cited in "Monas akan miliki penanggung jawab" [Monas Will Have a Guarantor], *Kompas*, 21 July 2001.

48. Ibid.

49. "Proyek pemugaran Monas senilai 8,7 milyar rupiah dimulai," [The Project of Fencing Monas Which Costs 8.7 Billion Rupiahs Has Begun], *Kompas*, 25 July 2002.

50. In Jakarta public garbage bins have always been stolen. "Even as they [are] made of concrete planted deep into the ground, the garage bins have still been stolen. But in the future, we will plant them even deeper, so that they will not be removed again," explained a sanitation officer about his strategy. See "550 tempat sampah untuk Monas" [550 garbage bins for Monas], *Warta kota*, 15 August 2002, 4.

51. "Proyek pemugaran Monas senilai 8,7 milyar rupiah dimulai."

52. "Penertiban Monas, pedagang siap melawan" [The Keeping Order of Monas, Traders Ready to Fight], *Kompas*, 31 July 2001.

53. "Tugu Selamat Datang memperindah kota" [The Welcome Monument Beautifies the Capital City], *Star Weekly*, 9 September 1961.

54. "Rampung, proyek penerangan Monumen Selamat Datang" [Ready, the Project of the Lighting of the Welcome Monument], *Kompas*, 2 July 2001.

55. The lighting was done by General Electric (GE) who assured the governor that the lighting will make the monument appear glorious. *Kompas* reported that GE had also installed the lighting for the Statue of Liberty in New York, Chain Bridge in Hungary, and the ancient monument of Candi Prambanan in Central Java. See "Rampung, proyek penerangan Monument Selamat Datang."

56. Ibid.

57. B. Nurbianto, "HI Circle, between History and Reality," *Jakarta Post*, 6 July 2002.

58. "Sutiyoso Has Failed to Perform Well," *Jakarta Post*, 6 July 2002.

59. In the riots, about one hundred buildings in Chinatown that architects considered valuable were burned and completely destroyed in two days.

60. P. Dundu, "Neraka Kota 'Oud Batavia'" [The Hell of Old Batavia], *Kompas*, 30 October 2000.

61. "Kota tua perlu dikembalikan fungsinya" [Old City Needs to Be Revitalized], *Republika*, 21 May 2001.

62. Ibid.

63. Cited in "Cagar budaya menopang wisata" [Heritage Preservation Harnessed Tourism], *Suara karya*, 25 April 2001.

64. "Wajah Batavia tempo doeloe tersimpan rapih di pelabuhan Sunda Kelapa" [The Face of Old Batavia Is Well Kept in the Sunda Kelapa Harbor], *Harian Buana*, 28 January 2001, 12.

65. Yuwono, "Restorasi Stadhuis dan Jakarta Kota."

66. For a recent debate on the proposal to build the Jakarta History Corridor, see "Membangun Koridor Sejarah Jakarta" [Building Jakarta History Corridor], *Kompas*, 4 September 2006; and "Ethos nasionalisme di balik misi Jakarta kota joang" [Nationalism behind the Mission of Jakarta the City of National Struggle], *Kompas*, 19 April 2006.

67. Yuwono, "Restorasi Stadhuis dan Jakarta Kota."

68. The middle class reacted to Jakarta's lack of security in various ways, one of which was the demand for more police protection. "To counter crimes that have been proliferating these days, citizens of Jakarta need police badly. We need the presence of police in sensitive corners, at quiet streets especially at night, in buses, in bazaar, in bus station, and train stations. It looks like there is no longer any security in every *jengkal tanah* [inch] of Jakarta today." "Patroli polisi, soal lama yang dilupakan" [Police Patrol, an Old Forgotten Practice], *Kompas*, 30 July 2002. Yet the demand for police protection has also been contradicted by the middle class's sense of distrust of the police, for, in their eyes, the police are exploitative and profiteering. Victims of theft and robbery have been reluctant to report their losses to the police, to avoid further trouble. "Calling the police would have spelled further trouble. At the very least, I would have had to give them 'cigarette money' before they commenced their 'investigation'." See Damar Harsanto, "Unreliable Police Data Causes Failures in Fighting Crime," *Jakarta Post*, 29 July 2002.

69. For a study of the mentalitet of the middle class in the 1990s, see van Leeuwen, "Lost in Mall."

70. Brochure of Lippo Karawaci, 2002.

71. Brochure of Kota Wisata, 2002.

72. "Duta Pertiwi mulai unjuk prestasi" [Duta Pertiwi Has Begun to Show Achievements], *Properti Indonesia*, August 2002.

73. Triyanto et al., "Pertarungan seru pusat belanja di CBD," 11.

74. Ibid.

75. Ibid., 12.

76. "Malls offer everything for everyone."

77. Triyanto et al., "Pertarungan seru pusat belanja di CBD," 14.

78. "Malls Offer Everything for Everyone," *Jakarta Post*, 14 July 2002, 20.

79. Hantoro et al., "Tambal sulam simbol kota," 72.

Chapter 2: The Regime, the Busway

1. Damar Harsanto, "The Revolution Has Begun on Jakarta's Streets," *Jakarta Post*, 27 December 2004.

2. Ibid.

3. "Bang Yos menjawab lugas" [Sutiyoso Responded Lucidly], *Tokoh Indonesia*, 16 May–19 June 2005, www.tokohindonesia.com.

4. Tweki Triardianto, "Jajak pendapat berkait HUT ke 476 Jakarta" [City Poll during the 476th Birthday of Jakarta: Attractive Even Though Chaotic], *Kompas*, 24 June 2003.

5. Darmaningtyas, "Pungli: Sumber masalah transportasi Jakarta" [Unauthorized Charge: Main Problem in Jakarta's Transportation], *Kompas*, 14 June 2003.

6. Is Surotho, "Angkutan umum: Nyaman hanya impian" [A Comfortable Public Transportation Is Only a Dream], *Suara pembaharuan*, 9 April 2002. See also Susanti, "Disjointed Jakarta."

7. Triardianto, "Jajak pendapat berkait HUT ke 476 Jakarta."

8. "Jakarta mirip kota kaki lima" [Jakarta Resembles City of Vendors], *Kompas*, 12 June 2000.

9. "Jalan tol macet, tanggung jawasiapa" [Toll Road Is Jammed, Who Is Responsible], *Suara karya*, 29 May 2001.

10. Kusno, *Behind the Postcolonial*, chap. 4.

11. Sidel, "'Macet Total'."

12. Ibid., 160.

13. Ibid.

14. For various meanings of *macet*, see Podo and Sullivan, *Kamus ungkapan Indonesia-Inggris*.

15. Pemberton, *On the Subject of "Java,"* 6.

16. Guattari, "Regimes, Pathways, Subjects," 18.

17. In this context, shock therapy is related to neoliberalism. For a discussion of neoliberalism, see Harvey, *A Brief History of Neoliberalism*.

18. Sukarno as cited in Abeyasekere, *Jakarta*, 210.

19. Suharto, *My Thoughts, Words and Deeds*.

20. Yudhoyono, "We Need Shock Therapy."

21. "President Tells Cabinet to Use Shock Therapy," *Jakarta Post*, 23 October 2004.

22. Ibid.

23. For a typological approach to the neoliberal state, see Harvey, *A Brief History of Neoliberalism*, 64–86. See also Ong, *Neoliberalism as Exception*.

24. As entered in a web messaging page by a resident of Jakarta on 19 December 2005, sedikitpitra.blogsome.com.

25. "Subway ke busway-buswayan" [From Subway to the Game of Busway], *Kompas*, 24 Feb 2003.

26. For the image of Sutiyoso at the end of his first term, see "Sutiyoso: Most Maligned Governor?," *Jakarta Post*, 11 November 2002.

27. For a discussion of the exemplary center, see Geertz, *Negara*.

28. "Despite a Few Bumps, New Busway Corridor a Hit with Jakartans," *Jakarta Post*, 17 January 2006.

29. "'Busway' Bukan untuk selesaikan kemacetan" [Busway Is Not Meant to Resolve Traffic Jam], *Kompas*, 9 May 2003.

30. "Sutiyoso Officially Opened the HCB," *Berita Jakarta*, 7 September 2006, www.beritajakarta.com.

31. "Bus TransJakarta mulai beroperasi hari ini" [TransJakarta Bus Starts Operating Today], *Republika*, 27 March 2003.

32. "Controversial Busway Project to Have 'Bus Marshals,'" *Jakarta Post*, 16 June 2003.

33. "New Busway Services Blamed for Traffic Woes," *Jakarta Post*, 23 January 2006.

34. Irzal Djamal, the head of the TransJakarta, cited in Damar Harsanto, "Orange Team to Replace Rude Busway Guards," *Jakarta Post*, 26 May 2005.

35. "City Holds Busway Writing, Photo Contest," *Jakarta Post*, 27 May 2005.

36. "Busway Offers School Visits," *Jakarta Post*, 23 July 2005.

37. Seno Joko Suyono and Evieta Fajar, "Ikhtiar seni di halte busway" [Arts in Busway's Shelter], *Tempo*, 12 February 2006, 72–73.

38. Susantono, "Busway," 50.

39. Tantri Yuliandini, "The Joys of Riding the Busway," *Jakarta Post*, 16 January 2006.

40. Rustam Effendi Sidabutar, head of the Transportation Department, as cited in Jenny Aipassa, "Singkirkan bus, amankan busway" [Getting Rid of the Bus, Making Way for the Busway], *Suara pembaruan*, 19 September 2005.

41. Ibid.

42. "East Jakarta Municipality to Move Vendors for Busway Construction," *Jakarta Post*, 29 August 2006, emphasis added. Hundreds of trees have been sacrificed to make way for the new transportation system. One tree resisted being removed. Several efforts were made to remove it, and workers concluded that the tree was possessed by a powerful spirit and does not want to bend to the new traffic authority. For a report on the fate of the trees, see Damar Harsanto, "Busway Project End of Line for Many Trees," *Jakarta Post*, 25 October 2005.

43. "Busway Work, Vendors Cause Traffic Jam," *Jakarta Post*, 20 September 2006.

44. Sibarani Sofyan, as cited in "Power of Example: If It's Built People Will Follow," *Jakarta Post*, 16 September 2006.

45. "New Busway Corridors to Operate This Year," *Jakarta Post*, 19 May 2006.

46. Sutiyoso feels that it would be beneficial for Jakarta to have a leader who is rather crazy. See "Sutiyoso: Pemimpin harus rada gendeng" [Leader Needs to Be a Bit Crazy], *Tempo*, 15 January 2006, 36.

47. "Bang Yos menjawab lugas."

48. "Sutiyoso: Pemimpin harus rada gendeng," 36.

49. In the last two years, as the governor was stepping down, images of him in a business suit have appeared on the cover of glossy magazines. The notion of "A Spectacular Decade of Jakarta Property" is from *Property Indonesia*, the July 2007 issue.

Chapter 3: "Back to the City"

1. "Arsitektur kedaerahan atasi kesenjangan" [Regional Architecture Overcomes Social Gaps], *Bisnis Indonesia*, 28 July 1999, 1.

2. "Rumah idaman," 7.

3. Ibid.

4. Ibid., 8–9.

5. Sukada, "Indonesian Architects Award," 14.

6. Ibid.

7. "Arsitektur korban ekonomi salah arah," 3. It is not surprising that the 1999 competition gives no award to residential architecture. Perhaps, after the 1998 riots, none is close to the ideal expectation of IAI.

8. Sukada, "Indonesian Architects Award," 14.

9. "Arsitektur korban ekonomi salah arah" [Architecture Victim of Economy Gone Astray], *Bisnis Indonesia*, 12 November 1999, 3.

10. Purnomo has put together his works in *Relativitas*. For an architectural appreciation of Purnomo's work, see Susanti, "Against Jakarta."

11. "Adi Purnomo: Settling Debts with Nature," 52.

12. Purnomo, *Relativitas*, 98–101.

13. "Major brand" architecture is architecture that sells the image of market-generated cosmopolitanism for the new, rich, urban middle class.

14. Purnomo, *Relativitas*, 99.

15. For Mamo's discussion on Tanjung Duren House, see Purnomo, *Relativitas*, 52–58. See also Tardiyana and Antar, *The Long Road Towards Recognition*, 58–59, 72–77.

16. The attention to local vocabulary is quite different from the postmodern architectural paradigm that was once adopted by architects during the New Order to justify their use of historical "local" elements as a decorative style in their search for

national identity. Yet the concern for the urban house marks a turn to the fascination with interior life, in other words, it reflects their belief that the urban fabric cannot be engaged with other than by domesticating it in the private sphere. The city fabric is engaged less as a coherent entity than as fragments to be picked up for the restoration of the whole in the interior. We could say that the intellectual and artistic position of Mamo (and other fellow architects such as Eko Prawoto) is a development out of the earlier tradition of the Yogya school, in its attention to what was in the era of independence, a concern with local cultural identity — an attention that could also be traced back to the earlier struggles of the Dutch architect, Henri Maclaine Pont.

17. Purnomo, *Relativitas*, 72.
18. For a discussion on the concept of magersari, see ibid., 66–70.
19. Mamo's architecture attempts to develop a new architecture (an approach no doubt related to the legacy of Yogyakarta's approach to architecture associated with Romo Mangunwijaya and his follower Eko Prawoto, a contemporary of Mamo) by way of developing a language of the kampung.
20. Sutiyoso as cited in Mustaqim Adamrah, "Squatters Face Eviction in the Wake of Fire," *Jakarta Post*, 13 August 2007. The latest fire that gutted a shanty town built under an elevated highway in North Jakarta and a tollgate heading to Soekarno-Hatta International airport has prompted the city government to evict all the shelters built in or next to public facilities.
21. Putra, "Menjawab tantangan dengan megaproyek," 26–27.
22. For a discussion of the functioning of the neoliberal state, see Harvey, *A Brief History of Neoliberalism*.
23. "From the Editor," 5.
24. Marudi Suharman, executive director of PT Bakrieland Development, as cited in Prasetyo, "Superblock terbesar di Jakarta," [The Largest Superblock in Jakarta], *Bisnis Properti* 35, 2006, 52.
25. Burhanuddin Abe, "Between Investment and Lifestyle," *Jakarta Post*, supplement edition, "High-Rise Living," 20 February 2007.
26. See Marshall, *Emerging Urbanity*; Olds, *Globalization and Urban Change*; Bunnell, Drummond, and Ho, *Critical Reflections on Cities in Southeast Asia*.
27. As stated by a United States–based design firm working for a project in Jakarta. See "Regatta: Sebuah ikon bagi Indonesia" [Regatta: The Icon of the Future of Indonesia], *Kompas*, 27 July 2006, 65.
28. This phenomenon is by no means confined to Jakarta for one can also see the growth of the superblock in several major cities in Indonesia, such as Bandung, Surabaya, and Medan.
29. "Ridwan Kamil: Champion of Good Design," *Jakarta Post*, 20 July 2006.
30. Ibid.
31. "Sutiyoso Gives up Fight over Senayan," *Jakarta Post*, 19 November 2005.

32. Indra Setiawan, as cited in Ferdinand Lamak, "Dari gelanggang olahraga hingga pusat belanja modern" [From a Sports Arena to a Modern Shopping Center], *Bisnis Properti* 35, July 2006, 16.

33. Ibid.

34. Ibid.

35. See Panangian Simanungkalit, "Lagi, APGbikin terobosan," [Again, APG Made a Breakthrough], *Bisnis Properti* 35, July 2006, 7.

36. See "Senayan City: Your City Starts Here," *Indonesia Design* 3, no. 12 (2006), 47.

37. The concept of the exemplary center is as follows: "The court-and-capital is at once a microcosm of the supernatural order—an image of . . . the universe on a smaller scale—and the material embodiment of political order." Geertz, *Negara*, 13. We may refashion Geertz's concept by assuming that the political order is now to be restored by a consumerist-based societal order exemplified by the superblock.

38. "Senayan City, a New Place to Be Seen," *Jakarta Post*, 8 October 2006.

39. "Senayan City: Your City Starts Here," 49.

40. Ibid., 49.

41. "Senayan City, a New Place to Be Seen."

42. Sibarani Sofian, as cited in "Power of Example: If It's Built People Will Follow," *Jakarta Post*, 16 September 2006. Emphasis added.

43. Urbane Indonesia, "Kontemplasi arsitektur Kepulauan dan Kelautan," 73.

44. Ibid., 69.

45. Ibid., 73.

46. See "Young Architect to Represent RI," *Jakarta Post*, 20 July 2006.

47. Ibid.

48. Chris Yoshii, as cited in "Power of Example."

49. Ibid.

50. If Senayan City and the Grand Indonesia occupy the north and the west corners of the Golden Triangle, the Rasuna Epicentrum at Kuningan takes up the third corner. Owned by PT Bakrieland Development, the Rasuna Epicentrum will become the largest superblock in Jakarta. It plans to occupy 44.7 hectares of land by incorporating the existing buildings into the new complex. As a whole, the superblock will have Taman Rasuna apartment, Pasar Festival, Aston Rasuna Residence, Rasuna Office Park, Klub Rasuna, and the new twelve-hectare Rasuna Epicentrum complex, which will consist of Media Walk and Life Style Center, the corporate tower of the Bakrie group, condominiums, and a TV studio.

51. "Ridwan Kamil." Kamil is fully aware of the global production of architecture and has written an extensive article on how Indonesian design could tap into the network. See Kamil, "Arus kapitalisme global dan masa depan arsitektur Indonesia." For a discussion of the globalization of design production, see Tombesi, "A True South for Design?"

52. For a discussion of "Global Intelligence Corps," see Olds, *Globalization and Urban Change*.

53. "Grand Indonesia, Jakarta," 31.

54. Ibid., 33.

55. Ibid., 32.

56. Quotes from the brochure for the marketing of the Kempinski Residence, Grand Indonesia.

57. I am indebted to Michael Leaf for coming up with the terms "state modernism" and "market modernism" as two useful analytical categories for an understanding of past and present urban transformation.

Chapter 4: Glodok on Our Minds

1. One estimate suggests that more than two thousand people were killed during the riots. The victims of rape are calculated to be somewhere between 168 and 468 people (of whom 20 to 60 died). See Colombijn, "What Is So Indonesian about Violence?," 34. For a report, list of documents, and discussion of the riots in Indonesia, see Pattiradjawane, "Peristiwa Mei 1998 di Jakarta: Titik terendah sejarah orang etnis Cina di Indonesia."

2. For a discussion of the causes of the May riots and the pattern of anti-Chinese riots in Indonesia in the late Suharto period, see Sidel, "'Macet Total'." For a discussion on Indonesians' (including ethnic Chinese's) perception of the May riots, see Siegel, "Thoughts on the Violence of May 13 and 14, 1998, in Jakarta," and Siegel, "Early Thoughts on the Violence of May 13 and 14, 1998 in Jakarta."

3. For a discussion on anti-Chinese activities in the formation of Indonesian nationalism in the early twentieth century, see Shiraishi, "Anti-Sinicism in Java's New Order." For a report on the killing of Chinese at the outbreak of the Indonesian revolution in Malang, see Kwee Thiam Tjing, *Indonesia dalem api dan bara*. On the massacre of Chinese during the beginning of Dutch colonial rule, see Blusse, "Batavia, 1619–1740."

4. Siegel suggests that anti-Chinese riots in Indonesia have taken the form of looting goods, burning houses and property, and killing on the spot those identified as Chinese, as if the word *Chinese* itself legitimizes the practices of theft and violence. As Benedict Anderson has stated in relation to Siegel's work on the peculiarity of the ethnic Chinese position: "Few Indonesians dream of wiping them out or of expelling them wholesale from the country." On the contrary, believing that "Chinese have unlimited access to goods . . . looters who ransacked small Chinese neighborhood stores allowed themselves to feel surprised and even annoyed when they discovered that the stores had not reopened for business the following week." Anderson, "Introduction," in *Violence and the State in Suharto's Indonesia*, 15.

5. Gang rape, as a technique of subjugation, was first exercised in parts of Aceh and

East Timor by elements of the Indonesian military under Suharto's regime. The rape of Sino-Indonesian women has been attributed—though without proof—to these elements of Suharto's security apparatus. It appears, however, that nonmilitary Indonesians of the lower classes also participated in the rapes. For a discussion of Indonesians' perceptions of the May gang rapes, including the reception and denial of these aspects of the riots, see Siegel, "Thoughts on the Violence of May 13 and 14, 1998, in Jakarta"; and Siegel, "Early Thoughts on the Violence of May 13 and 14, 1998 in Jakarta." See also Strassler, "Gendered Visibilities and the Dream of Transparency" and Heryanto, "Rape, Race and Reporting."

6. Siegel, "Thoughts on the Violence of May 13 and 14, 1998, in Jakarta," 111.

7. Ibid, 109.

8. Groups of Indonesians of ethnic Chinese descent have demanded that the government acknowledge the gang rape of ethnic Chinese girls and women during the May riots. For a report of the protest in front of the Presidential Palace during the rule of Abdurrahman Wahid, see "Keturunan Tionghoa berdemo di Istana Negara" [Indonesians Chinese Demonstrate at the Presidential Palace], *Indonesia Media*, June 2000, 10, 54. I would like to mention that there have been dishonesties on the Internet concerning the fact of gang rapes and in the circulation of the voices of the victims of the gang rapes. The most troubling one has been the circulation of gruesome pictures of mutilated bodies of women. These pictures were taken from the violence in East Timor. They were, however, used by the mobs and the Chinese community, mostly overseas, to represent the gang rapes during the May riots and to gain the attention of the public. For a discussion and a list of references on the denial that gang rapes occurred during the riots, see Pattiradjawane, "Peristiwa Mei 1998 di Jakarta," 239–47.

9. "Habibie temui pedagang" [Habibie Met Traders], *Kompas*, 27 May 1998.

10. "Trauma mematikan dan membangkitkan" [Trauma That Destroys and Constructs], *Sinar Glodok*, 12 May 2001. The victims of the May riots, especially of the gang rapes, often do not want to speak about the event.

11. See, among others, Gillis, ed. *Commemorations*; Wu, "Tiananmen Square"; Young, *At Memory's Edge*.

12. According to Walter Benjamin: "Architecture has always represented the prototype of a work of art the reception of which is consummated by a collectivity in a state of distraction." See Benjamin, "The Work of Art in the Age of Mechanical Reproduction," 239.

13. "Habibie temui pedagang."

14. The importance of this image of Glodok is reemphasized by the economic team of former President Abdurrahman Wahid (2000–2001). "The [economic] impact [of riots] is very big. The world will blow up the news if there is an incident [of rioting] in Glodok. Investors in Singapore are afraid to come, not to mention investors from other parts of the world." See "Investorpun takut" [Investors Are Afraid], *Warta kota*, 16 May 2000.

15. "Habibie temui pedagang."

16. Ibid.

17. See Siegel, "Early Thoughts on the Violence of May 13 and 14, 1998 in Jakarta," 96 n. 13.

18. Wang Gungwu, a historian of ethnic Chinese in Southeast Asia, has pointed out that the ethnic Chinese with whom he has spoken have been unable to express the specificity of the violence during the May riots. Memories of the gang rapes have dwelled silently and uncomfortably alongside the memories of arson, looting, and other anti-Chinese actions in Indonesia. Communication with Wang Gungwu in Singapore, 10 July 2002.

19. Berfield and Loveard, "Ten Days That Shook Indonesia," 38.

20. "Warga Tionghoa peringati tragedi Mei: Kami tak mau jadi korban lagi" [Indonesian Chinese Commemorated the May Tragedy: We Don't Want to Be Victimized Again], *Jawa Post*, 14 May 1999.

21. A building construction journal opened its report on the rebuilding of Glodok Plaza in this way: "The May riots still leaves traces in our memories. The residues of the riots can still be found today, for many building owners are still waiting for a safer environment. However, lately, there has been much rebuilding of public buildings that were destroyed during the riots. One of these is the shopping mall of Glodok Plaza." "Renovasi Glodok Plaza menerapkan konsep 'IT Mall'."

22. "Glodok Plaza si legendaris" [The Legendary Glodok Plaza], *Kompas*, 3 November 2000.

23. "Image baru Glodok Plaza" [The New Image of Glodok Plaza], *Mega Konstruksi*, www.megatika.com.

24. Ibid.

25. "Renovasi Glodok Plaza menerapkan konsep 'IT Mall'."

26. "Image baru Glodok Plaza."

27. "Glodok Plaza to Reopen in July 2001," *Jakarta Post*, 6 October 2000.

28. Surya Semesta Internusa, "Surya Semesta Internusa Will Boost Efficiency by Internal Merger," press release, 7 November 2000.

29. "Glodok Plaza si legendaris."

30. According to one report, the decision to completely clean the site of the remnants of the riots was based on a Chinese belief that fire connotes a bad omen. See "Dianggap tidak 'hoki,' Pasar Glodok diratakan" [Considered Unlucky, Pasar Glodok Is Razed], *Kompas*, 3 July 1999.

31. In the map of the municipality, Glodok is part of old Batavia. The municipality of Jakarta has for some time intended to turn the old part of Jakarta into a heritage town for nostalgic tourism. If the project is successful, tourists will be able to "explore the old city . . . with the taste of old time. Keroncong music [popular Hawaiian-like songs of the colonial time, quite often performed by a troop of musicians from various ethnic backgrounds, for example, indigenous, Eurasian, Chinese] will accompany the tourists who walk and enjoy old buildings, which might

be turned into theaters, hotels, plazas, cafes, museums, and souvenir shops." See Muzhar Muchtar, "Bangunan kuno, Jakarta dan pariwisata" [Old Buildings, Jakarta and Tourism], *Suara pembaruan*, 26 August 1998.

32. "Pancoran akan menjadi kawasan pejalan kaki" [Pancoran Will Become an Area for Pedestrians], *Kompas*, 2 September 1996.

33. Ibid.

34. "Habibie temui Pedagang."

35. "Doa, tabur bunga, dan orasi warnai peringatan tragedi Mei" [Prayers, Flowers, and Speech Colored the Commemoration of the May Tragedy], *Media Indonesia*, 14 May 2001.

36. As Michel de Certeau remarks: "Any autonomous order is founded upon what it eliminates: it produces a 'residue' condemned to be forgotten. But what was excluded re-infiltrates the place of its origin—now the present's 'clean' place." De Certeau, *Heterologies*, 4.

37. For a history of the Chinese mayors in colonial Indonesia, see Lohanda, *The Kapitan Cina in Batavia 1837–1942*.

38. See Ida Indawati Khouw, "Candra Naya Escapes Wrecker's Ball," *Jakarta Post*, 29 January 2000. Several seminars involving not only academicians but also government representatives, businesspeople, and the developers of the site have been staged to discuss Candra Naya. I had the chance to participate in a closed meeting with the owners of the Modern Land (a big business group, the owners of which include Chinese Indonesian businessmen), architectural preservation experts, and the feng shui master, who also is a spirit medium, on 19 July 2001.

39. The spirit medium conversed with Khouw Kui Lan, the spirit of the daughter of the last Chinese major in Batavia. Lady Khouw does not want to give way to the skyscrapers. She says that if her house is to be moved, it should be relocated to the site of the previous Chinese embassy in Indonesia (on land that was owned by her father) or the house should "move upward" along its vertical axis. This latter alternative suggests a means for Lady Khouw to take on the skyscrapers. If the owners do not follow her wish, disasters beyond imagination will occur and she will also ask Nyi Loro Kidul (the legendary queen of the South Seas) to deal with the problem. This story worries the owners even though they are Christians. On 11 September 2001, the youngest son of the owners of the skyscrapers was killed in one of the planes that crashed into the World Trade Center in New York City. Stories have been circulated among those who believed in the story of Lady Khouw that the death of the son is connected to the owners' disrespect of Candra Naya. The most recent news concerning the fate of Candra Naya is that it will stay.

40. For the activity of Sin Ming Hui, see Oei Tjoe Tat, *Memoar Oei Tjoe Tat*, chap. 5.

41. Note that there are differences in social class among the ethnic Chinese in Indonesia. The owners of the skyscrapers represent big Chinese Indonesian investors,

and they do not have to be physically on the site where their business is located. These ungrounded business deals are very different from the locally bound Chinese at Glodok who often speaking neither Chinese nor English must deal with customers, former rioters among them, on a daily basis. For a discussion of Chinese diaspora and transnationalism, see Aihwa Ong, "On the Edge of Empires."

42. Andreas Huyssen would perhaps identify this phenomenon as a "geographical spread of the culture of memory" against amnesia and "the loss of historical consciousness" of "lived memories," the expression of which "remains tied to the histories of specific nations and states." See Huyssen, "Present Pasts," 26–27.

43. Ibid., 26.

44. "Imlek di klenteng meriah, pertokoan sepi" [Chinese New Year in the Temple Is Festive, Shops Are Empty], *Warta kota*, 25 January 2001.

45. Barongsai is usually performed in the temple and on the streets during the Chinese New Year, religious rites, or public celebrations. Accompanied by beating drums, it attracted crowds (of Chinese and non-Chinese backgrounds). This carnival-like performance was banned by President Suharto, and this ban signified the erasure of the display of Chinese culture in public. Its return is significant; it has become a symbol of the change of political order. Barongsai can be seen in many places today, especially shopping malls and tourist areas. For a report on the mushrooming of traditional Chinese arts and culture after 1998, see Kleden and Sutarwiyo, "The Lionheart Beats Again."

46. For a reaction from the state as well as from communities in the capital city on the Chinese New Year in Glodok, see "Perayaan Imlek dijaga ketat 30,000 anggota satgas" [Chinese New Year Celebration Is Safeguarded by 30,000 Armed Forces], *Kompas*, 24 January 2001.

47. For a documentation and discussion of the process of banning signs of Chinese culture in Indonesia, see Coppel, *The Indonesian Chinese in Crisis*.

48. For a discussion of the proliferation of Chinese-language newspapers post-1998 in the major urban centers of Indonesia, see Agus Sudibyo, "Pers Tionghoa, sensibilitas budaya, dan politik" [Chinese Press, Cultural Sensitivity, and Politics], *Kompas*, 1 June 2001.

49. Kota Wisata belongs to the business group of Duta Pertiwi, which joins venture groups with business groups from Japan, Korea, and Thailand. Starting in 1996, it sought to promote housing for upper middle-income consumers. Located on the outskirts of Jakarta, it aims to feature architectural styles of various countries. See the website of Kota Wisata at www.kota-wisata.com. Kota Wisata began to promote Chinese architecture in 2001, a decision many believe would have been impossible during the reign of Suharto.

A shophouse contains a ground-floor shop that opens onto a public arcade and an upstairs residential space. It is considered a vernacular architectural building type that is associated with ethnic Chinese in Southeast Asia.

50. According to one Indonesian Chinese: "People have begun to try to revive Chinese

culture, although they still worry about the uncertain political circumstances." See "Imlek: Mengulang tradisi masa lalu" [Chinese New Year: Replaying the Old Tradition], *Kompas*, 24 January 2001.

51. The present memory of Chinese cultures is therefore "another form of forgetting, and forgetting a form of hidden memory." Huyssen, "Present Pasts," 27.

52. Ibid., 26.

53. Seno Gumira Ajidarma, "Jakarta, 14 Februari 2039," *Matra* (December 1999). The essay is reprinted with illustrations by Asnar Zacky and retitled *Jakarta 2039*. Citations in the following discussion are from the illustrated version. Seno's story is about the May riots, but it does not include the non-Chinese Indonesian middle class. That the essay was published in *Matra* requires comment. The main readers of *Matra* are middle-class Indonesians who were spared the extreme effects of the riots. Thus, in spite of the sacrifice of middle-class university students in the riots, this social group is likely the least critical of the May 1998 anti-Chinese riots. Perhaps this is the way Seno encourages the middle class to critically reflect on the violence. For an insightful commentary on the "mentality" of the non-Chinese Indonesian middle class during the May riots, see Siegel, "Early Thoughts on the Violence of May 13 and 14, 1998 in Jakarta."

54. See the back cover of *Jakarta 2039*. For a discussion of the denial of the occurrence of gang rapes, see Siegel, "Early Thoughts on the Violence of May 13 and 14, 1998 in Jakarta." Seno's story, in this sense, could be seen as producing a discourse about rapes, as Siegel puts it, "an actual event put into a framework suitable for the (news)papers and for the elaboration of stories." Siegel, "Early Thoughts on the Violence of May 13 and 14, 1998 in Jakarta," n. 31.

55. For a discussion of the concept of simultaneity in the novel and its political effect for the formation of new consciousness, see Benedict Anderson, *Imagined Communities*, chap. 2.

56. Seno, *Jakarta 2039*, back cover.

57. Ibid., 30–37 (emphasis added).

58. Ibid., 48–49.

59. Michael Roth and Charles Salas write: "The modern concept of trauma emphasizes the demand for representation and the refusal to be represented." See Roth and Salas, "Introduction," 2.

60. Seno, *Jakarta 2039*, 57.

61. Ibid., 72.

62. Ibid., 69.

63. Ibid., 70.

64. Ibid., 72.

65. In the last scene of Ajidarma's story, the policeman, after making his own decision to spare the lives of the two rapists, explained to his partner: "I am actually a son of a rapist. I accidentally *overheard* a conversation between my caretaker at the orphanage and a reporter. My caretaker said to the reporter that what he was

about to hear should be *off the record*. But I recorded it in my mind. My mother was raped by my father at the night of looting and burning on 14 May 1998. I was born nine months later on 14 February 1999. I am forty years old now. I don't know who my mother and my father are. I live with anger to rapists. In my mind, I have already killed my father. I don't know which one is more evil and wrong, to kill a rapist or to kill my own father." Ibid., 77–78 (emphasis added).

Chapter 5: The Afterlife of the Empire Style

1. "The Past in the Present" is the title of a workshop organized by Peter Nas in 2005 that reflects the emerging interest in the Netherlands in tracing the influences of Dutch architecture in the (post)colony of Indonesia. Papers presented in the workshop have been published in Nas, *The Past in the Present*. An exhibition was also held in 2007 in the Rotterdam's Museum of Modern Architecture.

2. There are an increasing number of comprehensive studies on Dutch colonial architecture in Indonesia. I adopt loosely the stylistic terms from them. Among others: Akihary, *Architectuur en Stedebouw in Indonesie 1870–1940*; Handinoto, *Perkembangan kota dan arsitektur kolonial Belanda di Surabaya, 1870–1940*; Handinoto and Soehargo, *Perkembangan arsitektur kolonial Belanda di Malang*; Sudradjat, "A Study of Indonesian Architectural History"; Sumalyo, *Arsitektur kolonial Belanda di Indonesia*; Wiryomartono, *Seni bangunan dan seni binakota di Indonesia*.

3. For a recent discussion on the postcoloniality of contemporary global architectural culture, see King, *Spaces of Global Cultures*.

4. I have made a more complicated argument on Sukarno's city building in *Behind the Postcolonial*, 49–70. For a recent assessment of Sukarno's Jakarta, see Fakih, *Membayangkan ibu kota*.

5. For an analysis of the concept of "development," see Heryanto, "The Development of 'Development'."

6. Ali Moertopo as cited in Bourchier and Hadiz, *Indonesian Politics and Society*, 106–7.

7. For a discussion on "global modernity" and its relation to "colonial modernity," see Dirlik, *Global Modernity*.

8. See Cowherd, "Cultural Construction of Jakarta."

9. Accessed online 15 June 2005 at www.semarang.go.id (no longer available).

10. Prijotomo, "The Indonesian Elements in the Architecture of 1900–1930s."

11. Historian M. C. Ricklefs calls the early twentieth century "a new colonial age." The new age is characterized by the initiation of the Ethical Policy, which was concerned with a humanitarian approach to colonialism. While remaining exploitative, "the exploitation of Indonesia began to recede as the main justification for Dutch rule, and was replaced by professions of concern for the welfare of Indonesians." See Ricklefs, *A History of Modern Indonesia since c. 1300*, 152.

12. For a discussion on the tension between civil servants and engineers, see van Doorn, *The Engineers and the Colonial System*.

13. For a general description of "classical-modern" style architecture, see Robert Adhi Ksp "Rumah bergaya klasik modern dengan warna perancis" [Houses in French Classical Modern Style], *Kompas*, 23 May 2003. See also the promotional webpages of Ciputra, www.ciputra.com and the website for CitraLand, www .citraland-manado.com.

14. As cited in "Membongkar pilar Yunani," 18. See also "Joglo=Jogya—Solo."

15. Suharto, as cited in Bourchier and Hadiz, *Indonesian Politics and Society*, 106–7.

16. Professor Eko Budihardjo has put together papers presented in the workshops in a series of books published by Penerbit Alumni in Bandung. Most of them have been reprinted more than twice. Among others: Budihardjo, *Menuju arsitektur Indonesia* (1983); *Jati diri arsitektur Indonesia* (1989); *Arsitek bicara tentang arsitektur Indonesia* (1987).

17. The design of the University of Indonesia was drafted by prominent Indonesian architects and academics led by Gunawan Tjahjono.

18. For a comprehensive treatment of the architectural work of Henry Maclaine Pont, see van Leerdam, *Architect Henri Maclaine Pont*.

19. See Langmead, *Dutch Modernism*, 17.

20. Liem, *Riwajat Semarang, 1416–1931*, 226.

21. The Preanger Hotel was refashioned by Wolff Schoemaker in 1930, and the new Javasche Bank Semarang Branch was designed by the Batavia-based architecture bureau of Fermont-Cuypers in 1935. For a report of the opening of the Javasche Bank in Semarang, see "Pemboeka'an gedong baroe dari Javasche Bank Semarang" [The Opening of the New Building of the Java Bank in Semarang], *Mata-Hari*, 14 December 1935. A picture of the building is included in the report.

22. See Dikken, *Liem Bwan Tjie (1991–1966)*.

23. Jameson, *Signatures of the Visible*, 225.

24. Mrázek, *Engineers of Happy Land*.

25. However, we could also ask another question about Lim's work that has to do with its relationship to the sociopolitical milieu of ethnic Chinese in Indonesia — which is generally ideologized in terms of its difference from "tradition" (insofar as this is identified with Indonesia) and modernity (insofar as this is associated with the West). The shophouses on the main street are largely owned by ethnic Chinese. It is tempting to suggest that the "modernization" of the facade of shophouses over time, from its Chinese-look in the 1920s into a more abstract "art deco" form in the 1930s, and later in the "aluminum facade" of the large-scale billboards in the 1980s could be seen as the Chinese Indonesian response to the erasure of their public identity. I am not suggesting that there are some putatively unique Chinese cultural elements in the architecture of Budi Lim, but, in a way, his modernist grammar of art deco transcends ethnic identity and identification into a discourse that has become symptomatic of the architecture of ethnic Chinese in Indonesia. I would argue (even though this needs a further study) that many Chinese Indonesians, following the suppression of their identities in the

public domain under Suharto's rule, found themselves "hiding" behind the trans-ethnic Empire style, art deco, and "Indonesian architecture."

26. This is certainly not because of the powers of evocation inherent in forms and styles themselves. The power lies in the investment of meanings by cohorts of architects, the advertising industry, and academics (including the author of this chapter) whose ideological assumptions sustain and project the influence of particular styles. All three major stylistic conventions that I have discussed in this chapter are the product of such constructions.

27. For a discussion of the irony of colonial legacies, see Chakrabarty, *Provincializing Europe.*

Chapter 6: Colonial Cities in Motion

1. Marco Kartodikromo, *Three Early Indonesian Short Stories,* 19. For the life history of Marco Kartodikromo, see Shiraishi, *An Age in Motion,* 81–91. For Marco's literary world, see also Tickell, "Introduction."

2. In the 1960s, Lynch, in his book, *The Image of the City,* sought to understand how people perceive their environments, a knowledge that he hoped could be used by professionals for designing cities. While I share with Lynch his belief that it is important to understand how people perceive cities, I find his assumptions problematic. Lynch believed that everyone "naturally" assumes a similar way of perceiving environmental form. He disregarded the question of whether social relations structure the experience of physical space. In this chapter I emphasize not only the importance of power relations in giving meaning to urban form but also the political effects of visually perceptible symbols. For other explorations on similar issues, see Dovey, *Framing Places;* Nas, *Urban Symbolism.*

3. Jameson, "Cognitive Mapping."

4. Textual materials might help us interpret the responses of people who experienced or altered buildings or spaces they used and created. They might capture the significance of particular buildings, but textual evidence cannot fully represent the meanings that people put into the building. Even if there is written documentation on someone's experience of a particular space, we can never be clear how much of the account can be transposed to represent the power of a particular place. Besides, human experience cannot always be verbally or textually stated, and what we want to know about someone's experience, quite often, remains unstated.

5. Shiraishi, *An Age in Motion;* Mrázek, *Engineers of Happy Land;* Siegel, *Fetish, Recognition, Revolution.*

6. Shiraishi, *An Age in Motion,* xi.

7. Doelriadi, "Zaman baharoe," *Persatoean Hindia,* 3 April 1920, 1.

8. As cited in Surjomihardjo, *Kota Yogyakarta,* 132.

9. Marco Kartodikromo, "The Corrupted Life of a Big City," 13.

10. Ibid., 13.

11. As cited in Mrázek, *Engineers of Happy Land*, 143.

12. Ibid.

13. Bhabha, "Of Mimicry and Man."

14. Shiraishi, *An Age in Motion*, 65.

15. For a discussion of the political implications of comparison, see Anderson, *The Spectre of Comparisons*; Culler and Cheah, *Grounds of Comparison*.

16. Anderson, *Language and Power*, 45.

17. Geertz, "Centers, Kings and Charisma," 130–31.

18. Kuntowijoyo, "The Making of a Modern Urban Ecology," 163.

19. Mulyadi and Soedarmono, *Runtuhnya kekuasaan 'kraton alit,'* 321.

20. Ibid.

21. Kuntowijoyo studies the case of Laweyan. Geographically, Laweyan and Kraton were only a few miles away from each other, however, they were two different worlds. The prime reason for the distance was more social than physical. At the beginning Laweyan was the center of Javanese "traders" and trade, which, in the eyes of the sultanate, was a realm of the world deemed marginal in, if not outside of, the hierarchical structure of Kraton. This detachment from the center however was a blessing in disguise. Laweyan prospered economically under its own Islamic trading network while socially it enjoyed autonomy unattainable within the structure of patrimonial relations. This social distance was wide enough to undermine the grip of the cultural power of Kraton and encourage the formation of alternative cultures. In Laweyan, the Sarikat (Dagang) Islam, the first popularly based indigenous organization in the Indies, was established. It derived its power from the combined forces of Islam, trade, and opposition to the cultures of Javanese aristocrats (priyayi). See Kuntowijoyo, *Raja, priyayi dan kawula*, 74–76.

22. Kuntowijoyo, "The Making of a Modern Urban Ecology," 163.

23. Marco Kartodikromo, *Student hidjo* was first serialized in *Sinar Hindia* newspaper, 1918. It was then published a year later in Semarang by NV Boekhandel en Drukkerij Masman and Stroink. After several press offenses and jail terms for political writings, Marco decided in 1918 to write novels.

24. We can reflect on the urban theories of Georg Simmel and Louis Wirth. Because their primary concern was with the urban experiences of the West, Simmel and Wirth overlook the ways in which urban modernity (in the colony) was formed out of the struggle against the colonial or monarchical order. The spatial coordinates of Wirth (the rural and urban split) and the temporal contradictions of Simmel (the old and new social relations based on money) do not take into account the disjuncture between the authority of the royal center and urban modernity especially in the context of a colony. See Wirth, "Urbanism as a Way of Life," and Simmel, "Metropolis and Mental Life."

25. Marco Kartodikromo, "Sama rata sama rasa," 3.

26. Kuntowijoyo, *Raja, priyayi dan kawula*, 80–81.

27. In 1894 the state railway company opened the east-west route of the Buitenzorg-Yogyakarta-Surakarta-Surabaya line. Shiraishi reports that a year later "in 1895, the East-West line . . . carried 5,759,000 passengers and earned 3,054,000 guilders from passenger fares and 6,588,000 from merchandise transportation." Shiraishi, *An Age in Motion*, 8.

28. As cited in Mrázek, "Tan Malaka," 34.

29. Marco Kartodikromo, *Mata gelap*.

30. Ibid., 103.

31. Ibid., 108.

32. Ibid.

33. Riyanto, *Iklan surat kabar dan perubahan masyarakat di Jawa masa kolonial (1870–1915)*, 111–12 (emphasis added).

34. Ibid., 127 (emphasis added).

35. For a discussion of the concept of unbound seriality, see Anderson, *The Spectre of Comparisons*.

36. Pramoedya Ananta Toer, *Bumi manusia*, p. 2, as cited in Cheah, *Spectral Nationality*, 270.

37. Marco Kartodikromo, "Semarang hitam," 7.

38. Marco Kartodikromo, "The Corrupted Life of a Big City," 20–22.

39. As cited in Shiraishi, "The Dispute between Tjipto Mangoenkoesoemo and Soetatmo Soeriokoesoemo," 101.

40. Ibid., 103.

41. Shiraishi, *An Age in Motion*, xiii.

42. Isolated by the colonial police, Minke (referred to historically as Raden Mas Tirto Adhi Soerjo [1880-1918]) died in 1918 in a hotel where he was staying upon his return from exile.

Chapter 7: Urban Pedagogy

1. Marco Kartodikromo, *Pergaulan orang buangan di Boven Digoel*, 1–2.

2. Shiraishi, *An Age in Motion*, 339.

3. Scott, *Seeing like a State*.

4. Shiraishi, *An Age in Motion*, 93.

5. As cited in Mrázek, "Sjahrir at Boven Digoel," 41.

6. Ibid.; Shiraishi, "The Phantom World of Digoel."

7. As cited in Shiraishi, *An Age in Motion*, 311.

8. Shiraishi, "The Phantom World of Digoel," 94.

9. Marco's reports were published as a serial (*cerita bersambung*) in *Pewarta Deli* from 10 October to 9 December 1931. See Toer, "Pengantar."

10. Shiraishi, "Digul," 184–85.

11. Shiraishi, "The Phantom World of Digoel," 94.

12. Shiraishi points out that "Digoel and its camps functioned both to refract and

to reflect the normal, that is, Digoel by definition demarcated the boundaries between the normal and abnormal, the cooperative and the recalcitrant, thereby separating the rational colonial order and the psychopathic fringe population.... Normalcy was thus contingent on a complex apparatus of policing that marked and partitioned colonial territories, subjects, and signs." Ibid., 118.

13. Ibid.

14. The album was published in 1939 as Karsten, *Het Indische stadsbeeld, voorheen en thans.*

15. Ir. Lemei wrote the preface for *Het Indische stadsbeeld.*

16. Thomas Karsten wrote the introduction for *Het Indische stadsbeeld.*

17. Karsten, *Het Indische stadsbeeld, voorheen en thans.* My textual interpretation is based on the Indonesian version translated by Warsono as *Wajah kota Hindia Belanda.*

18. "Glass house" is a term used by Pramoedya for his *Rumah kaca.*

19. As cited in Dick, *Surabaya, City of Work,* 196–97. For a discussion of Karsten's contribution to the Indies town, see Bogaers and de Ruijter, "Ir. Thomas Karsten and Indonesian Town Planning."

20. Karsten in Wertheim, *The Indonesian Town,* 35.

21. Ibid., 38.

22. For a discussion on markets, see Karsten, "Iets over de centrale pasar," which included section drawings of various markets proposed by Karsten.

23. Marco Kartodikromo, *Three Early Indonesian Short Stories.*

24. Ibid., 22.

25. Ibid.

26. Marco Kartodikromo, *Pergaulan orang buangan di Boven Digoel.*

27. For instance, in the 1920s, some of the Indonesian radicals who were looking for a spatial base to organize their operational units recognized with caution that "kampung populations are composed of various groups and classes, namely workers, petit bourgeoisie, officials, spies, etc., and the strength that resides in the kampung is not strong enough to build a communist society." See Shiraishi, *An Age in Motion,* 314.

28. Karsten in Wertheim, *The Indonesian Town,* 19.

29. Mrázek, *Engineers of Happy Land,* 57.

30. Tillema in Wertheim, *The Indonesian Town,* xi.

31. For a discussion on Tillema, see Coté, "Towards an Architecture of Association"; Mrázek, *Engineers of Happy Land.*

32. Karsten in Wertheim, *The Indonesian Town,* 55.

33. Ibid.

34. As cited in Cobban, "Kampungs and Conflicts in Colonial Semarang," 279.

35. Tillema, *Kromoblanda.*

36. Tillema, *Van wonen en bewonen.*

37. Mrázek, *Engineers of Happy Land,* 64.

38. Ibid., 65.

39. For some of the debates see Preij, "Het Koningspleinplan 1937"; *De ingenieur in Nederlandsch-Indië*, 294.

40. As cited in Mrázek, *Engineers of Happy Land*, 68.

41. Karsten as cited in Wertheim, *The Indonesian Town*, 69–70.

42. Wertheim, *The Indonesian Town*, 79.

43. Tillema as cited in Wertheim, *The Indonesian Town*, 82.

44. Ibid., 81.

45. Ibid., 81–82.

46. Mrázek, *Engineers of Happy Land*, 66.

47. Ibid.

48. Sarwoko et al., *Pembangunan perumahan dan hunian modern di Indonesia*, 46.

Chapter 8: "The Reality of One-Which-Is-Two"

1. See Oshikawa, "'Patjar Merah Indonesia' and Tan Malaka."

2. See ibid.

3. See Kusno, "Tan Malaka, Shanghai and the Politics of Geographical Imagining."

4. This chapter owes much to Benedict Anderson's analytical insights on Islam in Indonesia. See Anderson, "Religion and Politics in Indonesia since Independence."

5. For a discussion of culture as an invented tradition, see Hobsbawm, "Introduction: Inventing Traditions." For a discussion of culture as a way of life that consciously or unconsciously guides the practice of everyday life, see Clifford Geertz's formulation of "cultural system" in Geertz, *Local Knowledge*, 73–93 and 94–120; and *The Interpretation of Cultures*, 87–125 and 193–233.

6. Geertz, *Islam Observed*, 12.

7. See Anderson, "The Idea of Power in Javanese Culture"; Kathirithamby-Wells, "The Islamic City; Tjandrasasmita, *Pertumbuhan dan perkembangan kota-kota Muslim di Indonesia dari abad 13 sampai 18 masehi*; Reid, "The Islamization of Southeast Asia."

8. For a recent discussion, see Howell, "Sufism and the Indonesian Islamic Revival"; Hefner, "Print Islam"; Hefner, "The Political Economy of Islamic Conversion in Modern East Java."

9. For a discussion on the impact of the Java War on colonial policy, see Ricklefs, *A History of Modern Indonesia since c. 1300*, 109–30. For a discussion of this war as seen from the perspective of Java, see Sears, *Shadows of Empire*.

10. See Benda and Larkin, *The World of Southeast Asia*; Kumar, "Diponegoro (1787–1855)."

11. The "reality of one-which-is-two" is an expression coming out of *Jaka babad tingkir*, a nineteenth-century Javanese manuscript that I will discuss later in the chapter. See Florida, *Writing the Past, Inscribing the Future*.

12. Luqman, "Heboh peninggalan Sunan Kudus," 62.

13. The architect proclaimed: "I only evaluated things of concern to architecture, that is, the stylistic form. The history of Kudus tower is outside our discipline." Ibid., 62.

14. See Cholid and Darsono, "Takdir mendebat kubah mesjid"; see also Aqsha, van der Meij, and Meuleman, *Islam in Indonesia*, 388.

15. As historian Kathirithamby-Wells indicates: "Stylistically the early mosques at Melaka, Demak, Kadilangu and Banten adopted some local features such as the tiered pagoda roof, instead of the Moorish dome and minaret introduced during a later period." See Kathirithamby-Wells, "The Islamic City," 338.

16. As cited in Cholid and Darsono, "Takdir mendebat kubah mesjid," 107.

17. Changes and additions have been made to the Great Mosque of Kutaradja, but a picture of the original version built by the Dutch can be found in collection of photos compiled by Wachlin, *Woodbury and Page*. For a discussion of the Great Mosque in Java, see van Dijk, "The Changing Contour of Mosques."

18. As cited in van Dijk, "The Changing Contour of Mosques."

19. Florida, *Writing the Past, Inscribing the Future*.

20. *Kiblah* refers to the direction of prayer rather than the building. However, mosques often are invoked to orient its direction towards the Ka'bah in Mecca. During prayers, worshippers form a long row facing the kiblah wall, which often has a niche within that wall to emphasize the direction of Mecca.

21. Florida, *Writing the Past, Inscribing the Future*, 334.

22. *Jaka babad tingkir*, as cited in ibid., 335–36.

23. Oliver W. Wolters wrote that "localization" means that "the materials, be they words, sounds of words, books, or artifacts, had to be localized in different ways before they could fit into various local complexes of religious, social and political systems and belong to new cultural 'wholes'." See Wolters, *History, Culture and Religion in Southeast Asian Perspectives*, 52.

24. See Saliya, Hariadi, and Tjahjono, "Contemporary Expressions of Islam in Buildings," 8.

25. For a further discussion of Demak Mosque and its preservation by the government, see O'Neill, "The Mosque as a Sacred Space."

26. See Julius Pour and Tonny Widiastono, "Mesjid agung Demak: Antara legenda dan kenyataannya" [Demak Mosque: Between Legend and Reality], *Kompas*, 21 March 1987.

27. See: O'Neill, "Islamic Architecture under the New Order."

28. The idea of building Istiqal Mosque was already in circulation in 1950. The then-minister of religion K. H. A. Wahid Hasyim and H. A. Anwar Tjokroaminoto initiated the idea with the support of Muslim communities. President Sukarno took the project up at the end of 1954 by forming a "national" committee. Sukarno determined the site of the mosque was to be at the location of the Dutch fortress.

For Sukarno, this "colonial monument" had to give way to the "national monument" of the Istiqal Mosque. A competition was held, but none of the entries satisfied Sukarno. The project was then given to Silaban, an architect of Christian background from Tapanuli, North Sumatra. Silaban actually won second place, but it was clear that first place was reserved for Sukarno, who himself was an architect. The construction began in the August 1961 and the mosque was opened by the second president, Suharto, on 22 February 1978. The mosque is so big that it dwarfs buildings in the area including the early twentieth-century Roman Catholic cathedral. For documentation of the process of building Istiqal Mosque, see Salam, *Masjid Istiqal*; and "Irama kolom dan ruang Silaban." See also O'Neill, "Islamic Architecture under the New Order."

29. As cited in O'Neill, "Islamic Architecture under the New Order," 157. Sentences in brackets have been added by me and are from Sukarno's speech on Istiqal Mosque, *Bung Karno dan Islam*, 242. Sukarno also indicated: "Brothers, I am not the nine wali who built Demak Mosque in just one night. I am just a human being. I am not a wali, I am not a magician. I just happened to be a human being bestowed by God to hold a very high ideal." Sukarno, *Bung Karno dan Islam*, 236.

30. The "international style" imagined by Sukarno includes the dome (instead of the three-tiered roof of a Javanese mosque) and such materials as bronze, marble, "pualam" stone, steel, and concrete. He cannot tolerate using wood or structures with tile roofs. See Sukarno, *Bung Karno dan Islam*, 240–41.

31. Domes have become a popular icon for mosques today, a phenomenon that seems to have emerged significantly only in the late Suharto era. The president's political incorporation of Islam in the last part of his rule and his resignation in 1998 had the effect of relaxing the pressure to build mosques in the vernacular style. The dominance of the dome today can be gleaned from the newspaper reports, which I summarize below. In 2003, about twenty-five kilometers west of the capital city, a mosque much anticipated by the population of Tangerang, which cost over five million US dollars, has finally been completed. The Al A'zham Grand Mosque, built on a 2.5 hectare plot of land in front of the new Tangerang mayoralty office, is expected not only to be the center of the recently established municipality, but also to be the largest mosque in the world. The main feature of this mosque is the giant dome (forty-four meters high with a diameter of sixty-three meters) that is sustained by five lesser domes without supporting columns. Hamidi Rusadi, the chairman of the Grand Mosque Welfare Council revealed that his team had made a number of comparative studies in places known to have the largest domes in the world, like Medina in Saudi Arabia, Istanbul in Turkey, Selangor in Malaysia, Agra in India, and Surabaya in East Java. The sixty-three meters diameter of Al A'zham's overcomes all of these mosques. The council is considering contacting the Guinness World Records company to register the dome. Behind the celebra-

tion of this achievement is also the attempt of the city of Tangerang to become a "religious city." While prioritizing the development of infrastructure for education and business investment, Tangerang also, despite intense criticism, imposed a law that prohibits prostitution, alcoholic drinks, and public kissing. In this regard, the dome operates as the symbol of the moral core of the city, which aspires to become one of the country's international gateways. For the news about the return of the dome, see Multa Fidrus, "Al A'zhom Mosque, Pride of Tangerang," *Jakarta Post*, 6 October 2006; Fidrus, "Tangerang to Be 'Religious' City: Mayor," *Jakarta Post*, 30 December 2005.

32. For an account of the two ex-presidents of Indonesia's *politics* of mosque building, see Kusno, *Behind the Postcolonial*, 1–4; see also O'Neill, "Islamic Architecture under the New Order." However by using a secular "political" framework of analysis, something quite substantial is missing from these accounts. In this chapter, I propose a reading of the discourses of mosque building by the two previous presidents through their "mentalities" or the cultural behavior within which they were embedded.

33. See "Arsitektur tidak hanya bentuk fisik yang teraga."

34. A slight modification of this syncretism can be seen in the beliefs among Indonesian architects that the principle of modern architecture, no matter in the East or West, is at bottom the idea of traditional Javanese building culture. Ir. Sidharta formulates it in this manner:

> Let's for a while leave behind the socio-cultural explanation [of architecture] and look at the *Joglo* [Javanese roof structure] from the climatic and technical lenses. The original *Joglo* has a frame structure that holds all the weight of the roof. Therefore the wall is not bearing any weight. Isn't this kind of structural system what constitutes modern architecture promoted by Walter Gropius, Mies van der Rohe and other master architects? The roof structure of *Joglo* also composes other principles of modern structure. Ir. Henri Maclaine Pont [the Dutch architect] in his "Javaansche Architectuur" published in Djawa in 1923–1924 pointed out that the structure of *Joglo* is a structure of tent, a "membrane structure" [presumably part of modern architecture]. (Sidharta, "Menuju arsitektur Indonesia modern," 66)

Chapter 9: Guardian of Memories

1. Anderson, "Cartoons and Monuments," 174.

2. Van Dijk, *A Country in Despair*, 203.

3. For a discussion on security discourses after 1998, see van Dijk, "The Privatization of the Public Order."

4. In less than six months after Suharto stepped down, urban residents across Java and Sumatra saw in their cities many poskos that were built by PDI, the political party of Megawati. As many as 862 poskos were found in the region of Madiun,

1,000 in Magetan, and 380 in Ponorogo. "Posko gotong royong PDI terlalu ban-yak" [Too Many Gotong Royong Posko of PDI], *Kompas*, 17 December 1998. By the beginning of 1999, in Semarang, there were already 813 poskos; in Kendal, 843; in Kudus, 627; in Demak, 400; in Jepara and Kati, 750; and in Cilacap, over 1,200 poskos. In Jakarta there were over 1,500 poskos, and in some areas, one could find a posko every fifty meters. "Posko Gotong Royong PDI: Bukan balas dendam terhadap kuningisasi" [The Gotong Royong Posko of PDI: Not Revenge on Golkar], *Kompas Cyber Media*, 14 January 1999.

5. The average size of the posko is around two by two square meters and, depending on the building materials, each one costs around forty dollars.

6. "Ancaman dari posko-posko PDIP" [Threats from the Poskos of PDIP], *Demo-krasi dan Reformasi*, 9–14 August 1999, 28.

7. "Posko gotong royong untuk amankan warga kota Solo" [Posko Gotong Royong to Bring Security to the Citizens of Solo], *Suara Pembaruan*, 19 October 1998.

8. "Posko parpol harus di bongkar" [Poskos of Political Parties Must Be Dis-mantled], *Kompas Cyber Media*, 5 June 1999.

9. "Ancaman dari posko-posko PDIP," 28.

10. Her critics perhaps know about her concerns, and they often criticize her by look-ing at what has gone wrong with the posko. For instance, the ex-president Gus Dur, in his critique of Megawati, claims that some people have been using the posko for "drinking, gambling, embezzling, and sexual transactions." "Gus Dur komentari posko gotong royong PDI" [Gus Dur comments on Posko PDI], *Kom-pas*, 12 January 1999. The municipal authority also challenges Megawati by pro-claiming that the placement of many of her poskos disturbs the aesthetics and the "visual comfort" (*kenyamanan*) of the city. See "Posko akan ditertibkan" [Poskos Will Be Disciplined], *Pikiran rakyat*, 14 September 2002.

11. See Bourchier and Hadiz, "Introduction," 8.

12. Sukarno, "Tahun vivere pericoloso," 5–6.

13. As suggested in Mrázek, *Engineers of Happy Land*, 213.

14. "PDI Perjuangan, si raja posko" [PDI-P, the King of Poskos], *Demokrasi dan Re-formasi*, 5–10 April 1999, 28.

15. "Beribu pesan bertebaran di jalan" [Thousands of Messages on the Streets], *Kom-pas*, 31 March 2000.

16. See Anderson, "The Idea of Power in Javanese Culture."

17. A leader of a PDI branch made this statement. Cited in "Posko gotong royong PDI terlalu Banyak."

18. The pyramid shape of the pendhopo's roof is also associated with the mythical Mount Meru. The master pillars, which support the roof, symbolize a concentric circle. The structure connotes the master's sphere of influence that integrates sub-jects from the surrounding as well as the outer realms.

19. For a discussion of the formation and transformation of the Indonesian "middle

class" in relation to the fear of the "underclass," see Siegel, *A New Criminal Type in Jakarta*.

20. For a reference to *posko taktis*, see *Jurnal pelaksanaan manunggal TNI masuk desa*, 34.

21. See: Santoso, "Operasi pengamanan ABRI: Dari hutan belantara ke perkotaan" [The Security Operation of the Indonesian Army: From Jungle to the City] *Tempo interaktif*, 2 February–15 March 1997.

22. As cited in ibid.

23. Ibid.

24. Kusno, *Behind the Postcolonial*, chap. 4.

25. Sadikin however worked independently and, at the height of Suharto's power, had become one of the most established critics of the New Order regime.

26. Sadikin, *Gita jaya*, 160.

27. Ibid., 168, 112.

28. Ibid., 112.

29. Ibid., 168.

30. Ibid., 138.

31. Barker, "State of Fear"; Barker, "Surveillance and Territoriality in Bandung."

32. Brongtodiningrat, *The Royal Palace (Karaton) of Yogyakarta*.

33. Wolters, *History, Culture and the Region in Southeast Asian Perspectives*; Moertono, *State and Statecraft in Old Java*; Anderson, "The Idea of Power in Javanese Culture."

34. Reid, "The Structure of Cities in Southeast Asia, 15th to 17th Centuries"; Kathirithamby-Wells, "The Islamic City."

35. As cited in Breman, *The Village on Java and the Early-Colonial State*, 36.

36. Brousson, *Batavia awal abad 20*, 121.

37. Onghokham, *The Thugs, the Curtain Thief, and the Sugar Lord*, 161.

38. Nas and Pratiwo, "Java and De Groote Postweg, La Grande Route, the Great Mail Road, Jalan Raya Pos."

39. What was the response of the Javanese king(s) and commoners to this change in "cosmology"? Partly as a result of the extension of the road network of the Grote Postweg, Prince Diponegoro decided to start the Java War in 1825 for he believed the road extension had violated his symbolic "sphere of influence." Liem Thian Joe states in his chronicle: "Because the Dutch wanted to replace one of the Prince's residence with a wide street, the Prince resisted and thus the war lasting for years erupted." Liem, *Riwajat Semarang, 1416–1931*, 96.

40. Wachlin, *Woodbury and Page*, 81.

41. Soon hotels were built adjacent to the spot of the "rest-houses." For example, one of the first hotels in the Indies, Hotel Preanger in Bandung.

42. Scidmore, *Java, the Garden of the East*, 176.

43. Liem, *Riwajat Semarang*, 99.

44. Scidmore, *Java, the Garden of the East*, 179, 176.

45. In Breman's words: "Each new arrival or departure had to be reported immediately and in detail to the district head." Breman, *The Village on Java and the Early-Colonial State*, 40.

46. Ibid.

47. Onghokham, *The Thugs, the Curtain Thief, and the Sugar Lord*, 126.

48. Ibid.

49. Burger as cited in Breman, *The Village on Java and the Early-Colonial State*, 41.

50. Suhartono, *Apanage dan bekel*, 157.

51. Scott, *Seeing like a State*.

52. See also Nordholt and van Till, "Colonial Criminals in Java."

53. De Groot, H. A., "De uitoefening der politie op Java III: De wachthuizen," *De Locomotief*, 20 December 1893.

54. See Shiraishi, *An Age in Motion*.

55. Brousson, *Batavia awal abad 20*, 120.

56. In suggesting the formation of spatial boundaries and legal differences, we are also talking about the privileged group imposing power on others by law and restriction. While different ethnic groups were asked to maintain their own legal systems, the colonial state also imposed restriction and mobility on those groups. For instance, the subsequent imposition of "passport regulation" (*passenstelsel*) (1821–1906), "residential regulation" *wijkenstelsel* (1841–1915), and the *politieirol* (1848–1910s) contributed much to the emergence of the "Kampong Cina" (Chinese camp). See Lohanda, *Growing Pains*, 36–48.

57. We can see the effect of this gardu system in Haji, *Hikayat Siti Mariah*. What is peculiar about the story is that it represents the era of the Cultivation System as the time of peace and order. No reference is made to the fact that the exploitative era was in fact marked by social unrest, banditry, and an unprecedented sense of insecurity, especially among the European communities. The only indication of the real time is the constant portrayal of the night watch and the gardu. The story could thus be seen as taking place inside a "European" kampung under the watch of the gardu. Little is known about the street beyond that community.

58. Marieke Bloembergen (through communication) indicates that in Arsip Nasional Republik Indonesia, Arsip Binnenlands bestuur, BB 3540, one can find information concerning "Java-wide research on the possibility to dispose of the gardoe and ronda services (1924), also a short report on the outer province (1927)"; BB 3539, idem., including the outer provinces, 1928–33.

59. Bloembergen, "Between Public Safety and Political Control," 3.

60. Ibid., 7.

61. Neytzel de Wilde, "Hal polisi," 109.

62. Ibid., 108.

63. Bloembergen, "Between Public Safety and Political Control," 7.

64. Ibid., 16.

65. Lombard, *Nusa Jawa*, 278.

66. Liem, *Riwajat Semarang*, 109.

67. Blusse, "Batavia, 1619-1740."

68. According to Liem, before then the Chinese in Semarang demarcated their territories at the entrance to their kampung by placing temples, the earth deities (Thow Tee Kong—a local, indigenous deity refashioned in Chinese codes), and inscriptions of Buddhist sayings for peace, such as "Lam Boe O Mie Too Hoet Kiat An." Liem, *Riwajat Semarang*, 60.

69. Ibid., 33–34.

70. Ibid., 34.

71. Ibid., 91.

72. Ibid., 92.

73. Ibid., 96.

74. Ibid., 108-9.

75. "Penjerahan kampoeng pada gemeente" [The Administration of the Kampung Is Now under the Municipality], *Sin Tit Po*, 30 January 1925.

76. Kwee Thiam Tjing published his account under the pseudo-name Tjamboek Berdoeri, *Indonesia dalem api dan bara*. I am using this version for my citations. The book was republished in 2004 by Elkasa Jakarta with an illuminating introduction by Benedict Anderson on the author and his time.

77. Ibid., 65.

78. Ibid., 65-66.

79. Ibid., 68.

80. Ibid., 221.

81. Mohamad Hatta cited in Ken'ichi, "Modern Japan and Indonesia," 20. Ken'ichi remarked that Hatta's statement made on radio should be understood within the context of Japanese military censorship. Yet, the statement still indicates an important effect of Japanese occupation on the subjectivity of Indonesians. For Kwee Thiam Tjing (Tjamboek Berdoeri), who was an ethnic Chinese, "the new environment (under the Japanese military) had eliminated the freedom which once existed at least in the mind of the people." See Kwee, *Indonesia dalem api dan bara*, 156.

82. Ken'ichi, "Modern Japan and Indonesia," 21.

83. Kwee, *Indonesia dalem api dan bara*, 138. In *Indonesia dalem api dan bara*, Kwee recorded how Japanese occupation affected the subjectivity of Indonesians.

84. Ibid., 153.

85. Joesoef, "Keamanan di kota Bandoeng."

86. According to Kurasawa, the government announced on 11 January 1944 a number of tasks of the tonarigumi, which included assisting security in the neighborhood by combating air raids, espionage and criminals; notifying people of government instructions, increasing food production and distributing goods, promoting mutual aids among inhabitants and serving the government in military affairs. See Kurasawa, "Mobilization and Control."

87. See Yoshihara and Dwianto, *Grass Roots and the Neighborhood Associations*.

88. Kurasawa, "Mobilization and Control," 286.

89. S. Ozu, "Roeangan wanita: Tonarigumi" [Space for Women: Tonarigumi], *Sinar Baroe*, 2603 (5 July 1943), 3.

90. "Setahun keibodan: Langkah menoejoe keamanan: Tjorak persamaan dan persahabatan" [The First Year of Keibodan: A Step towards Security, Community, and Friendship], *Sinar Baroe*, 2604 (1 May 1944).

91. "Keibodan dan pendjaga kampoeng" [Keibodan and the Guarding of the Kampung], *Sinar Baroe*, 2603 (19 May 1943), 2.

92. As told to Bill Frederick by an informant in 1977, see Frederick, "Indonesian Urban Society in Transition," 49–50.

93. "Pendjagaan kampoeng" [Guarding the Kampung], *Kanpo Sinar Baroe*, 2 (August 1943), 4.

94. "Solo: Menjaga keamanan kampong" [Solo: Guarding the Kampung] *Sinar Baroe*, 18 2603 (18 August 1943).

95. "Setahun keibodan," 3.

96. "Tonari gumi di lantik dengan resmi oleh S. P. Pakoealaman-Ko" [Tonarigumi Is Made Official by S. P. Pakoealaman-Ko—a Javanese Aristocrat], *Sinar Baroe*, 2604 (6 January 1944), 2.

97. Lombard, *Nusa Jawa*, 278.

98. Cribb, "Law and Order in Occupied Jakarta, 1946."

99. "Penghapusan pas militer sepandjang djalan-raja (hoofdwegen)" [The Abolition of the Street Pass], *Soeloeh ra'jat*, 13 November 1947.

100. "Jang didjamin ketertiban dan keamanannja" [To Guarantee Order and Security], *Soeloeh ra'jat*, September 1947.

101. "Commando post TNI," *Soeloeh ra'jat*, 20 October 1947.

102. "Maksoed satoe-satoenja mendjaga keamanan bersama" [The Only Aim Is to Provide Security for All], *Soeloeh ra'jat*, 15 December 1947.

103. For a discussion on the importance of appearances, especially clothing in Indonesia across various orders, see Nordholt, *Outward Appearances*.

104. For an analysis of "pemuda" style, see Frederick, "The Appearance of Revolution." See also Anderson, *Java in a Time of Revolution*.

105. Pramoedya, *Di tepi kali Bekasi*, 99.

106. Ibid., 123.

107. *Kedaulatan rakyat*, 20 May 1946. Cited in Lapian, *Semangat'45 dalam rekaman gambar IPPHOS*, no page number.

108. Soedjarwo, *Lukisan revolusi rakjat Indonesia, 1945–1949*, no page number.

109. Frederick, "The Appearance of Revolution."

110. Soedjarwo, *Lukisan revolusi rakjat Indonesia*, no page number.

111. This area remained a war zone for most of the revolutionary period. Newspapers were filled with reports such as "civilians living close to the demarcation line have been continuously harassed" and "patrollers and posts of the Dutch army were

fired on twenty times." See "Keadaan militer" [The Military Situation], *Soeloeh ra'jat*, 19 June 1947.

112. "Awas intimidasi dan provokasi" [Beware of Intimidation and Provocation], *Kedaulatan rakjat*, 12 December 1949.

113. Sekretariat Negara, *30 tahun Indonesia merdeka, 1945–1955*, 353, fig. 416.

114. Ekadjati, "Tulak bala," 20.

115. Ibid., 23.

116. As cited in "Ancaman dari posko-posko PDIP," 28.

117. For an account of neighborhood watch in a city in Java during the New Order, see Siegel, *Solo in the New Order*, chaps. 2 and 3.

118. Hudijono, *Gardu*, ix–x.

119. Ibid., cover.

BIBLIOGRAPHY

Abeyasekere, Susan. *Jakarta: A History*. Singapore: Oxford University Press, 1987.

"Adi Purnomo: Settling Debts with Nature." *Tempo*, 3 January 2005.

Ai, Maeda. *Text and the City: Essays on Japanese Modernity*. Durham, N.C.: Duke University Press, 2004.

Akihary, Huib. *Architectuur en Stedebouw in Indonesie 1870–1940*. Geeuwenbrug, Netherlands: Grafiplan, 1988.

AlSayyad, Nezar, ed. *Forms of Dominance: On the Architecture and Urbanism of the Colonial Enterprise*. Aldershot: Avebury, 1992.

Anderson, Benedict. *Java in a Time of Revolution: Occupation and Resistance, 1944–1946*. Ithaca, N.Y.: Cornell University Press, 1972.

———. "Religion and Politics in Indonesia since Independence." *Religion and Social Ethos in Indonesia*, edited by J. A. C. Mackie, 21–32. Melbourne: Monash University, 1977.

———. "Cartoons and Monuments: The Evolution of Political Communication under the New Order." *Language and Power: Exploring Political Cultures in Indonesia*, 152–93. Ithaca, N.Y.: Cornell University Press, 1990.

———. "The Idea of Power in Javanese Culture." *Language and Power: Exploring Political Cultures in Indonesia*, 17–77. Ithaca, N.Y.: Cornell University Press, 1990.

———. *Language and Power: Exploring Political Cultures in Indonesia*, Ithaca, N.Y.: Cornell University Press, 1990.

———. *Imagined Communities*. London: Verso, 1993.

———. *The Spectre of Comparisons: Nationalism, Southeast Asia and the World*. London: Verso, 1998.

———. "Introduction." *Violence and the State in Suharto's Indonesia*, edited by Benedict Anderson, 9–19. Ithaca, N.Y.: Southeast Asia Program Publications, Cornell University, 2001.

Aqsha, Darul, Dick van der Meij, and Johan H. Meuleman, eds. *Islam in Indonesia: A Survey of Events and Developments from 1988 to March 1993*. Jakarta: INIS, 1995.

"Arsitektur tidak hanya bentuk fisik yang teraga: Memperkenalkan konsep arsitektur Pancasila" [Architecture Is Not Only Physical: Introducing the Concept of Pancasila Architecture]. *Konstruksi*, December 1985.

"Bang Yos menjawab lugas" [Sutiyoso Responded Lucidly]. *Tokoh Indonesia*, 16 May–19 June 2005. www.tokohindonesia.com.

Barker, Joshua, "State of Fear: Controlling the Criminal Contagion in Suharto's New Order." *Indonesia* 66 (October 1998), 7–43.

———. "Surveillance and Territoriality in Bandung." *Figures of Criminality in Indonesia, the Philippines and Colonial Vietnam*, edited by Vicente Rafael, 95–127. Ithaca, N.Y.: Southeast Asia Program Publications, Cornell University, 1999.

Benda, Harry J., and John A. Larkin, eds. *The World of Southeast Asia: Selected Historical Readings*. New York: Harper and Row, 1967.

Benjamin, Walter, "The Work of Art in the Age of Mechanical Reproduction." *Illuminations*, edited by Hannah Arendt and translated by Harry Zohn, 217–52. New York: Schocken Books, 1969.

Berfield, Susan, and Dewi Loveard, "Ten Days That Shook Indonesia." *Asiaweek*, 24 July 1998.

Bertrand, Romain. "Inhabiting Jakarta: Interstitial Imaginings in a Globalized Cityscape." Paper presented at the International Network on Globalization, Tokyo, Rikkyo University, June 2001.

Bhabha, Homi. "Of Mimicry and Man: The Ambivalence of Colonial Discourse." *The Location of Culture*, 85–92. New York: Routledge, 1994.

Bloembergen, Marieke. "Between Public Safety and Political Control: Modern Colonial Policing in Surabaya (1911–1919)." Paper presented at the First International Conference on Urban History, University of Airlangga and Netherlands Institute for War Documentation, Surabaya, 23–25 August 2004.

Blusse, Leonard. "Batavia, 1619–1740: The Rise and Fall of a Chinese Colonial Town." *Journal of Southeast Asian Studies* 12 (1981), 159–78.

Bogaers, Els, and P. de Ruijter. "Ir. Thomas Karsten and Indonesian Town Planning, 1915–1940." *The Indonesian City; Studies in Urban Development and Planning*, edited by Peter J. M. Nas, 71–88. Dordrecht: Foris Publications, 1986.

Bourchier, David, and Vedi Hadiz, eds. *Indonesian Politics and Society: A Reader*. London: Routledge Curzon, 2003.

———. "Introduction." *Indonesian Politics and Society: A Reader*, edited by David Bourchier and Vedi Hadiz, 1–24. London: RoutledgeCurzon, 2003.

Boyer, Christine. *The City of Collective Memory: Its Historical Imagery and Architectural Entertainments*. Cambridge, Mass.: MIT Press, 1994.

Breman, Jan. *The Village on Java and the Early-Colonial State*. Rotterdam: CASP 1, 1980.

Bresnan, John, "The United States, the IMF, and the Indonesian Financial Crisis." *The Politics of Post-Suharto Indonesia*, edited by A. Schwartz and J. Paris, 87–112. New York: Council on Foreign Relations Press, 1999.

Brongtodiningrat, K. P. H. *The Royal Palace (Karaton) of Yogyakarta: Its Architecture and Its Meaning*. Translated by R. Murdani Hadiatmaja. Yogyakarta: Karaton Museum Yogyakarta, 1975.

Brousson, H. C. C. Clockener. *Batavia awal abad 20 (gedenkschriften van een oud-koloniaal)* [Batavia at the Beginning of the Twentieth Century]. Translated by Achmand Sunjayadi. Jakarta: Komunitas Bambu, 2003.

Bunnell, Tim, Lisa Drummond, and K. C. Ho, eds. *Critical Reflections on Cities in Southeast Asia*. Singapore: Time Academic Press, 2002.

Chakrabarty, Dipesh. *Provincializing Europe: Postcolonial Thought and Historical Difference*. Princeton, N.J.: Princeton University Press, 2000.

Cheah, Pheng. *Spectral Nationality: Passages of Freedom from Kant to Postcolonial Literatures of Liberation*. New York: Columbia University Press, 2003.

Cholid, Mohamad, and Budiono Darsono. "Takdir mendebat kubah mesjid" [Takdir Debates over the Mosque's Dome]. *Tempo*, 7 May 1988, 107.

Cobban, James. "Kampungs and Conflicts in Colonial Semarang." *Journal of Southeast Asian Studies* 19, no. 2 (1988), 266–91.

Colombijn, Freek. "What Is So Indonesian about Violence?" *Violence in Indonesia*, edited by Ingrid Wessel and Georgia Wimhofer, 24–46. Hamburg: Abera-Verl, 2001.

Colombijn, Freek, et al., eds. *Kota lama, kota baru: Pejarah kota-kota di Indonesia sebetum dan sesudah kemerdekaan*. Yogyakarta: Ombak Press, 2005.

Coppel, Charles A. *The Indonesian Chinese in Crisis*. Kuala Lumpur: Oxford University Press, 1983.

Coté, Joost. "Towards an Architecture of Association: H. F. Tillema, Semarang and the Discourse on the Colonial 'Slum'." *The Indonesian Town Revisited*, edited by Peter J. M. Nas, 319–47. Munster/Berlin: Lit Verlag, 2002.

Cowherd, Bob. "Cultural Construction of Jakarta: Design, Planning and Development in Jabotabek, 1980–1997." PhD dissertation, MIT, 2002.

Cribb, Robert. "Law and Order in Occupied Jakarta, 1946." Paper presented at the conference on Decolonization and Daily Life in Asia and Africa, Netherlands Institute for War Documentation, Amsterdam, 11–13 December 2003.

Crinson, Mark, ed. *Urban Memory*. London: Routledge, 2005.

Culler, Jonathan, and Pheng Cheah, eds. *Grounds of Comparison: Around the Work of Benedict Anderson*. London: Routledge, 2003.

De Certeau, Michel. *Heterologies: Discourse on the Other*. Minneapolis: University of Minnesota Press, 1986.

De ingenieur in Nederlandsch-Indië 5, no. 1 (1938) (special issue).

Dick, Howard W. *Surabaya, City of Work: A Socioeconomic History, 1900–2000*. Athens: Ohio University Press, 2003.

Dikken, Judy den. *Liem Bwan Tjie (1991–1966)*. Rotterdam: Colofon, 2002.

Dirlik, Arif. *Global Modernity*. Boulder, Colo.: Paradigm Publishers, 2006.

Dovey, Kim. *Framing Places: Mediating Power in Built Form*. London: Routledge, 1999.

Ekadjati, Edi S. "Tulak bala: Sistim pertahanan tradisional kasus desa Karangtawang, Kabupaten Kuningan, Jawa Barat" [Tulak Bala: Traditional System of Defense;

The Case of Karangtawang Village, Kuningan District, West Java]. *Tulak Bala*, edited by Ajip Rosidi, 9–26. Bandung: Pusat Studi Sunda, 2003.

Escobar, Arturo. *Encountering Development: The Making and Unmaking of the Third World*. Princeton, N.J.: Princeton University Press, 1995.

Fakih, Farabi. *Membayangkan ibu kota: Jakarta di bawah Soekarno*. Yogyakarta: Penerbit Ombak, 2005.

Firman, Tommy. "The Restructuring of Jakarta Metropolitan Area: A 'Global City' in Asia." *Cities* 15, no. 4 (1998), 229–43.

———. "Indonesian Cities under the 'Krismon'." *Cities* 16, no. 2 (1999), 69–82.

Florida, Nancy. *Writing the Past, Inscribing the Future: History as Prophecy in Colonial Java*. Durham, N.C.: Duke University Press, 1995.

Forty, Adrian, and Susanne Küchler, eds. *The Art of Forgetting*. New York: Berg, 1999.

Foucault, Michel. "The Subject and Power." *Michel Foucault: Beyond Structuralism and Hermeneutics*, edited by Paul Rabinow and Hubert L. Dreyfus, 208–26. Chicago: Chicago University Press, 1982.

———. "Governmentality." *The Foucault Effect: Studies in Governmentality*, edited by Graham Burchell, Colin Gordon, and Peter Miller, 87–104. Chicago: Chicago University Press, 1991.

Frederick, William. "Indonesian Urban Society in Transition: Surabaya, 1926–1946." PhD dissertation, University of Hawaii, 1978.

———. *Visions and Heat: The Making of the Indonesian Revolution*. Athens: Ohio University Press, 1988.

———. "The Appearance of Revolution: Cloth, Uniform, and the Pemuda Style in East Java, 1945–1949." *Outward Appearances: Dressing State and Society in Indonesia*, edited by Henk Schulte Nordholt, 199–248. Leiden: KITLV Press, 1997.

"From the Editor." *Indonesia Design* 1, no. 5 (2004), 5.

Geertz, Clifford. *Islam Observed*. New Haven, Conn.: Yale University Press, 1968.

———. *The Interpretation of Cultures*. New York: Basic Books, 1973.

———. *Negara: The Theatre State in Nineteenth-Century Bali*. Princeton, N.J.: Princeton University Press, 1980.

———. "Centers, Kings and Charisma: Reflections on the Symbolics of Power." *Local Knowledge*, 121–46. New York: Basic Books, 1983.

———. *Local Knowledge*. New York: Basic Books, 1983.

Gillis, John R, ed. *Commemorations: The Politics of National Identity*. Princeton, N.J.: Princeton University Press, 1994.

Goenawan Mohamad. "City." *Sidelines*. Translated by J. Lindsey, 28–29. South Melbourne: Hyland House, 1994.

Gouda, Frances. "The Unbearable Lightness of Memory: Fragmentations of Cultural Memory and Recycling the Dutch Colonial Past." "Tempoe doeloe: Koloniale cultuur in Nederlands-Indie," special issue, *Groniek historisch tijdschrift* 40 (spring 2007), 9–28.

"Grand Indonesia, Jakarta." *Indonesia Design* 3, no. 12 (2006), 31.

Guattari, Felix. "Regimes, Pathways, Subjects." *Incorporations*, edited by Jonathan Crary and Stanford Kwinter, 16–35. New York: Urzone 1992.

Haji Mukti. *Hikayat Siti Mariah*. Edited by Pramoedya Ananta Toer. Jakarta: Lentera Dipantara, 2003.

Handinoto. *Perkembangan kota dan arsitektur kolonial Belanda di Surabaya, 1870–1940* [Architecture and Urban Development under Dutch Colonialism in Surabaya]. Surabaya: Universitas Kristen Petra, 1996.

Handinoto, and Paulus H. Soehargo. *Perkembangan arsitektur kolonial Belanda di Malang* [Architectural Development during Dutch Colonialism in Malang]. Surabaya: Universitas Kristen Petra, 1996.

Hantoro, J. et al. "Tambal sulam simbol kota" [Fixing the Symbols of the City]. *Segitiga emas* 2 (April 2001), 72.

Harootunian, Harry. *Overcome by Modernity: History, Culture and Community in Interwar Japan*. Princeton, N.J.: Princeton University Press, 2000.

Harvey, David. *A Brief History of Neoliberalism*. New York: Oxford University Press, 2005.

Hefner, Robert W. "The Political Economy of Islamic Conversion in Modern East Java." *Islam and the Political Economy of Meaning: Comparative Studies of Muslim Discourse*, edited by William R. Roff, 53–78. London: Croom Helm, 1987.

———. "Print Islam: Mass Media and Ideological Rivalries among Indonesian Muslims." *Indonesia* 64 (October 1997), 77–103.

Heryanto, Ariel. "The Development of 'Development'." Translated by N. Lutz. *Indonesia* 46 (1988), 1–24.

———. "Rape, Race and Reporting." *Reformasi: Crisis and Change in Indonesia*, edited by Arief Budiman, Barbara Hatley, and Damien Kingsbury, 299–334. Melbourne: Monash Asian Institute, 1999.

Heuken, Adolf. *Historical Sites of Jakarta*. Jakarta: Cipta Loka Caraka, 2000.

Highmore, Ben, ed. *Everyday Life Reader*. London: Routledge, 2002.

Hobsbawm, Eric. "Introduction: Inventing Traditions." *The Invention of Tradition*, edited by Eric Hobsbawm and Terence Ranger, 1–15. Cambridge: Cambridge University Press, 1983.

Howell, Julia Day. "Sufism and the Indonesian Islamic Revival." *Journal of Asian Studies* 60 (August 2001), 701–30.

Hudijono, Anwar. *Gardu: Refleksi sosial menuju kehidupan yang demokratis* [The Security Post: Social Reflection toward a Democratic Life]. Jakarta: Grasindo, 2004.

Huyssen, Andreas. "Present Pasts: Media, Politics, Amnesia." *Public Culture* 12, no. 1 (2000), 21–38.

———. *Present Pasts: Urban Palimpsests and the Politics of Memory*. Stanford: Stanford University Press, 2003.

"Irama kolom dan ruang Silaban" [The Rhythm of Columns and the Space of Silaban]. *Tempo*, 26 May 1984.

Jameson, Fredrick. "Cognitive Mapping." *Marxism and the Interpretation of Culture*, edited by Cary Nelson and Lawrence Grossberg, 347–57. Urbana: University of Illinois Press, 1988.

———. *Signatures of the Visible*. New York: Routledge, 1990.

Jellinek, Lea. *The Wheel of Fortune*. Honolulu: Hawaii University Press, 1991.

Joesoef, R. "Keamanan di kota Bandoeng" [The security of the city of Bandung]. *Tjahaja*. 2602 (western year: 1942)."Joglo = Jogya—Solo." *Tempo*, 1 June 1984.

Jurnal pelaksanaan manunggal TNI masuk desa [Journal for the Operation of Indonesian Army in the Village]. Jakarta: Ministry of Information, 1991.

Kamil, M. Ridwan. "Arus kapitalisme global dan masa depan arsitektur Indonesia" [Global Capitalism and the Future of Indonesian Architecture]. *Desain arsitektur: Majalah eksplorasi desain dan Arsitektur*, 3 June 2000. http://darsitektur.tripod .com.

Karl, Rebecca. *Staging the World: Chinese Nationalism at the Turn of the Twentieth Century*. Durham, N.C.: Duke University Press, 2002.

Karsten, Thomas. "Iets over de centrale pasar." *Locale techniek* 7, no. 2 (1938), 63–66.

———. *Het Indische stadsbeeld, voorheen en thans*. Bandoeng: Stichting Technisch Tijdschrift, 1939.

Kathirithamby-Wells, J. "The Islamic City: Melaka to Jogjakarta, c. 1500–1800." *Modern Asian Studies* 20, no. 2 (1986), 333–49.

Ken'ichi, Goto. "Modern Japan and Indonesia: The Dynamics and Legacy of Wartime Rule." *Japan, Indonesia and the War*, edited by Peter Post and Elly Touwen-Bouwsma, 14–30. Leiden: KITLV Press, 1997.

King, Anthony. *Spaces of Global Cultures: Architecture, Urbanism, Identity*. London: Routledge, 2004.

Kleden, Hermien, and Adi Sutarwiyo. "The Lionheart Beats Again." *Tempo*, 8 January 2001, 42–43.

Kumar, Ann. "Diponegoro (1787–1855)." *Indonesia* 13 (April 1972), 69–118.

Kuntowijoyo. "The Making of a Modern Urban Ecology: Social and Economic History of Solo, 1900–1915." *Lembaran sejarah* 3, no. 1 (2000), 163–85.

———. *Raja, priyayi dan kawula* [The King, the Priyayi and the Kawula]. Yogyakarta: Ombak, 2004.

Kurasawa, Aiko. "Mobilization and Control: A Study of Social Change in Rural Java, 1842–45." PhD dissertation, Cornell University, 1988.

Kusno, Abidin. *Behind the Postcolonial: Architecture, Urban Space and Political Cultures in Indonesia*. New York: Routledge, 2000.

———. "Tan Malaka, Shanghai and the Politics of Geographical Imagining." *Singapore Journal of Tropical Geography* 24, no. 3 (2003), 327–39.

Kwee Thiam Tjing (Tjamboek Berdoeri). *Indonesia dalem api dan bara*. Malang, 1947.

Langmead, Donald. *Dutch Modernism: Architectural Resources in the English Language*. Westport, Conn.: Greenwood Press, 1996.

Lapian, A. B., ed., *Semangat '45 dalam rekaman gambar* IPPHOS [The Spirit of 1945 in the Visual Documentation of IPPHOS]. Jakarta: Sinar Harapan, 1985.

Leaf, Michael, "Suburbanization of Jakarta: A Concurrence of Economics and Ideology." *Third World Planning Review* 16, no. 4, 1994, 341–56.

———. "Building the Road for the BMW: Culture, Vision and the Extended Metropolitan Region of Jakarta." *Environment and Planning A* 28, no. 9, 1996, 1617–35.

Lee, Leo Oufan. *Shanghai Modern: The Flowering of a New Urban Culture in China.* Cambridge, Mass.: Harvard University Press, 1999.

Lefebvre, Henri. *Everyday Life in the Modern World.* New Brunswick, N.J.: Transaction Books, 1984 [1968].

Liem, Thian Joe. *Riwajat Semarang, 1416–1931.* Semarang-Batavia: Boekhandel Ho Kim Yoe, 1933.

Lohanda, Mona. *The Kapitan Cina in Batavia 1837–1942.* Jakarta: Penerbit Djambatan,1996.

———. *Growing Pains: The Chinese and the Dutch in Colonial Java, 1890–1942.* Jakarta: Yayasan Cipta Loka Caraka, 2002.

Lombard, Denys. *Nusa Jawa: Silang Budaya 2: Jaringan Asia* [The Spheres of Java: Cross Culture 2: The Asian Network]. Jakarta: Gramedia, 1996. Originally published 1990 as part of *Le carrefour Javanais: Essai d'histoire globale.*

Luqman, A. "Heboh peninggalan Sunan Kudus" [Controversy over the Heritage of Sunan Kudus]. *Tempo,* 2 August 1986, 62.

Lynch, Kevin, *The Image of the City.* Cambridge, Mass.: MIT Press, 1960.

Marco Kartodikromo. *Mata gelap: Tjerita jang soenggoeh kedjadian di tanah Djawa.* [Blind Eyes: A Real Story That Took Place in Java]. Bandoeng: Bookerji Insulinde, 1914.

———. "Sama rata sama rasa" [Equal Height, Equal Feeling]. *Sair rempah-rempah* [The Poems of Spices]. Semarang: Druk. N. V. Sinar Djawa, 1918.

———. "The Corrupted Life of a Big City." *Three Early Indonesian Short Stories,* translated by Paul Tickell, 19–23. Melbourne: Monash University, Centre of Southeast Asian Studies, 1981.

———. "Semarang hitam." *Three Early Indonesian Short Stories,* translated by Paul Tickell, 7–12. Melbourne: Monash University, Centre of Southeast Asian Studies, 1981.

———. *Three Early Indonesian Short Stories.* Translated and introduced by Paul Tickell. Melbourne: Monash University, Centre of Southeast Asian Studies, 1981.

———. *Pergaulan orang buangan di Boven Digoel* [The Social Life of People in Exile in Boven Digoel]. Jakarta: Kepustakaan Populer Gramedia, 2002.

———. *Student Hidjo.* Yogyakarta: Bentang, 2005. First published as a serial in *Sinar Hindia* newspaper in 1918; published 1919 by NV Boekhandel en Drukkerij Masman and Stroink.

Marshall, Richard. *Emerging Urbanity: Global Urban Projects in the Asia Pacific Rim.* New York: Spon Press, 2003.

"Membongkar pilar Yunani" [Dismantling the Greek Column]. *Tempo*, 1 September 1984, 18.

Ministry of Information. *Jurnal pelaksanaan manunggal TNI masuk desa*. Jakarta: Ministry of Information, 1991.

Moertono, Soemarsaid. *State and Statecraft in Old Java: A Study of the Later Mataram Period, 16th to 19th Century*. Ithaca, N.Y.: Southeast Asia Program Publications, Cornell University, 1981.

Mrázek, Rudolf. "Tan Malaka: A Political Personality's Structure of Experience." *Indonesia* 14 (1972), 1–48.

———. "Sjahrir at Boven Digoel: Reflections on Exile in the Dutch East Indies." *Making Indonesia*, edited by Daniel S. Lev and Ruth. T. MacVey, 41–65. Ithaca, N.Y.: Southeast Asia Program Publications, Cornell University, 1996.

———. *Engineers of Happy Land: Technology and Nationalism in a Colony*. Princeton, N.J.: Princeton University Press, 2002.

Mulyadi, M. Hari, Soedarmono, and colleagues. *Runtuhnya kekuasaan 'kraton alit': Studi radikalisasi sosial 'wong Sala' dari kerusuhan Mei 1998 di Surakarta* [The Collapse of the Palace Power: A Study of the Radicalization of Common Solo Folks during the May 1998 Riots in Surakarta]. Surakarta: Lembaga Pengembangan Teknologi Perdesaan, 1999.

Murray, Alison. *No Money, No Honey*. Singapore: Oxford University Press, 1991.

Nas, Peter, ed. *Urban Symbolism*. Leiden: Brill, 1993.

———, ed. *The Past in the Present: Contemporary Architecture in Indonesia*. Rotterdam: NAI Press, 2007.

Nas, Peter J. M., and Pratiwo. "Java and De Groote Postweg, La Grande Route, the Great Mail Road, Jalan Raya Pos." *Bijdragen tot de taal-, land-en volkenkunde* 158, no. 4 (2002), 707–25.

Neytzel de Wilde, A. "Hal polisi" [About the Police]. *Kitab peringatan oentoek Hindia Belanda ketika S. B. Maharadja Poeteri tjoekoep 25 tahoen bertachta keradjaan, 1898–1923* [Album for the Netherlands East Indies in the Celebration of the Dutch Princess for Her Twenty-five Years of Ruling the Monarchy, 1898–1923, 108–11]. Batavia: G. Kolff and Co., 1923.

Nordholt, Henk Schulte, ed. *Outward Appearances: Dressing State and Society in Indonesia*. Leiden: KITLV Press, 1997.

Nordholt, Henk Schulte, and Hanneman Samuel, eds. *Indonesia in Transition: Rethinking "Civil Society," "Region" and "Crisis."* Yogyakarta: Pustaka Pelajar, 2004.

Nordholt, Henk Schulte, and Margreet van Till. "Colonial Criminals in Java." *Figures of Criminality in Indonesia, the Philippines and Colonial Vietnam*, edited by Vicente Rafael, 47–69. Ithaca, N.Y.: Southeast Asia Program Publications, Cornell University, 1999.

Oei Tjoe Tat. *Memoar Oei Tjoe Tat*. Compiled by Pramoedya Ananta Toer. Jakarta: Hasta Mitra, 1995.

Olds, Kris. *Globalization and Urban Change: Capital, Culture and Pacific Rim Mega-*

Projects. Oxford Geographical and Environmental Studies Series. Oxford: Oxford University Press, 2002.

Olick, Jeffrey, "Collective Memory: The Two Cultures." *Sociological Theory* 17 (November 1999), 333–48.

O'Neill, Hugh. "Islamic Architecture under the New Order." *Culture and Society in New Order Indonesia*, edited by Virginia M. Hooker, 151–65. Kuala Lumpur: Oxford University Press, 1993.

———. "The Mosque as a Sacred Space." *Indonesian Heritage: Architecture*, edited by Gunawan Tjahjono, 94–95. Singapore: Archipelago Press, 1998.

Ong, Aihwa. "On the Edge of Empires: Flexible Citizenship among Chinese in Diaspora." *Positions* 1 (1993), 745–78.

———. *Neoliberalism as Exception: Mutations in Citizenship and Sovereignty*. Durham, N.C.: Duke University Press, 2006.

Onghokham. *The Thugs, the Curtain Thief, and the Sugar Lord: Power, Politics and Culture in Colonial Java*. Jakarta: Metaphor Publishing, 2003.

Oshikawa, Noriaki. "'Patjar Merah Indonesia' and Tan Malaka: A Popular Novel and a Revolutionary Legend." *Reading Southeast Asia*, edited by Takashi Shiraishi, 1–39. Translation Series 1. Ithaca, N.Y.: Southeast Asia Program Publications, Cornell University, 1990.

Pattiradjawane, Rene L. "Peristiwa Mei 1998 di Jakarta: Titik terendah sejarah orang etnis Cina di Indonesia" [The May 1998 Incident in Jakarta: The Most Devastating History of Ethnic Chinese in Indonesia]. *Harga yang harus dibayar: Sketsa pergulatan etnis Cina di Indonesia* [The Price That Has to Be Paid: A Sketch of the Struggles of Ethnic Chinese in Indonesia], edited by I. Wibowo, 213–52. Jakarta: Gramedia dan Pusat Studi Cina, 2000.

Pemberton, John. *On the Subject of "Java."* Ithaca, N.Y.: Cornell University Press, 1994.

Podo, Hadi, and Joseph Sullivan. *Kamus ungkapan Indonesia-Inggris*. Jakarta: PT Gramedia, 1989.

Prakash, Gyan. "The Urban Turn." *Sarai Reader 02: The Cities of Everyday Life*, 2–7. Delhi: Sarai, Centre for the Study of Developing Societies, 2002.

Pramoedya A. Toer. "Letter to a Friend from the Country." *From Surabaya to Armageddon*, 69–76. Singapore: Heinemann Books, 1955.

———. *Rumah kaca: Sebuah roman sejarah* [House of Glass]. Jakarta: Hasta Mitra, 1988.

———. *Di tepi kali Bekasi*. Jakarta: Lantera Dipantara, 2003. First published 1951.

Prasetyo, Arief. "Superblock terbesar di Jakarta" [The Largest Superblock in Jakarta]. *Bisnis Properti*, 2006.

Preij, W. "Het Koningspleinplan 1937." *Locale techniek* 7, no. 1 (1938), 8–15.

Prijotomo, Josef. "The Indonesian Elements in the Architecture of 1900–1930s." *Arsitektur Nusantara menuju keniscayaan*, compiled by Johanes Adiyanto, 147–56. Surabaya: Wastu Lanas Grafika, 2004.

Purnomo, Adi. *Relativitas: Arsitek di ruang angan dan kenyataan* [Relativity: Architecture in the Real and Imagined World]. Jakarta: Borneo Publication, 2005.

Putra, Dian. "Menjawab tantangan dengan Megaproyek" [Facing Challenge with Megaproject]. *Proyeksi*, 16 July–15 August 2006.

Rabinow, Paul. *French Modern: Norms and Forms of the Social Environment*. Cambridge, Mass.: MIT Press, 1989.

Reid, Anthony. "The Structure of Cities in Southeast Asia, 15th to 17th Centuries." *Journal of Southeast Asian Studies* 11, no. 2 (1980), 235–50.

———. "The Islamization of Southeast Asia." *Charting the Shape of Early Modern Southeast Asia*, 15–38. Singapore: Institute of Southeast Asian Studies, 2000.

"Renovasi Glodok Plaza menerapkan konsep 'IT Mall'" [Glodok Plaza Renovates the Concept of an Information Technology Mall]. *Indo Construction* 1 (December 2000), www.indoconstruction.com.

Ricklefs, M. C. *A History of Modern Indonesia since c. 1300*, 2nd ed. Stanford: Stanford University Press, 1993.

Riyanto, Bedjo. *Iklan surat kabar dan perubahan masyarakat di Jawa masa kolonial (1870–1915)* [Newspaper Advertisement and Social Change in Colonial Java]. Yogyakarta: Tarawang Press, 2000.

Robinson, Michael, and Gi-Wook Shin, eds. *Colonial Modernity in Korea*: Cambridge, Mass.: Harvard University Asia Center, 1999.

Robison, Richard, and Vedi Hadiz. *Reorganising Power in Indonesia: The Politics of Oligarchy in an Age of Markets*. New York: RoutledgeCurzon, 2004.

Rossi, Aldo. *The Architecture of the City*. Translated by Diane Ghirardo and Joan Ockman. Cambridge, Mass.: MIT Press, 1982. First published 1966.

Roth, Michael and Charles Salas. "Introduction." *Disturbing Remains: Memory, History, and Crisis in the Twentieth Century*, edited by Michael Roth and Charles Salas, 1–16. Los Angeles: Getty Research Institute, 2001.

"Rumah idaman" [The Dream House]. *Indo Construction*, February 2002.

Sadikin, Ali. *Gita Jaya: Catatan H. Ali Sadikin, gubernur kepala daerah khusus ibukota Jakarta, 1966–1977* [Gita Jaya: Notes of Ali Sadikin, the Governor of Jakarta, 1966–1977]. Jakarta: Pemda Khusus Ibu kota Jakarta, 1977.

Said, Edward. *Beginnings: Intention and Method*. New York: Columbia University Press, 1985.

Salam, Solichin. *Masjid Istiqal: Sebuah monumen kemerdekaan* [Istiqal Mosque: An Independence Monument]. Jakarta: Pusat Studi dan Penelitian Islam, 1991.

Saliya, Yuswadi, Hariadi, and Gunawan Tjahjono. "Contemporary Expressions of Islam in Buildings: Indonesian Experience." Paper presented at the seminar on Contemporary Expressions of Islam in Building, sponsored by the Aga Khan Award for Architecture, Yogyakarta, 16–19 October 1990.

Sarwoko, G., L. D. The, Sutjipto, and Wenny Purwanti. *Pembangunan perumahan dan hunian modern di Indonesia* [Housing Development and Modern Living in Indonesia]. Jakarta: Yayasan Mitra Purna Caraka, 1995.

Scidmore, E. R. *Java, the Garden of the East*. Singapore: Oxford University Press, 1984.

Scott, James. *Seeing like a State: How Certain Schemes to Improve Human Conditions Have Failed*. New Haven, Conn.: Yale University Press, 1998.

Sears, Laurie. *Shadows of Empire: Colonial Discourse and Javanese Tales*. Durham, N.C.: Duke University Press, 1996.

Sekretariat Negara. *30 tahun Indonesia merdeka, 1945–1955*. Jakarta: Sekretariat Negara Republik Indonesia, 1997.

"Senayan City: Your City Starts Here." *Indonesia Design* 3, no. 12 (2006), 47.

Seno Gumira Ajidarma. *Jakarta 2039*. Yogyakarta: Galang, 2001.

———. "Dari Jakarta" [From Jakarta]. *Djakarta: The City Life Magazine*, 21 July 2002.

Shiraishi, Takashi. "The Dispute between Tjipto Mangoenkoesoemo and Soetatmo Soeriokoesoemo: Satria vs. Pandita." *Indonesia* 32 (October 1981), 93–108.

———. *An Age in Motion: Popular Radicalism in Java, 1912–1916*. Ithaca, N.Y.: Cornell University Press, 1990.

———. "The Phantom World of Digoel." *Indonesia* 61 (1996), 93–118.

———. "Anti-Sinicism in Java's New Order." *Essential Outsiders: Chinese and Jews in the Modern Transformation of Southeast Asia and Central Europe*, edited by Daniel Chirot and Anthony Reid, 187–207. Seattle: University of Washington Press, 1997.

———. "Digul." *Mencari demokrasi* [Searching for Democracy], edited by F. X. Baskara and T. Wardaya, 159–88. Jakarta: Institut Studi Arus Informasi, 1999.

Sidel, John T. "'Macet Total': Logics of Circulation and Accumulation in the Demise of Indonesia's New Order." *Indonesia* 66 (October 1998), 159–94.

Sidharta. "Menuju arsitektur Indonesia modern: Permulaan perkembangan arsitektur modern di Eropa dan Amerika" [Toward Modern Indonesian Architecture: The Beginning of Modern Architecture in Europe and America]. *Rekaman kongres nasional 2, ikatan arsitek Indonesia* [Proceedings of the National Conference 2, Association of Indonesian Architects] Jakarta: Bidang Sinfar IAI, 1984.

Siegel, James. *Solo in the New Order: Language and Hierarchy in an Indonesian City*. Princeton, N.J.: Princeton University Press, 1986.

———. *Fetish, Recognition, Revolution*. Princeton, N.J.: Princeton University Press, 1997.

———. *A New Criminal Type in Jakarta: Counter-Revolution Today*. Durham, N.C.: Duke University Press, 1998.

———. "Early Thoughts on the Violence of May 13 and 14, 1998 in Jakarta." *Indonesia* 66 (October 1999), 75–108.

———. "Thoughts on the Violence of May 13 and 14, 1998, in Jakarta." *Violence and the State in Suharto's Indonesia*, edited by Benedict Anderson, 90–123. Ithaca, N.Y.: Southeast Asia Program Publications, Cornell University, 2001.

Silver, Christopher. *Planning the Megacity: Jakarta in the Twentieth Century*. New York: Routledge, 2007.

Simanungkalit, Panangian. "Lagi, APG Bikin Terobosan" [Again APG Made a Breakthrough]. *Bisnis Properti*, 35, July 2006.

Simmel, Georg. "The Metropolis and Mental Life." *The Sociology of Georg Simmel*, edited by K. Wolff, 409-24. New York: Free Press, 1964.

Slyomovics, Susan. *The Object of Memory: Arab and Jew Narrate the Palestinian Village*. Philadelphia: University of Pennsylvania Press, 1998.

Soedjarwo, ed. *Lukisan revolusi rakjat Indonesia, 1945-1949* [Paintings of Indonesian Revolution, 1945-1949]. Yogyakarta: Kementerian Penerangan Republik Indonesia, 1949.

Strassler, Karen, "Gendered Visibilities and the Dream of Transparency: The Chinese-Indonesian Rape Debate in Post-Suharto Indonesia." *Gender and History* 16, no. 3 (2004), 689-725.

Sudradjat, Iwan. "A Study of Indonesian Architectural History." PhD dissertation, University of Sydney, 1991.

Suharto. *My Thoughts, Words and Deeds*. Jakarta: PT Citra Lamtoro Gung Persada, 1991.

Suhartono. *Apanage dan bekel: Perubahan sosial di pedesaan Surakarta 1830-1920* [Apanage and the Village Chief: Social Change in the Village of Surakarta 1830-1920]. Yogyakarta: PT Tiara Wacana Yogya, 1991.

Sukada, Budi. "Indonesian Architects Award: The Long Road Towards Recognition." *The Long Road Towards Recognition: Selected Works of Indonesian Architects*, edited by Ahmad Tardiyana and Yori Antar, 13-15. Jakarta: Gramedia, 2005.

Sukarno. "Tahun vivere pericoloso: Pidato presiden RI pada tanggal 17 Agustus 1964" [President's Speech on Independence Day, 17 August 1964]. Tjetakan 2 (Jajasan Prapantja), 1964.

————. *Bung Karno dan Islam: Kumpulan pidato tentang Islam, 1953-1966* [Sukarno and Islam: Speeches on Islam]. Jakarta: CV Haji Mas Agung, 1990.

Sumalyo, Yulianto. *Arsitektur kolonial Belanda di Indonesia* [Dutch Colonial Architecture in Indonesia]. Yogyakarta: Gadjah Mada University Press, 1993.

Surjomihardjo, Abdurrachman. *Kota Yogyakarta: Sejarah perkembangan sosial, 1880-1930* [Yogyakarta: A History of Social Development, 1880-1930]. Yogyakarta: Yayasan untuk Indonesia, 2002.

Susanti, Dewi. "Against Jakarta." *East Asian Architecture* 104 (July 2006), 32-47.

————. "Disjointed Jakarta: Hyper-Traditional Planning Attitudes versus Rhizomatic Growth in a Postcolonial City." *Traditional Dwellings and Settlement* 190 (2006), 971-97.

Susantono, Bamrang. "Busway . . . Why Busway?" *Gatra*, 14 January 2006.

"Sutiyoso: Pemimpin harus rada gendeng" [Leader Needs to Be a Bit Crazy]. *Tempo*, 15 January 2006, 36-39.

Suyono, Seno Joko, and Evieta Fajar. "Ikhtiar seni di halte busway" [Arts in Busway's Shelter]. *Tempo*, 12 February 2006, 72–73.

Tardiyana, Achmad, and Yori Antar, eds. *The Long Road Towards Recognition*. Jakarta: Gramedia, 2005.

Thongchai, Winichakul. *Siam Mapped: A History of the Geo-body of a Nation*. Honolulu: Hawaii University Press, 1994.

Tickell, Paul. "Introduction: Mas Marco Kartodikromo and Early Indonesian Literature." *Three Early Indonesian Short Stories*, translated and introduced by Paul Tickell, 1–5. Melbourne: Monash University, Centre of Southeast Asian Studies, 1981.

Tillema, Henry F. *Van wonen en bewonen, van bouwen, huis en erf*. Tjandi-Semarang, 1913.

————. *Kromoblanda: Over 't vraagstuk van "het wonen" in Kromo's groote land*. Vol. 5, part 2. 's Gravenhage: Uden Masman, De Atlas and Adi Poestaka, 1923.

Tjahjono, Gunawan, ed. *Indonesian Heritage: Architecture*. Singapore: Archipelago Press, 1998.

Tjandrasasmita, Uka. *Pertumbuhan dan perkembangan kota-kota Muslim di Indonesia dari abad 13 sampai 18 masehi* [The Emergence and Development of Islamic Cities in Indonesia, 13th to 18th Centuries]. Kudus: Penerbit Menara Kudus, 2000.

Toer, Koesalah S. "Pengantar." *Pergaulan orang buangan di Boven Digoel* [The Social Life of People in Exile in Boven Digoel], by Marco Kartodikromo, xi–xxvi. Jakarta: Kepustakaan Populer Gramedia, 2002.

Tombesi, Paolo. "A True South for Design? The New International Division of Labour in Architecture." *Architecture Research Quarterly* (ARQ) 5, no. 2 (2001), 171–80.

Triyanto, G. et al. "Pertarungan seru pusat belanja di CBD" [Sharp Competition of Shopping Centers in the Central Business District]. *Segitiga emas* 2 (April 2001), 11–14.

Urbane Indonesia. "Kontemplasi arsitektur Kepulauan dan Kelautan" [Reflection on the Architecture of Archipelago]. *Indonesia Design* 3, no. 15 (2006), 69–73.

Van Dijk, Kees. *A Country in Despair: Indonesia between 1997–2000*. Leiden: KITLV Press, 2001.

————. "The Privatization of the Public Order: Relying on the Satgas." *Violence in Indonesia*, edited by Ingrid Wessel and Georgia Wimhöfer, 152–67. Hamburg: Abera Verlag, 2001.

————. "The Changing Contour of Mosques." *The Past in the Present: Architecture in Indonesia*, edited by Peter J. M. Nas, 45–66. Rotterdam: Nai Publishers, 2006.

Van Doorn, J. *The Engineers and the Colonial System: Technocratic Tendencies in the Dutch East Indies*. Comparative Asian Studies Programme 6. Rotterdam: Comparative Asian Studies Programme, 1982.

Van Leerdam, Ben F. *Architect Henri Maclaine Pont: Een speurtocht naar het wezenlijke van de Javaanse architectuur*. Den Haag: CIP—Gegevens Koninklijke Bibliotheek, 1995.

Van Leeuwen, Lizzy. "Lost in Mall: An Ethnography of Middle Class Jakarta in the 1990s." PhD dissertation, University of Amsterdam, 2005.

Wachlin, Steven, ed. *Woodbury and Page: Photographers Java*. Leiden: KITLV Press, 1994.

Walkowitz, Daniel J., and Lisa Maya Knauer, eds. *Memory and the Impact of Political Transformation in Public Space*. Durham, N.C.: Duke University Press, 2004.

Warsono, R., trans. *Wajah kota Hindia Belanda* [The Face of the Indies Town]. Jakarta: Pusat Penelitian dan Pengembangan and Fakultas Teknik Universitas Tarumanagara, n.d. Originally published 1939 by Stichting Technisch as Karsten, *Het Indische stadsbeeld voorheen en thans*.

Wertheim, W. F., ed. *The Indonesian Town: Studies in Urban Sociology*. The Hague and Bandung: W. van Hoeve, 1958.

Wessel, Ingrid, and Georgia Wimhofer, eds. *Violence in Indonesia*. Hamburg: Abera-Verl, 2001.

Williams, Raymond. *The Long Revolution*. Harmondsworth: Penguin, 1965.

Wirth, Louis. "Urbanism as a Way of Life." *American Journal of Sociology* 44, no. 1 (1938), 1–24.

Wiryomartono, Bagoes. *Seni bangunan dan seni binakota di Indonesia* [Building and Urban Design in Indonesia]. Jakarta: Gramedia, 1995.

Wolters, W. Oliver. *History, Culture and Religion in Southeast Asian Perspectives*. Singapore: Institute of Southeast Asian Studies, 1982.

Wu Hung. "Tiananmen Square: A Political History of Monuments." *Representations* 35 (Summer 1991), 84–117.

Yates, Frances. *The Art of Memory*. Chicago: University of Chicago Press, 1966.

Yeoh, Brenda. "Postcolonial Cities." *Progress in Human Geography* 25, no. 3 (2001), 456–68.

Yoshihara, Naoki, and Raphaella Dewantari Dwianto. *Grass Roots and the Neighborhood Associations: On Japan's Chonaikai and Indonesia's* RT / RW. Jakarta: Gramedia Widiasarana Indonesia, 2003.

Young, James. *At Memory's Edge: After-Images of the Holocaust in Contemporary Art and Architecture*. New Haven, Conn.: Yale University Press, 2000.

Yudhoyono, Bambang Soesilo. "We Need Shock Therapy." Interview with *Time Asia Magazine*, 1 November 2004.

Yuwono, Martono. "Restorasi Stadhuis dan Jakarta Kota" [The Restoration of the "Stadhuis" and the Old Jakarta]. Paper presented at the Architecture of the Jakarta Historical Museum, 21 August 2002.

Zurbuchen, Mary, ed. *Beginning to Remember: The Past in the Indonesian Present*. Seattle: University of Washington Press, 2005.